D1273693

Islam, Politics,
and Social Movements

COMPARATIVE STUDIES ON MUSLIM SOCIETIES

General Editor, Barbara D. Metcalf

1. William R. Roff, ed.,
Islam and the Political Economy of Meaning

2. John Davis,
Libyan Politics: Tribe and Revolution

3. Yohanan Friedmann,
Prophecy Continuous:
Aspects of Aḥmadī Religious Thought and Its Medieval Background

4. Katherine P. Ewing, ed.,
Sharī'at and Ambiguity in South Asian Islam

5. Edmund Burke, III, and Ira M. Lapidus, eds.,
Islam, Politics, and Social Movements

Islam, Politics, and Social Movements

EDITED BY

Edmund Burke, III, and Ira M. Lapidus

CONTRIBUTORS

Ervand Abrahamian · Hamid Algar · Joel Beinin
Edmund Burke, III · Julia Clancy-Smith · Fanny Colonna
Sandria B. Freitag · David Gilmartin · Ellis Goldberg
Nikki R. Keddie · Ira M. Lapidus · Paul Lubeck
Ted Swedenburg · John O. Voll · Peter Von Sivers

UNIVERSITY OF CALIFORNIA PRESS
Berkeley   Los Angeles   London

University of California Press
Berkeley and Los Angeles, California
University of California Press, Ltd.
London, England
© 1988 by
The Regents of the University of California
Printed in the United States of America
1   2   3   4   5   6   7   8   9

Library of Congress Cataloging-in-Publication Data

Islam, politics, and social movements / edited by Edmund Burke, III,
and Ira M. Lapidus.
    p.   cm. — (Comparative studies on Muslim societies; 3)
                      Includes index.
              ISBN 0-520-05758-9 (alk. paper)
    1. Islamic countries—History.   2. Islam and politics.   I. Burke,
Edmund, 1940–   .   II. Lapidus, Ira M. (Ira Marvin)   III. Series.
                      DS35.63.164 1988
909′.097671—dc19   87-17352
                                                             CIP

We thank the publishers of E. Abrahamian, "'Ali Shari'ati:
Ideologue of the Iranian Revolution," *MERIP Reports* (January 1982):
24–28, and of N. R. Keddie, "Iranian Revolutions in Comparative Perspective,"
American Historical Review 88 (1983): 579–98, for
permission to reproduce these articles.

CONTENTS

MAPS / *vii*

PREFACE / *xiii*

LIST OF ABBREVIATIONS / *xvii*

PART ONE · ISLAMIC POLITICS OR SOCIAL MOVEMENTS?

1. Islamic Political Movements: Patterns of Historical Change
   Ira M. Lapidus / 3

2. Islam and Social Movements: Methodological Reflections
   Edmund Burke, III / 17

PART TWO · NINETEENTH-CENTURY ANTI-COLONIAL RESISTANCE AND MILLENARIANISM IN THE MAGHRIB AND THE SUDAN

3. Rural Uprisings as Political Movements in Colonial Algeria, 1851–1914
   Peter Von Sivers / 39

4. Saints, Mahdis, and Arms: Religion and Resistance in Nineteenth-Century North Africa
   Julia Clancy-Smith / 60

5. The Transformation of a Saintly Lineage in the Northwest Aurès Mountains (Algeria): Nineteenth and Twentieth Centuries
   Fanny Colonna / 81

6. Abu Jummayza: The Mahdi's Musaylima?
   John O. Voll / 97

v

PART THREE · ISLAM AND NATIONALISM: SECULAR OR COMMUNAL?

7. The Roots of Muslim Separatism in South Asia: Personal Practice and Public Structures in Kanpur and Bombay
Sandria B. Freitag | 115

8. The Shahidganj Mosque Incident: A Prelude to Pakistan
David Gilmartin | 146

9. The Role of the Palestinian Peasantry in the Great Revolt (1936–1939)
Ted Swedenburg | 169

PART FOUR · THE WORKING CLASS BETWEEN NATIONALISM, COMMUNISM, AND ISLAM

10. Islam, Marxism, and the Shubra al-Khayma Textile Workers: Muslim Brothers and Communists in the Egyptian Trade Union Movement
Joel Beinin | 207

11. Muslim Union Politics in Egypt: Two Cases
Ellis Goldberg | 228

12. Islamic Political Movements in Northern Nigeria: The Problem of Class Analysis
Paul Lubeck | 244

PART FIVE · REVOLUTION IN IRAN

13. Imam Khomeini, 1902–1962: The Pre-Revolutionary Years
Hamid Algar | 263

14. 'Ali Shari'ati: Ideologue of the Iranian Revolution
Ervand Abrahamian | 289

15. Iranian Revolutions in Comparative Perspective
Nikki R. Keddie | 298

LIST OF CONTRIBUTORS | *315*
GLOSSARY OF SELECTED TERMS | *317*
INDEX | *321*

MAPS

1. North Africa

2. The Aurès Mountains

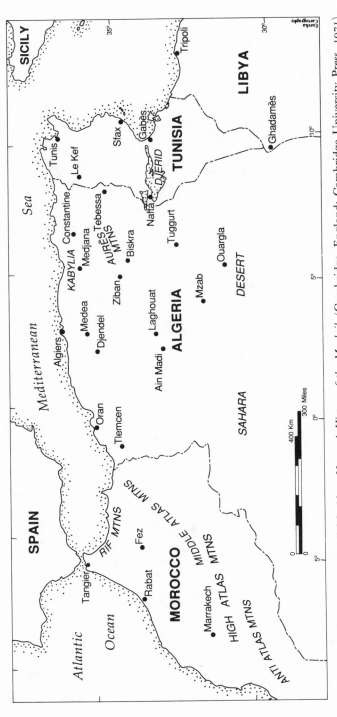

1. North Africa. Based on Jamil M. Abun-Nasr, *A History of the Maghrib* (Cambridge, England: Cambridge University Press, 1971) pp. 314–15.

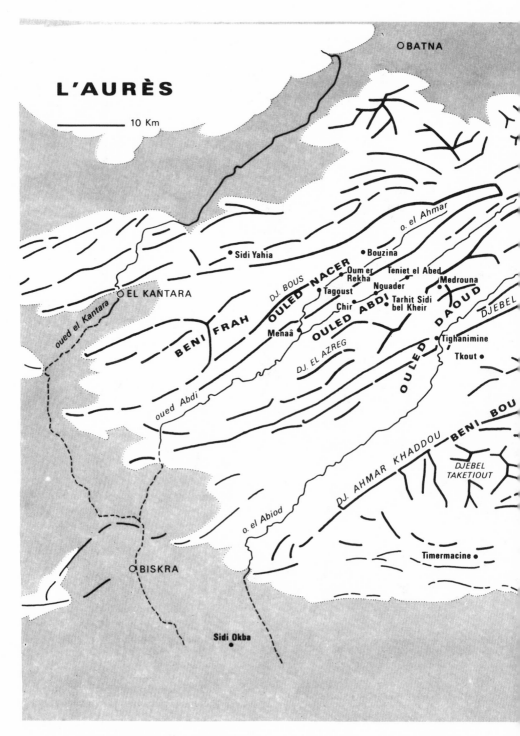

2. The Aurès Mountains. Source: *Annales: Economies, sociétés, civilsations* 35, nos. 3–4 (1980): 646–47.

O TIMGAD

KHENCHELA

O U D J A N A

ZELLATOU

SLIMANE

KIMMEL

DJEBEL CHERCHAR

oued el Arab

BENI BARBAR

Ciar

Khanga Sidi Hadji

o. Bedjer

ZERIBET EL OUED

CARTE M-C LAPEYRE

PREFACE

This book is based on a conference held at the University of California at Berkeley in June 1981 to examine movements of social protest and political resistance in Muslim countries in the nineteenth and twentieth centuries. The papers presented here include many of the original conference papers, revised for this publication, plus additional contributions to round out the volume. Since the Iranian revolution of 1978–79, a veritable cascade of books and articles has poured forth on this subject. These studies have chiefly focused on the contemporary resurgence of Islamic activism, particularly in its Shi'i forms. Although this literature has made some notable contributions to our understanding of the evolution of Islamic doctrine and the views of particular thinkers, it lacks methodological self-consciousness and tends to overemphasize the contemporary Middle East at the expense of historically more grounded and culturally more inclusive views. With this in mind, the conference was organized in Berkeley in June 1981 to attempt to situate historically the diverse responses of Islamic societies to the changes they have undergone since 1750 and to explore the strengths and weaknesses of differing research strategies. Thus was set in motion the process of dialogue and debate of which the present book is one result.

The essays in this volume examine selected case studies of social movements in Islamic societies during the nineteenth and twentieth centuries from different methodological perspectives. The book brings together specialists on the Islamic world from Africa to the Indian subcontinent, including the Maghrib, Egypt, the Arab East, Iran, and India, and it covers the period from the early nineteenth century to the present. The focus is on popular political movements in Islamic societies: how they arise, how they spread, why they have taken the forms they have, and how these have changed over time.

Part one attempts to situate the essays included in this book in their historical and methodological contexts, as well as in the context of the history of Islamic popular political movements. In Chapter 1, Ira Lapidus provides a framework for understanding the essays in the context of a history of Islamic political movements. In Chapter 2, Edmund Burke discusses the methodological traditions in which such studies have been conducted and looks at how the contributions included here seek to move beyond them. Finally, his paper places the essays in the context of an alternative history of collective action in the Islamic world.

Part Two examines the resistance of rural Muslim populations to European imperial hegemony, a topic which plays an important part in the histories of many parts of the world. In successive chapters Peter Von Sivers, Julia Clancy-Smith, Fanny Colonna, and John Voll take up the subject of resistance and rebellions in nineteenth-century Algeria and the Sudan. They emphasize two aspects of the movements in particular. One is the micropolitics of anti-colonial resistance in an environment of scarcity. The other is the interplay of popular and official religion in the conduct of politics in rural areas. Through these contributions we come to see how recent writings have moved beyond the old paradigms to develop new insights and questions more thoroughly rooted in the social and cultural history of the region.

With the defeat of the Ottoman empire in 1918, the subsequent abolition of the caliphate, and proclamation of the new Turkish republic, a system of legitimation and symbolic identity that had lasted 1,300 years came to an end. In the harsher realities of the interwar period, Muslims were compelled to rethink their political situations. In Part Three the focus is on the emergence of a nationalist consciousness in India and Palestine between the wars, and the reasons why, in the first case, a Muslim identity, and in the second, a secular nationalist one emerged. The essays by Sandria Freitag and David Gilmartin on India stress how different segments of the Muslim elite sought to manipulate religious symbols the better to advance their own programs and interests. Ted Swedenburg's essay on the Palestinian revolt of 1936–39 reexamines the role of Islamic and secular nationalist appeals in the mobilization of the peasantry and the interplay of communal, class, and national solidarities.

Part Four considers the subject of Islamic and working-class formation in Egypt in the 1940s and in contemporary Nigeria. Essays by Joel Beinin, Ellis Goldberg, and Paul Lubeck consider the development of the labor movement, and the complex relationship of the workers' struggle to the national struggle. Through a close examination of empirical cases, they also discuss the allied question of religion-based and class-based politics in the two countries.

The Iranian revolution of 1978–79, the subject of Part Five, continues to influence developments throughout the Islamic world. Contrasting chapters by Hamid Algar and Ervand Abrahamian consider the respective roles of Ayatullah Khomeini and 'Ali Shari'ati in the unfolding of the revolutionary process, while Nikki Keddie's chapter places the revolution in the context both of the constitutional revolution of 1906–11 and of the social science literature on the theory of revolutions. The question of which is more important in great social upheavals, the role of individuals or that of social processes, is thereby posed. This book brings us face to face not only with the empirical variety of the historical experience of Islamic peoples, but also with the rather different historiographical traditions of writing about social movements in the Maghrib, Sudanic Africa, the Arab East, India, and Iran.

In any work dealing with Islamic subjects, transliteration presents special problems. To simplify the book for the reader we have used a system of modified transliteration from Arabic, Persian, Urdu, and Hausa. In general we omit diacritical marks, but we have retained the single open quote to represent the Arabic ayn. Standard Arabic words used in variant versions in different Muslim countries have generally been spelled in their Arabic form, but geographical and proper names and terms particular to each Muslim region have been left in the form to which people reading the regional literatures are accustomed.

The editors are grateful for the help we have received in the preparation of this book. We would especially like to thank the participants in the original conference on which this book is based, for their contributions in both written and oral form: Hamid Algar, Julia Clancy-Smith, Fanny Colonna, Dale Eickelman, Ernest Gellner, David Gilmartin, Roger Joseph, Suad Joseph, Nikki Keddie, Paul Lubeck, Barbara Metcalf, Irwin Scheiner, Peter Von Sivers, David Skinner, and John Voll. We are especially grateful to Ellen Sheeks, Jean Auka, and Laurence Michalak of the Center for Middle Eastern Studies at the University of California, Berkeley, who organized this conference and contributed mightily to its practical success, and to Wendy Fassett and Susan Mattern, who have contributed much editorial assistance.

We would also like to acknowledge the financial assistance of the Graduate Division, the Center for Middle Eastern Studies, and the Institute of International Studies of the University of California, Berkeley; and the Faculty Research Committee of the University of California at Santa Cruz. We are particularly grateful to the Director of the Institute, Professor Carl Rosberg, and the Management Services Officer, Karin Beros, for their generous support.

Barbara Metcalf has been invaluable as a colleague, as a critic, and as our editor at the University of California Press.

ABBREVIATIONS

AGT	Archives Générales Tunisiennes, Dar el-Bey
AME	Archives du Ministère des Affaires Etrangères, Paris
AMG	Archives du Ministère de la Guerre, Vincennes
AN-Aix	Archives Nationales, Gouvernement Général de l'Algérie, Aix-en-Provence
AN-Paris	Archives Nationales, Paris
ARGT	Archives de la Résidence Générale de France à Tunis, Nantes
BPP	British Parliamentary Papers
CHEAM	Centre des Hautes Etudes sur l'Afrique et l'Asie Moderne, Paris
FO	Foreign Office
IJAHS	*International Journal of African Historical Studies*
IJMES	*International Journal of Middle East Studies*
IOR	India Office Records
JAH	*Journal of African History*
JMH	*Journal of Modern History*
NEPU	Northern Elements Progressive Union
PRP	People's Redemption Party
ROMM	*Revue de l'Occident Musulman et de la Méditerranée*
SKMTWU	Shubra al-Khayma Mechanized Textile Workers' Union
SVN	Selections from the Vernacular Press, India

PART ONE

Islamic Politics
or Social Movements?

ONE

Islamic Political Movements: Patterns of Historical Change

Ira M. Lapidus

The chapters in this volume include studies of Islamic resistance in Algeria and the Sudan, riots and protests in late nineteenth- and early twentieth-century India, guerrilla war in Palestine, labor movements in Egypt and Nigeria, and the revolution in Iran. These movements are examined in order to explore their self-conception and symbols, the economic and political conditions under which they developed, and their relation to agrarian and capitalist economic structures and to established state regimes and elites. While this is a small sample of such movements in Islamic countries, many of these studies are pioneering works in their field and suggest new insights into the relationship between religious *mentalité* and political action in Muslim countries. They also tell us a great deal about the variations among Muslim populations and about historical changes in the character of politico-religious ideas and social action.

These studies can be grouped into two historical epochs. Those by Von Sivers, Clancy-Smith, Colonna, and Voll present a premodern form of Islamic society and political action. Although they discuss events in the epoch of imperial domination in Algeria and the Sudan, they show a stage of Islamic society before the transformation ultimately wrought by imperialism and capitalist domination. The remainder of the articles consider the contemporary era, in which Muslim peoples are attempting to adjust to the profound changes that colonial and capitalist intrusion have caused. Thus we see attempts at new forms of political organization in India and Palestine, labor movements in Egypt and Nigeria, and revolution in Iran. In these cases Islamic beliefs and rhetoric do not belong to the once-established system of old societies, but represent an effort to generate and legitimate new forms of political and social action in radically changing societies. The two periods may overlap in time, but there is a profound difference of historical moment.

THE PRE-MODERN SOCIETIES: ALGERIA AND THE SUDAN

The contributions of Von Sivers, Clancy-Smith, and Colonna on Algeria and of Voll on the Sudan suggest some hypotheses about a premodern mode of Islamic political and social action. Von Sivers explores Algerian resistance to the expansion of French military power and administrative control to the whole (and not just a part) of the country, the universal imposition of taxes, and the substitution of new elites for old in the period between 1850 and 1900. The resistance, however, was differentiated by economic and ecological characteristics. In regions where peasantries were self-sufficient, resistance was led by landlords and tribal chiefs who were attempting to maintain their position against French efforts to reduce their power. This was the case in the great al-Muqrani revolt of 1871–72 and the revolt in the Adélia in 1901. Both revolts needed the support of large coalitions of mountain and desert peoples rallied by appeals to defend Islam and wage jihad against the French in order to have any prospect of success.

In mountain and desert regions where populations exceeded the carrying capacity of the land, peasants and nomads could not be self-sufficient. They had to exchange specialized products such as olive oil, honey, wax, animals, and wheat. Under such conditions peasants and nomads were prepared to fight to protect their access to vital trade routes and markets. This helps account for the involvement of the Kabyle peoples who joined the al-Muqrani revolt at a time when they had experienced little direct pressure from French rule but were economically vulnerable. Similarly, the populations of the Aurès who had a high risk of being cut off from markets responded to the French appointment of outside tax-collectors with open resistance. Also, sheep- and camel-herding nomads in the south of Algeria, who required access to markets and control of oases to obtain dates and wheat, found their freedom of movement constrained by the French and sought out religious leaders such as Si Sulayman and Ibn 'Ayash to legitimate armed resistance.

What, then, is the role of Islam in the Algerian resistance? Our authors see this in different ways. Von Sivers regards economic interests, the struggle for livelihood, as the central reason for Algerian resistance. In his view, religious leaders in the Aurès and in the desert regions helped broaden the appeal of resistance and gave raids a greater legitimacy. They gave an ideological boost to pragmatic motives for action. Islam was a kind of tonic for protest.

Clancy-Smith leaves aside the economic issues (in practice though not in principle) to concentrate on the social and religious aspects of Muslim resistance to French imperialism. Her central theme is the role of the Rahmaniya Sufi *tariqa* (brotherhood) and its great shaykh, Mustafa ibn 'Azzuz (d. 1866), but her analysis begins logically with the local resistance movements led by Abu Ziyan of Zaatcha in 1849 and Muhammad ibn 'Abdallah in 1851–55. Resistance begins with local lineages that oppose taxation, try to maintain their political autonomy, and mount a millenarian anti-colonial jihad. Islam in the form of the Rahmaniya order became important because it legitimated this resistance and provided intelligence, communications, and, above all, military supplies along its networks of kinship, *zawiya* (Sufi hospices), brotherhood, and trade connections. Ibn 'Azzuz, based at Nafta in Tunisia after his *hijra* (migration) from French-occupied Algeria, was not a frontline leader of revolt but mobilized his brotherhood to maintain the flow of *baraka* and *barud*—sanctity and guns. Perhaps the crucial contribution of Ibn 'Azzuz was that he could stimulate simultaneous action among otherwise unorganized peoples.

Clancy-Smith also sees the limits of this kind of resistance. Ibn 'Azzuz operated not in a millenarian but in a political context sensitive to the larger North African balance of power and to the need to protect his own base of operations in Tunisia. He used his authority to help demobilize the Tunisian revolt of 1864 and to dampen Algerian resistance. When the political interests of the Rahmaniya in Tunisia, or that of the tribes, or the risk of serious defeat so required, the resistance effort was abandoned for a more cautious policy. As Ross Dunn has also shown in his study of Tafilalt in Morocco, resistance may be articulated in religious terms, but its religious inspiration does not necessarily override pragmatic interests. Ideals, Muslim or other, are only one consideration among many. Islam in this case is the aspect of resistance that supplies the motivating emotion, legitimation, and leadership to unite and mobilize groups across lineage and factional lines. It supplies the networks of communication and flow of weapons. In the end it also provides the discourse to allow for adjustment of political action to the larger strategic situation. In Clancy-Smith's view, Algerian rebellions can only be understood in their Islamic context.

Colonna shows in other ways how Islamic considerations are intrinsic to the organization of nineteenth-century Algerian society and therefore to the Algerian resistance movements in the Aurès. Her contribution is based on a more extended series of articles on the Derduriya order published in other places. Colonna's studies concentrate not so much on the outbreak of an anti-French rebellion in 1880 as on the social and religious forces that generated the rebellion. Behind the outburst of 1880 lies a long struggle among religious leaders and brotherhoods representing the interests of rival lineage coalitions. In this combined struggle for tribal and religious supremacy, the capacity to mobilize material resources and political power was considered a sign of divine favor. Conversely, the reputation for sanctity and spiritual achievement was the basis of social recognition, political leadership, and the acquisition of wealth.

The French disturbed the local distribution of power by giving the lands of one lineage to another and thereby forced the defeated lineage to find new strategies to maintain its position and that of its followers. These new strategies depended on renewed struggle for control of the two critical and interrelated resources—religious prestige and land.

Thus in 1870 Si Lhachemi broke with the Rahmaniya to establish the Derduriya. His personal history of wandering and pilgrimate to Mecca, his reputation as a preacher, healer, and clairvoyant, his feats of bodily renunciation, all were resources on which he drew to assert a new religious authority and a new religious order. Si Lhachemi also went to work with his people bringing land into cultivation by steady hard labor. His strategy to survive in competition with other lineages in a political environment created by the French was a combination of cultivating a reputation for personal sanctity, defending religious principles, and acquiring land.

In these three chapters, then, we have a subtle shift of perspective. Beginning with the question of resistance movements against the French, we gradually discover that the central issue is not resistance but the role of Islam in segmentary societies where Sufi authority is the basis of large-scale social organization. Islam is connected to resistance because it is essential to the organization of the society, whether for purposes of internal struggle for power or for resistance to state authorities. Religious authority and doctrine not only were tools in the struggle against the French, but are an intrinsic part of the struggle for existence within Algerian society.

Turning to the Sudan, we see a similar cultural and political system: a society of scattered tribal peoples living in the cultural expectation that a saintly leader will arise to lead them to safety. In the Sudan holy men abound, wandering through the region, sometimes proclaiming themselves a *khalifa* (lieutenant) of the Mahdi, or even the Mahdi himself, to rally support. Local peoples conceive of unification and defense in terms of the coming of a holy savior.

In the late nineteenth century the Sudan was undergoing drastic changes due to the imposition of a centralized state regime after the Turko-Egyptian conquest. In reaction to the consolidation of the new state, Muhammad ibn 'Abdallah al-Mahdi united various groups to oppose the new regime and set up his own state. The Mahdist movement was based on the growing importance of Sufi brotherhoods, which espoused a more scripturalist and universalist version of Islam and were hostile to local Muslim holy men. Voll shows us that while Egyptian rule was being resisted by the Mahdists, in the Dar Fur region a local holy man, Abu Jummayza, was organizing a struggle for regional autonomy against the Mahdist state.

Voll also shows how variants of Islamic belief were associated with different types of social structure. Ecstatic Sufi leaders, Mahdist doctrine, and jihad ideology were associated with the integration of segmentary units into larger political movements. Reform Islamic teaching, hostile to ecstatic Sufism, was associated with state formation and national-scale resistance movements. Colonna, too, has shown how reform ideology may be used in local-level competition for religious prestige and political influence.

In both Algeria and the Sudan we are witnessing political action in societies organized into small-scale family, clan, lineage, or tribal groups in which Islam, represented by Sufi holy men and privileged religious lineages or Sufi brotherhoods, plays a role in defining, symbolizing, and organizing these small groups, either within or across kinship lines, to create coalitions, alliances, and new political movements among otherwise unrelated peoples. In these accounts of Algeria and Sudan we see the fluid interplay of various levels of segmentary organization, tribal coalitions, and state forces, all of whom depend on Islamic concepts for legitimation and some of whom depend on Islamic religious teachers for organization. Though all elements borrow from the Muslim ideological repertoire, the ideology expressed, whether Mahdist or reformist, depends on the political purposes of the competing forces. Thus "resistance" to foreign rule was only one expression of a complex political system which could involve internal struggles as well as resistance to colonial states.

TRANSITIONAL MUSLIM SOCIETIES:
INDIA, PALESTINE, EGYPT, NIGERIA

Our next group of studies brings us into an era in which we can no longer take for granted the operation of a pre-modern system of societies. By the late nineteenth and early twentieth centuries, foreign imperial regimes had been consolidated in many Muslim regions, and the autonomy of parochial communities had been overcome by strong central governments. The traditional forms of Muslim religious organization were often suppressed. The breakdown of the old political system was accompanied by extensive economic change, disruption of small groups, migration to the cities, and development of new social strata. The new era was marked by efforts to define new modes of political action as well as new modes of Islamic religious belief. Therefore, the chapters that deal with India, Palestine, Egypt, Nigeria, and Iran examine the role of Islamic conceptual vocabulary, symbols, and authority in the reorganization of Muslim communities living through unprecedented situations.

The Indian case turns on the quest for political identity. Before the consolidation of the British raj, the Mughal empire contained a heterogeneous Indian population. The empire was officially Muslim, but the dominant elite included a Hindu aristocracy and cultivated a syncretic cultural style which drew heavily on Indian symbols. The Muslim subject population did not have an empire or an Indian identity but was divided into numerous small groups organized around lineages (*biradari*) and ethnic or caste communities (*jamatbandi*), as well as Sufi *turuq* and other forms of religious organization. The dissolution of the Mughal empire entirely disrupted the old system of society and opened the way for a century-long struggle to define new forms of Muslim political organization. In this struggle among Muslims, two main forces came to the fore. One was the reformist ulama typified by the Fara'idi movement in Bengal, the jihad of Sayyid Ahmad, and the Deoband College, which sought to define a standard Islamic practice and to suppress local Indian Muslim cults in order to create a new form of universalistic Muslim identity in the subcontinent. The reformers denounced saint worship, cultic practices, and local rituals and called for a purified form of Islam guided by the teaching of the Quran and the example of the prophet. The reform movement was organized through colleges and schools, and sometimes through direct preaching and community action.

The primary alternative took shape in the early twentieth century with the emergence, out of the matrix of the old Mughal political aristocracy and their descendants, of a Western-educated professional, lawyer, journalist, and secular-minded elite which also wished to create an India-wide Muslim identity. This elite gave rise to the Muslim League in 1906. Subsequent Muslim disappointment with British policy led to a new Muslim political consciousness. After 1912, Muslim journalists helped to form a more emotional, populist, and combative sense of Muslim identity. A new generation was coming to power on a national rather than a religious concept of the Indian Muslim community, emphasizing the collective political aspect of Muslim loyalties rather than the individual religious vocations of Muslim believers. In 1940 an influential section of this elite committed itself to the demand for Pakistan as a new state for the Muslim population.

Freitag and Gilmartin explore the new communal symbols and politics from a novel point of view. While conventional histories stress the impact of the British system of rule and British concepts upon the development of Muslim communal consciousness, Freitag and Gilmartin probe the roots of social and political consciousness by examining the local situations in which it was forged.

In Freitag's discussion of Kanpur and Bombay the central theme is the disparity between the appeal to universal Islamic symbols and the factionalized social structure of the Muslim population. The late nineteenth century had bequeathed Kanpur a legacy of sharp class cleavage between *ashraf* nobles and lower-class corporate groups, as well as different modes of Islamic culture, but nonetheless a shared allegiance to Muslim symbols such as the Quran, the mosque, and the Urdu language, and the shared sense that Muslims were in decline before powerful British and Hindu enemies. Ulama schools, public preaching, and newspapers were the main mechanisms for fostering this common identity, but the sense of unity had yet to overcome the divisions of the Muslim community. Shared cultural values had yet to find public expression.

The first step toward forming an overarching Muslim identity was the agitation over the partial demolition of the Kanpur mosque in 1913. Freitag shows that the threat to the mosque invoked Muslim symbols of mourning, martyrdom, and defense of Islam, gave the Muslims a common cause, and made possible an extraordinary public protest. After 1913, however, this enlarged community consciousness could not be translated into organizational cohesion. Between 1913 and 1931 Muslim movements such as Tanzim (missionary) religious preaching and processions enhanced collective self-awareness but did not overcome neighborhood factional and class divisions. Thus the political tensions of 1931 led once again to rioting.

As opposed to Kanpur, in Bombay Muslims had no historic cultural basis for Muslim unity. The city was given over to its extraordinary linguistic and ethnic diversity, its highly factionalized quarters, competing *muharram* processions, and frequent local riots. The riots of 1929 helped crystallize the first sense of a city and indeed of an India-wide Muslim identity in Bombay. These riots stemmed from efforts to organize masses of Indian millworkers into labor unions, while Pathans took on the role of strikebreakers. In the heat of the struggle, labor disputes and class issues were translated in the minds of Muslims into a Hindu-Muslim struggle. Modern communication transmitted to Bombay the sensitivity to Muslim symbols developed elsewhere and allowed frustrated Pathans to define their problems in terms of the need for Muslim political organization and state protection. The need for a public structure for fragmented Muslim communities led to attachment to subcontinent-wide Muslim symbols.

Gilmartin's study of Muslim symbols and political consciousness in the Punjab complements Freitag's analysis of Kanpur and Bombay. Here too the defense of a mosque as the symbol of an embattled Muslim community was manipulated to shape Muslim political consciousness in the face of the underlying pluralism of elites and community bodies. While the Muslim population of Lahore was poor and working-class, it was led by local landowning families and quarter chieftains. British-educated professionals such as lawyers and journalists sought to define a community which would allow Muslims to compete for power within the British system, while the ulama, focusing on the religious education of individual believers, attempted to define the Muslim community as a self-governing religious body operating under Muslim law and Muslim religious leadership. Lahore was thus divided among ulama, professionals, lenders, and traditional landed notables.

Transcending the fragmented leadership in Lahore was an ideal Muslim community represented in symbolic terms by the Quran and the mosque. Muhammad Iqbal taught that the Muslim *umma* was constituted simply by the allegiance of Muslims to the symbols of Islam. Thus the fate of the Shahidganj mosque was an issue to rouse the passions of all Muslims, and it led to riots. Still, none of the several elites could seize control of the agitation to create an organized political body. Lahore Muslims finally had to turn to Sayyid Jamaat 'Ali Shah, a leading Punjabi rural Sufi *pir*, to take the position of *amir-i millat* (head of the Muslim community). Gilmartin makes the point that this was a reversion to a type of religious authority effective in segmentary rural societies. The effort to use charismatic Sufi authority to unite urban Muslims with other religious leaders was bound to fail. The failure to translate shared sentiment into the unified Muslim community left, as Gilmartin tellingly observes, only one option: the quest for a still more potent symbol for public expression of Islamic identity, but one nonetheless divorced from the actualities of Muslim politics. This was to be Pakistan. While in Algeria and Sudan we have seen Muslim symbols and authorities as part of a complete political system, we see India in transition from an older type of plural segmentary society toward a new national political identity mediated by symbols divorced from political actualities which nonetheless generate an Indian Muslim consciousness.

The Palestinian case discussed by Swedenburg is another example of a society in which new needs for political organization bear an uneasy relationship to meaningful symbols. Swedenburg shows how nineteenth-century Palestinian peasant society was grouped into *hamula* or clan units and Qays-Yemen tribal moieties. As in Algeria and Sudan, religious sentiment helped to overcome the fragmentation of society. Worship at the shrines of saints, the festival of Nabi Musa, and the celebration of the *mawsim* in honor of the prophet all attracted pilgrims from numerous villages and towns. Folk religious practices helped to unify a highly segmentary society.

In the 1920s and 1930s this folk community and folk culture were disrupted. In 1920 the festival of Nabi Musa could still be the occasion for a demonstration of anti-Zionist, anti-British, and pro-Arab feelings, but in the decades that followed, patron-client ties were broken by landlords who sold their land to the Jews, and the centralization of state power under the British mandate transformed the conditions of life. Universalistic Islamic reform ideas and nationalist concepts were advanced to cope with the changed political situation.

The 1936–39 revolt represented a genuine peasant movement and reveals the transitional quality of Palestinian identity and political organization. Palestinian resistance was mobilized in part by old *hamula* and factional considerations, and in part by Islamic reformers, as in the case of Shaykh al-Qassam and the Young Men's Muslim Association. Al-Qassam was a marriage registrar for Muslim courts, a chief organizer of peasant action and a major inspiration for the outbreak of the Arab resistance. At the same time a younger generation of intelligentsia represented by the Istiqlal Party and others was formulating the Palestinian cause in Arab nationalist terms. The difficulties of maintaining an organized Palestinian movement have to do not only with the strength of Jewish and British opposition, but also with the inherent difficulty of finding unifying Islamic religious or national symbols in a still incompletely integrated society with multiple political leadership. Without either compelling symbols or unified cadres, the Palestinian movement was bound to be disunited.

The chapters by Beinin, Goldberg, and Lubeck introduce yet other examples of the effort to fuse Islamic symbols and loyalties with contemporary social and political movements. Beinin and Goldberg examine the union movement in the Egyptian textile, sugar, and oil industries. Beinin sees the textile industry as a test case of "the political and ideological struggle between two mutually antagonistic worldviews for hegemony over . . . the Egyptian working class." The

Communist view stresses class struggle; it conflicts with the Muslim Brothers' view of Islam as the basis of social solidarity and cooperation. At Shubra al-Khayma, one of the few places with an industrial working class, large-scale production had brought a proletariat into being in the 1930s. Muslim Brothers and others, some of whom would later become Communists, organized the first labor unions in 1937 and 1938. The Shubra al-Khayma Mechanized Textile Workers' Union (SKMTWU) was an active and militant union that won various victories in the 1940s, victories which made the union tougher and more politically self-conscious, independent of political domination, militant, nationalist, and ideologically oriented. Communists assumed leadership of the movement in the early 1940s, and the union was dissolved by the Egyptian government in April 1945.

The increasing influence of the Communists provoked a reaction among Muslim Brothers long active in mutual aid and other union activities. The Muslim Brothers believed, not in class antagonism, but in an "organically interdependent society." Though they denounced the exploitation of workers, they stressed social responsibility and the need for owners and the government to provide employment and to create a just Islamic society free of materialistic values. In particular the union defended the principle of equal pay for skilled workers. In practice the Muslim Brothers retreated from strikes and militant action and even helped to break a strike in 1946. They attacked communism as contrary to Islam, split with the leftist movement, and opened their own campaign for leadership in the union movement aided by the dissolution of the Communist-led labor unions. The Muslim Brothers, however, despite a period of growing influence, were not primarily committed to the special interests of labor but to a larger program of anti-Communist, anti-colonialist, and national political goals, and above all to an Islamic moral vision. The Muslim Brothers wanted to spread Islam rather than build unions. According to Beinin, "the moral appeal was not consistently developed into a concrete program for worker political action." The Muslim Brothers ultimately failed to organize the mills because their view of Islam solidarity did not accord with the realities of class conflict. The disjunction of Muslim ideology and actuality made it an inappropriate or ineffective ideology for labor-union action.

Goldberg gives a parallel analysis of the role of the Muslim Brothers in the highly industrialized Egyptian sugar and oil industries, but sees a more constructive Muslim Brothers contribution. Goldberg chronicles the formation in 1942 of the first Union of Sugar Industry Workers. The union stressed communal solidarity and close links among workers, foremen, and managers, rather than class antagonism. Its critical function was to defend the material interests of workers but it was also to provide them with legal aid and welfare benefits such as sick pay and loans. In particular the union defended the right of skilled workers for equal pay with foreigners. Its rhetoric stressed moral and religious solidarity and national unity in opposition to foreign economic exploitation.

Thus the sugar union expressed the moral sentiments of members who were often peasants in transition to industrial work roles, the material interests of foremen who had particular economic and status concerns, and a general interest in integrating millworkers into the national struggle.

Similarly, the first Union of Oil Workers, also founded under the auspices of Muslim Brothers, attempted to unite workers with different interests and to articulate these interests in general moral and religious terms. Again the primary union orientation was opposition to *foreign* managers and owners. Class antagonism was experienced in national terms.

Lubeck's analysis of workers and political parties in Kano, Nigeria, reveals in another Muslim-worker context the tendency to define worker and peasant interests in communal rather than class terms. Here, too, class consciousness is absorbed into national consciousness. Whereas Freitag and Beinin see Islamic values, as represented by important local movements, at odds with political and social realities, Lubeck and Goldberg see them as absorbed and transmitted by class interest. "Class-based deprivation," Lubeck says, "is the prism through which Islamic culture is perceived." *Talakawa* (rural under-class) and *leburori* (workers) make a "selective interpretation of Islamic ideology."

Striking in the Nigerian situation, however, is how both elites and oppressed classes adopt, albeit with different emphases, the same symbols and concepts. Implicitly they choose to emphasize the overall community at the same time as they attempt to differentiate interests within that community. There are two major reasons for this strong tendency to absorb Islamic considerations into the Nigerian workers' movement. One is the increasing identification of all classes of Kano society with Islam in opposition to British colonial rule. The other is the fact that the working class is recruited largely from mobile peasants and from rural Quran students who come to the cities in the dry season to work in factories or at menial labor. Lubeck points out that some 14 percent of workers were originally Islamic students. Many others are *mallams*, religious scholars employed as tailors in factories. In unions, *mallams* are important leaders; workers with an Islamic education are the most militant members. For these workers the industrial system is taken to be an expression of foreign capitalist domination. Their class interest, as in Egypt, is filtered through a religious and nationalist concept of solidarity.

Lubeck applies a similar analysis to the Northern Elements Progressive Union in northern Nigeria. NEPU is a Nigerian political party founded in the late 1940s to oppose British rule and the domination of the emirate aristocracy in northern Nigeria. NEPU, backed by status-deprived petit-bourgeois civil servants and Quranic schoolteachers, or *mallams*, criticized the privileges that the aristocrats held at the expense of the *talakawa*. It protested against forced labor, unfair taxation, and inadequate educational opportunities, and it denounced these abuses as un-Islamic. NEPU called for a return to a true Islam and the abolition of class privilege and imperial rule. The electoral victory of

NEPU's successor, the People's Redemption Party (PRP) in 1979 led to reforms which abolished certain patrimonial abuses. Lubeck points out, however, how difficult it is for a populist movement to achieve political reform, since they have so many diverse constituencies. They include elements which agree on the Islamic rhetoric but are opposed to each other in terms of real interests. His analysis concludes with a point also made by Beinin, Freitag, and Gilmartin, about the preference for a communal or populist orientation and the difficulty of wedding communal symbols to the needs of political action. This problem seems to be characteristic of transitional societies.

THE IRANIAN REVOLUTION

The Iranian revolution is a special case of the problem of defining cultural and political identity and political action in a changing society. For various reasons, Iranian national identity has already been established alongside and above lineage, tribal, and other parochial ties. This identity is expressed in secular linguistic, political, and territorial terms, but these secular aspects coincide with the Shi'i religious realm. The problem in Iran, then, is not to create a new unit of organization but to define the values and symbols that will prevail in an existing national society. The Islamic revolution may therefore be understood as a struggle to reject the Pahlavi regime with its Western supporters and Westernizing cultural orientation in favor of a more truly Islamic identity. Just what this true Islamic Iranian identity is or should be is a matter of dispute in Iran and among our contributors.

Keddie gives a full analysis of modern Iranian history to examine the links among ideologies and Iranian politics. Abrahamian and Algar offer biographical portraits of two leading revolutionary figures, Shari'ati and Khomeini, which implicitly display not only portraits of very different persons and beliefs but two different assessments of the ideological and political nature of the Iranian revolution.

Keddie begins her assessment with a brief historical review. She points out that the political structure of Iran has been characterized by weak, decentralized state regimes and strong Shi'i ulama with doctrinal authority, considerable economic support from the populace, and juridical, educational, and social power. The ulama are allied with the bazaar merchant and artisan classes in opposition to Iranian states and foreign influence.

The historic division in the society between the state and the organized ulama and their followers manifested itself in the struggles of the 1890s and in the first decade of the twentieth century and were again reenacted in the 1970s. In the 1970s the resistance to the Pahlavi regime developed around a coalition of students, unemployed urban workers, guerrilla activities, and ulama. The revolution, Keddie argues, was due to the discontent of the poor, the middle classes, and the national minorities with the regime of the shah; it represented a protest against an oppressive regime, economic hardship, and American and other Western influence. Thus it was an assertion of a national identity based on a blend of Islam and Third World liberal and leftist tendencies. The ultimate victory of one element in the opposition coalition, the ulama, over the remainder of the movement is portrayed by Keddie not as intrinsic to the revolution but, rather, due to such contingent circumstances as Khomeini's leadership and the tactical need to oppose Westernization.

Abrahamian's portrait of Shari'ati gives us the archetypal opponent to this concept of the Iranian revolution. Shari'ati represents the effort to synthesize Marx and Fanon, socialism and Shi'ism, to create an anti-imperialist and anti-capitalist, Iranian concept of revolution. Shari'ati taught that Iran needed a double revolution: a national revolution to sweep away foreign rule and revive national identity, and a social revolution to end exploitation and create a classless society. Shi'ism he regarded as both the expression of an Iranian identity and as an intrinsically radical religion of struggle against injustice. Shi'ism embodied both the national struggle against foreign domination and the revolutionary struggle for social justice. In Shari'ati's view, Shi'ism was not a set of religious beliefs and practices in the traditional sense, but the symbol of the Iranian revolutionary cause.

Algar represents an alternative view which stresses the particularly Islamic nature of the revolution and in particular its embodiment in the charismatic figure of Khomeini. Khomeini is the embodiment both of the truth and of the nation. The revolution and the republic are the expression of his vision of an Islamic society, a vision which called for the elimination of the Pahlavi regime, foreign imperialist influences, and secular intellectuals in favor of ulama leadership. Algar sees Islamic Iran as an *umma*, a religiously defined community owing obedience to Khomeini, its Imam.

Algar's biographical study of Khomeini presents his life as directed toward the cultivation of the qualities essential for this role. He points out that Khomeini's personal spiritual development combines the study of law with *hikmat* and *'irfan* or the pursuit of mystical truths; that Khomeini has experiential mystical knowledge and has combined the roles of contemplative, teacher, scholar, and warrior. He has reached spiritual heights that qualify him to lead a Muslim community in its worldly struggles. He also has a personal history of opposition to arbitrary government oppression, a lifetime commitment to the institution of the ulama as the leaders in the struggle against oppressive regimes and foreign powers, and a long commitment to political activism which would lead to the transformation of society under the leadership of the ulama. Khomeini has thus made himself into a figure of unquestioned moral authority, "the normative embodiment of tradition," the renewer of Islam and Islamic society.

From Algar's point of view, it may be argued that while the liberals and the leftists played a vanguard role, the ultimate victory of Khomeini and the

Islamic Republican Party was not due to circumstances or tactical considerations but reflects the central position of specifically Islamic religious symbols and leaders rather than "Islamo-Persian" revolutionary symbols and loyalties. Khomeini and the ulama were indispensable to the mobilization of the masses and the legitimation of the revolutionary regime. It may be argued that by contrast with Islamic movements in India, Egypt, and elsewhere, in Iran Muslim symbols and religious leadership and political organization have come together to effect a national revolution. At the same time it must be recognized that in all Muslim countries, Islamic values and institutions exist in a symbiotic relationship with political and social organizations and ideologies—whether parochial, national, or revolutionary—that are non-Islamic.

CONCLUSION

In these chapters we can distinguish at least three modes of the relationship of Islamic values and elites to political and social movements. The first is the premodern, exemplified by nineteenth-century Algeria and the Sudan, in which Islamic symbols and leaders are intrinsic to the structure of societies. Resistance movements built around Islamic symbols and leaders are, then, a variation upon the operation of the political system.

The second type is exemplified in what I have called transitional societies, the Islamic movement in India, Palestine, Egypt, and Nigeria. In these societies, Islamic symbols and concepts become a powerful source of inspiration and legitimation in the struggle for social and political justice and for communal and political identity. In India, Egypt, and Nigeria we see how Muslim symbols constitute a moral vocabulary emphasizing communalism, nationalism, solidarity, and unity. The preferred Muslim rhetoric excludes or is hostile to parochial and class concepts of political action. At the same time a manifest difficulty is encountered in fitting Muslim rhetoric to actual situations. In India the unifying symbols and the rhetoric of united Muslim political action did not overcome the division of Muslims into numerous parochial bodies and the rivalries among their elites, including factional chiefs, ulama reformers, Sufi *pirs*, and secularized professionals. The rivalry of elites complicated the problem of defining identity and divorced acceptable universal symbols from local roots. In Palestine no unifying Muslim symbol emerged. The numerous elites—*hamula* chiefs, religious preachers, and secularized modern educated nationalists—appealed to different concepts of political organization. In these cases Islamic symbols were imperfectly related to organizational structures. They failed either to mobilize or to reflect structural conditions.

Similarly, in the case of the Egyptian and Nigerian labor movements, the Muslim moral economy favored collective opposition to foreign domination, and appeals for moral justice. Beinin finds that Islamic affiliation operated against worker interests in the Egyptian textile industry. Goldberg and Lubeck allow for its effectiveness in mobilizing transitional peasant populations and in combining labor unionism and anti-imperialist political action. They argue for the existence of a fusion of national, class, and religious consciousness. Still, this consciousness does not articulate internal differences. The labor and political movements built on it are often coalition movements in which the partners have conflicting interests and are united only by a common enemy. Here, too, the fit among symbols, interests, and organizations remains imperfect.

Only in the Iranian revolution did historical conditions allow an effective junction of Islamic symbols, leaders, and political action. In Iran, national identity had already been achieved on both a secular and a religious basis, the political regime was highly centralized, and the opposition was closely identified with a national religious establishment. In that moment, Islamic symbols could again express, as they did in the very different world of the nineteenth century, the integration of cultural identity and worldly actuality.

TWO

Islam and Social Movements: Methodological Reflections

Edmund Burke, III

Scholarly concern with the Islamic roots of culture and politics is very recent. Dominated by the paradigm of modernization, the academic literature until quite recently stressed the impact upon Islamic elites of European ideas and cultural models, notably the modernizing efforts of such nineteenth-century reformers as Muhammad 'Ali of Egypt and Ottoman sultan Mahmud II, and the impact of secularism on culture and politics. An important subsidiary theme was the study of nationalism, which by the 1950s became the dominant ideology throughout the region. Today, in the wake of the Islamic revival, we are inclined to wonder if the concern with secular nationalism was all a mirage.[1]

It is important to consider the reasons for this important mental revolution. At issue, in part, is the nature of historical understanding. The built-in obsolescence of social thought derives from its rootedness in particular historically conditioned ways of thinking and feeling. Our angle of vision as observers constantly shifts with the passing of years: now one aspect of the past, now another, seems most significant to us. Partly also it has to do with the nature of the historical process itself. In a given society, particular cultural or structural features acquire prominence by the ways the changes they are subjected to affect them. (Thus, for example, one can account for the emergence of secular nationalism under the specific set of conditions that prevailed in the post-1919 world.) Similarly, under particular historically determined conditions of stress, social or cultural faultlines which had hitherto remained dormant may become activated. They can produce social earthquakes of sufficient magnitude to bring down not only regimes and classes, but also worldviews—the ways contemporaries have conceptualized their self-understanding. The Iranian revolution was one such seismic event. It swept away not only a regime but a view of the world. Today we find the ideas of particular politicians and modernization theorists obsolete not because they were wrong or inappropriate to their time, but because they no longer seem to apply under present conditions. Thus it is useful to remind ourselves that under another set of conditions, secular nationalism may regain its salience. If and when it does, however, it will surely do so in a different manner.

The current interest in Islam and politics can be seen to be a product of a particular historical moment. In the enthusiasm to comprehend the current upsurge of Islamic militancy, this basic fact is often forgotten. Secularism was not a mirage: it was rooted in long-term global processes of change, notably the rise of a world capitalist system centered on western Europe and of a class of bureaucrats interested in state centralization. The history of popular political movements in Muslim societies from 1918 to 1978 is incomprehensible unless one is willing to look at it from this perspective.

In this mood of sober reexamination, it is appropriate to note a related factor that shapes the development of the field. The epistemological ground on which studies of popular political action in Islamic societies is situated is notoriously spongy and subject to periodic cave-ins. Not only is it difficult to spot a trend except by hindsight, because of the extent to which we are all prisoners of present ways of thinking, but it is also perilous to advance an explication of the so-called Islamic revival without reproducing the concerns of the ambiant political culture of our own society, with its deeply grounded fears and phantasms about Islam. The discourse on the Other, especially the Muslim Other, is politically saturated. This is not to disqualify non-Muslim appreciations of Islamic social movements, however. The views of the cultural outsider will invariably differ to some degree from those of an insider, but this fact by no means invalidates them. While we cannot escape completely from these constraints, a degree of methodological self-consciousness is indispensable.[2]

ISLAMIC MOVEMENTS, OR SOCIAL MOVEMENTS?

The Islamic revival has exposed what might be viewed as a basic division in the field. Thus beyond a general agreement that it is important to study the historical roots of the modern Islamic revival and that its unfolding presents important regional variations, it is apparent that the presuppositions, the sources, and even the subject itself are rather differently conceived by the authors of the essays included here. As one engages this issue, one notes important differences over even so basic a matter as the definition of the subject. Is it *Islamic* political movements? Or *social* movements in Islamic societies? These contrasting questions frame a basic difference in the field.

An initial approach is to view the essays in this book as representative of two major traditions of scholarship on popular political action in Muslim societies. Drawing on what might be called the new cultural history (or the new Orientalism), one tradition pursues the Islamic dimension of these movements.

It explores how and to what effect particular movements (millenarians in nineteenth-century Sudan, Muslim nationalists in twentieth-century India, clergy in twentieth-century Iran) have deployed the cultural and religious resources of Islam in an attempt to mobilize and legitimate insurgent (anti-incumbent as well as anti-colonial) political movements.

A second approach derives from the new social history. It places the study of collective action in its sociological as well as its Islamic context. Its unit of analysis is not so much the movement as the system of relations (economic, political, and social) in which it developed. (Chapters included in this book which adopt this approach examine the study of anti-colonial resistance in nineteenth-century Algeria and twentieth-century Palestine, Islam, nationalism and the labor movement in Egypt and Nigeria, and revolution in Iran.)

Clearly, both costs and benefits are associated with each approach. In part, they seek to explain rather different phenomena. The study of social movements inevitably is concerned with how social protest arises and especially with the social and political structures within which such movements arise, regardless of the cultural idiom in which grievances are expressed. The study of Islamic movements, on the other hand, takes as its subject the Islamic concepts and rhetoric used by insurgent movements in different political and economic settings throughout the Muslim world. It is concerned less with explaining why the movements occur than with why they have adopted the forms they have and to what effect.

In part the differences between the two approaches spring from the principal sources utilized in each: for one, indigenous Islamic religious writings, often produced by the leadership of particular movements; for the other, sources (both indigenous and foreign) primarily concerned with the material conditions and political context in which the movements have arisen. But the two approaches also reflect different strategies for historical study and rather different assessments of the outcomes of these movements. Both have lengthy and respected intellectual lineages, though the eclecticism of current practice has tended to blur this fact.[3]

The first is associated with the work of the German sociological historian Max Weber. It postulates that the structure and action of a group are derived from its commitment to a particular belief system, on which the goals, standards of behavior, and legitimacy (and, ultimately, the power) of the authorities spring. In the Weberian system, challenges to established political systems spring from charismatic individuals able to galvanize large groups of followers in dedication to a particular idea.

The second approach draws its inspiration (if not always the weighting it gives to particular factors) from the work of Karl Marx. Marxists postulate that classes arise from common positions in the organization of production and that changes in society are the result of shifts in the organization of production. For them, shared aims and beliefs derive from shared interests and are mediated through each class's specific internal structure and relationship to other classes. Social movements emerge from shared interests as well, though they are shaped by internal structure, relationship to other classes, and common consciousness.

There is also a third tradition of studies of social disorder, although it is not represented in this volume. It is the important family of analysis derived from the work of the French sociologist Emile Durkheim. Durkheimians begin with the idea that the integration of societies rests on a shared consciousness, the disruption of which causes anomie, individual disorientation, and eventual conflict. Social change is the villain: it leads to social disintegration and disorder. Thus, in the familiar phrase, modernization causes revolution. We can recognize studies influenced by this approach by their concern with the psychological states and attitudes of the actors and with the social controls that restrain or favor their expression.[4]

Until the last few decades, the great majority of studies of social movements in Islamic societies tended (either implicitly or explicitly) to be situated within the Weberian tradition, though often without much methodological self-awareness. For those of a more methodological turn of mind, the work of Talcott Parsons (and, through him, of neo-Weberian sociologists and anthropologists like Robert Bellah, S. E. Eisenstadt, Clifford Geertz, and Victor Turner) has been especially influential.[5] Studies of Islamic movements have drawn productively on the works of these and other scholars. They have helped us to see more clearly the roles Islam has played in politics, as well as sensitizing us to the many ways the cultural and religious norms and precepts of Islam have been invoked in different societies and different settings.

The Iranian revolution and the resurgence of Islamic militancy throughout the Middle East have coincided with, and in part stimulated, a renewed concentration on Islamic movements, most of it drawing either explicitly or implicitly upon the Weberian tradition. Two subjects in particular have been emphasized: the transformation of Islamic religious doctrine, and the changing role of Muslim religious scholars, the ulama. The first has yielded valuable insights into the modern origins of Islamic fundamentalism, from the revival of *hadith* studies and the emergence of neo-Sufism in the eighteenth century to the emergence of contemporary movements in Islamic societies.[6] Studies of the second topic have emphasized the transformation of the role of the ulama and Muslim religious institutions more generally in the modern era.[7]

An increasing number of studies have drawn on other important intellectual traditions in the study of social protest. The so-called new social history, best identified with the work of Eric Hobsbawm, George Rudé, Edward P. Thompson, and Charles Tilly, has been especially influential. Nondoctrinaire and sensitive to the role of culture in shaping the choices socially available, these neo-Marxist historians and social scientists have played an important role in renewing the history of the origins of the European working class.[8] Their studies have provided us with a much more complex and richly informed understanding of the behavior of the crowd and of the ideology of social protest. The study of protest in Islamic societies has recently been invigorated by focusing their questions and approaches on social movements in Islamic societies.[9]

BLURRED GENRES

The debate between the new Orientalism and the new social history is unproductive as posed. It is one in which the two sides go past one another, never agreeing on what is to be explained, what sources are appropriate, or what questions to ask of them. But it does not have to be sterile.[10] One general characteristic of the social sciences recently has been a tendency toward the convergence of its diverse currents in broader explanations. For example, one rarely encounters either Weberian or Marxian analysis in an undiluted form. Rather, the time is one of blurred genres.[11] In some ways it makes sense to see this convergence as a product of deep tendencies in contemporary social thought toward a more historical, global, and comparative understanding of the world around us, of the relation of thought to action, and of parts to wholes. Thus while the essays included here can be seen as rival traditions of scholarship, eternally locked in segmentary opposition, this view is ultimately unsatisfactory. For despite sharp differences in orientation, their approach and findings converge closely. This convergence is indeed one of the chief contributions of this volume.

Three areas of substantial overlap can be distinguished. One is the shift from the study of writings by the religious elite—Islam as a normative system—to the study of popular culture—Islam as it is actually experienced by most Muslims. Two strategies have so far emerged, both of which are represented in this volume. One derives from the work of Geertz and other anthropologists and examines the ways elite discourse makes use of systems of symbols of identity and legitimacy. The other seeks to examine semi-autonomous forms of popular culture among workers and peasants and is influenced by the writings of British historian E. P. Thompson.

As we have become more knowledgeable about elite discourse, scholars have turned increasingly to the study of popular culture, the point of intersection of culture and politics. On the one hand, as we become better informed about the positions adopted by different Sufi *turuq* (brotherhoods), traditionists and schools of law, we are better able to ascertain their relative political positions within the existing system of religious discourse. On the other hand, the progress of knowledge about the impact of change on different class, ethnic, and other groups in Muslim societies from Morocco to India has enabled us better to grasp the nature of the stakes in particular cases, and also of the outcomes.

The theme of how various groups have invoked Islamic symbols and arguments to justify their political actions is an important one. It is taken up in many of the essays included here, especially in the chapters by Sandria Freitag and

David Gilmartin on the origins of Muslim nationalism in India. They stress the rivalry for leadership of various groups within the Indian Muslim elite and how each one sought to manipulate Islamic and other symbols of identity and legitimacy to its own advantage. The theme is also taken up in Part Five, "Revolution in Iran," which taken as a whole suggests that the outcome of the revolutionary process was far from preordained. Rival groups advanced conflicting remedies for the crisis of Iranian society, each of which was expressed in Islamic language and made use of Islamic symbols and arguments.

Popular culture in different parts of Islamic Africa is explored in a number of our contributions. Fanny Colonna's study of the Derduriya provides a richly detailed portrait of the popular culture of rural Algeria, and of a group who refused to follow the path of millenarian rebellion. John Voll's study of Abu Jummayza, a major rival of the Sudanese Mahdi, Muhammad Ahmad, builds upon a generation of studies of the popular culture of the Sudanic lands of Africa to present a fascinating study of the treacherous crosscurrents of the Sudanese political and religious world in the 1880s. Colonna, a sociologist, and Voll, a historian, provide converging views of rural popular culture in a time of change.

Since the 1950s, enormous changes have occurred in our understanding of movements of collective action. The work of European historians such as George Rudé, Eric Hobsbawm, and Edward Thompson have accustomed us to look not only at what rebels have said to justify their actions, that is, at their ideologies, but at what they have done as well. In the process what had once seemed like random archaic violence now appears to have been patterned: with hindsight it appears that the targets of the crowd were selected for their real or symbolic importance in the eyes of the rebels (although certainly some random looting and violence did occur as well). Thompson has argued that eighteenth-century English bread rioters were guided by a "moral economy," a religiously grounded sense of justice which not only propelled them into action but also provided the rituals of rebellion (such as the "setting of the price") according to which their actions were patterned. It is tempting to see the actions of Muslim crowds as being similarly directed.

The idea that the moral vision of workers and artisans in Muslim societies was shaped by peculiarly Islamic notions of justice is invoked by a number of the contributors to this volume. Taking a cue from Thompson, one can even refer to an "Islamic moral economy" as a shorthand description of the culturally patterned ways this sense of justice was invoked by crowds throughout the Islamic world.[12]

A second area of convergence has been the writing of political history, where the key change has been the shift in focus from the level of elite discourse and action to that of the local group. Again two strategies can be distinguished: the first, influenced by the writings of Ernest Gellner, among others, has sought to examine the behavior of rural elites in the context of the politics of segmentary tribes and economic scarcity.[13] The other strategy has come at the problem of rural politics from the opposite end. Influenced at least in part by the literature on African protest and resistance, it has focused on the problem of scale: how, in a world of kinship politics, to build coalitions that knit together larger units for political purposes.[14] Both ideological and organizational factors have received consideration in this approach.

As research develops on the role of Islam in politics, it becomes increasingly clear that the question of how and why particular groups behaved as they did cannot be satisfactorily answered by referring only to the influence of the religious and political elites. The decisive arena seems more and more to be the level of local politics. The pulling and tugging of factions, the pressures of political and economic exploitation at the level of everyday life, the influence of local political and religious figures shaped the responses of particular groups. The more we look, the more the micropolitics of protest appears an affair not of heroic poses and radical flourishes, but of bets artfully hedged, old grudges paid off in kind, and (sometimes) old solidarities reemphasized.

The history of colonial Algeria constitutes a particularly important terrain for the discussion and analysis of how these dynamics operated, although the theme is one that runs through most of this book. In the chapters by Peter Von Sivers and Julia Clancy-Smith we can observe the many forms taken by nineteenth-century Algerian resistance, which varied according to the eco-logical niche occupied by the group in question, the alliances of local elites, and the charisma of local marabouts or Sufi shaykhs. Collectively these authors raise an important question: why did some groups respond to millenarian appeals to jihad against the French, while others remained prudently outside the circle of violence, awaiting a better day? Seen from this angle, there was nothing inevitable about anti-colonial resistance, and, with a shift in the political winds, even the most charismatic leader might find himself suddenly deserted. The result of this line of investigation is to call into question the nationalist paradigm—which has tended to assume the broad appeal of resistance—and to focus attention on the micropolitics of the anti-colonial struggle.

One can also put the question the other way around. What is to be expected in times of crisis is that individuals draw back into basic kinship groups and other solidarities, those on which they depend directly for support and suste-nance. What is unusual is the effort to forge alliances with strangers whom they have every reason to distrust. For those who sought to organize large-scale movements of popular protest (or expand those already begun), the question was, accordingly, how to surmount the basic limitations on the scale of political action.

The chapters in Part Three, which take up the development of nationalism in the 1920s and 1930s in two societies particularly noted for their factionalism and ethnic minorities, Palestine and India, also depict responses to the question of scale.

In the aftermath of World War I, moreover, the situation was more than usually fluid. The destruction of the Ottoman empire and the abolition of the caliphate in 1924 removed at one stroke the central focal point of the identity of Sunni Muslims everywhere, leaving many in anguish and despair. The emergence of a Muslim nationalism in India was one result of this situation. It was to lead eventually to the establishment of Pakistan. In the process a nationalism had to be constructed that could bridge the huge ethnic, religious, and other gaps between the various elements of the Muslim populations of India. How Muslim politicians attacked the problem of expanding the scale of political action is addressed in the chapters by Freitag and Gilmartin.

The question of scale presented itself in a different fashion in mandate Palestine, where Christian and Muslim elites were able to put together (not without many difficulties) a coalition based on a secular nationalist program. The chapter by Ted Swedenburg considers the problems of including the Muslim rural populations, who found themselves caught between the exploitation of the Palestinian absentee landowning elite and the Zionist schemes of land purchase and colonization. Swedenburg's contribution pushes us to examine the reasons for the seeming incoherence of the Palestinian responses and the continuing importance of Islamic appeals to mobilize the rural populations. In particular, it raises the question of the role of Islamic appeals in the mobilization of the peasantry in the 1936–39 revolt. His focus on rural society permits us to see the linkages by which different elements were mobilized, and how and why the revolt took the form it did.

Do different social groups in Muslim societies invoke religion in distinctive ways? The question is an important one, and the effort to connect particular currents of thought and politics with particular social groups marks a third point of convergence visible in these pages. While such a sociology of Islamic social movements is not yet fully possible, it is clear that the more successful authors are at specifying the nature of popular beliefs and in locating them socially, the more persuasive their analyses are. In different parts of the Islamic world, different ethnic, ecological, and historical contexts have in practice yielded a different range of popular political movements.

One place that we begin to see how these linkages worked is in Egyptian society in the 1940s, where research into the rivalry between the Egyptian Communists and the Muslim Brothers for influence in the new working class has enabled scholars to begin to specify the connections between culture and politics, and between elite and popular thought and action. The chapters by Joel Beinin and Ellis Goldberg seek to trace the ways in which elite and popular levels of discourse connected to particular groups. Similarly, in the case of northern Nigeria Paul Lubeck examines the employment of the languages of religion, nationalism, and class by different social groups. He discusses the development of populist politics and its use by a portion of the political elite and organized works in Kano, but also the upsurge of millenarian social movements like the 'Yan Tatsine since independence, in an effort to explain the limited appeal of the latter.

Finally, this volume is a step toward a comparative history of Islamic societies. As a result of the work of such scholars as Fernand Braudel, Barrington Moore, Jr., Theda Skocpol, Immanuel Wallerstein, and Eric Wolf, awareness of the ways changes at the local level have been affected by regional, state, and global developments has been heightened.[15] Their work has been especially suggestive for the history of the Middle East, where the impact of extralocal causes is so evident. By shuttling back and forth in a disciplined and focused fashion between the local factors, on the one hand, and the more global explanatory factors, on the other, important analytical gains can be realized. These are especially evident in the study of protest movements. (Comparative history in this sense consists in placing a particular protest movement in its multiple contexts—it does not necessarily involve a comparison of two or more cases.) Thus, by situating the movements discussed here in a broad context, it is possible to see more clearly the connections between changes within groups and those affecting the state, society, and economy from the local level to the global. All three tendencies operate to deepen and sharpen explanations of popular political movements. As a result, instead of ascribing particular developments to Islam, we find ourselves in these essays seeking to understand the ways specific religious and cultural currents influenced the behavior of particular groups in particular circumstances, and how the social and political settings in which movements occurred helped shape the choice of strategies and thus the outcomes as well. The convergences of modern scholarship on popular political movements in Islamic societies have sharpened our sense of what is a good question and also of what might constitute a convincing explanation.

COLLECTIVE ACTION IN THE ISLAMIC WORLD: AN INTERPRETATIVE FRAMEWORK

The study of popular political movements can teach us much about the historical transformations Muslim societies have experienced since the end of the eighteenth century. What we learn, however, is a product of the questions we ask, the connections we make, and the historical context in which we situate these movements. On this level, beyond the blurring of genres, basic epistemological options once again become relevant. Depending on whether one is interested in tracing the history of Islamic political movements (and the religious ideas that have inspired and to a degree shaped them) or collective action in Muslim societies (and the social and economic contexts in which they have arisen), two rather different interpretative strategies may be suggested. A brief consideration of each concludes this chapter and helps to make clear the differences between the two approaches, as well as the reasons for some of the convergences noted in the previous section.

Ira Lapidus adopts the first perspective, placing the cases discussed in this book within the framework of a history of Islamic political movements. He focuses on changes in Islamic political symbols and concepts and the role of elites in shaping styles of political action. Lapidus's approach stresses the relationship of Islamic symbols, leaders, and political action. It provides a necessary and helpful context in which to consider the patterns of Islamic political action, one rooted in the tradition of cultural history deriving ultimately from Max Weber.

Drawing on the tradition of the new social history, the cases discussed in this book can be situated within a second context, however. It is the history of collective action in Islamic societies. Clearly this is a daunting proposition. Although we are only beginning to see the outlines of such a history, enough is presently visible to make possible a brief sketch. In the remainder of this section, I draw on the preliminary findings of my work in progress on the history of Middle Eastern protest since 1750 in an effort to develop its implications for the cases included in this work.[16]

Instead of privileging ideology as the central analytic category, a comparative history of collective action focuses on the movement (regardless of the cultural idiom in which it expresses itself). Such an undertaking begins with a consideration of the patterns of collective action—what the rebels did, where they gathered, the slogans they chanted, the targets of their wrath. But it is ultimately concerned with tracing the connections between changes in the patterns of protest and the changing structures of the society. To place our cases in the context of the history of the forms of collective action, it is first necessary to understand the ways Islamic societies were transformed from the nineteenth century to the present.

For purposes of analysis, one can say that since 1750, social movements in the Islamic world have emerged as a result of the intersection of three main kinds of change. The first was the indigenous self-strengthening movement in the region. Under its aegis the state bureaucracy sought to increase its control of the society, modern armies were established, and modern schools and methods of communications developed. In the Ottoman provinces this process was known as the *tanzimat* movement. It led inevitably to a collision between reform-minded state bureaucrats and local elites, eager to defend their traditional rights and liberties. The *tanzimat* also stimulated conflict with peasants and artisans, for whom the encroachment of the state was experienced primarily in the form of military conscription and increased taxation. The development of a centralized state proceeded in similar fashion in the Indian subcontinent, with the British operating in the background until the Great Mutiny in 1857. Thereafter, the Indian experience came to resemble that of other colonial dependencies in the Middle East. Analogous changes were also experienced, though in attenuated form, in Sudanic Africa, the Maghrib, and Qajar Iran, where the state was less deeply rooted and the opponents of centralization more powerful.[17] The incorporation of the Middle East into the world economy stimulated a second and in some ways more far-reaching type of change, which affected even relatively isolated regions with weak states. Its effects, however, were differentially greater upon those societies, such as Egypt and the Arab East, that stood astride major world communications links. Economic incorporation led to the rise of a new urban middle class whose fortunes were linked to Europe, and to the emergence of an urban-based class of landowners engaged in commercial agriculture for export. It also resulted in the decline of artisans and peasants unable to adapt to the changing economic tides. To the fiscal and other pressures of the centralizing state were added, therefore, additional ones along economic lines of cleavage.[18]

The third major axis of change was provided by the establishment of European hegemony throughout the region. Since European power was based on the local elites, this had a distorting impact on internal processes of change, working to undermine the legitimacy of collaborating groups and/or diverting social movements from their internal targets to the European rulers. This can be observed first in such places as India and Algeria, but, ultimately, similar social patterns arose even in such formally independent countries as Iran. In the long run, while European dominance shored up the precarious power of old elites, who capitalized upon their position to maintain control of the nationalist movement when it emerged, it ensured that when new classes made their long-deferred emergence onto the political scene after World War II, they swept all before them.[19]

Each of these vectors of change worked in favor of certain groups in the society and against others. Those possessing privileged ties to the state or to European business interests were often in a position to profit disproportionately, while urban artisans and rural agriculturalists found themselves squeezed on all sides. Following the establishment of European political control, groups willing to serve as intermediaries gained substantially, while overt opponents suffered from various forms of political and economic discrimination. The complex sequence of changes thus set in motion intersected with one another, generating powerful crosscurrents and back eddies that eroded established interests and molded new ones. Social protest and resistance found fertile ground in the circumstances thus created.

Three major types of collective action were generated by the intersection of these forces of change: urban-based popular disturbances; movements of peasant protest; and movements directed against European political dominance and in defense of social identity. Far from it being the case that Islamic societies tend to generate only a very limited repertoire of social-movement types, we can distinguish important differences between them. Each type of movement had its own specific patterns and repertoires of collective action, and its own history. As we will see, the social composition, ideologies, targets, and basic patterns of movements varied in relation to changing structures and *mentalités*.

Some patterns were culturally specific, such as the Iranian Shi'i memorial processions which, put to new uses, provided one of the central motifs of the Iranian revolution. Others were more widely disseminated, such as the basic repertoire of urban protest until the twentieth century in many Islamic societies.

PHASE ONE:
THE LONG NINETEENTH CENTURY (1750–1914)

If we seek to place the cases discussed in this book in the framework of patterns of collective action, we get some interesting results. One major finding is the persistence into the nineteenth century of basic movement patterns from earlier Islamic times, and their connection to the perduring structures of social action. Thus urban social movements were given their distinctive forms by the persistence of political and religious institutions which served to organize life in the cities, notably the quarter, the guild, the Sufi *tariqa*, and the mosque. Rural movements tended to be shaped by the local agrarian structures—especially local social solidarities (agnatic, religious, and economic)—which were the links between the local community and the outside world.

A central feature of urban movements prior to the twentieth century was the central role of the ulama as go-betweens and legitimators of the crowd's anger. Urban protest movements tended to follow a basic scenario, which began with the gathering of the crowd at the central mosque. After much discussion, the demands of the crowd were fixed and ulama intermediaries appointed. The crowd then proceeded from the mosque to the citadel, where its demands were presented to the local authorities by the ulama. Violence was often symbolic and generally limited, casualties were few, and the targets of the crowd selected rather than random: grain storehouses, the homes and shops of profiteering officials and merchants. Insofar as its social composition is known to us, the crowd appears to have been drawn from artisans, workers, and Islamic students (*talib*). The solidarities of the urban quarter, Islamic guilds, Sufi brotherhoods (and in the Ottoman empire, local janissary units) provided whatever coherence the crowd had, and very often the leadership as well.[20]

A second type of protest is constituted by peasant jacqueries and other rural disturbances. These could take a variety of different forms depending on local agrarian structures. The possibilities of rural popular political action were largely shaped by the patterns of social segmentation and the extent to which the gaps between groups were bridged by religious and economic connections. Feuds and other honor-related violence aside, three basic types of rural movements can be discerned. First, there were the rebellions based on the village and/or tribal structures, sparked by particular grievances, and legitimized solely by local cultural values. Where translocal interests were placed in jeopardy, however, larger-scale rebellions involving several groups might occur and were generally structured by overarching social solidarities, among which tribal or village alliance networks and Sufi *turuq* played a major role. It is in this way that we may understand such important rural uprisings as the 1858 Kisrawan rebellion, the 1864 Tunisian rebellion, and the 1902 Shawiya rebellion in Morocco.[21] Finally, if the crisis were particularly intense, rural groups could further raise the stakes by invoking Islamic millenarian appeals. The Sudanese Mahdiya is an example of this movement type.

In the nineteenth century, patterns of resistance to European encroachment, our third sort of movement, either followed the course of an Islamic *levée en masse* (in which the central authorities and urban ulama invoked the doctrine of jihad and sought to organize a coherent resistance effort, like that of the Amir 'Abd al-Qadir in Algeria) or, as occurred in rural areas after his defeat, tended to build on the basic repertoire of rural rebellion outlined above. As we will see, these traditional forms of protest and resistance underwent important changes after 1900.

The chapters in Part Two clearly develop the millenarian and Sufi context of rural protest and resistance in Islamic Africa. In Algeria, the Sufi-led revolts against the French discussed by Peter Von Sivers and Julia Clancy-Smith represent the dominant form of anti-colonial resistance in the nineteenth century. Fanny Colonna's examination of the case of the Derduriya shows that millenarian resistance was not the only available option, however. The strategy pursued by this Sufi order, which involved a refocusing of the group's energies upon investment in land, placed them in a strong position after World War I. Colonna argues that it is no accident that they became local leaders of the Islamic reformist movement in the 1930s. Finally, John Voll's discussion of the case of the Sudanese Mahdi and his rival, Abu Jummayza, explores the influence of the millenarian and Sufi populist tradition of Islam in Sudanic Africa. In each case, the patterns of protest were linked to particular agrarian structures and cultural traditions. By the postwar period, as Paul Lubeck shows, fundamental societal changes led to the emergence of nationalism in such African societies as Nigeria and to new forms of popular political action. One result was the marginalization of the older millenarian Sufi tradition, even though it continues to exist in the form of movements like that of the contemporary 'Yan Tatsine rebels of northern Nigeria.

THE SECULAR AGE:
FROM WORLD WAR I TO THE OCTOBER WAR

The last popular protests in which the ulama played an important role occurred prior to World War I. Between 1840 and 1914, the central political dynamic began to change as a result of the adoption of major reform programs in Egypt, the Ottoman empire, and India (in the latter case, under British auspices). Strong centralizing states came to replace the remnants of the old janissary/Mamluk system. In the cities, governments moved to destroy the independent power of the urban-based military elites and to assert their own dominance. As a result of the new repressive capacity of the state, protest became less common. At the same time, far-reaching social changes undermined urban and rural structures and the ways of life embedded in them. Throughout the region a gradual shift both in the targets of the crowd's wrath and in the forms it assumed can be observed. The old repertoire of collective action, based on the gathering of the crowd at the mosque, solemn processions to the seat of government, and the presentation of petitions to the authorities, faded out everywhere.

The urban crowd reemerged as a political force in the early twentieth century with the Iranian constitutional revolution of 1906–11, the Young Turk revolution of 1908, and the Moroccan revolution of 1908. By this time one can already catch a glimpse of emerging patterns of popular protest: the first strikes, boycotts, and student demonstrations occurred prior to 1914. Also evident from this period is the emergence of nationalism as an important political ideology.

The Ottoman defeat in 1918, followed by the rise of a Turkish republic and the abolition of the caliphate in 1924, shattered the old political framework. A new style of politics was beginning and, with it, new forms of popular political movements. After 1919, urban politics was dominated for two generations by various forms of nationalism, and popular political action assumed new forms. Collective action in the interwar period is examined by the chapters in Parts Three and Four that treat India, Palestine, and Egypt. As the old urban social structures were gradually undermined by change, the control exercised by the urban notables began to break down. New political actors emerged.[22]

The chapters by Freitag and Gilmartin provide a view of the complexities that resulted in the Indian subcontinent. After the split between the Congress party and the Muslim League in 1916, Indian Muslim notables found themselves in a difficult position. On the one hand, their control over urban politics was contested by both the urban ulama and rural notables. On the other hand, they found themselves challenged from below by a new communal populist leadership as well as by the emerging working-class movement. Cleavages between generations further aggravated the situation. Through their examination of the political use of Islamic symbols and the role of communal disturbances in defining a Muslim political identity, Freitag and Gilmartin help explain why Muslim nationalism assumed the forms it did.

In the Arab world, by contrast, nationalism ruled the streets. In spite of the emergence of new political forces, the urban notables were able to maintain their control over politics until after World War II. Their situation differed greatly from that of Indian Muslims, as Ted Swedenburg's essay on the Palestinian revolt of 1936–39 shows. He argues that the course of Palestinian politics under the British Mandate was shaped by the ways Palestinian agrarian structures and popular culture were transformed in the nineteenth and twentieth centuries. While urban notables followed a secular strategy, the largely Muslim peasantry of Palestine could most readily be mobilized by appeals to religion. His examination of the role of Shaykh 'Izz al-Din al-Qassam and his followers in the outbreak of the revolt helps us to see how much patterns of protest had changed since the nineteenth century. Despite al-Qassam's reliance upon religious appeals, the organization of his movement, no less than its social base and its strategy and tactics, differed from nineteenth-century ulama-led movements. The internal dynamics of the nationalist coalition, landlord dominance, Ottoman (and later British) centralizing agencies, and Zionist strategies of settlement and land acquisition had permanently transformed Palestinian social realities and possibilities of collective action.

A second new form of popular political action in the interwar Islamic world was the emergence of a labor movement. The first stirrings of workers' protest are visible in Turkey, Egypt, and India before 1914. Thereafter it developed in parallel with the implantation of industry. The forms of collective action utilized by protestors drew on the repertoire of European workers' movements— strikes, boycotts, factory occupations, and the like. But they were inspired by Islamic notions of social justice, and often recruited worker activists from such Islamic religious networks as Sufi brotherhoods and Quran schoolteachers, as the chapters by Goldberg, Beinin, and Lubeck in Part Four demonstrate. Connections between the class struggle, the national struggle, and the Islamic struggle for justice in an immoral world are intricate, as these chapters show, and the Islamic experience of working-class formation differed in important respects from that of the West. Just how much becomes clear in Beinin's chapter, which considers the experience of the Shubra al-Khayma textile workers and the confrontation between the organizers of the Communists and those of the Muslim Brothers. There, and later in Nigeria, as we see in Lubeck's chapter, the limits of Islamic populism are shown.

IN THE SHADOW OF THE IRANIAN REVOLUTION

Part Five situates historically one of the major political events of our time: the Islamic revolution in Iran in 1978–79. Despite their seeming archaisms, the forms of protest, the repertoire of collective action, and the symbolic language of protest utilized by the insurgent forces in Iran were of modern origin, as Nikki Keddie's contribution argues.

The role of leadership in movements of collective action is emphasized in the contrasting portraits of two of the major leaders of the revolution: Imam Khomeini and 'Ali Shari'ati, examined in the chapters by Hamid Algar and Ervand Abrahamian. Here as well we come to appreciate the major ideological struggle within the world of Iranian Shi'ism which culminated in the splintering of the revolutionary coalition following Khomeini's accession to power. These two contributions enable us to see, through the prism of two extraordinary individuals, some of the constraints and possibilities of the Iranian tradition of collective action.

The Iranian revolution shattered a number of basic assumptions made by

Western scholars about how revolutions occur.[23] While most political scientists assumed that revolutions are made by those on the left and are secular in ideology, the Iranian revolution was avowedly Shiʻi and anti-Marxist. Although the literature on revolutions stressed the central role of peasant rebellions in setting off revolutionary upsurges, the peasantry played almost no role in the Iranian revolution. Indeed, the Iranian revolution was an almost exclusively urban phenomenon. Although the successes of guerrilla forces in the overthrow of colonial governments led many experts to assume that this was the chief route to success in the postwar era, in the Iranian revolution guerrilla groups played only a very modest role. By contrast, the events in Iran in 1979 witnessed the largest mass demonstrations in history—which were, moreover, almost entirely peaceful. Finally, against those who argue that incumbent forces can maintain control through a unified display of repressive force, Iran offers the example of a regime that deployed unprecedented repressive power and maintained its unity to the very end, yet still lost. Social scientists are still working to salvage something from the wreckage of battered concepts in the wake of the Iranian revolution.

In her chapter, Keddie situates the Iranian revolution in the context both of theories of revolution, and of Iran's turbulent political history. She shows how in both 1905–11 and 1978–79, an alliance among the ulama, the bazaar, and secularized liberals and urban radical intelligentsia made the revolution possible. Whereas in 1905–11 this alliance broke down, it remained strong in 1978–79. Both revolutions grew out of earlier rehearsals. In both instances, there were significant social and economic dimensions to the crisis that immediately preceded the onset of the revolutions. Social forces let loose by the political decay of the regimes then coalesced and sought to overthrow them.

The contrasts Keddie develops between the two revolutions are even more illuminating. Thus, for example, she notes that post–World War II Iranian society was much more decisively disrupted by the changes set in motion by the shah's reforms. These were further exacerbated by the OPEC price increase, which led to a huge influx of revenues to the state coffers and set off a hyperinflationary spiral resulting in windfall gains for the few and misery for the many. As a result, the social forces that composed the opposition coalition in 1979 were vastly stronger than they had been at the beginning of the century. Conversely, their opponents were much weaker: the reactionary landlords, for example, had their wings clipped by the shah following the introduction of land reform, while the traditional ulama were transformed by changes in the system of religious education. If, following Keddie's analysis, it was to some extent inevitable that the Iranian regime would have provoked an Islamic popular challenge, she argues that it was by no means foreordained that events would escalate into revolution or that the group around Ayatullah Khomeini would win control once it occurred. While Leninist interpretations of the Iranian revolution abound, it is important to insist that the specific outcome of the confrontation was by no means predictable (in fact, to our knowledge no one did predict it).

The essays on the revolution in Iran bring us full circle—back to the questions with which we started, of the role of personalities, ideas, and social and economic factors in social movements. In the work on Iran, as in other essays included in this book, we see the contributions which both the new Orientalism and the new social history have begun to make in the study of popular political movements in Islamic societies. It is clear that each makes significant contributions to our understanding and that the field can only benefit from increased dialogue and debate. In retrospect, then, the question is not so much that of *Islamic* movements versus *social* movements. Rather, it is how the new methodological advances can be incorporated to the enrichment of both. The chapters in this book together make an important statement about where research on Islam and social movements is going. They provide us with a variety of fruitful approaches that can usefully be adapted to other studies. Their interaction cannot fail to enrich the study both of Islamic history and of social movements.

NOTES

1. On the subject of secularization, modernization, and nationalism, see, among others, Niyazi Berkes, *The Rise of Secularism in Turkey* (Montreal: McGill University Press, 1964); Bernard Lewis, *The Emergence of Modern Turkey* (London: Oxford, 1961); Albert Hourani, *Arabic Thought in the Liberal Age* (London: Oxford, 1962); and Serif Mardin, *The Genesis of Young Ottoman Thought* (Princeton: Princeton University Press, 1962).

2. The subject of discourse on Islamic societies has attracted considerable interest recently. For a representative sample of works on the subject see Malcolm Kerr, ed., *Islamic Studies: A Tradition and Its Transformation* (Santa Monica: Undena University Press, 1981); Henri Moniot, ed., *Le mal de voir* (Paris: Collection 10/18, 1976); Edward Said, *Orientalism* (New York: Pantheon, 1979); and Jean-Claude Vatin, ed., *Connaissances du Maghreb: sciences sociales et colonisation* (Paris: C.N.R.S., 1984). See also Jean-François Clement, "Journalistes et chercheurs des sciences sociales face aux mouvements islamistes," *Archives de Sciences Sociales des Religions* 55 (1983): 85–104.

3. It is symptomatic of the absence of methodological self-consciousness in the profession that many historians are surprised to discover that they belong to a tradition of social analysis.

For a discussion of the chief intellectual lineages in the study of social movements, see Charles Tilly, *From Mobilization to Revolution* (New York: Addison-Wesley, 1978).

4. Representative examples include Samuel P. Huntington, *Political Order in Changing Societies* (New Haven: Yale University Press, 1968); Chalmers Johnson, *Revolutionary Change* (Boston: Little, Brown, 1966); and Ted Robert Gurr, *Why Men Rebel* (Princeton: Princeton University Press, 1969).

For a critique of the Durkheimian school, see Charles Tilly, "Does Modernization Breed Revolution?" *Comparative Politics* 5 (1973): 425–47.

5. Talcott Parsons, *The Social System* (New York: Free Press, 1964); Robert Bellah, *Beyond Belief* (New York: Harper and Row, 1970); S. E. Eisenstadt, *The Political Systems of Empires* (New York: Free Press, 1963); Clifford Geertz, *The Interpretation of Cultures* (Stanford: Stanford University Press, 1974); and Victor Turner, *The Ritual Process* (Chicago: Aldine, 1969).

6. See Marshall Hodgson, *The Venture of Islam*, 3 vols. (Chicago: University of Chicago Press, 1974); also, among others, Hamid Enayet, *Modern Islamic Political Thought* (Austin: University of

Texas Press, 1982); Fazlur Rahman, *Islam* (New York: Holt, Rinehart and Winston, 1966); John Voll, *Islam: Continuity and Change in the Modern World* (Boulder: Westview Press, 1982).

7. See Nikki R. Keddie, ed., *Scholars, Saints, and Sufis: Muslim Religious Institutions since 1500* (Berkeley and Los Angeles: University of California Press, 1972); Hamid Algar, *Religion and State in Iran 1785–1906* (Berkeley and Los Angeles: University of California Press, 1969); Michael Fisher, *Iran: From Religious Dispute to Revolution* (Cambridge, Mass.: Harvard University Press, 1980); Dale Eickelman, *Moroccan Islam: Tradition and Society in a Pilgrimage Center* (Austin: University of Texas Press, 1976).

8. Eric Hobsbawm, *Primitive Rebels* (New York: Norton, 1956), and, with George Rudé, *Captain Swing* (London: Lawrence and Wishart, 1969); George Rudé, *The Crowd in History* (New York: Harper and Row, 1964); Edward P. Thompson, *The Making of the English Working Class* (New York: Alfred A. Knopf, 1963), and *Whigs and Hunters: The Origins of the Black Act* (London: Allen Lane, 1975); Charles Tilly, *The Vendée* (New York: John Wiley, 1964), and, with Louise Tilly and Richard Tilly, *The Rebellious Century, 1830–1930* (Cambridge, Mass.: Harvard University Press, 1975); and William Sewell, *Work and Revolution in France* (London: Cambridge University Press, 1980).

9. See, for example, Ervand Abrahamian, *Iran between Two Revolutions* (Princeton: Princeton University Press, 1981); Hanna Batatu, *The Old Social Classes and the Revolutionary Movements of Iraq* (Princeton: Princeton University Press, 1978); and Edmund Burke, III, *Prelude to Protectorate in Morocco: Precolonial Protest and Resistance, 1860–1912* (Chicago: University of Chicago Press, 1976).

10. An interesting debate between William Sewell, Jr., and Theda Skocpol centers on many of the issues discussed here. William Sewell, Jr., "Ideologies and Social Revolutions: Reflections on the French Case," *JMH* 57 (1985): 57–85, and Theda Skocpol, "Cultural Idioms and Political Ideologies in the Revolutionary Reconstruction of State Power: A Rejoinder to Sewell," *JMH* 57 (1985): 86–96.

11. Clifford Geertz, "Blurred Genres," *American Scholar* (1980): 165–79.

12. For an attempt to do this see my "Understanding Arab Social Movements," *Arab Studies Quarterly* 8 (1986): 333–45. It is important in making this extension of the term *moral economy* to be aware of the specifically British and Christian concept behind Thompson's usage.

13. Ernest Gellner, *Saints of the Atlas* (London: Weidenfeld, 1973).

14. For the literature on African resistance see T. O. Ranger, "The People in African Resistance: A Review," *Journal of Southern African Studies* 4 (1977): 125–46; and Ranger's unpublished paper, "From Proto-Nationalist Revolt to Agrarian Protest: A Historiographical Shift."

See also Robert Rotberg and Ali Mazrui, eds., *Protest and Power in Black Africa* (Oxford: Oxford University Press, 1970); Jean Bazin and Emmanuel Terray, eds., *Guerres de lignages et guerres d'états en Afrique* (Paris: Archives Contemporaines, 1982); and Donald Crummey, ed., *Banditry, Rebellion and Social Protest in Africa* (London: Heinemann, 1986).

15. Fernand Braudel, *Civilization matérielle et capitalisme*, 3 vols. (Paris: Armand Colin, 1976); Barrington Moore, Jr., *Social Origins of Dictatorship and Democracy* (Boston: Beacon Press, 1966); Theda Skocpol, *States and Social Revolutions* (New York: Cambridge University Press, 1979); Immanuel Wallerstein, *The Modern World System*, 2 vols. (New York: Academic Press, 1974, 1980); and Eric Wolf, *Peasant Wars of the Twentieth Century* (New York: Harper and Row, 1969), and *Europe and the People without History* (Berkeley and Los Angeles: University of California Press, 1983).

16. See my unpublished paper "Arab Protest and Resistance, 1750–1930," presented at the American Historical Association Annual Meeting, December 1983.

17. On the self-strengthening movement in the Middle East see Richard Chambers and William Polk, eds., *Beginnings of Modernization in the Middle East* (Chicago: University of Chicago Press, 1968), and Robert Ward and Dankwort Rustow, eds., *Modernization in Turkey and Japan* (Princeton: Princeton University Press, 1966). See also Carter Findley, *Bureaucratic Reform in the Ottoman Empire* (Princeton: Princeton University Press, 1980); Nikki R. Keddie, *Roots of Revolution: An Interpretive History of Modern Iran* (New Haven: Yale University Press, 1981); and Afaf Lutfi al-Sayyid Marsot, *Egypt under Muhammad Ali* (Cambridge, England: Cambridge University Press, 1984).

18. On the economic incorporation of the Middle East see Charles Issawi, *An Economic History of the Middle East and North Africa* (London: Methuen, 1982); and Roger Owen, *The Middle East in the World Economy, 1800–1914* (London: Methuen, 1981).

19. The history of European imperialism in the Middle East and the Islamic world is in need of renewal. In the interim, see, for example, M. S. Anderson, *The Eastern Question* (London: St. Martin's Press, 1966); David Landes, *Bankers and Pashas* (Cambridge, Mass.: Harvard University Press, 1962); and L. Carl Brown, *International Politics and the Middle East: Old Rules, Dangerous Game* (Princeton: Princeton University Press, 1984).

20. On urban protest, the debate over the case of late-eighteenth-century Egypt among Gabriel Baer, Afaf Lutfi al-Sayyid Marsot, and André Raymond is of interest. André Raymond, "Quartiers et mouvements populaires au Caire au XVIIIème siècle," in P. M. Holt, ed., *Political and Social Change in Modern Egypt* (London, 1968), pp. 104–16; Afaf Lutfi al-Sayyid Marsot, "The Role of the Ulama in Egypt during the Early Nineteenth Century," in ibid., pp. 264–80; and Gabriel Baer, "Popular Revolt in Ottoman Cairo," *Der Islam* 54, no. 2 (1977): 213–42. Cf. also my "Understanding Arab Social Movements."

21. On the Kisrawan rebellion, see D. Chevallier, "Aux origines des troubles agraires libanais en 1858," *Annales ESC* 14 (1959): 35–64, and Y. Porath, "The Peasant Revolt of 1858–61 in Kisrawan," *Asian and African Studies* 2 (1966): 77–157. On the 1864 Tunisian revolt, see B. Slama, *L'Insurrection de 1864 en Tunisie* (Tunis: Maison Tunisienne d'Edition, 1967). On the Shawiya rebellion of 1902, see E. Burke, "Mouvements sociaux et mouvements de résistance au Maroc: La Grande Siba de la Chaouia, 1903–1907," *Hesperis-Tamuda* 17 (1976–77): 149–63.

22. Philip Khoury, "Syrian Urban Politics in Transition: The Quarters of Damascus during the French Mandate," *IJMES* 16 (1984): 507–40.

23. See, for example, Theda Skocpol, "Rentier State and Shi'a Islam in the Iranian Revolution," *Theory and Society* 11 (1982): 265–83; and the replies by Eqbal Ahmad, Nikki Keddie, and Walter Goldfrank.

PART TWO

Nineteenth-Century Anti-Colonial Resistance and Millenarianism in the Maghrib and the Sudan

THREE

Rural Uprisings as Political Movements in Colonial Algeria, 1851–1914

Peter Von Sivers

The most common form of political movement in the Middle East and North Africa prior to the twentieth century was the rural uprising. With the exception of the original great Arab-Islamic movement of the seventh century A.D. (which had its roots in the city of Mecca) and the urban social and religious movements, with their political overtones, in tenth- and eleventh-century Syria and Iraq, political movements were usually initiated by nomads or peasants. On the one hand, the predominance of political movements of rural origin occasions little surprise, given the numerical insignificance of urban populations prior to twentieth-century industrialization and urbanization. On the other hand, this predominance should not be taken as an indication that the countryside was somehow more predisposed than the city to the formation of political movements. On the contrary, there are numerous indications pointing to the existence of formidable social and economic barriers against the formation of such uprisings in the countryside. Until the twentieth century, political movements in the Middle East and North Africa were rural more by default than by design.

In this chapter, Algeria, during the second half of the nineteenth century, is used as an example in analyzing some of the social and economic barriers that kept political movements from effectively uniting the countryside. Although French colonial occupation of the country provided the single most potent stimulus for the formation of rural resistance movements, social and economic conditions inherited from the pre-French period did, in fact, impose considerable limits on these movements. I shall first sketch the general background for an understanding of these rural uprisings and then describe demographic and agricultural conditions of full and incomplete self-sufficiency, before discussing specific revolts in fully self-sufficient and then incompletely self-sufficient regions; finally, I shall analyze the crucial role played by Islam in all these insurrections.

BACKGROUND FOR RURAL UPRISINGS IN ALGERIA

As is well known, Algeria had been for centuries a province of the Ottoman empire when the city of Algiers was attacked and taken by the French in 1830. In the sixteenth and seventeenth centuries, Algeria had been a strategically important advance naval base for the Ottomans against the Habsburgs in Spain, as well as a possession made lucrative by its successful corsair campaigns against the Christians. In the eighteenth century this strategic and financial importance had evaporated, primarily because of the decline of Spanish power and the shift of the profitable trans-Atlantic trade from Spain to the Netherlands and England. As a consequence, Algeria's agricultural resources had been tapped more systematically to provide both for the Ottoman military and administrative contingent in the country and for the required tribute to Istanbul. By the time of the English continental blockade, Algeria had acquired some importance as a wheat producer for Napoleon's armies. The French attack on Algiers in 1830 was directed toward gaining control of Algeria's wheat-derived wealth.

After a decade of extensive debates over the question of whether direct or indirect control should be exercised over Algeria, the French government eventually opted for total conquest and direct colonial control. Between 1840 and 1851 all of northern Algeria was wrested from 'Abd al-Qadir and al-Hajj Ahmad, the two indigenous leaders who had assumed leadership of the western and eastern portions (respectively) of the country after the Ottoman collapse. After 1851 a system of French military government, complete with garrisons, outposts, and local tribal administrators, was built up, and European immigrants were encouraged to settle on tracts of farm or brush lands expropriated from the indigenous Arabic- and Berber-speaking population. An analysis of indigenous uprisings has to begin at this lowest level of full colonial control and the establishment of colonial farming settlements on expropriated land by the French.

The heroes of the Algerian revolts against French colonial rule were a varied lot. Scions of old religious and secular families sacrificed their lives as readily as did obscure religious charismatics and peasants. Most uprisings occurred in the steppes and deserts of the northern Sahara, but a good number happened in the mountains and plains of North Africa. Some rebellions broke out spontaneously; others had been planned long in advance. Some insurrections were put down as quickly as they emerged; others dragged on for years or even decades. About the only constant that can easily be distinguished in the dozen or so revolts during the period between the completion of the French conquest in most of northern Algeria (1851) and the beginning of nationalism around World War I (1914) is of a fiscal nature. All revolts erupted in areas that had been exempt from, or only occasionally within reach of, the arm of the Ottoman tax authorities and now, in the second half of the nineteenth century, were subject to the regular taxes or tributes instituted by the French everywhere in Algeria.

Amid this diversity of resistance movements it is tempting to make that one constant—former freedom from regular Ottoman taxation—the center for the interpretation of Algerian history in the second half of the nineteenth century. However, the trouble with such an interpretation is that the documents of the period contain neither direct complaints against nor even indirect hints about the French-imposed taxes. One would have to engage in a good deal of liberty with the sources in order to transform the Algerian uprisings into tax revolts against cruel colonial exploiters.

If concrete taxes are ruled out as an explanation, perhaps some more general theory invoking the insurrectionists' traditional autonomy can be formulated. According to this theory one might think that those populations that were imbued with traditions of autonomous leadership tended toward revolt, while those with a long history of subjection to Ottoman leaders and tax agents did not possess the leadership infrastructure to rebel. However, although it is true that the populations of the Kabylia and Aurès mountains and the Saharan steppes and deserts possessed strong traditions of autonomy in a political sense, the same was not true in the economic sphere. Mountain, steppe, and desert populations were crucially dependent on market exchange with the wheat producers of the northern plains and valleys. These wheat producers were among the economically most self-sufficient populations in Algeria, yet they were precisely the ones subjected to Ottoman taxation and were traditionally rather inactive politically. Thus, unless a careful distinction is made between economic dependency and political autonomy, and a convincing explanation for the disparity between the two is found, this more general theory will also be of little value. In the following section I shall analyze the sources of this disparity.

DEMOGRAPHY AND DEGREES OF SELF-SUFFICIENCY

Historically, Algeria—indeed, the Maghrib as a whole—has always been an area of low population density. However, population distribution has also historically been quite unequal, with important consequences that I shall investigate below. Prior to the great cholera epidemic of 1867, the average density in northern Algeria was perhaps 20 persons per square kilometer; some mountain regions held as many as 170 persons per square kilometer; and in the steppes and deserts of the northern Sahara the density sank as low as 2 persons per square kilometer.[1] These figures may be contrasted with those of the Netherlands, the most populous country of Europe, which during the early eighteenth century, at the time of its transition from a self-sufficient to a market-dependent agriculture, had up to 100 persons per square kilometer.[2] The average population density in northern Algeria, though comparatively low, was nevertheless high enough to require an agriculture based on the plow and the cultivation of wheat rather than, for instance, the stick and hoe for the cultivation of tubers, as obtained in the even more sparsely populated areas of Africa south of the Sahara.[3] Thus, even though on the average not many mouths had to be fed in the Algeria of the early nineteenth century, demographic pressure was nevertheless great enough to make the employment of the plow, with its corresponding requirements of labor and degree of productivity, necessary.

Plows in early-nineteenth-century Algeria were ox-drawn, and for each wheat field under cultivation another field was left fallow. Ox-power and the two-field system, of course, did not represent the highest form of labor intensity and productivity on the plow-wheat level of agriculture. A team of oxen was capable of plowing at best about ten hectares (called *zawija*: the amount of land a team of oxen could plow in a day) per season, and the total employment for a man in the cultivation of wheat was at the most ninety days, concentrated in the planting and harvesting seasons.[4] However, since in the absence of a high population density there was no incentive for peasants to work harder and more efficiently, the invention, or adoption from abroad, of more productive technologies such as horse-drawn plows or the three-field system with legumes as intermediate crops between wheat and fallow, was unnecessary.[5] Prior to the coming of the French, the level of agricultural technology was perfectly adapted to the requirements of low population densities.

With the modest demographic density, the low labor requirements of cereal agriculture were not accidental. Modest demographic density made the exchange of goods costly when considered in terms of the distances separating peasants from each other and therefore put a premium on self-sufficiency. Peasant producers could not afford to invest all available labor time in wheat production: an adequate amount of time had to be reserved for a range of other activities in order to maintain a self-sufficient household. Horticulture, arboriculture, apiculture, poultry farming, pastoralism, dairy farming, hunting, exploitation of forests, cloth-making, construction of shelter all demanded attention for full self-sufficiency to be assured.[6] Although wheat was the central food staple, peasant activities on the plains had to be fully diversified if all the requirements of conditions of sparse population density were to be met.

Land values in this system of diversified self-sufficiency agriculture based on wheat cultivation were at an intermediate level. On the one hand, wheat required less intensive labor than vegetables or fruits and therefore wheat fields tended to remain communal property (*'arsh*) while gardens and groves constituted private properties (sing. *mulk*). On the other hand, the margin of arable land left in the brush and forest zones was too small not to result in some valorization of wheat fields over brush and forest land. This valorization was expressed in the institution of sharecropping, through which the members of a community recognized the permanence of each other's wheat and fallow lands by contracting for farming rights on these lands. Owners granted owners of other lands the right to plant and reap wheat on their lands in return for a share of the harvest. To further complicate matters, small landowners often sought sharecropping contracts for themselves as well, so that in a given area, systems of interlocking sharecropping arrangements existed.[7] Even though cropland was not private de jure, it was almost recognized as such de facto.

The existence of sharecroppers (*khamamisa*) in Algeria was thus indicative of residual communal interest in preserving a just distribution of wheat land, which was similar to a communal interest in guaranteeing free access to pastures, brushlands, and forests. All members of a given community were entitled, through the institution of sharecropping, to a scattering of their wheat fields over what was regarded as the communal patrimony. Thus the risk of harvest failure was spread over a variety of rich and poor, moist and dry, flat and steep lands. However, at the same time, the higher value placed on wheat land (as compared to that of pastures, brushlands, and forests) can be seen in the right of the owners to hire and fire sharecroppers at will at the end of the agricultural year or even to farm, at the risk of communal disapproval, without sharecropping at all. As such, the Algerian-Maghribi *khammas* system reflected a somewhat higher level of private ownership than did the Syrian *musha*, an institution of periodic land redistribution among the members of a community.[8] However, in neither country was the population density high enough in the early nineteenth century to warrant full private ownership of the wheat lands, and therefore it is preferable to talk of "landlords" rather than "landowners," as we shall see later in this article.

Some landlords were obviously less in need than others of making recourse to land distribution via sharecropping. Whenever these landlords received outside support—from the Ottomans prior to the French expedition of 1830 to Algiers, or from Amir 'Abd al-Qadir or Ahmad Bey prior to the completion of the French conquest in 1851—they took on large numbers of sharecroppers without becoming sharecroppers themselves. Enough support was given to landlords in strategically important geographical positions (for example, the Muqrani or Bin Sharifa families in northcentral Algeria) to ensure their loyalty. Similarly, some two dozen religious families in charge of pilgrimage, placed where potentially dangerous crowds assembled, were coopted through official recognition and thus became wealthy landlords without being themselves actively engaged in agriculture.[9]

While in most of the northern Algerian plains area what is called in this article full self-sufficiency (with or without widespread sharecropping) defined the relationship between demography and agricultural resources in the early nineteenth century, population densities in many mountain and desert areas were too high when measured against the food supplies that could be provided by prevailing agricultural technologies or when compared with Algeria as a whole, for full self-sufficiency to be possible. The demand for wheat exceeded the supply that could be gleaned from narrow valley floors or mountain terraces and arid steppes. Therefore both mountain peasants and nomads, who were unable to achieve full self-sufficiency, had to concern themselves with product specialization in order to have the means for acquiring necessary cereals through market exchange. In the mountains these special products were olive oil, honey, and wax; in the desert, animals, animal products, and textiles. Mountain and desert dwellers carried these products to the markets in the northern plains where wheat was available.

Therefore, viewed solely from the angle of full self-sufficiency, both mountains and deserts were overpopulated in the sense that, with available technologies, not all members of the community could be adequately provided for. But this overpopulation could nevertheless be maintained, thanks to the flexibility of the wheat-based self-sufficiency system predominant in the northern Algerian plains. This system supported not only the wheat producers on the plains but also those engaged in product specialization and market exchange on its fringes, that is, in the mountains and in the desert.

From budgets established by the French during the nineteenth century for a number of Algerian households it can be concluded that the degree of product specialization needed for market exchange by mountain and desert households was very small. In the case of one Kabyle mountain household of medium wealth, only about 14 percent of the family's annual production was marketed. Goods produced with the market in mind were honey and wax, and 74 percent of these products did end up in the market. Specialization for the exchange of animals and animal products, as well as olive oil, was significantly lower: 51 and 15 percent, respectively, of these products were directed toward the market. Money acquired through market exchange was for the most part spent on textiles—55 percent of all market expenditures. The remaining expenditures were split up more or less evenly among soap, cosmetics, coffee, tobacco, construction materials, farm implements, payment for services (of smiths, shepherds, and so forth), and the payment of taxes. Food supplies, particularly wheat staples, were adequate, and no grain had to be bought on the market; but wheat self-sufficiency was possible only because two adult sons of the eleven-member household emigrated during the six winter months to Algiers to earn their living there as street vendors of souvenirs.[10] Thus for dependency on wheat supplementation from the markets in the plains the household substituted dependency on labor contributed to the market in Algiers.

In the case of a moderately wealthy nomadic household of the tribe of al-Arba'a in the northcentral Sahara, the product specialization was even smaller, amounting to less than 7 percent of its annual production. Goods for the market consisted of a wild resin (akin to gum arabic and used for the manufacture of glue and pharmaceuticals) and textiles, such as carpets, burnooses, haiks (white overcoats), and braids or ribbons. The resin harvest was marketed in its entirety; 34 percent of the textiles were traded. An additional "product" offered to the market was caravan service for the transportation of dates from the oases to the north and of wheat from the north to the oases. The profits from this trade amounted to one-fifth of the value of the resin and textiles sent to the market. The purchase of wheat for this nomadic household made up nearly 53 percent of its expenditures; dates, coffee, olive oil, beef meat, and household furnishings absorbed more or less equal, and small, amounts of its remaining expenditures.[11]

The Kabyle and Saharan examples date from 1884–85 and in a strict sense are not fully applicable to the early nineteenth century discussed so far in this section of the article. However, they constitute the earliest quantified budgets available, and we must do with what we have. Moreover, since the market supplement could only have increased during the earlier part of the century along with the increasing penetration of Algeria by French colonial capital and cheap industrial goods, the examples can still be regarded as generally representative of the early 1800s. What emerges, then, is a surprisingly small market dependency and one even smaller in nomadic than mountain households.[12] But we shall see how crucial even the small market dependency was in terms of political activism.

On the basis of the preceding description of self-sufficiency, as well as the presentation of the two examples of product specialization and market dependency, one can create a scale ranging from full self-sufficiency to complete market integration and relate this scale to the Algerian revolts. At the point of full self-sufficiency, so it can be hypothesized, the temptation to revolt was almost nil. Under conditions of low population density and the availability of basic food supplies, peasants usually endured even steep tax rates, unless, of course, the very basis of their self-sufficiency was affected.

A much greater readiness for revolt seems to have existed in a range on the scale where, strangely enough, partial self-sufficiency coexisted with only a slight market dependency. Under conditions of low population density, markets were small and fragmented and therefore presented an irresistible invitation for political competition. Whoever possessed enough power to control a local, isolated market could influence its prices, and this was of crucial importance because only those competitors who could prevent their incomplete self-sufficiency from being eroded by an increased market dependency were politically successful. Limited market dependency stimulated strong political assertiveness precisely to keep this dependency low. Thus, as long as the demographic density remained low and either full self-sufficiency or a high degree thereof was necessary, a substantial part of the population had few hesitations about asserting itself in rebellions.

The close connection among partial self-sufficiency, political action and avoidance of increased market dependency seems to have lasted in rural Algeria until well into the twentieth century, at least as far as the mountain populations are concerned. The fact that the War of Independence (1954–62) found its strongest support in the mountains of the Constantinois and Algérois, which were least affected by colonialism, seems to support my theory that even up to twenty years ago the idea of insurrection as a means of preventing increased dependency on outsiders retained its allure. It apparently mattered little to the mountain populations that most of the leaders of the war were of urban origin or that they justified their insurrection in part by decrying the plight of Algeria's rural population, which the French kept in what the revolutionaries regarded as feudal backwardness and isolation (without, however, troubling themselves much about how the peasants themselves perceived their situation).

National integration was such a self-evident goal for the urban revolutionaries that during the war they failed to notice the disparity between mountain revolts directed against outside interference and urban revolution directed toward the achievement of national integration. This disparity was obscured by a genuinely shared passion to get rid of the French. But immediately after Independence the fundamental incompatibility of rural and urban concerns broke into the open, expressed in armed clashes between the so-called "interior *wilayas*" and the government in Algiers, and was only eventually resolved, through the use of force, in favor of national integration. At present, integration continues to prevail, although lately the Kabyle language has become a rallying point for local opposition, perhaps because it is the last and least reducible element capable of preventing a final social integration now that economic and political integration into the Algerian state have become irreversible facts.

At what point on the scale between full self-sufficiency and complete market integration the latter can become powerful enough to undermine political activism as a means of compensation for partial self-sufficiency and market dependency is difficult to determine. One can perhaps take a clue from the Ouarsenis, a region southwest of Algiers for which detailed household data exist. The large majority of the Ouarsenis inhabitants in the early 1970s were small and landless peasants. The small peasants, those with up to 2 hectares of land, were self-sufficient for only 37 percent of their overall food demands and, moreover, had to turn to the market for 60 percent of their wheat requirements. Wages earned through labor on large farms provided most of the money spent in the market, but a certain amount of capital was realized from agricultural surpluses. For the so-called landless farmers, who lived off pastoralism on public brush and forest lands, food self-sufficiency was even lower, comprising only some 16 percent of their needs; they bought their staples on the market, except for meat, milk, some vegetables, and wild food.[13] Small and landless farmers were notoriously passive politically. The fact that the well-touted program of a thousand flourishing socialist villages, in which these peasants were supposed to be provided with enough land to achieve full food self-sufficiency, barely got beyond the stage of one hundred villages was due in part to bureaucratic ineptitude and in part to peasant inertia. The silent but massive rural exodus in Algeria is perhaps the most telling evidence of the increasing attractiveness of the urban labor market. Complete market integration in the cities obviously appears a more promising possibility than does full self-sufficiency in the countryside.

The shift from self-sufficiency to market integration as a principal goal, which must have occurred sometime after Independence for most rural people in Algeria, must be assumed to be a consequence of rising demographic densities. The tantalizing question of whether this shift entailed a parallel relationship between varying degrees of market integration and urban militancy on the other end of the scale, in analogy to the relationship between varying degrees of self-sufficiency and rural rebelliousness discussed above, would be interesting to pursue but goes beyond the framework of this paper. I raise the question only to suggest ways the skeleton of my theory that nineteenth-century Algerian revolts were conditioned by factors such as demographic density, self-sufficiency, and market integration might be filled out. The social factor of demographic density is particularly crucial for this theory, in that it determines whether the economic goal of full self-sufficiency or complete market integration predominates and pushes those who are close to but not quite capable of reaching either into compensatory political action. Thus social demographic pressures must be viewed as preceding economics and politics.

REVOLTS IN REGIONS OF FULL SELF-SUFFICIENCY

The large majority of Algerians—those living in the northern plains—were more or less self-sufficient, if necessary with the aid of sharecropping, until well into the twentieth century, as we have seen in the previous section. The replacement of sharecropping by salaried labor, the emigration of peasants, the rural exodus from nonmountain and nondesert areas, and the appearance of market dependency are for the most part contemporary phenomena. During the nineteenth century, when the relatively sparse population could still be fairly easily accommodated through the self-sufficiency system, usually enough was produced to support, in addition, the administration and armies first of the Ottomans, then of 'Abd al-Qadir and Ahmad Bey and finally of the French, although the voracious colonial ambitions of the last required hefty subsidies from metropolitan France to supplement indigenous taxes, and this double source of income made the French position in Algeria considerably stronger than that of their predecessors.

The self-sufficiency system was weakened in two ways by the fiscal demands of the French colonial system. First, the French extended over the whole country a tax system which, as mentioned above, had been limited during the Ottoman period to the top 20 percent of the most productive districts of Algeria. But it is undeniable that the taxes consisted of a hodge-podge of traditional, reformed, and new fiscal dues, contained no incentives or progressive scales, and affected the peasants unevenly. On the whole it appears that the tax rate remained more or less the same from the Ottomans to the French, with the important difference, however, that all mountain and desert districts, where formerly only irregular or no taxes at all had been levied, were now officially added to the rolls.[14]

Second, the French-appointed local Algerian leaders, who were responsible for the collection of taxes, the maintenance of civil and military peace, and the collection of fines, performed their duties with devastating enthusiasm. Under the Ottomans there were perhaps fifty local leadership positions with official blessing, whereas the French created a formidable body of some one thousand local administrators. Furthermore, the fifty Ottoman-recognized local leaders did not collect taxes from the people of their own districts, as their French-appointed colleagues did, but either performed as tax collectors elsewhere or were merely responsible for local military and civil security within their own district. Since they could legitimately collect dues from sharecroppers, some of these Ottoman-supported leaders were able to transform themselves from active farmers into rent-collecting landlords. But never more than a small percentage of the peasants of a given district under an Ottoman-recognized local leader had payed sharecropping rents prior to the coming of the French. By contrast, the passion with which the one thousand French-appointed local leaders set to work to use the commissions given them from the taxes and fines collected while performing their duties enabled the majority of them to transform themselves from ordinary farmers into landlords and tax agents in one and the same district. In the end, during the early twentieth century, a thirteen hundred–strong landlord class had emerged, with individual properties of more than one hundred hectares and hundreds of thousands of collective sharecroppers.[15]

However, the overwhelming majority of self-sufficient farmers endured the double squeeze on their resources by the French and the new breed of landlords without resorting to revolt. Therefore, we must assume that somehow self-sufficiency still appeared possible to Algerian peasants in the second half of the nineteenth century. Insurrections occurred in only two of what I have called full self-sufficiency regions. Of these two insurrections—the great Medjana-Kabylia revolt of 1871–72 and the smaller uprising of Adélia-Margueritte in the Djendel of 1901—the first, of course, was the largest and most dangerous of all revolts between the French conquest and Independence; the second, an important link roughly midway between the events of 1871–72 and the period of germination of the War of Independence, between 1945 and 1954. In the Medjana, the well-established military family of the Muqrani controlled most local leadership positions, and two members of the family were among the leaders of the revolt. In the Djendel, the old military family of the Awlad bin Sharifa dominated local leadership positions until 1871, when less prominent leaders of local and outside origin were appointed. Both the Medjana and the Djendel had been strategic districts adjacent to mountain regions where safe passage to eastern and western Algeria was crucial and where the Ottomans therefore had granted considerable liberty to the local leaders. Thus, while the peasants in these regions had little incentive to revolt, their leaders, faced with the loss of power and prestige, had plenty.

Members of traditional leadership families, if they played a shrewd political game and kept a certain distance from the French, enjoyed an obvious advantage over newly appointed leaders in terms of familiarity and popularity during the second half of the nineteenth century. They were already landlords with long-established sharecropping rights and were recognized by the sharecroppers without demurral. Even if the traditional leaders were unable to prevent the introduction of French taxation, they at least were seen as paying taxes like everybody else. Moreover, if they continued, and capitalized on, the established customs of calculated generosity, they provided some return for the numerous illegal dues they collected *sub rosa* from the peasants. For instance, both Muhammad al-Muqrani and Abu 'Alim bin Sharifa distributed large quantities of wheat from their stores to the peasants of their districts and even, in the case of al-Muqrani, to the neighboring Kabyle peasants who were stricken in 1867–78 with both famine and cholera.[16] Al-Muqrani was able to display this largesse thanks to a substantial annual income of 250,000 francs, inherited from his father's time, which had been increased by Muhammad's own French-granted annual emolument of 25,386 francs.[17] For his part, Bin Sharifa collected some 109,760 francs, including 26,760 in commissions and emoluments, in 1860.[18] How immense these revenues were can be seen if they are compared, as one German traveler in 1857 did, with the salary of a Prussian minister, which amounted at that time to about 20,000 francs.[19] The two leaders clearly had secure economic positions from which, should provocation be sufficient, defiance of French colonial power could be contemplated.

Muhammad al-Muqrani decided the time had come to throw down the gauntlet in March 1871, and he assembled some 25,000 troops and a total of 100,000 followers for his purposes. He was soon joined by Shaykh al-Haddad, head of the Rahmaniya brotherhood in the Kabyle mountains, who contributed some 120,000 troops and a total of 600,000 supporters. During the summer of 1871 the revolt spread to the eastern Sahara. Initially, the colonial government found itself in a critical situation, since Napoleon III's regime in France had collapsed in September 1870 in the war with Prussia, and French reinforcements were not available for the colonies. In the end, however, better training and greater tactical adroitness helped the French regain their initiative, and in January 1872 the last rebels were forced to surrender.[20]

The list of circumstances contributing to this revolt is well known. Among the earliest irritants were French efforts to abolish the upper echelons of the local leadership and to create the first colonial settlements. Irritation turned into apprehension and finally to fear in 1871, when al-Muqrani realized the threat posed by the French in the form of a civilian prefect. The full list of contributing causes for the revolt does not need to be repeated here; I shall simply subsume them all under the general heading of self-sufficiency, this paper's central concept of analysis. Al-Muqrani's political actions were clearly determined by considerations which can only be understood in terms that landlords of self-sufficient sharecroppers would find significant. He was not at all restrained by the type of property concerns that a twentieth-century American or European would consider important: Neither land value nor investment in infrastructure and equipment was critical; but unimpeded production, as we have seen in the previous section, was essential. The ultimate concern was not economic gain but freedom of political action and economic independence.

Al-Muqrani was a leader who had to use force, even if it was disguised behind well-accepted traditions, in order to extract rents from economically self-sufficient farmers. He must have been quite persuasive in convincing the farmers of the Medjana that it was not his benign patriarchal demands but the brutal power of the French infidels that was responsible for the squeeze on their self-sufficiency income. However, it should also be noted that he was not able to muster more than a sixth of the manpower that the militarily much less experienced religious leader al-Haddad and his son were able to mobilize among the Kabyle mountain people. Objectively, the latter had much less reason for revolt than did the people of the Medjana, since colonialism had not yet penetrated into the Kabyle valleys and landlordship was still only feebly developed. Yet as peasants who lived in areas of relatively higher demographic density and incomplete self-sufficiency, as we have seen in the previous section, they had a much stronger interest in political action and a keener perception of the French threat than did their more self-sufficient brethren in the Medjana. Al-Muqrani was quite aware of the weakness of motivation behind his uprising, and it was he who originally initiated the alliance with the Kabyles, only to be absorbed eventually by their stronger insurrectional movement.[21]

The Adélia revolt reinforces on a smaller scale the motivations of leadership revolts in full self-sufficiency districts. As far as is known, the Banu Sharifa never dreamed of revolt and, like the great majority of both their traditional and their newly elevated colleagues, opted for enrichment via French-tolerated landlordship over sharecroppers in conjunction with their traditional leadership positions. This option, however, worked no better for the Banu Sharifa than it had for al-Muqrani. By 1887 the French had reduced the political influence of the Banu Sharifa in the Djendel to such a degree that they could be replaced in leadership positions by local peasants.[22]

One such replacement, a certain 'Ali al-'Arbi Quyidar, was appointed local administrator of Adélia in 1899. Quyidar was from the Djendel but was not a native of Adélia and lived in modest circumstances with an annual income of perhaps 2,500 francs. His personal file indicates that he tried to use his position to become a landlord but had wealthy competitors who pursued similar ambitions more successfully.[23] Two of these competitors were Ya 'qub bin Bashir and Talbi bin Jilali, the latter reportedly a "rich" peasant. During the annual celebration of the local saint's in April 1901, at which some three to four hundred local farmers congregated, the two appointed each other as leader and deputy (sultan and *khalifa*) of a movement in support of Abu 'Amama, an insurgent from southwestern Algeria who had led a revolt in 1881 and was now trying to keep his insurrection alive from his Moroccan exile. During the morning of Friday, 26 April, the two headed a band of about one hundred farmers armed with rifles and sticks on a rampage first against Quyidar and then against the nearby colonial village of Margueritte where they forced the inhabitants to convert to Islam. One villager, who dared to laugh in disbelief in the face of the insurgents, was shot and killed, but French police arrived in the afternoon and dispersed the band of would-be revolutionaries. Thus ended this modest effort at revolt.[24]

In the early 1860s Adélia had been a *commune mixte* of 9,000 hectares, populated by little more than 2,000 inhabitants. By 1900 it had shrunk to 4,000 hectares, 5,000 hectares of fields and former common brush and forest land having passed to the French colonialists. Algerian peasants were clearly "squeezed" for land, as one of the investigative reports expressed it. Three-quarters of the active male population worked for wages in the European vineyards which had been planted on former brush land, while at the same time maintaining their own farms. Additional labor came from Kabylia and Morocco. Apparently a small number of Algerian peasants were able to enlarge their holdings, presumably at the expense of their hapless neighbors who were thus brought down to the level of marginal farmers. In 1900, twelve small-to-medium landowners were wealthy enough to undertake the pilgrimage to Mecca. Talbi bin Jilali, who had gone to Mecca once already, was given authorization to go again.[25] All the circumstances of the revolt indicate that the uprising of Adélia was a repetition in miniature of al-Muqrani's revolt minus mountain peasants and minus a strong, official, traditional indigenous leader to head the revolt.

As the last of the strictly rural revolts prior to the War of Independence, Adélia is important for two reasons. First, aspiring small-to-medium landowners appeared on the insurrectional scene after the major political leaders and landlords had given up all residual hopes of revolt. This type of landowner later provided a major source of support to the War of Independence. Second, the small-to-medium landowners maintained close lay relations with the local village Islam, which was based on the veneration of saintly figures. In spite of the generally syncretistic tendencies of this village Islam, with its thamaturgic rituals, a few fundamentalist traits were predominant. The fact that in Adélia smoking was prohibited during the assemblies at the saint's tomb, and the proselytizing fervor there (even if directed against Christians who, according to strict law, did not have to convert) demonstrated certain elements of fundamentalism.[26] This fundamentalism—that is, Islam stripped of its syncretisms and redefined in its allegedly pristine state—developed between the two world wars into a major factor in the nationalist movement which then, in turn, launched the War of Independence. The uprising of Adélia-Margueritte in the

Djendel was certainly small, and of no great threat to the French when compared to the great revolt of Medjana-Kabylia. However, it foreshadowed the direction in which political activism was to go under those self-sufficient farmers with lands of medium size who had inherited the mantle of leadership from their more illustrious predecessors of the Ottoman and early French times.

While al-Muqrani found the strongest support for his revolt among the Kabyle mountain people, the Adélia insurgents planned to join Abu 'Amama's nomads in the northwestern Sahara. It is interesting that both revolts, involving full self-sufficiency peasants led by ambitious leaders in traditionally independent regions of Algeria in the northern plains, had close actual or projected links with mountain and desert peoples in areas of incomplete self-sufficiency: the only potential countryside revolts were precisely those that occurred in formerly independent self-sufficiency regions but were clearly dependent on the support of the incompletely self-sufficient, and more traditionally rebellious, rural populations in the mountains and deserts. One suspects, therefore, as has been suggested above in the case of al-Muqrani, that the uprisings of self-sufficiency farmers could become viable only with the help of mountaineers or nomads. It was in terms of this need for more general support that Medjana and Adélia foreshadowed the War of Independence.

REVOLTS IN REGIONS OF INCOMPLETE SELF-SUFFICIENCY

In contrast to the insurrections of Medjana and Adélia, most of the revolts in the incompletely self-sufficient mountain and desert areas were relatively isolated affairs and displayed a number of interesting common traits. Since the Kabyle participation in the 1871–72 revolt has already been discussed above in conjunction with the Medjana uprising, I shall concentrate in this section on the insurrectional events that involved the Aurès mountains as well as the northern Sahara.

The Aurès mountain-dwellers resembled their Kabyle colleagues in that their economic circumstances created a high degree of both political sensitivity and impetuosity: incomplete self-sufficiency made any interference with their access to the market a major threat. A small but important wheat supplement from the plains was required to satisfy their cereal needs. Therefore, market exchange was crucial and political action necessary if traditionally favorable market conditions were endangered.

Only political autonomy and strong local leadership could guarantee effective political action. The recognized leaders in the Aurès, as in Kabylia, were local Islamic teachers and thaumaturges such as Si Sadiq or Muhammad bin Amzyan who, in 1856 and 1879 respectively, led small local revolts involving no more than a few hundred followers. Since neither of these men was a direct farmer, and as both were dependent on alms given by the local peasants, they were free to exercise political leadership functions analogous to those of the landlords in the plains whose incomes derived from sharecroppers' dues.

Both Si Sadiq and Bin Amzyan revolted in protest against the French-appointed intruders from the plains and their local collaborators who now collected taxes and regulated market conditions. The first victims of their revolts were the functionaries of Arab and Turkish descent from the plains who had been assigned to the predominantly Berber-speaking Aurès and who, in addition to the misfortune of their descent, were universally regarded as being puppets in the hands of the wealthy landlord families in the nearby north-eastern plains of the Sahara. These landlord families, the Banu Shanuf and Banu Gana, possessed enormous wealth and were in the same league as al-Muqrani and Banu Sharifa discussed above. But, in contrast to the latter, they did not use their leadership positions for revolt. The extension of political influence into the Aurès, with all its attendant financial rewards, obviously outweighed any gains that could be realized through revolt, in the eyes of the Banu Shanuf and Banu Gana. In this regard it should be noted that al-Muqrani was never given the opportunity of ruling in or over Kabylia. This entirely new political structure of alien landlord-leaders from the plains superimposed on traditional local leadership was clearly a serious impediment to mountain freedom, particularly that crucial freedom of descending to the markets on the plains and dealing there on long-established and well-understood terms.[27]

Mountain political rebelliousness can be seen again, with only a few variations, in the desert among the camel nomads in the central Sahara. These nomads depended for their small wheat supplement on supplies brought to the oases by the sheep camel nomads who lived to the north of the pure camel nomads and between the oases and the wheat regions of northern Algeria. The camel nomads had only precarious access to the oasis markets, which were jealously guarded by the sheep/camel nomads. With great regularity and gusto these two nomadic groups raided each other.[28]

However, as far as justification for action more substantial than that of ordinary raids was concerned, the camel nomads of the deep south had to depend on the counsel of religious leaders from the sedentary north, who possessed a legitimacy provided by permanent saintly tombs and associated centers of religious learning and practice that was not available to the camel nomads. Such willing religious leaders appeared in great numbers during the time when the French began to coopt secular and religious leaders in the Sahara. Just as in the Kabyle and Aurès mountains, these coopted leaders were seen by the tribes as threats to their freedom of movement between the southern pastures and the northern oases. The most prominent revolts among the pure camel nomads were those led by Muhammad ibn 'Abdallah between 1850 and 1861 and Abu Shusha in 1871–72: both men came originally from northern Algeria and both adopted religious names for their purposes. These revolts were highly flexible affairs; at times they shrank to the size of mere raids, and for the most part they remained marginal events occurring deep in the Sahara.

More important and complex was a series of three revolts of the sheep/camel nomads who controlled most of the oases in the northern Sahara and conducted the trade between these oases and the wheat markets of the Algerian plains further to the north. As such, the sheep/camel nomads were both incompletely self-sufficient producers and landlords, and it was this peculiar combination which made them particularly dangerous in revolt. Economically incomplete self-sufficiency required access to the wheat markets in the north, which, as we have seen above, stimulated protective political activism. In part this activism was expressed through the political institution of landlordism thrust upon the fully self-sufficient date-palm farmers in the oases. These farmers were share-croppers under the domination of sheep/camel nomads, and although they mainly grew dates, they also produced sufficient quantities of wheat and vegetables to take care of their food needs. The surplus dates which the sheep/camel nomads collected from their sharecroppers were shipped by caravan to the northern wheat markets. In return, the caravans of the sheep/camel nomads brought wheat back to the oases for distribution on the oases' markets to the camel/nomads of the far south. Among the sheep camel nomads incomplete self-sufficiency and landlordism were mixed in a curious way that amounted to a collective landlordship over the date sharecroppers by nomadic tribes; there was no parallel for this in the Algerian north, where the landlords were organized in families or, at most, in clans.

This mixture was politically highly explosive: incomplete self-sufficiency and landlord interest in sharecropper rents made political activism a necessity. General justification could be provided through appeal to saints who had their tombs in the oases. Some of these tombs possessed adjoining centers of religious learning and practice run by respected families who lived among the sheep/camel nomads. Many members of these families became highly alarmed when the French began to exercise control over the northern wheat markets and Saharan oases, and three families revolted to protect both their incomplete self-sufficiency and their landlord rights.

The first of these insurgents was Si Sulayman, the French-appointed head of the Awlad Sidi Shaykh Sharaqa (or eastern branch of the family descending from Sidi Shaykh). He and his successors led an initially formidable revolt from 1864 to 1883 which at one point engulfed most of southwestern and south-central Algeria but later dwindled into a series of raids.[29] The two other insurgents were bin 'Ayash of the Banu 'Azid, who revolted in 1876, and Abu 'Amama of the Awlad Sidi Shaykh Gharaba (or western branch of the family), who rose up in 1881 to take the banner of revolt from Si Sulayman's successors, whose insurrection had by this time degenerated into insignificant raids. Si Sulayman's vanquished successors returned to the French fold in small groups after 1883, but Abu 'Amama remained in unrepentant exile in northern Morocco until his death in 1908.[30] Interestingly, in all three of these revolts the date farmers demonstrated their primary concern as self-sufficiency by being reluctant participants at best, getting on the bandwagon late and jumping from it at the earliest signs of reversal. The backbone of these revolts was provided by the sheep/camel nomads, who were fiercely protective of their freedom of movement and landlord interests in the oases.

The returning penitents of the Awlad Sidi Shaykh were amply rewarded for their renewed loyalty after 1883; prestigious leadership positions were distributed by the French, who badly needed a stable border while preparing for the extension of their diplomatic—later colonial—influence into southeastern Morocco.[31] For similar reasons a leadership position was bestowed on a son of al-Muqrani's, al-Makki, sometime between 1900 and 1910, in one of the valleys of Kabylia.[32] Traditional landlord families, if they repented after revolting, were likely to remain loyal and provide better leadership than obscure *nouveaux riches* landlords—or at least this is what the French colonial administrators thought, after they became disturbed by what they feared was the disappearance of indispensable traditional families from leadership positions.[33]

THE ISLAMIC FACTOR IN THE REVOLTS

So far this analysis has focused on what can be called the minimum conditions necessary to stimulate revolts. Dependency on market exchange in a society which was predominantly organized around full self-sufficiency produced compensatory political activism if this dependency was threatened—thus can the minimum conditions for insurrections in Algeria during the second half of the nineteenth century be most succinctly described. However, as has been seen in the discussion of revolts in the last two sections, each revolt was wholly or partly organized and led by religious figures. These figures may indeed have taken as their point of departure a secular quest for freedom of political action in compensation for unavoidable economic dependency created by their specific circumstances, as has been maintained in the analysis so far. But in all the revolts discussed in these two sections, the religious organizers and leaders aspired to much more, that is, to a more or less clearly articulated overall purpose. This purpose was the goal of freedom for Islam which, because Islam recognizes no lord but God, could be viewed as being compromised by the colonial infidel. The analysis of this paper will be complete only if the relations between the socioeconomic and political conditions and the religious goal are understood.

As is well known, the idea of freedom of Islam from infidel control was part of the inherited corpus of classical Islamic ethics and law. The central concept in this corpus, next to that of the absolute sovereignty of God, was the notion of solidarity among brothers in the faith. In the rural Algeria of early modern times the concept of Islamic brotherhood was embodied in the institution of the *zawiya* (pl. *zawaya*), the communal center for instruction, prayer, pilgrimage, mystical retreat, and healing. Islamic brotherhood had a universal meaning reflected in the tolerance displayed by what may best be called the ecumenical coexistence of a multiplicity of *zawaya*, which was only occasionally violated by the claims of the followers of a particular saint to exclusive representation of brotherhood. It is interesting to observe that the beginnings of most of the revolts discussed above coincided with a rejection of this tolerant ecumenism and the assumption of an exclusive representative universality. In some cases, as with Si Sadiq, al-Haddad, or Abu 'Amama, *zawaya* were expressly transformed from ecumenical congregations into exclusively representative insurrectional movements. Evidently only brotherhood expressed in terms of exclusive representation was capable of mobilizing interest and manpower for pursuit of the goal of liberating Islam from the infidel.

The ideal of a universal ecumenical Islamic brotherhood, even when betrayed by insurrectionists claiming exclusive representation, functioned as an essential element in the relationship between specific minimum conditions and a universal goal in the Algerian insurrections. It would clearly be a mistake to assume that the revolts occurred only because minimum conditions existed in some parts of the country. Raids, market brawls, and brigandage would have been much more typical responses, had minimum conditions alone acted as triggers. Indeed, the frequency with which these types of disturbances occurred alongside the revolts during the second half of the nineteenth century provides vivid evidence of how the minimum conditions could produce violent action without the aid of religious universal goals. However, raids, market brawls, and brigandage could acquire the status of insurrections only if they were given a larger and more legitimate significance and direction. While the minimum conditions could be claimed for justifying tribal, familial, or individual action, the proclamation of a universal, in this case Islamic, goal was necessary to organize an insurrection of widespread and respectable appeal.

In the context of nineteenth-century Algeria, universality was associated with religion, although, as shown above, it was not the ecumenical but the exclusively representative version that was employed for the purpose of revolt. The concept of universality was much older than Islam and, in fact, even older than revealed religion: it went back beyond the empires of the Persians and Greeks to the world-encompassing realms claimed by the Mesopotamian and Egyptian dynasties. The notion of exclusively representative universality in the form of political movements thus was not truly religious in origin, although universality and revelation obviously have been in close alliance in the historical process. Once the independent status of universality was recognized again as a result of secularization in modern times, it could be associated anew with nonreligious concepts, among which the notion of the nation has been the most successful. Movements claiming exclusive representation of the total population in a specific territory and sharing a specific cultural heritage appeared, reminiscent of earlier world-claiming realms. Religious opinion notwithstanding, universality was a nonreligious concept that could be used by both religious insurrectionist and secular nationalist movements in nineteenth- and twentieth-century Algeria.

Of course, before the goal of national independence could be proclaimed in Algeria, a set of new, transregional minimum conditions had to come into existence. The nineteenth-century regional mountain- or desert-area option of political action in compensation for economic dependency on the plains had to give way, at least partially, to integration into a national market and the expectation of benefits to be derived from this integration. The goal of national independence and integration made sense only in terms of these new minimum conditions arising from a unified market structure. Yet, as was argued in another context above, there are grounds for assuming that traditional mountain regionalism acted as a functional minimum condition in the War of Independence, together with national, market integration.

CONCLUSION

In this chapter I have analyzed the social factor of demographic density and the economic and political consequences of this density in nineteenth-century Algeria. If density was low, as it was in Algeria until well into the twentieth century, the only logical economic goal for most rural people was self-sufficiency. If these people achieved full self-sufficiency and had traditionally been governed and taxed by outside powers, the idea of revolt was both objectively and subjectively foreign. These peasants were relatively flexible economically, and politically they lacked leaders with whom they could identify. Fully self-sufficient peasants with local leader-landlords of their own were more amenable to insurrectional action, especially when goaded into it by these leaders. These agreed to rise in revolt if the local leader-landlords felt their freedom of political action to be so threatened by the French that they convinced the peasants that they, too, were being thwarted in their efforts to maintain self-sufficiency. Not all fully self-sufficient farmers were persuaded by this appeal to defend a shared interest with their local leader-landlords, who, after all, could be as exacting as the French themselves. Therefore, the call for revolt by local leaders usually produced only a modest and reluctant response among the peasants of traditionally fully self-sufficient regions.

The idea of revolt had the widest appeal in regions of incomplete self-sufficiency. As I have discussed above, mountain peasants and desert nomads compensated for their lack of economic self-sufficiency by political activism in order to assure continuous access to vital market exchange on the most favorable terms possible. On the leadership level, religious figures who were dependent on alms from the local population were as sensitive to French interference as the secular leader-landlords in the plains. If these religious figures possessed substantial and traditionally recognized influence, they could persuade the peasants or nomads in their area that the French threat to the favorable market exchange necessary to supplement their incomplete self-sufficiency was so malign that indigenous religious leadership was the only thinkable alternative to French rule. In the incompletely self-sufficient regions the call for revolt tended to be more persuasive precisely because religious leaders were usually more closely bound up with the economic concerns of the peasants and nomads than were landlords in the fully self-sufficient regions.

Full or incomplete self-sufficiency, market dependency, and compensatory political activism, however, constituted only the minimum conditions for the revolts of the nineteenth century. What I have called a universal goal had to be invoked in order to provide sufficient justification for an insurrectional movement. Appeal to a universal form of justice, embodied by an exclusively representative Islamic movement, had to be made in order to overcome any hesitation among potential followers to whom the minimum conditions were too particularist. Universalism, as defined during the nineteenth century in religious terms, was the indispensable basis for the rebellions.

Given this combination of minimum conditions and universal goals, the Algerian uprisings of 1851 to 1914 should not be misconstrued as gropings toward a sense of Algerian nationality in response to the threat of French colonial exploitation or as proto-nationalist responses to capitalist disruption of the economy.[34] Since there was no unified national market, the control of which might have inspired Algerian rural leaders of all stripes to unified revolt, there was also no capitalist disruption, as it were, during the nineteenth century that could have seriously affected either full or incomplete self-sufficiency agriculture. The relative insignificance of wheat supplements in incomplete self-sufficiency regions lends support to my assertion that the revolts were defensive in the sense that self-sufficiency was still more understandable and accessible than market integration, in spite of French interference. Given the low population, an integrated national market was so remote a concept that most Algerian peasants continued their traditional self-sufficiency and only when threatened on these grounds did they think of compensatory political action in terms of insurrectional movements. It was this prevalence of self-sufficiency that limited the effectiveness of the Algerian revolts in the second half of the nineteenth century.

NOTES

1. These are rough estimates. In 1830 the population was estimated at 2.5 million, of which about 2.4 million lived in northern Algeria. The agriculturally usable surface of northern Algeria is about 140,000 square kilometers. For the figures in Kabylia see Lucien Boyer-Banse, "La condition économique des populations agricoles indigènes dans le Département d'Alger," *Bulletin de la Société Géographique d'Alger* 11 (1906): 189–209.

2. Jan de Vries, *The Dutch Rural Economy in the Golden Age, 1500–1700* (New Haven: Yale University Press, 1974).

3. On this question see Ester Boserup, *The Conditions of Agricultural Growth* (Chicago: Aldine, 1966).

4. Hippolyte Lecq and Charles Rivière, *Traité pratique d'agriculture pour le Nord d'Afrique*, 2 vols. (Paris: Challamel, 1928–29); Joost van Vollenhoven, *Etude sur le fellah algérien* (Paris, 1903).

5. Ester Boserup, "The Impact of Growth on Agricultural Output," *Quarterly Journal of Economics* (1975): 257–70.

6. Djilali Sari, "L'équilibre économique traditionnel dans l'Cuarsenis," *Revue d'Histoire et de Civilisation du Maghreb* 9 (1970): 57–78.

7. Georges Rectenwals, *Le contrat de khamessat en Afrique du Nord* (Paris: Pedrone, 1912).

8. Jacques Weulersse, *Paysans du Syrie et du Proche Orient* (Paris: Gallimard, 1946), pp. 99–109.

9. Peter Von Sivers, "Les Plaisirs du collectioneur: capitalisme fiscal et chefs indigènes en Algérie (1840–60)," *Annales ESC* 25 (1980): 679–99.

10. Figures calculated from Vincent Darasse, "Paysans et colporteurs émigrants de Tabou-Douchd-el-Baar (Grande Kabylie)," *Revue des Deux Mondes* 5 (1885): 459–502.

11. Figures calculated from Auguste Geoffrey, "Arabes pasteurs," *Ouvriers des Deux Mondes*, 2d series, 1 (1887): 409–64.

12. Auguste Geoffrey, "Bordier (fellah) berbère de la grande Kabylie (Province d'Alger), *Ouvriers des Deux Mondes*, 2d series, 2 (1890): 53–92.

13. Figures calculated from Djilali Sari, "La désorganisation de l'agriculture traditionnelle dans l'Quarsenis," *Etudes Rurales* 47 (1972): 39–72.

14. On the complicated tax system see A. Bochard, *Les impôts arabes en Algérie* (Paris: Guillaumin, 1893), and Alex-Henry Dupuy, *Les impôts arabes en Algérie* (Algiers: Gojosso, 1910).

15. Peter Von Sivers, "Algerian Landownership and Rural Leadership, 1860–1914: An Authoritative Approach," *Maghreb Review* 4 (1979): 58–62.

16. Archives de l'Ancien Gouvernement Général d'Algérie, in Archives Nationales de France, Dépôt d'Outre-Mer, Aix-en-Provence (An-Aix) (for al-Muqrani), and 5H2, 1I11, 92I1, 1II.

17. AN-Aix 6H27 and 1KK430.

18. AN-Aix 1I11 and 92I1.

19. Max Hirsch, *Reise in das Innere von Algerien* (Hamm: Grote, 1862), 229.

20. The most detailed account of this revolt is found in Louis Rinn, *Histoire de l'insurrection de 1871 en Algérie* (Algiers, 1891).

21. Rinn, *Histoire*, pp. 197–99.

22. AN-Aix 5H17, under El Hadj Ben Khalfa Ben Rahmani.

23. AN-Aix C248 (Alger), under Kouider, Ali Larbi Ben Kouider Ben Mohammed.

24. AN-Aix F 80, 1690, "Révolte indigène dans le douar Adélia, 7 mai 1901, Rapport général."

25. AN-Aix F 80, 1690, "Rapport sur les causes du soulèvement de Margueritte, 13 mai 1901."

26. Ibid.

27. Peter Von Sivers, "Insurrection and Accommodation: Indigenous Leadership in Eastern Algeria, 1840–1900," *IJMES* 6 (1975): 259–75.

28. Augustin Bernard and N. Lacrois, *L'évolution du nomadisme en Algérie* (Paris: Jourdan, 1906).

29. Peter Von Sivers, "Alms and Arms: The Combative Saintliness of the Awlad Sidi Shaykh in the Algerian Sahara, 16th–19th Centuries," *Maghreb Review* 8, nos. 5–6 (1983): 113–23.

30. On these revolts see Peter Von Sivers, "Insurrection," and "Secular Anxieties and Religious Righteousness: The Origins of the Insurrection of 1881 in the Nomadic and Sedentary Communities of the Algerian Southwest," *Peuples Méditerranéens* 18 (1982): 145–62.

31. Ross E. Dunn, *Resistance in the Desert: Moroccan Responses to French Imperialism* (Madison: University of Wisconsin Press, 1977).

32. AN-Aix 16H31, under Mokrani, Si El Hadj El Mekki Ben El Hadj Mohammed El Mokrani, Commune mixte d'Akbou.

33. Peter Von Sivers, "Indigenous Administrators in Algeria, 1846–1914: Manipulation and Manipulators," *Maghreb Review* 7 (1982): 116–21.

34. Elbaki Hermassi, *Leadership and National Development in North Africa* (Berkeley and Los Angeles: University of California Press, 1972); Annie Rey-Goldzeiguer, *Le royaume arabe* (Algiers: Société Nationale d'Edition et de Diffusion, 1979).

FOUR

Saints, Mahdis, and Arms: Religion and Resistance in Nineteenth-Century North Africa

Julia Clancy-Smith

A central problem for the historiography of North Africa during the early stages of imperialism (see Map 1) concerns the nature of the response of indigenous societies to increasing loss of independence or outright foreign rule.[1] Anti-colonial resistance movements of the nineteenth and twentieth centuries represented one of several possible replies to Western domination, others of which ranged from evasion or emigration to accommodation or open collaboration. Resistance itself could assume various guises: refusal to pay taxes, anti-European propaganda, or the mobilization of large numbers of people for armed insurrection.

Studies of the response of a region, as defined by a specific political economy, or of identifiable socio-religious groups or institutions such as the ulama or Sufi *turuq* (sing. *tariqa*) have produced typologies characterizing the behavior of native elites when confronted with Western imperialism.[2] Scholarly investigations of those opting for militant resistance in Africa during the past century have mainly focused on such figures as the Sudanese Mahdi or Muhammad al-Sanusi (who made use of somewhat unusual historical conjunctures to attempt a form of primitive state-building), on flamboyant tribal leaders such as Abu Himara, or on the instigators of the great revolts, like that of 1864 in Tunisia. The peripheral movements often led by apocalyptic visionaries—and they were legion in parts of the Maghrib at certain times—have, unfortunately, received less attention. The most recent work has begun to stress the complexity of this response and to show that the decision for or against militant activism was shaped by a number of factors besides an implacable hatred for the conqueror. Local politics, ecology and economies, self-interest and personality were as important in determining the strategies adopted by secular or religious elites as were the actions and policies of European powers or colonial regimes.[3]

All studies must sooner or later address the issue of the relationship between religion and resistance. Islam in its various manifestations has rightfully been assigned a double role—that of conferring legitimacy upon the leadership of a movement, and that of providing the ideological basis for unusual forms of cooperation, since the forces working against unified resistance were frequently as strong as those for it. But within these configurations, the interplay between religion and politics could itself be extraordinarily complex.

The historical treatment of Algeria in the rebellious half-century stretching from 1830 until the 1880s illustrates many of the issues raised above. Despite the significance of this period to the evolution of modern Algeria, the number of recent studies devoted to the question of insurrection is surprisingly limited; a comprehensive work on the subject remains to be done.[4] Existing studies tend to concentrate on the Amir 'Abd al-Qadir or to cluster around certain dates, such as that of the 1871 uprising. Viewed from the perspective of the entire nineteenth century, the history of Algeria appears as a succession of revolts, directed first against the Turkish ruling caste and then against the European invader. Yet the interconnections between movements within the same period or the continuities between the "Turkish" and French eras are often over-looked. Furthermore, dealing with anti-colonial movements within the frame-work of modern, national boundaries poses a methodological problem since the existence of crucial links between Algeria and the rest of the Maghrib or Mashriq go unperceived. Finally, if the involvement of the Sufi orders and their leadership in resistance during the past century is a constant in the literature, the precise nature of this involvement merits further study.

The following paper deals with a period, a region, and several movements that have received scant scholarly attention, perhaps because these revolts were deemed of only marginal importance or because the behavior of those involved was ambiguous at times and not always amenable to neat typologies. It focuses on a Rahmaniya *zawiya* and its shaykh, Mustafa ibn 'Azzuz (d. 1866), whose activities influenced political events in the region between the Ziban in the southern Constantine and the Tunisian Djerid during the "middle ages" of the rebellious half-century. That an activist like Sidi 'Azzuz was a member of the Rahmaniya is hardly surprising. Not only did the *tariqa* of 'Abd al-Rahman al-Qujtuli al-Azhari (d. 1793) claim the largest following in eastern Algeria, as well as in parts of the Beylik, but several of its *zawaya* were implicated in the uprisings which periodically broke out in the Constantine until the 1870s. Firmly in keeping with the spirit of the Neo-Orthodox Sufi revival of the eighteenth century, the order was among the most socially dynamic, putting great emphasis on education, among other things. The Rahmaniya was not one of the more militant of the Algerian *turuq* in the first half of the nineteenth century: however, the extension of French military conquest and rule into eastern and southeastern Algeria would change this.[5]

A case study of Shaykh Mustafa ibn 'Azzuz, among the earliest of the Rahmani militants, is instructive for several reasons. Because of the way he

employed his authority as a Sufi notable and a saint to encourage resistance in
Algeria for two decades (ca. 1844–66), Sidi 'Azzuz represents another type of
response to Western imperialism, one studied little, if at all. Religious figures
like 'Azzuz, who might be termed the behind-the-scenes activists, were numerous in the past century, and their political behavior was thus in reality far more
typical of the men of religion in many ways.[6] What distinguishes them from an
'Abd al-Qadir or a Shaykh al-Haddad (a Rahmani *muqaddam*, or head of a
local Sufi *tariqa*, whose entry into the 1871 uprising helped turn a local rebellion
into a generalized insurrection) is the fact that they pushed others to revolt by
providing the moral-ideological bases for mobilization and/or the material
means for collective action but preferred to leave the actual leadership to
someone else.

In preaching jihad either from within Algeria or from across the borders,
Sufi notables such as Sidi 'Azzuz often relied on a combination of tactics in
dealing with colonial authorities or their allies—evasion, emigration, and even
outward accommodation—in order to resist or, at times, to hedge their bets in
unstable political environments. If Shaykh 'Azzuz illustrates the complex and
historically ambiguous rapport of the men of religion with power, the use that
he and his followers made of the Rahmani centers in southeastern Algeria and
the Beylik reveals the importance of the *zawiya* as an institutional component of
resistance. And while the saint of Nafta was part of a long North African
tradition—that of the militant *murabit* (pl. *murabitin*)—he was also one of the
first to realize the value of European military *baraka* for those seeking to limit
French expansion in the eastern Maghrib during the past century. It was after
the Ibn 'Azzuz emigrated from the Ziban to the Djerid in 1844 that rebellion in
Algeria became increasingly a Tunisian problem.

The period dealt with here—roughly the two decades between the final
defeat of the Amir in 1847 and the great regional insurrections such as that of
Muqrani in 1871—might be regarded as a transitional point in the evolution of
anti-colonial resistance in Algeria. The kinds of political action undertaken
during these decades were situated between the earlier attempt to organize a
Muslim state as a defense against the conqueror and the later uprisings, which
were as much a result of the malfunctioning of the colonial system, with its
heavy administrative reliance on a privileged group of indigenous notables, as
they were attacks on the very fact of foreign domination itself. This same period
was obviously not without its continuities both from previous and to subsequent
movements in terms of some of the political figures involved, the strategies
employed, and, above all, the role played by religion in resistance. The oases
and tribal groups of southern Algeria studied here had long been accustomed to
withstanding assaults by Turkish tax columns, and even crushing defeats by the
French army in the late 1840s and 1850s did not prevent many of them from
making common cause with the rebels of 1871. Furthermore, during the
"middle ages" the Tunisian connection was to become vital for insurrection in

Algeria, since through the southeastern oases in particular came arms, mahdis, and mobilizers.

From 1830 until the establishment of a protectorate over Tunisia, the idée fixe of colonial administrators was security for their African colony, a concern that revolved around the matter of borders, contraband arms, and the Muslim Confrèries. By the 1870s the eastern frontier of Algeria had developed into such an obsession that the Beylik represented France's version of the route to India. Diplomatic and military correspondence for the pre-1881 period contains endless references to attempts to secure the borders, control the movements of groups or individuals, and eliminate the arms trade between Algeria and Tunisia so as to reduce political unrest. One of the clauses of the 1880 Bardo Treaty—imposed upon the Bey after yet another border incident had furnished the pretext for military occupation—stipulated that the ruler end the traffic in armaments between the two countries by severely restricting the sale of weapons and gunpowder. Moreover, by the eve of the Protectorate, there were several thousand Algerians in the Beylik, many of whom had long been viewed as real or potential threats to the security of "French" Algeria.[7]

The *hijra* (migration) of Algerians to Morocco and the Beylik began quite soon after the French invasion. With the defeat of the Amir and his forces and then following each of the uprisings, large groups emigrated to Tunisia, either to settle permanently or to go from there to the Mashriq. Others came during periods of economic distress or at the urging of religious figures preaching the duty of Muslims to depart from Christian-held territories. Once in Tunisia, some of the former rebels renounced politics for the pursuit of commerce or religious studies, and a few became protégés of France, while others continued to engage in anti-French activities, frequently combining religion, resistance, and commerce. Since the larger of the *turuq* offered an organizational structure and material base of support and maintained close contacts with other Sufi centers in Algeria and elsewhere, the nucleus for these activities was often a *zawiya*. The city of Tunis harbored a number of these political émigrés, as did the border towns, especially those in the Djerid and the region of Le Kef (Ar. *al-Kaff*). The attitude of the Beys toward the newcomers was usually one of solicitude—several of the Amir's supporters and several leaders of the 1871 insurrection were welcomed by the Bardo—as long as their presence did not stir up trouble among the Beylik's more turbulent subjects. The rulers normally refused to extradite Algerians sought by colonial officials for whatever reason, since they felt it was their duty as fellow Muslims to provide refuge. Ceaseless protests from French consuls in Tunis were countered by promises from the Beys to keep undesirable individuals away from the borders, although without much success. Until 1881 and even after, the southern and Saharan regions of the Beylik were regarded by colonial authorities as a "quasi-permanent center of political disorder" largely because of the Algerian community established in the area.[8]

Among the first to emigrate to the Djerid was Shaykh Mustafa ibn 'Azzuz, who left al-Borj in the Ziban, where he had been *al-shaykh al-akhbar* (head) of the Saharan branch of the Rahmaniya, when the French army moved against Biskra late in 1843.[9] The oases of the Ziban were located, as were those of the Djerid, on the main pilgrimage route from Morocco to the Hijaz, which meant that they shared continuous relations of a religious, commercial, and, at times, political nature. Moreover, the Ziban had a long history of opposition to the Turkish central government. Al-Borj, like its neighbor Zaatcha, had been taxed only intermittently by the Bey of Constantine, and in the early part of Sidi Mustafa's life had successfully withstood at least one siege. The traditional hostility of the region toward their Turkish rulers explains why so many of the oases supported 'Abd al-Qadir in his struggles against Ahmad, the last Bey of Constantine. Furthermore, one of Shaykh Mustafa's brothers had been a *khalifa* (official) of the Amir, and it was his capture and imprisonment by the French that led to the Shaykh's departure for southern Tunisia to organize a base of resistance there.

That Mustafa ibn 'Azzuz could undertake this task was due to the reputation his family enjoyed in eastern Algeria and particularly in the Saharan regions.[10] The Ibn 'Azzuz were a powerful clan of religious notables, long established in the Ziban, whose prestige and authority rested on their claims to sharifian descent as well as on their learning and saintliness. A certain affluence naturally accompanied the family's status, and the Ibn 'Azzuz not only controlled extensive properties in the al-Borj but dominated the surrounding sedentary and tribal populations, who as clients owed part of their surplus to the saintly lineage. Moreover, the father of Mustafa, Sidi Muhammad, had been revered as a *wali* and a disciple of the founder of the Rahmaniya *tariqa*; his tomb in al-Borj was the object of local pilgrimage as well as a source of family income. It was Muhammad ibn 'Azzuz who first introduced the new *tariqa* into this area of Algeria at the end of the eighteenth century. The rapid extension of the Rahmaniya there was largely due to the strategy pursued by Sidi Muhammad and his *muqaddams*, that of incorporating local saintly lineages and their *zawaya* into the *tariqa*, frequently by concluding marriage alliances.

By the time of Muhammad ibn 'Azzuz's death in 1819, the southern branch of the Rahmaniya had affiliated *zawaya* and mosques in the southern Aurès, the Oued Souf, and the Oued Righ, as well as in the Ziban. As a result, the Ibn 'Azzuz had ties of one sort or another with most of the religious notables in the entire region: the Ibn 'Uthman of Tolga, the saints of Khanqa Sidi Naji, the Sidi 'Ali family of El-Oued, to name but a few. The Ibn 'Uthman, a wealthy sharifian clan, and the Ibn 'Azzuz intermarried for several generations, and the post of *al-shaykh al-akhbar* passed alternately between the two families until a rift occurred at the end of the nineteenth century.[11] The *zawiya* of the Ibn 'Uthman in Tolga had long been a prestigious center of Islamic learning, and its library housed a rich collection of manuscripts acquired in Cairo and elsewhere during the *hajj*. Furthermore, the range and level of education offered by the Tolga *zawiya*, surprisingly advanced for a relatively small oasis, attracted students and scholars from all over. It was here that Mustafa ibn 'Azzuz studied the Muslim sciences with the celebrated *'alim* Shaykh 'Ali ibn 'Umar, who then bestowed his *baraka* (blessing) and the post of *al-shaykh al-akhbar* upon Sidi Mustafa just prior to his departure for the Djerid.

Once in the Beylik, Shaykh 'Azzuz and his family and followers founded mosque-*zawiya* in the oasis of Nafta; it soon became one of the largest and most powerful Rahmaniya establishments in Tunisia. The city of Nafta was itself a major Islamic center and, as the "port" of Tunis to the markets of the Sahara and southern Constantine, was the nearest oasis to the rather fluid border between Algeria and the Beylik. The choice of the Djerid was therefore a calculated one, since it placed the Ibn 'Azzuz just beyond the reach of the French military and at the intersection of several pilgrimage and commercial routes through which Shaykh 'Azzuz was able to keep in touch with and influence political events in Algeria. It was from Nafta that Sidi 'Azzuz supported the revolt of Zaatcha (1849), that of the "Sharif" of Ouargla, Muhammad ibn 'Abdallah (1851–55), and perhaps several others. In addition, the Rahmaniya *zawiya* in Nafta served as a refuge for Algerian émigrés and political dissidents during the shaykh's lifetime and even afterward. Sidi 'Azzuz never appeared at the head of an insurrection himself and, ironically, was best known in Tunisia for his role in quelling a rebellion. Nevertheless, his hostility toward the French was proverbial, and the memory of it lingered on among the populations of the south until the twentieth century. Finally, in undertaking the religious and social functions expected of any prosperous North African *tariqa*, the Nafta *zawiya* became active in the contraband arms trade flowing between the Tunisian coast and the southern Constantine.[12]

The traffic in munitions of all kinds developed into a going concern in the Maghrib during the nineteenth century and provided income for diverse groups of people; some made large fortunes from it. Many of the tribes of the Sahara traded in European rifles, and British gunpowder, reputed to be of the highest quality, was a much-sought-after commodity. During outbreaks of hostilities, the market price for a firearm could increase threefold, and powder by even more. The problem of adequate military supplies for 'Abd al-Qadir's regular army was so acute that the sale of arms by one of his soldiers was punished as severely as desertion—by death. Moreover, as a recent study has shown, access to European military technology constituted a key factor in the emergence of several regional "strongmen" in Morocco at the end of the nineteenth century.[13]

Given the number of revolts occurring in Algeria during the past century, the supply of armaments could never satisfy demand; the same could be said for Morocco and Tunisia in certain periods. Of course, not all the imported munitions were used against the French conqueror. Interminable tribal warfare as well as struggles for power among indigenous notables also served to keep demand high. Although there were groups in Algeria who had traditionally engaged in the manufacture of simple firearms and gunpowder (the Kabyles and Mzabites, for example), these could not be made in sufficient quantities. Furthermore, sulphur, one of the three components needed for producing gunpowder, had for the most part to be imported. When French officials placed severe restrictions on the availability of sulphur as well as firearms and gunpowder in the 1840s and attempted to prohibit overland commerce between the colony and its neighbors, the clandestine trade in arms increased sharply. And with continual advances in European military technology, after 1850 in particular, the problem for North Africans became not only that of quantity but of the quality of weaponry as well.[14]

The British were very active in the distribution of arms and, especially, gunpowder in the Maghrib, as were the Spanish and a number of commercial establishments in Italy and Marseilles. By mid-century, the trade in armaments between Tunisia and southern Algeria had become a British monopoly due to the industriousness of their Maltese protégés in the Beylik. Because of its distance from Tunis and proximity to Malta, the coastal region between Sfax and Djerid grew into the center for this segment of the contraband traffic. Most of the imported munitions intended for southeastern Algeria were introduced there via the oases of the Djerid, although several other routes existed for the northern Constantine: caravans organized in Sousse normally used the ThalaTebessa road, while those from Tunis went by way of Le Kef and Suq Ahras. Smaller quantities of powder and firearms also came into Algeria with pilgrims returning from the Hijaz or from visits to shrines in Tunisia or with Saharan tribes and merchants who moved between southern Tripolitania and the markets of the Oued Righ and the Mzab.[15]

Although the contraband arms trade existed prior to the arrival of Mustafa ibn 'Azzuz in the Djerid and would continue well into the twentieth century, the Rahmaniya Shaykh is noteworthy for the manner in which he drew upon *tariqa* networks and institutions to carry on his behind-the-scenes jihad against the French. And while the participation of a *wali* in the traffic in munitions may seem somewhat paradoxical, Shaykh 'Azzuz was, in fact, part of a tradition found in certain parts of the Maghrib which enlarged the protective powers of the saint and his *zawiya* to include that offered by firearms. When a Turkish tax expedition threatened Ain Madi (Ar. 'Ayn Mahdi) in the early decades of the nineteenth century, the inhabitants wrote to Ahmad Tijani, in Fez at the time, requesting that he save them—either by his presence in the oasis or by sending them arms. The Ibadiyya communities of the Mzab habitually stored munitions in their mosques, and Darqawa *zawaya* housed both arms depots and workshops for their repair. Further east, the Sanusi centers in Cyrenaica had by the end of the century evolved into veritable arsenals in response to the growing threat of European occupation.[16] The association between *baraka* and *barud* (saintliness and fighting) naturally found expression in the popular discourse and imagery surrounding saints and particularly mahdis. The almost universal claim of an aspiring apocalyptic leader was that "gunpowder counted for nothing against him" or that adversaries' bullets would be miraculously deflected from his person.[17] Even those promising to inaugurate the millennium and supposedly armed only with the grace of God often took pains to provide their forces with munitions. Abu Ziyan and Muhammad ibn 'Abdallah, both of whom led movements with millenarian dimensions, were supplied with European firearms and British powder, much of which reached them through the Rahmaniya *zawiya* in Nafta.

As head of a large and strategically situated Sufi center that came to have a number of affiliated *zawiya*, Sidi 'Azzuz could draw on several types of networks—kinship, religious, commercial—in order to adapt traditional institutions to new political conditions. Moreover, the Shaykh's involvement in the international arms trade and in insurrection in Algeria and the expansion of his *tariqa* as well as the growth of his spiritual authority were interrelated phenomena that cannot be divorced from the climate of crisis prevailing in the region at the time.[18] Nor can personality be discounted, for even the enemies of 'Azzuz regarded him as a charismatic figure who was tremendously influential in preaching and whose reputation for both *'ilm* (religious knowledge) and *baraka* attracted throngs of followers to his *zawiya*. In a biographical notice devoted to him, the Tunisian historian Ibn Abi al-Diyaf described Shaykh 'Azzuz as an "*'alim, wali, 'arif*" who performed miracles, initiated the tribes into his "way," and urged people to accomplish their religious duties, much in the manner of the Islamic *mujaddid*.[19] Many of the tribal groups in the Djerid (the Ghrib and Maraziq', for example) were affiliated with the Nafta Rahmaniya, as were most of the Frashish tribe located near Thala and the eastern branch of the Namamsha, who moved between the southern Constantine and Tunisia. And as so often happened, the saint of Nafta came to be held in such high esteem by tribal clients and sedentary adepts that those initiated into the *tariqa* by him began referring to themselves as either Rahmaniya or 'Azzuziya. The shaykh was not without spiritual competitors in the area, since the Tijaniya and Qadiriya, among other orders, enjoyed a following in the oases, but relations between the Tijaniya elite and the Rahmaniya really became less than amiable after Sidi Mustafa's death, precisely when the Tijaniya began to dominate the south.[20]

In mapping out the geography of Sidi 'Azzuz's clientele, several patterns emerge. The shaykh had followers in the border regions, perhaps even as far north as Ain Drahem (Ar. 'Ayn Draham), and above all in areas that maintained economic ties with cities and markets in the eastern Constantine, such as Tebessa. Moreover, the oases that traded with the Djerid—Ghadamès, Gabès, Ouargla, Tuggurth, Laghouat—also counted adepts. In addition, there were several 'Azzuziya *zawaya* in Benghazi and the Hijaz, probably founded during one of Sidi Mustafa's pilgrimages to Mecca and through which he kept in touch with events in the east. Most important for resistance in Algeria, however, were the pilgrims, students, and agitators who flocked to Nafta from eastern Algeria, for upon their return they served as the saint's emissaries, informants, and distributors of munitions.[21]

As noted above, the arms traffic was linked to the interregional and international trade between the Mediterranean, the interior, and the desert. After being purchased from Maltese importers in the southern Tunisian ports, the powder was brought in caravans to the Djerid by tribes specializing in the transport of contraband, several of whom were "'Azzuziya." Obliged to traverse areas where security was frequently lacking, the caravans were placed under the safe-conduct of Shaykh Mustafa, whose protection was also sought by merchants and travelers coming from the west into the Djerid. Once in Nafta, the shipments of munitions were "placed between the hands of Sidi 'Azzuz" and stored in or near the *zawiya*, whose space was considered *haram* (sacred) and therefore inviolable.[22] Since figures regarding quantities are only found in French sources, it is hazardous to make estimates; the most reliable data for the early 1850s held that as many as two caravans per month were involved, each carrying several thousand kilos of gunpowder. The munitions were then sold to clients or merchants, often from the Oued Souf (whose inhabitants were inveterate traders in all sorts of contraband articles), or to tribes such as the Sha'amba, who supplied the markets of the Mzab. Via the Djerid–Oued Souf route, British powder and firearms reached the Ziban, the Kabylia, and even as far as the province of Oran.[23]

Distribution was not limited to the *zawaya* or adepts affiliated with Sidi 'Azzuz. One of his more notable clients was the Tijani *al-shaykh al-akhbar* of the Tijaniya Sidi Muhammad al-'Id of Temassine, regarded by most French officials as one of their staunchest allies. In all probability, at least one of the Rahmaniya centers established by Mustafa ibn 'Azzuz sometime after 1850 in the region of Kasserine and linked to the 'Azzuz family by kinship was also involved in the arms traffic between the Beylik and Algeria. The village of Thala, which then consisted mainly of a large arms depot and the 'Azzuziya *zawiya*, was located on one of the caravan routes between either Tunis or Sousse and Tebessa. And when the Oued Souf was under close French military surveillance, caravans loaded with powder from the Djerid used this route to introduce munitions into the Constantine.[24]

The political activities of Shaykh 'Azzuz and his immense religious prestige naturally brought him to the attention of both the rulers of Tunisia and the French. During his lifetime, the saint of Nafta enjoyed the favor of the Beys, especially Ahmad (reigned 1837–55), over whom 'Azzuz apparently exerted a great deal of influence and whom he even visited on several occasions. The Beys of Tunis pursued the same strategy of bestowing honors and privileges upon the Rahmaniya in Nafta as they did for other powerful religious establishments in

Tunisia and even in Constantine province. At the time of 'Azzuz's death, the *zawiya* was among the wealthiest of the Djerid, and to his heirs the shaykh left extensive properties as well as a string of benefactors. Several family members achieved considerable social mobility, chiefly through ties to the central government.[25] In return for patronage, the Bardo could normally rely on provincial religious notables, like Sidi 'Azzuz, to act as its emissaries or as intermediaries between ruler and ruled during periods of unrest. When increased taxation in 1851 provoked unusual opposition, particularly in the south, the shaykh attempted to divert resentment away from Ahmad Bey by blaming the taxes upon the French. However, he carefully maintained a certain distance from the local representative of the government, whose efforts at centralization were extremely unpopular in the Djerid. Finally, the Bardo acted as a protector by ignoring repeated demands from French authorities that the saint be kept away from the borders or interned and may have even given sub-rosa encouragement to him.[26]

French Arab Bureau officers naturally viewed Mustafa ibn 'Azzuz as a "dangerous" individual, and some went so far as to recommend invading the Djerid in order to end his "incessant intrigues," which went beyond furnishing the material means for rebellion. In addition to being "the most active agent in the contraband powder trade between Gabès and Oued Souf," the shaykh's *zawiya* in Nafta served as a haven and meeting place for political figures from Algeria, among them several of Amir 'Abd al-Qadir's *khalifa*s; it even welcomed British agents in the early 1860s.[27] Moreover, in terms of his influence, the Rahmaniya leader was feared as another amir during a period when many in Algeria looked to the south or to the Beylik for deliverance. Expectations centered either upon holy warriors (Ar. *mujahidin*) coming out of the Sahara with their armies to expel the infidels or on other Muslim rulers, particularly the Bey of Tunis or the Ottoman Sultan, whose military support was repeatedly looked for during rebellions and was always rumored to be just on the way. In this respect, another dimension of the *zawiya* as an institutional component of resistance emerges—that of functioning as a center for the creation and/or dissemination of propaganda aimed at maintaining a certain level of political ferment among the population at large. Indeed, an officer of the Arab Bureau assigned to the region of Biskra in the 1850s commented that "the Djerid is the foyer for hostile propaganda toward France due to the presence there of the ben Azouz."[28]

Sidi 'Azzuz acted as a sort of propagandist (Ar. *da'i*) in a manner reminiscent of the Shi'i movement in the Maghrib many centuries earlier. Rumors, prophecies, and information regarding political events in the Maghrib, Europe, and the Muslim East were all diffused over wide areas and among isolated groups of people. Sufi leaders like Shaykh 'Azzuz were particularly well equipped to engage in propagandist activities since as ulama their words carried great weight and as heads of *zawaya* they could make use of pilgrims and travelers to

carry letters or could transmit via their adepts bits of news designed to stir up
the tribes or the more complacent city-dwellers.[29] Thus, from his base of
operation in the Djerid, the Rahmaniya leader carried on the work of the
Tuwala, a secret association of religious notables formed sometime during the
mid-1840s in western Algeria and in which both Mustafa and one of his
brothers participated until its discovery by the French in 1851. The association's goal of driving the infidel from North Africa was to be achieved by
pushing local popular religious figures, often with mahdist pretensions, to revolt
and by exhorting the populace to support these movements. When the French
army was sufficiently distracted by a number of simultaneous outbreaks, the
signal for a mass uprising would then be given—or so the Tuwala reasoned.[30]

Although the conspiracy came to naught before the appointed hour for
expelling the conqueror, two uprisings in eastern Algeria during the period
bear the marks of the Tuwala strategy. Moreover, they reveal continuities with
earlier resistance and resisters as well as the multifaceted nature of the pursuit
of the millennium. The revolt led by Abu Ziyan, a minor landholding notable
from Zaatcha and a former *khalifa* of the Amir, was preceded by an intense
propaganda (one might even say "publicity") campaign in the spring of 1849.
Rumors and prophecies announcing that deliverance was at hand began
circulating, as did news of political problems in France which—or so the
reasoning went—had weakened the resolve to hold onto Algeria. Letters
calling for jihad flooded the Ziban, Hodna, the Sahara, and the Aurès, and
support was even solicited from native *qaids* nominally allied with the French
and the Bey of Tunis.[31] While the Zaatcha revolt has not received much recent
scholarly attention (the colonial literature on it is relatively extensive), it was an
event of immense significance for all parties to the conflict. For the French army
aiming at pacification, the siege was the longest and most costly since 1830; and
because it sparked a number of uprisings among both tribal and sedentary
groups over an enormous area, the outcome was intended as a permanent lesson
for the unruly inhabitants of the south. To the latter, the struggle that eventually centered upon the small oasis represented an Armageddon in miniature
and test case not only for the political future of the Ziban but for the rest of
Algeria as well. Indeed, the significance of the Zaatcha revolt did not end with
the defeat: the determined resistance of Abu Ziyan and his forces created a
heroic epic that remained in the popular collective memory long afterward.[32]

The causes of the revolt, its timing, and the events leading up to the outbreak
of hostilities were the result of a complicated set of conjunctures that cannot be
dealt with here. Moreover, as so often happened, the nature of the movement
changed over time. Thus, at Zaatcha were combined elements of a traditional
oasis tax revolt—particularly in terms of its carefully planned organization—
and an effort to maintain regional political and economic autonomy with an
anti-colonial jihad that had more or less explicit millenarian dimensions. Abu
Ziyan's eventual claims of being the *khalifa* (or precursor) of the Mahdi

certainly played a part in his ability to attract a large and rather diverse following that included not only *muhajidin* from most of the surrounding oases and tribes and figures involved in earlier rebellions but participants from Tunisia (among them two of Sidi 'Azzuz's brothers), Morocco, and even the Hijaz, giving a pan-Islam coloring to the movement.[33] Yet as was so often the case with aspiring apocalyptic leaders, large-scale mobilization depended on more than fitting the paradigm of the Mahdi (or his deputy), which offered the possibility of joining religious with politico-military authority. Equally necessary was the backing of the more established men of religion in a given region, and numerous examples of would-be mahdis whose movements never got off the ground due to the lack of such support can be offered for nineteenth-century Algeria.[34] Thus, the uprising headed by Abu Ziyan reached the proportions it did in part because of the backing of several of the most influential Rahmani centers in the area, those of Sidi Khalid, Nafta, Sidi Masmudi, and, eventually, Sidi Khanga Naji. Moreover, it was in all likelihood Shaykh 'Azzuz who prevailed upon Sidi 'Abd al-Hafidh, shaykh of the Khanga Sidi Naji *zawiya*, to give in to pressures from his followers in the Aurès and move against the French near Biskra in September 1849 as a diversionary tactic.[35]

The fifty-two-day siege of Zaatcha resulted in its total destruction and the submission of the rest of the oases in the Ziban. The goal of pacification had hardly been achieved, however, for the opposition simply moved further south and eventually into Tunisia, while benefitting from the bitter resentment caused by the events of 1849. Almost immediately following was the movement led by the so-called *sharif* of Ouargla, Muhammad ibn 'Abdallah, which kept the Oued Righ and Oued Souf in a state of low-grade rebellion from 1851 until 1855 and involved some of the same personalities and strategies.[36] Significant here is the increasingly "international" cadre of resistance in Algeria, although unlike in Zaatcha, religion, while playing an important role in mobilization, was not sufficient to sustain long-term unified action. Moreover, if Shaykh 'Azzuz continued to act as before, the posture he assumed toward colonial authorities and his behavior in the final denouement of the movement merit closer examination.

This second revolt, a long-drawn-out affair, once again grew out of the interplay among political conjuncture, changing economic conditions, and the activities of the behind-the-scenes agitators. Beginning in 1851, another propaganda campaign was undertaken by Sidi 'Azzuz as well as by other supporters of the "*sharif*," among them the successor to Sidi 'Abd al-Hafidh; and numerous meetings of the Saharan clients of the Nafta *zawiya* were held. As in the past, shipments of arms, with 'Azzuz acting as middleman, began arriving in the southern Constantine from Gabès via the Djerid. The backing of the shaykh was particularly crucial because of his large following in the oases of Ouargla, Tuggurth, and the Oued Souf, where he and his father had founded a number of *zawaya* and *kuttab* (Quranic schools). It is perhaps not coincidental that after

Sidi 'Azzuz made the *hajj* in 1851, the Ottomans started sending emissaries to the region. Later, Turkish officials in Tripoli were to furnish material assistance to Muhammad ibn 'Abdallah in the hope that he would continue the work of the Amir. There is also reason to believe that the "sharif" enjoyed the support of the Sanusi in Cyrenaica, with whom he had stayed during his extended travels in the Muslim East. Somewhat problematic is the position of the Tijaniya leadership, whose *zawiya* at Tamasin (near Tuggurth) was second only to Ain Madi and therefore enormously influential. While in theory a French protégé, Shaykh Muhammad al-'Id seems eventually to have opted for covert participation in the revolt, perhaps under pressure from his clientele.[37]

The "*sharif*" of Ouargla, Muhammad ibn 'Abdallah (the name is itself significant), although more typical in many ways of a messianic figure than Abu Ziyan, was a *khalifa al-mahdi* with slightly tarnished credentials, since he had briefly served as a French official in Tlemcen in 1841. Failing miserably as a "secular" holder of power, he became a wandering ecstatic on the margins of the religious establishment and won a certain notoriety by carrying his spiritual devotions to the extreme. After nearly a decade in the east, the "*sharif*" returned to the region of Laghouat and the Mzab and initiated his career sometime in 1850 by performing miracles among the tribes, preaching jihad, and carrying out raids (Ar. *ghazwat*) against those allied to the French. In fact, throughout the wide-ranging movement, the "*sharif*" employed the tribal *ghazwa* as a principal instrument of holy war. However, in his letters seeking support from the tribes, he urged jihad rather for the "love of God" or the defense of Islam, frequently designating himself as the "protector of religion" (*haris al-din*).[38]

The concerted call for holy warfare began in September 1851 and appears to have been timed to coincide with political events in France, where the republic was once again in trouble, and in Algeria, where events in Kabylia were diverting attention from the south. As was so often the case, several other "*sharifs*" began operating in various parts of Algeria at the same time—Abu Baghla in the northern Constantine and a second in the Hodna. Prophecies then current among the population also helped the cause. One held that after a twenty-year stay, the foreigners would inevitably leave Algeria; a slightly different version predicted the coming of the millenarian leader Mawlay al-sa'a ("the master of the hour") in the year 1270/1853. Growing discontent with French-appointed *qaids* in the south, together with traditional rivalries and regional alliances, won over many of those who had long opposed the Ibn Jallab family, the rulers of Tuggurth, then nominally allied to the French. Finally, resentment caused by increasing colonial interference with Saharan trade and commerce may also have been a factor.[39]

The rebellion really got underway, however, when a struggle within the Ibn Jallab brought to power Sulayman ibn Jallab, who then threw in his lot with Muhammad ibn 'Abdallah in 1852. Once again, it is impossible to give a detailed account of the shifting fortunes of the movement. For our purposes, it is sufficient to note that the rebellion was aided not only by the Ibn 'Azzuz and the *qaid* of Tozeur but by another former *khalifa* of 'Abd al-Qadir, Ahmad ibn al-Hajj of Sidi Uqba, who, from his base in the Nafzawa, cooperated with Shaykh 'Azzuz to assure a steady supply of arms from the coast. Lacking the military capability to finish with the rebels in the earlier stages of the revolt, the French, by then firmly in control of Biskra (a key market for southeastern Algeria), cut the oases off from the customary grain supplies in 1852 and 1853. Yet as long as markets in neighboring Tunisia remained open to the "*sharif,*" Sulayman ibn Jallab, and their forces, this tactic met with only limited success. A series of poor harvests in the Beylik the following year meant economic hardship for the inhabitants of Oued Souf and Oued Righ and difficulties in provisioning the rebellion. Several military reverses, as well as dashed hopes of large-scale assistance from the Bey or the Ottoman Sultan, gradually eroded support for the movement. After a final defeat by the French and their tribal allies at the end of 1854, the two leaders and their followers fled from Tuggurth to the Djerid to prepare for a second round of hostilities.[40]

To legitimize their cause, the stated aim of which was to retake Biskra and punish collaborators, Muhammad ibn 'Abdallah and the now ex-Sultan Sulayman called on prominent religious figures for help: the Tijaniya leader at Temassine, Sidi 'Umar Abayda of Kairouan, and Shaykh 'Azzuz. The shaykh was responsible for mobilizing armed supporters by prevailing upon his numerous adepts in the region to join the movement. Use was also made of 'Azzuz's oratory skills, but his call for jihad shows little, if any, evidence of apocalyptic arguments. It was, rather, a "patriotic" appeal for the defense of religion and "to replace the flag of France with that of Islam." Indeed, even before the revolt entered its Tunisian phase in 1855, whatever millenarian fervor had existed at first had largely disappeared.[41] The response it elicited in the southern regions of the Beylik was probably due to the fact that a great deal of political unrest already existed, caused by drought, crop failures, and unusually heavy taxation by the Bey in order to finance the Crimea expedition. Thus, the "*sharif*'s" arrival appears to have coincided with a nascent opposition movement against the central government.[42]

The religious backers of the "*sharif*" achieved their task as mobilizers, and by the spring of 1855 large numbers had joined Muhammad ibn 'Abdallah and Sulayman Jallab, then camped in the Nafzawa, including the shaykh of the redoubtable Awlad Yaqub, Muhammad Abu Allaq. Yet even successful mobilization and the material and moral support of such Sufi notables as 'Azzuz and Sidi al-'Id did not necessarily lead to political action, for the "*sharif*" had attempted the impossible—to bridge tribal *soff* alliances and unite traditional tribal enemies under a single banner. Most significantly, when the movement began to falter, largely due to a falling out between its principal leaders, Shaykh 'Azzuz did not step in to assume control. Consequently, the planned attack against Biskra, intended as the prelude to a general insurrection in the Constantine, never materialized, and by August 1855 the assembled forces started dispersing. Muhammad ibn 'Abdallah and a band of followers continued to keep the Sahara in a state of unrest for years afterward, but not before both the *"sharif"* and Sulayman Jallab offered to put down their arms in exchange for administrative posts from the French military, an offer which was refused.[43]

They were not the only ones to assume a decidedly ambiguous stance toward the rulers of Algeria. At the same time that he was aiding the *"sharif"'s"* movement, the Saint of Nafta endeavored to stay in the good graces of colonial authorities, although he had been residing in the Beylik for years. Due to a network of well-placed informants, Sidi 'Azzuz was aware of his reputation, and in order to dispel the rumors concerning his hostility toward France he paid a visit sometime in 1853 to a fellow Algerian then serving the French as an interpreter. During the ensuing discussion, the shaykh declared that, far from being an opponent, he had willingly accepted the act of divine providence that had placed Algeria in the hands of France and that he abhorred the shedding of blood in the name of God. Not satisfied with this, he later sent letters to the governor-general and the director of the Arab Bureau to reaffirm his devotion.[44] The Saharan explorer Henri Duveyrier had a similar experience while traveling through the Djerid in 1860. Welcoming the Frenchman to his *zawiya*, the shaykh addressed him in language inspired by the recent Tunisian reform proclamation, the *'ahd al-aman*, and assured him that "Muslims, Christians, Jews, all those created by God were his children." Completely won over by Sidi 'Azzuz, Duveyrier later described him as an enlightened individual much above the ordinary.[45]

This seemingly contradictory behavior was in reality not uncommon for religious notables caught in situations analogous to that of Shaykh 'Azzuz; it reveals quite simply an awareness of the limitations upon, as well as the opportunities for, political action. In effect, the Rahmaniya Shaykh had to balance a number of related interests—those of family, *tariqa*, clientele—within an uncertain and shifting context which included the central government and European powers as well. The prestige, spiritual authority, and wealth that the Ibn 'Azzuz commanded were largely dependent on a constant stream of disciples to the Nafta *zawiya* and on the freedom of movement for members of the *tariqa* hierarchy to collect offerings and initiate new adepts into the holy way. Since a large part of his following came from across the borders and since the Ibn 'Azzuz family retained properties in the Ziban—several of his brothers had even returned there to live—the shaykh had to be somewhat circumspect, at least outwardly, in his relations with French authorities. And the question of adepts became particularly important in the period, since the Nafta Rahmaniya could by no means claim a monopoly or even a near-monopoly on sanctity in the region. Moreover, the shaykh's conciliatory gestures toward the colonial regime were probably related to the fact that—prophecies to the contrary notwithstanding—there existed an equally widespread belief regarding France's intent to extend military control over southern Tunisia. In all likelihood too, the Bey, under increasing pressure from the French consul in Tunis, requested that Sidi 'Azzuz be more discreet in his anti-French activities.[46]

Paradoxically, the Sufi leader was best known in the Beylik during the following decade for his role in defusing rebellion rather than encouraging it. After a tax revolt that began late in 1863 had turned into a full-scale insurrection by the spring of 1864, al-Sadiq Bey appealed to some of the more influential men of religion for help in quelling the uprising. While Sidi 'Azzuz's part in ending the Revolt of 1864 has perhaps been overrated, he used his authority as a Sufi notable to secure the submission of several tribes and their leaders, and he served as an intermediary by transmitting a list of grievances to the ruler. Allegedly the shaykh also relied on the more Machiavellian tactic of sowing dissension among the ranks of the rebels in order to hasten the breakup of the movement, which finally occurred late in 1864 and for which he was richly rewarded.[47] Thus, despite the fact that the Great Revolt was partially a reaction against increasing European interference in the affairs of nineteenth-century Tunisian society, Sidi 'Azzuz, the fomenter of rebellion across the border, was instrumental in demobilizing a movement that threatened the social order of the Beylik.

One does not have to search very far for explanations regarding the shaykh's action, especially if the later stages of the 1864 Revolt are interpreted as partially a threat from below that might alarm those who possessed wealth. Within the relatively centralized Tunisian state of the past century, Sufi notables like 'Azzuz, and the ulama in general, enjoyed only an uneasy quasi-autonomy vis-à-vis the central government; moreover, it was not unheard-of for the ruler to demote a leading religious figure who had incurred beylical dis-favor.[48] Yet ties to the Bardo and self-interest do not alone account for 'Azzuz's behavior when confronted with an event such as that of the Great Revolt. Neither an apocalyptic visionary nor a social revolutionary, the Rahmaniya leader consistently used his authority as a Sufi and saint either to preserve the social status quo or to attempt to restore it whenever circumstances rendered this feasible. Whether encouraging resistance in Algeria or putting down sedition in the Beylik, Sidi 'Azzuz not only responded to the political milieu in which he operated but strove to shape it to his own purposes. In so doing, he showed an awareness of the strength of the adversary and perhaps an awareness—however dim—of the international forces at play in the eastern Maghrib during the second half of the nineteenth century. Like 'Abd al-Qadir, Sidi 'Azzuz had an interest in the bases of France's power, and like the Sanusi, he seems to have sensed that Algeria would not satisfy French ambitions in North Africa.[49] In urging the tribes to submit to the Bey in 1864, the shaykh argued that prolonged turmoil would only invite French military intervention in the Beylik. To decrease the chances of this happening, he undertook another propaganda campaign in Algeria, designed to stir up unrest there so as to divert attention from events in Tunisia.[50]

During the years that separated the end of the 1864 Revolt from his death, the Saint of Nafta, deceived by the Bey's unfulfilled promise of pardon for the rebels, abandoned this world for the next. As might be expected, his tomb in the Djerid immediately became the object of local and regional pilgrimages which continued until after World War I. A tradition of resistance to Western imperialism remained among the saint's descendants, some of whom emigrated to the Hijaz after the establishment of the Protectorate; a grandson was expelled from Tunisia in 1912 for attempting to incite the inhabitants of Nafta to leave the Beylik for the Mashriq.[51]

What conclusions concerning the interplay between religion and politics in the nineteenth-century Maghrib can be drawn from the case study of a *tariqa* notable such as Mustafa ibn 'Azzuz? By providing the material and ideological bases of collective action, 'Azzuz and others like him permitted anti-colonial resistance in Algeria to last as long as it did. At the same time, their activities may have helped to hasten the French occupation of Tunisia, although transformations in the European balance of power during the 1870s were obviously the determining factor. As behind-the-scenes propagandists who frequently operated from across the border, these activist men of religion were difficult to detect and reduce to political quiescence by whatever means. As heads of networks of *zawaya*, they not only commanded considerable resources and the loyalties of diverse groups of people but also had systems of communication and information at their disposal. And in areas such as southern Tunisia or Algeria, the Sufi elite exercised a near-monopoly over learning, sanctity and, consequently, moral authority. In legitimizing the actual leaders of a movement and exhorting the hesitant to take up arms for jihad, figures like 'Azzuz bestowed unity—however temporarily—on inherently fragile alliances, because they used religion as a language with its own potent meanings and universal symbols.

Of course, the participation of the men of religion in the realm of earthly politics had structural as well as social limits in the form of tribal politics, the restraints imposed by ecology, and the jealously guarded prerogatives of central governments. Several of the most decisive factors for sustained rebellion in the south—assured access to key markets and bridging factional *soff* quarrels— were quite beyond the competence of an influential religious man such as Sidi 'Azzuz. Nevertheless, even in a world turned upside down, traditional institutions lent themselves admirably to new situations and the various kinds of social action that these situations call for. The nature of the *turuq*, which in North Africa encompassed more or less implicitly political elements, was to a great extent responsible for this. With a mass following that was often expressed in patron-client relationships and tending toward integration into local or regional economies, a major *tariqa* or one of its branches presented certain possibilities for collective action. Moreover, many of the roles assumed by populist Sufi leaders or saints—mediation, protection, education—implicated them at times in the realm of politics, either to confer legitimacy or to contest it. In a later period and in a different context, these same political elements would produce quite the opposite effect. By the turn of the century, the leadership of the Sufi orders, far from resisting, helped buttress the colonial regime in Algeria and, to a lesser degree, in Tunisia.[52]

What the above suggests is that typologies such as those offered by B. G. Martin—who characterized the response of Sufi leaders to Western imperialism in nineteenth-century Africa as either "radical, moderate or conservative"—or by M. Brett render static and rigid what was historically an exceedingly complex and rich social reality.[53] The fact that Shaykh 'Azzuz initiated adepts into the mysteries of the holy way and taught the foundations of the *Shari'a* while encouraging them to armed insurrection was in no way contradictory. Likewise, his apparent ambivalence toward the conquerors of Algeria represented a rational and calculated response to changing political conditions which might, on occasion, demand bowing to force majeure, or at least appearing to do so. Finally, one can legitimately speculate about the degree to which involvement in the international arms trade played a role in the rise to prominence of the Saint of Nafta, both in terms of his ability to supply much-needed weapons to followers and with respect to family fortunes and that of the *zawiya*. This is not to deny the importance of Sidi 'Azzuz's reputation for piety, religious learning, and *baraka*, for within the social and political order of the past century the flow of grace and the flow of arms were mutually reinforcing.

NOTES

1. This paper is based on the following archival collections: Archives du Ministère des Affaires Etrangères, Paris (AE); Archives du Ministère de la Guerre, Vincennes (AMG); Archives Nationales, Gouvernement Général de l'Algérie, Aix-en-Provence (AN-Aix); Archives de la Résidence Générale de France à Tunis, Nantes (ARGT); Archives Nationales, Paris (AN-Paris); Archives Générales Tunisiennes, Dar el-Bey (AGT); and the reports of the Centre des Hautes Etudes sur l'Afrique et l'Asie Moderne, Paris (CHEAM). For place references, please see Map 1.

2. For example, B. G. Martin, *Muslim Brotherhoods in 19th Century Africa* (London: Cambridge University Press, 1976); A. Nadir, "Les ordres religieux et la conquête française," *Revue Algérienne des Sciences Juridiques, Politiques et Economiques* 9 (1972): 819–72; M. Brett, "Mufti, Murabit, Marabout and Mahdi: Four Types in the Islamic History of North Africa," *ROMM* 29 (1980): 5–16.

3. Despite the numerical importance of Mahdist-led movements in eighteenth- and nineteenth-century Algeria and Morocco, there are few studies aside from P. Von Sivers, "The Realm of Justice: Apocalyptic Revolts in Algeria, 1849–1879," *Humaniora Islamica* 1, no. 1 (1973): 47–60; and A. Hammoudi, "Aspects de la mobilisation à la campagne, vus à travers la biographie d'un mahdi mort en 1919," *Islam et Politique au Maghreb* (Paris: Editions du Centre National de la Recherche Scientifique, 1981). Among the best such recent studies are E. Burke, III, *Prelude to Protectorate in Morocco: Precolonial Protest and Resistance, 1860–1912* (Chicago: University of Chicago Press, 1976); R. Dunn, *Resistance in the Desert: Moroccan Responses to French Imperialism, 1881–1912* (Madison: University of Wisconsin Press, 1977); and A. Green, *The Tunisian Ulama, 1873–1915* (Leiden: Brill, 1978).

4. The literature written during the colonial period on revolts is quite extensive. Aside from the works of C. R. Ageron and C. A. Julien, which deal with insurrection within a general historical framework, P. Von Sivers has done the most on the subject recently: see "Insurrection and Accommodation: Indigenous Leadership in Eastern Algeria, 1840–1900," *IJMES* 6 (1975): 259–75, and his chapter in this volume.

5. There exists no work on the Rahmaniya comparable to J. Abun-Nasr's *The Tijaniyya: A Sufi Order in the Modern World* (Oxford: Oxford University Press, 1965), aside from the dissertation by M. Sahli, "Etude d'une confrérie religieuse algérienne: la Rahmaniya," Ecole des Hautes Etudes en Sciences Sociales, Paris, 1979. Information on the order can be found in M. al-Niyal, *Al-Haqiqa al-tarikhiya lil-tasawwuf al-islamiya* (Tunis, 1965); M. Gouvion and E. Gouvion, *Kitab Aayane al-Marhariba* (Algiers, 1920); O. Depont and X. Coppolani, *Les confréries religieuses musulmanes* (Alger: A. Jourdan, 1897); and AGT, D–97–3, among others.

6. Some examples of other behind-the-scenes agitators: Sidi 'Abd al-Malik, shaykh of the Rahmaniya *zawiya* in al-Kaff; Sidi Hajj Muhammad ibn Bash-Tarzi, the Rahmaniya shaykh of the city of Constantine; Sidi Muhammad al-'Id, the Tijaniya shaykh of Temassine.

7. Sources for this are: AE, Tunisie, Correspondance Politique, vols. 10–66; ARGT, cartons 414–23; AN-Aix F80 and 16H series and *Documents diplomatiques, affaires de Tunisie*, vols. 54–57 (Paris, 1881).

8. There is no study of the Algerian *hijra* to the Beylik in the nineteenth century. Information here is based on the archival sources listed in n. 7 above. The quote is from D. Camisoli, "La frontière Algero-Tunisienne," *Revue historique de l'Armée* 11 (1955): 72.

9. AN-Aix, 10H76; AMG, Algérie, M1317, H230bis.

10. No study exists of the Ibn 'Azzuz; references are found in the secondary works listed in n. 5 above and in Ahmad ibn Abi al-Diyaf, *Ithaf ahl al-zaman bi-akhbar muluk Tunis wa 'ahd al-aman*, 8 vols. (Tunis, 1963–66), biographical notice 370, pp. 142–43; M. ibn Ashur, *Tarajim al-alam* (Tunis: Al-Dar al-Tunisiyah lil-Nashr, 1970), as well as in the archival collections listed in n. 1 above.

11. In contrast to the Ibn 'Azzuz, the Ibn 'Uthman had a tradition of accommodation with the central government, whether Turkish or French; see AMG, Algérie, H230bis. This attitude may have been the cause of the dispute between the Tolga *zawiya* and those at Khanga Sidi Naji, Masmudi, and Sidi Khalid. The rift was as much the result of the anti-French policies of the 'Azzuz as a struggle over property and prestige in the region; see Sahli, "Etude," pp.82–84.

12. For the Djerid, see A. Henia, *Le Jarid, ses rapports avec le Beylik de Tunis (1678–1840)* (Tunis, 1980), and M. Rouissi, "Une oasis du sud Tunisien, le Jarid: un essai d'histoire sociale," Thèse de IIIème cycle, Ecole des Hautes Etudes en Sciences Sociales, Paris, 1973. On Ibn 'Azzuz in the Djerid, see AN-Aix, 10H43, 16H67; AMG, Tunisie, 28bis, 29; CHEAM, no. 2053; and AGT, D–97–3.

13. R. Dunn, "Bu Himara's European Connexion: The Commercial Relations of a Moroccan Warlord," in *IJAHS* 21 (1980): 235–53.

14. On indigenous manufacture and trade in firearms and powder, see AN-Aix, F80 1426; for a discussion of the nineteenth-century European armaments industry and its impact on sub-Saharan Africa, see the collection of articles in *JAH* 12 (1971): 173–254.

15. There is no study of the arms trade between Algeria and Tunisia in the nineteenth century; what follows is based on AE, Tunisie, Correspondance Politique, vols. 12-supra and Missions et Documents, vol. 8; ARGT, 414–23, 3219; AN-Paris, F[17] 2957[2]; AN-Aix, 1H, 16H sous-série; and AMG, Tunisie and Algérie. Designating this trade as contraband expresses the French point of view.

16. Abun-Nasr, *The Tijaniyya*, p. 60; CHEAM, no. 8; E. Evans-Pritchard, *The Sanusi of Cyrenaica* (Oxford: Oxford University Press, 1949); and F. E. de Neveu, *Les Khouan* (Paris: A. Guyot, 1846).

17. For just a few examples of this association, see C. Richard, *Etude sur l'insurrection du Dhara* (Alger: A. Besancenez, 1846), p.16; and A. Hanoteau, *La Kabylie et les coutumes Kaybles*,3 vols. (Paris: Impr. nationale, 1872–73), vol. 1, p. 467.

18. A discussion of the relationship between the appearance of the saint in the Maghrib and surrounding sociohistorical conditions is found in A. Hammoudi's "Sainteté, pouvoir et société: Tamgrout aux XVIIème et XVIIème siecles," *Annales ESC* 35 (1980): 615–41.

19. Ibn Abi al-Diyaf, *Ithaf,* biographical notice 370, pp. 142–43.

20. On the tribal followers see AMG, Tunisie, 29, 30; AE, Tunisie, Missions et Documents, vol. 8. The 'Azzuziya-Rahmaniya of Nafta were in no way related either through kinship or spiritual ties to the purely local *tariqa* of Sidi 'Ali 'Azzuz found near Zaghouan; see AGT, D–97–3, Civil Controller's report on the "'Azzouzia." On relations between the orders, see AMG, Algérie, M1317.

21. Sahli, "Etude," pp. 82–84; ARGT, 989, 1218; AN-Aix, 1H12.

22. ARGT, 423; AE, Tunisie, Missions et Documents, vol. 8, and Correspondance Politique, vol. 14.

23. Estimates are found in AE, Tunisie, Correspondance Politique, vols. 14, 22, 23; ARGT, 415–17, 423. On the Oued Souf and contraband see AN-Aix, 22H26.

24. AE, Tunisie, Missions et Documents, vol. 8; ARGT, 415; AN-Aix, 1H12, 16H2, 16H3 and 25H16²; also C. Monchicourt, *La region du Haut Tell en Tunisie* (Paris: A. Colin, 1913), pp. 313–14, 412. The Rahmaniya *zawiya* of Sidi Yusuf in al-Kaff also distributed gunpowder to Algerian pilgrims in the 1870s: ARGT, 423.

25. Ibn Abi al-Diyaf, *Ithaf*; ibn Ashur, *Tarajim al-alam;* also Green, *The Tunisian Ulama,* p. 175; and AMG, Tunisie, 29. The Bey of Tunis sent gifts to both the Tijaniya in Temassine and the saints at Khanga Sidi Naji: AFT, D–173–3, E–29–2.

26. ARGT, 414; AN-Aix, 1H8, 10H18. For an analysis of the relationship between the Tunisian central government and the men of religion, see M. Cherif, "Hommes de religion et pouvoir dans la Tunisie de l'époque moderne," *Annales ESC* 35 (1980): 580–97.

27. AN-Aix, 10H18, 10H43; AE, Tunisie, Missions et Documents, vol. 8.

28. AN-Aix, 10H18; AMG, Algérie, M1317.

29. AN-Aix, 1H8–11.

30. On the Tuwala, see AN-Aix, 1H7; Nadir, "Les ordres religieuses."

31. AMG, Algérie, H131.

32. The only recent study of Zaatcha is Von Sivers's "Realm of Justice"; among the works written in the nineteenth century are C. Borcher, "Le siège de Zaatcha," *Revue des Deux Mondes* 10 (1851): 70–100, and Gen. Herbillon, *Insurrection ... eu 1849: relation du siège de Zaatcha* (Paris: J. Dumaine, 1863); for the significance of the revolt, see AN-Aix, 10H76, and AMG, Algérie, H137. Sidi Sadiq, shaykh of the Rahmaniya *zawiya* at Masmudi, who led an insurrection and exhorted his forces to follow the example set at Zaatcha: AN-Aix, 10H43.

33. AN-Aix, 1H9, 10H76; AMG, Algérie, H131, H230bis; Herbillon, Insurrection. For a somewhat different interpretation of the Zaatcha revolt as a movement, see Von Sivers, "Realm of Justice." The reputation Abu Ziyan had earned as a formidable marksman during an earlier siege of Zaatcha (1831) by the Bey of Constantine also won him considerable support.

34. Examples are found continually in the AN-Aix, 1H sous-série, such as 1H10 (1853), a would-be *khalifa al-mahdi* arrives from the Djerid in the southern Constantine, supposedly in the company of the son of Abu Ziyan, but fails to gain support; 1H11 (May 1854), another such figure arrives from Mecca in Nafta and, again unsuccessfully, attempts to win adherents among the Namamsha.

35. AMG, Algérie, H133; AN-Aix, 10H76.

36. There is no study on the movement led by the "*sharif*" of Ouargla aside from Louis Feraud's articles on the ibn Jallab, "Les Ben Djellab," in *Revue Africaine* 25 (1881): 121–37, 198–222, and ibid, 26 (1882): 46–50. What follows is mainly based on AN-Aix, 1H7–14, and AMG, Algérie, H133–37, M1317.

37. AN-Aix, 10H52: ARGT, 423; AE, Tunisie, Correspondance Politique, vols. 14, 15; Léon Roches expresses doubts about Sidi al-'Id's loyalty in AN-Aix, 25H16².

38. A number of these letters were intercepted by the French and can be found in AN-Aix, 1H9. There are striking similarities between figures like Muhammad ibn 'Abdallah and their counterparts in medieval Europe; see N. Cohn, *The Pursuit of the Millennium* (Oxford: Oxford University Press, 1970).

39. AMG, Algérie, H137, M1317; AN-Aix, 10H18.

40. AN-Aix, 1H8; ARGT, 423; and AE, Tunisie, Correspondance Politique, vol. 14; also Feraud, "Les Ben Djellab."

41. AE, Tunisie, Correspondance Politique, vol. 15; ARGT, 423. M. Cherif in "Les mouvements paysans dans la Tunisie du XIXème siècle," *ROMM* 30, no. 2 (1980): 31–32, notes the almost total absence of millenarian movements in nineteenth-century Tunisia in contrast to Algeria in the same period. His point merits further investigation.

42. AE, Tunisie, Correspondance Politique, vols. 13–15; ARGT, 423.

43. AE, Tunisie, Correspondance Politique, vol. 15; ARGT, 423; AN-Aix, 10H18. Only in 1862 was the "*sharif*" captured and delivered up to the bey. Von Sivers, "Realm of Justice," p. 57, points out that under certain conditions, movements like that of the "*sharif*" had a tendency to degenerate into brigandry.

44. AE, Tunisie, Missions et Documents, vol. 8.

45. H. Duveyrier, *Sahara Algérien et Tunisien: journal de route* (Paris: Challamel, 1905), p. 49; and Lt. Duveyrier, "Excursions dans le Djerid," *Revue Algérienne et Coloniale* 2 (1860): 543.

46. Duveyrier, *Journal*, pp. 41, 48–49; AN-Aix, 16H3, 25H16²; CHEAM, no. 2503; and AGT, D–97–3. E. Gellner's saints behaved in a not dissimilar fashion during the French advance into the High Atlas in 1916: *Saints of the Atlas* (Chicago: University of Chicago Press, 1969). This in no way ended Sidi 'Azzuz's political activities in Algeria or the arms trade through the Djerid.

47. On the revolt, see ibn Abi al-Diyaf, *Ithaf*, vol. 5, and B. Slama, *L'insurrection de 1864 en Tunisie* (Tunis: Maison Tunisienne de l'Edition, 1967); additional information on the Ibn 'Azzuz's role can be found in ARGT, 417; AE, Tunisie, Correspondance Politique, vols. 23, 25; and U.S. National Archives, Tunisia, Despatch Book, vol. 8.

48. C. L. Brown, *The Tunisia of Ahmad Bey* (Princeton: Princeton University Press, 1974), and Green, *The Tunisian Ulama*.

49. Duveyrier, *Journal*, p. 49.

50. AE, Tunisie, Correspondance Politique, vol. 23; ARGT, 417.

51. Ibn Abi al-Diyaf, *Ithaf*, biographical notice 370, p. 143. The incident concerning his grandson, al-Makki ibn 'Abd al-Krim ibn Tarzi ibn 'Azzuz, is reported in AE, Tunisie, nouvelle série, vol. 37. Green, *The Tunisian Ulama*, p. 223, reports that one of Mustafa ibn 'Azzuz's four sons, al-Makki ibn 'Azzuz, created a society in the Hijaz just prior to World War I that conducted an anti-French campaign in Tunisia and Algeria.

52. The roles and functions of the saint and *turuq* in North African society are discussed in Gellner, *Saints*, and P. Shinar, "Note on the Socio-Economic and Cultural Role of the Sufi Brotherhoods and Maraboutism in the Modern Maghreb," *Proceedings of the First International Congress of Africanists* 1 (1962): 272–85; see also J. P. Mason, "Oasis Saints of Eastern Libya in the North African Context," *Middle Eastern Studies* 17, no. 3 (July 1981): 357–74, for a slight variation on the theme of the saint.

53. Martin, *Muslim Brotherhoods*, pp. 8–9; Brett, "Mufti, Murabit, Marabout and Mahdi."

FIVE

The Transformation of a Saintly Lineage in the Northwest Aurès Mountains (Algeria): Nineteenth and Twentieth Centuries

Fanny Colonna

Cases like that of the Derduriya brotherhood (*tariqa*, pl. *turuq*) and the different modes of anti-colonial resistance adopted by successive generations of its leaders are doubtless not unique to the Aurès Mountains nor even to Algeria. But such cases are strategic ones for reexamining the idea of historical determinancy, which is part of the legacy of earlier generations of Orientalists and positivists. Despite the continuities of geography and society, the projects of Si Lhachemi, the founder of the order, and of his grandnephew, the chief leader of the reformist Salafiya movement in the Aurès in the 1930s (about which I have written elsewhere), are dramatically different.[1]

Their study, moreover, necessarily leads us to call into question the prevailing periodization of Algerian history: in this instance, the end of the period of heroic resistance and the beginning of the national liberation movement. I shall argue that historical turning points like this one, which separate societies and their histories into *befores* and *afters*, are not inherent in the order of things but, rather, are socially produced. They derive from the ways modes of religious control and mobilization were adapted to new social forms of production. To attempt to capture the indeterminancy of history, as we shall see, is to see how

The present work is based on three different types of sources. First, fieldwork interviews were conducted in five short stays, of ten days to a month, from 1973 to 1977 inclusive, in the western part of the Aurès region—more precisely, in the Oued Abdi and the Oued al-Ahmar (Bouzina). The investigation was concerned only exceptionally with religion, although in addition to economic facts, it furnished the political and social grammar of the events reported in the archives. Second, archival sources relating to the colonial history of Algeria were explored at Archives d'Outre-Mer, Aix-en-Provence. Finally, the colonial literature on the Aurès, notably the numerous articles of Emile Masqueray written between 1876 and 1886, was reread. In the present circumstances it has not been possible for me to mention my informants by name. However, they are all herein thanked for their assistance.

the development of such periodizations may also come to constitute a stake in the game for specific groups.

The present study is the product of extensive fieldwork in three villages in the north of the valley of the Oued Abdi in the northwest Aurès Mountains in eastern Algeria (see Map 2).[2] I have sought at each step of my research to confront the results of my oral inquiry with the testimony, partial and incomplete as it is, of the French colonial archives. I have also sought to confront the product of my research with materials gathered by the colonial ethnologist and historian Emile Masqueray, whose work on the Aurès is still fundamental. Finally, I have been led to examine the consciousness of the group via some of its intellectuals, whether traditional or not. This method of shuttling between the oral sources and the written record I think took me further in both time and understanding than written sources alone could have done.

TRADITION ABRIDGED

The villages in which the action takes place—both in 1880 and in 1937— belonged to the Rahmaniya *tariqa*, which, as we know from the colonial archives, was of recent creation.[3] According to oral tradition the *zawiya* of Tibermacine, which is located south of Ahmar Khaddou, in the north of the valley of Oued Abdi, originally belonged to the Rahmaniya Sufi *tariqa*. Oral sources dating from the sixteenth century also refer to a Qadiriya *zawiya* in that corner of the valley. Only later do we hear reference to the family of F., the lineage from which was to spring both the Derduriya *tariqa* and (in the 1930s) the local leadership of the reformist Islamic movement (known in Arabic as the Islah movement).[4] The opposition between the Rahmaniya and the Derduriya was thus built-in, and in the oral tradition, the F. lineage are late arrivals.

Why under those conditions, did Si Lhachemi decide in 1870 to split with the Rahmaniya, rather than working to reinforce it or trying to attain a more important position within it? Was it because of rivalries within the brotherhood itself? According to a tradition that dates from the 1847 conquest of the Aurès, the F. extended their religious and economic control over a great part of the upper valley of the Oued Abdi and beyond it to the west. They had extensive landholdings at Nirdi (north of Oued Ahmar), as well as at K and at Z, the family birthplace located in a fertile depression of the Oued Taga south of Lambèse. Their landholdings chiefly consisted of grain fields, although they also had abundant flocks of sheep. A tacit equilibrium existed between them and the Banu A., who controlled the south of the valley.

The French conquest to the region and the subsequent investiture of the Banu A. with the governorship broke this equilibrium. The French authorities took a huge parcel of land in the Oued Taga from the F. and bestowed it upon the Banu A. In this way hatred came to reinforce what had been till then only a rivalry. At first the two families played the same game: from early on, both pursued religious careers, studied the religious sciences (*'ilm*), and taught the local population. In the process, they made the villages of Menaa, in the south, and K, in the north, centers of culture, and the Oued Abdi an "enlightened" valley. According to tradition in about 1880 there were no illiterate adults in either K or Z. Both families had reputations for possessing charisma and were able to build up considerable fortunes by acting as mediators in local disputes. The Banu A., however, were the older and stronger family. This is the only way to explain the fact that the French authorities chose to rely on them. They also had been loyal to the Turkish government in pre-French times, whereas the F. seemed to have shunned them.

At the outset of our story, therefore, the situation was composed of a complex series of elements: rivalries within a Sufi *tariqa,*which enabled the lineage to keep its place in the local religious establishment; order disturbed and then restored by the French conquest; the calling into question of the political and religious equilibrium in the valley between the strong lineage to the south and the more fragile one to the north. Here as well the French conquest upset the old equilibrium and selected the targets inside and outside the valley whom disorder would benefit. Faced with circumstances that threatened their symbolic and economic situation, the F. could not remain passive. Perhaps, given the intensity of the crisis, this is how they came to change the game altogether.

If we consider the historical transformation in the strategies pursued by different groups in colonial Algerian society, we can observe that sometime between 1880 and 1930 it first became possible to pursue lineage-based strategies as distinct from tribal strategies. For the pre-colonial period, it can be shown that the rise of a clerical family tended to occur together with the establishment of a homogeneous tribe and the conquest of a territory from another group.

The history of the F. conforms to this rule. One of five lineages of a tribe, the H., who originated elsewhere, the F. came to the upper Oued Abdi, where they founded Z, a village with two mosques. The opening of a *zawiya* there centered on the holy lineage of F. is to be connected with the eastward progression of the H. toward the spring, their alliances with the former inhabitants, and the various pacts by which the saint flourished.

At first the lineages of the tribe of H. as a whole were on an equal footing from the standpoint of wealth, though within the tribe there was a division of labor between agriculture and saintliness. Though the saintly lineage of course received donations of labor from the others, as befitted those who consecrated their time to God, because of the spiritual context in which it was offered it is difficult for an outsider to estimate the degree to which it may be called exploitation. Certainly it was not so regarded by the group itself. The French conquest and the need to respond to it changed all this. At this point, then, the strategy pursued by the F. deviated from that of the other lineages, becoming, in effect, an attempt to create the conditions for a veritable extraction of surplus. The establishment of the Derduriya by Si Lhachemi thus marks the beginning of a new game in the Aurès region.

It is unlikely whether much would be known today about Si Lhachemi if his preaching and his personality had not constituted one of those affairs of local politics that set off the opening of a file in the French military archives in 1880. There were many religious lineages like his in the Aurès at the time, all of which at one time or another produced preachers or organizers of Sufi *turuq*. Despite the haziness of his memory as it survives in the group, he was singularly different from the other literate figures of his time. Who was Si Lhachemi, and of what was he accused?

THE AFFAIR OF THE DERDURIYA

Even though there is every reason to believe that the Derduriya affair itself was the result of a conspiracy organized by the French-appointed village-headmen shaykhs of the Oued Abdi, the study of the chief allegations in the files is quite instructive. The leader, Si Lhachemi, was accused of establishing his power and authority in three or four of the villages in the rich and open valley of the Oued Abdi. These villages are geographically close to one another. All are situated to the north of Chir. All contained members of the tribe to which Si Lhachemi belonged, as well as of the Aith F., the dominant lineage in his tribe. This is to say that this "agitation" involved relatively few people—certainly fewer than 5,000 in all.

As we will see, the charges made by the witnesses who testified against Si Lhachemi were vague and insubstantial. Filtered through dim memories of a conflict, only the result of which—the imposition of the authority of the shaykh—was in the end significant, we come to understand what it was about: the extortion of labor power, and who was entitled to benefit from it. The rest is the obscure quarrels of hillfolk desperately trying to cope with the unprecedented consequences of French domination.

To plunge into this file is to confront head-on the dense micropolitical world of an isolated corner of rural Algeria. A first fact noted in the depositions taken by the military authorities was the establishment of a private Quranic tribunal (*qadi*, *'adl*, and so forth), which it was alleged was intended to cut off the faithful of the Derduriya from the rest of the community.[5] This local court had the exclusive privilege of hearing cases of inheritance, which were very numerous in this region of *mulk* (privately held) land. There was constant debate over the location of the frontier between the zone governed by customary law and that under Quranic law.[6] Furthermore, Si Lhachemi was accused of building roads on the mountain between the villages affiliated to his brotherhood. Such roads would certainly have been very expensive to construct.[7]

Most serious in the eyes of the shaykhs was the fact that the members of the brotherhood claimed to obey only the authority of their master in all the circumstances of life, not only those that concerned their salvation. Thus all power and authority escaped or threatened to escape the shaykhs—certainly a bad example for the other villages of the region. The Shaykh of Hallaoua put it very well: "He forbids the people of my village, almost all of whom are members of the brotherhood, from obeying me or working for me. They only obey him, and I feel my power ebbing away."[8] Si Lhachemi was thus accused of forbidding his followers to provide the French or their local agents, the shaykhs, with corvée labor that they otherwise commonly extorted from their villagers. This is in fact the only concrete charge in the entire dossier, which is otherwise a tissue of allegations whose reality seems dubious. The sources speak of the French authorities as ratifying the selections of the local governor (Ar. *qaid*), in appointing the shaykhs. This *qaid* was from a very important clerical family of the southern valley, the Ibn 'Abbas of Menaa, a detail that gives us an idea of local power and authority at the time.

We can see that Si Lhachemi's preaching called into question local forms of control and function and established others for his own profit. Nonetheless, the recorded testimony does not breathe a word of the inevitable consequences of this mini-revolution, nor of Si Lhachemi's appropriation of the labor-power of his followers. Instead, it speaks only of authority. Here we can see clearly the impact of the spell of a charismatic relationship, which even enemies do not dare or cannot call a relationship of exploitation.

The final accusation—but can we really believe it?—was that of collusion with the *sharif*. The *sharif* in question was Si Muhammed bin 'Abdallah, the unfortunate leader of the June 1879 rebellion which occurred nearby.[9] The shaykhs complained that "he's behaving exactly like the *sharif* before the insurrection."[10] Although this is a weighty accusation, it appears probable, given the marginal status of the sharif, Muhammad Jarallah, a foreigner to the tribe he sought to incite to rebellion. He served as the instrument of the Lhalha, the clerical lineage who led the rebellion and were based north of the Oued el Abiod.

The roots of the 1879 rebellion lie in the state of total economic insecurity in the Aurès Mountains and more generally in eastern Algeria during those years. In 1877–1878 the grain harvest was very poor, and in 1879–1880, despite the fact that climate and harvests tended to vary more in the mountains than elsewhere in Algeria, it was a year of famine at A. and at K. Given the geographic and chronological proximity of the rebellion, the accusations against Si Lhachemi must have seemed plausible to the French authorities. As we shall soon see, however, armed actions were not part of the charisma of the F., who had long been sedentary agriculturalists. It seems reasonable, therefore, to draw the preliminary conclusion that while Si Lhachemi may have known in advance about the 1879 rebellion, he was not involved in it.

BETWEEN TWO EXILES...

Did the Derduriya really exist, in the sense of a fully constituted and autonomous brotherhood? Or was the name only a rubric in the colonial system of
classifying the Sufi orders, a reflection of the local idiom, as one speaks today, for
example, of the Hassiniya of Khanga in speaking of the great family of the Bin
Hassin and their clients? One wonders. In any event, what is clear is that there
was just one person of sufficient stature in the region to incite suspicion and
jealousy. Only Si Lhachemi was at the center of a highly structured political
and economic organization, and also (however indirectly) encouraging resistance to the central power. What happened there at that moment was a double
accumulation—of saintliness and of wealth. There can be no doubt that in this
apocalyptic period they constituted a power upon which the whole tribe could
draw. The tradition bears witness to this, even though it does not assign a major
role to the person who seems at first glance to have been responsible.

According to the sources, Si Lhachemi was born between 1809 and 1823—
1820 seems most likely—at A., which at that time was a prosperous village in
an isolated corner of the valley of the Oued Abdi. (Today it is still not connected
to the outside world by a road.) According to French sources, his father, Si 'Ali
bin Si Amar, was *muqaddam* (head) of the Rahmaniya *tariqa*, "of the Tunisian
branch."

> Si Lhachemi early left his people and went to the Regency of Tunis where he lived
> a long time. He visited *zawaya*, taught children to read, so we are told, and
> prepared himself for the role he would later take on. Joined by his father in 1867,
> he traveled with him to Mecca. Upon his return, he once again took up residence
> in Tunisia. Only in 1870 did he return to Medrouna, where he distinguished
> himself by his public displays of piety, at least until the death of his father in early
> 1871. In the process he acquired the reputation of being a saint. As soon as he was
> freed of the influence of his father he emerged from the shadows and began an
> active propaganda effort. He acquired many partisans.[11]

This is alleged to have occurred around 1876. Before concluding this "portrait of an agitator" from which there is already much to infer, it is useful first
to consider several notable events that concern the Aurès, and especially Si
Lhachemi's tribe and lineage. In 1845, at the time of the conquest of the region
by the French, the village of K. was taken by assault and burned "simply as an
example," according to the report of the Bedeau column.[12] Two villages were
burned on this occasion (the other was Nara). According to the report, it seems
that K. was the point of convergence of the seditious groups, who were drawn
from Nara, Menaa, and the Beni Frah—villages situated in the south and west
of the valley. The Awlad 'Abdi—here a well-defined entity, not including the
H.—"requested *aman*" (amnesty), for fear of seeing their fruit trees cut down.
"In deed, these trees formed one of the chief sources of wealth of the region,"
according to the report. Here in passing is one of the keys to the geography of

insurrections, and to war in the mountains in general. A sedentary way of life inscribed in the land by centuries of labor does not facilitate just any form of resistance. This is why the Banu 'Abdi permitted the French column to cross their lands, and why the H. did not join the resistance of the Twaba pastoralist nomads in 1879.

We do not know the date that Si Lhachemi left his village and went into exile, but it was sometime after the French conquest in 1845. Between that date and his return in 1870 a number of devastating blows struck the F. In 1859 the French seized 700 hectares of land in the Oued Taga and gave it to their arch-rivals, the Banu A. A rebellion led by the local Rahmaniya *tariqa* occurred in 1859 in Ahmar Khaddou. It was followed by a general famine in 1868. The al-Muqrani rebellion of 1871 did not mobilize the Aurès, properly speaking, but it did involve the northern piedmont, from Khenchela to the Belezma. With the latter, as we shall soon see, the H. were historical allies.

Thus the years that Si Lhachemi spent traveling in Tunisia as a schoolmaster (*muaddib*) were terrible ones for his tribe and his villages, and he knew it. In Tunisia, he spent his time "frequenting the *zawaya*" and "teaching the Quran to children"—most likely at Nafta in the nearby Djerid oases, the seat of the "Tunisian branch" of the Rahmaniya brotherhood. This seems the more likely since many Algerian students of the religious sciences were drawn to Nafta because they could not proceed as far as Tunis.[13]

At Nafta his students would have found in Si Lhachemi a respected foreign teacher, who lived (doubtless rather poorly) from his *'ilm* (religious knowledge) in a society at once close to and different from his own. The Djerid region of Tunisia was more ethnically diversified than the Aurès. It also had a higher literacy rate, was more deeply penetrated by strict orthodoxy, and was much more fully integrated into the relatively coercive, centralized, nineteenth-century Tunisian state. Finally, it was locally better organized to respond to and resist this coercion.[14]

In the Djerid, Si Lhachemi would have met all sorts of shaykhs and would have been introduced to Arabic poetry and the mystical tradition. At the mosque—whichever one he frequented in the Djerid—he would have been a devoted student of the traditional sciences (*'ulum al-naqliya*) and the rational sciences (*'ulum al-'aqliya*). Finally perhaps, as a bachelor, he would have been tempted to proceed on to Tunis. There he would have lived in one of the thirty-seven *madrasas* for provincial students in the city. Life in the *madrasas* of Tunis, with their poorly lighted little rooms and crowded conditions, must have been picturesque. In the evening, the students cooked their meals on the *babur* in front of the door, or else supper was provided for them as a pious act by bourgeois families. All the knowledge which the east of the Arab west could offer in the middle of the nineteenth century could be found there.[15]

In 1867, Si Lhachemi and his father went on the pilgrimage to Mecca and Medina. As was the custom of the time, they stayed in the Arab east for a year before returning to the Maghrib. In 1870 they returned to their village in the Aurès, and soon thereafter the father died. A short while later, Si Lhachemi married for the first time. (He eventually had two wives, by whom he had two children, a son, 'Ali, and a daughter, Messaouda.) In 1880 he was placed under arrest by the French authorities and sent to Calvi in Corsica where, according to the sources, he lived in exile for eight or ten years.[16]

His public preaching thus lasted at most ten years, and more likely six years. After his return from exile he was a beaten man, "worried and sick," very much alone, but very rich. His authority over his disciples continued, though by this time they were relatively few in number (around 500). He died in 1899 in a Florentine-style palace, betrayed by his son, having repudiated his two wives for fear of being poisoned, and aided only by two of his followers who had accompanied him to Calvi. His is a curious and an atypical biography. Si Lhachemi came from the mountains but passed a good quarter of his life in the lowlands, in touch with all the currents of the east. His mother tongue was Berber, but he made his living by his knowledge of the Arabic language and culture. A member of a lineage from a mountain valley peopled by tree-cultivating sedentary folk, he spent most of his adult life in exile.

This portrait of the saint as agitator is not very satisfying. But the tradition provides us with two others: that of a prereformist scripturalist, and that of a saint and Sufi master, known for his moral and spiritual teaching and his miracles. Everything predisposed him to be both at once. Si Lhachemi consis-tently denied having engaged in political agitation against the French. Instead, he claimed to be only a Sufi master. But to understand this claim we must determine what being a Sufi master meant in the Aurès during the nineteenth century.

A SUFI MASTER AND A SAINT

Si Lhachemi is only a figure, scarcely distinct from that of the others, who from the beginning of the nineteenth century, and perhaps even earlier, pursued and realized the project of making the H. into a special tribe "who provide *tolba* [Quranic schoolteachers] to all the other tribes." The case of Si Lhachemi and the Derduriya invokes a continuity with the past, one that is entirely congruous with continuity invoked on the scale of the country by the scriptuary pre-reformist *tariqa*, the Rahmaniya to whom the F. remained affiliated until the founding of the Derduriya by Si Lhachemi. However, the tradition carries only a pale shadow of his sermons (which seem to have been unusual in more than one respect), and only a dim image of the social cataclysm that inspired them.

Colonial observers wondered about the sources of Si Lhachemi's inspiration. Because they had not previously encountered someone who spoke as he did, they speculated about whether he might have been influenced by the Sanusiya *tariqa* (a favorite bête noire of theirs). Finally, they concluded that the Aurès project was "too lightweight," and thus that this was an unlikely source. The word *autodidact* appears to fit Si Lhachemi better—although the organization of the Derduriya was the expression of a social as well as a political idea. In any event, it need not have been borrowed ready-made from that of a previously existing *tariqa,* rather than devised independently. It was characterized by autonomous justice, refusal to provide forced labor for the French, and the integration of work with the religious life. One can hypothesize that the model he proposed was a reflection of Si Lhachemi's experiences during his stay in the Regency of Tunisia—a discovery of the political, in contrast to unilateral and unavailing resistance. Significantly, in the middle of the nineteenth century the central Tunisian state increased its fiscal pressure on the peasantry. The Tunisian people, however, had a very long experience of defense and negotiation by which local communities dealt with threats of state encroachment. A key to this system was the role of the shaykhs. The judicial and administrative structure of rural Tunisia was highly complex. Might not Si Lhachemi have noticed in Tunisia something more political than "municipal"?[17] Would not this have inspired in him new ideas about the organization of the society, especially about how much it has to surrender to the state when its authority can no longer be opposed directly? The traditional relationship of the tribes of the Aurès with the centralizing state apparatus, whatever most historians say, appears to have been an unfortunate choice between paying tribute or going to war.[18] However, the unprecedented situation in the Aurès following the suppression of the 1871 al-Muqrani rebellion and the establishment of civilian rule called for new responses. Si Lhachemi wanted to show that other choices besides surrender or death were possible and that other strategies might lead to a new balance of forces. This was the case in the Regency of Tunisia—especially, perhaps, in the Djerid, where local groups had negotiated a variety of different relations with the state.

Contrary to the civilizing aspects of Lhachemi's thought and activities, his spiritual message, of which the villagers still retain a memory, embraced all aspects of life, including a quite atypical exaltation of the benefits of agricultural labor. "He made his followers dig in a square marked out by four stones. He told them: if you do this daily, you will be rich by the end of the year." Then, taking off his burnous, he preached by example. A number of families owe to him the decisive turn in their family fortunes. When he was consulted on really serious matters—inheritance, disinheritance, plans for emigration or marriage—it seems his advice all ran in the same direction: hoarding and accumulation. He also encouraged teaching and working (including women's work such as weaving), always with the aim of increasing the family's holdings. While the market in land went up, particularly after the Senatus Consulte of 1863, his stubborn insistence on the importance of landowning is testimony to the insecurity of those troubled times.

Finally, although people speak most often about his reputation for puritanism and austerity (which K and A have inherited), he was capable of prodigious feats similar to those of the other saints of the mountains: healing, clairvoyance, foretelling the future. Some of his descendants are reputed to have such abilities even today.

Si Lhachemi was quite prominent, and in most respects his was a normal career for a rural Sufi master: the quest for knowledge, pilgrimage, withdrawal from society, and preaching. From what we know of his preaching, it was characterized by the lessons of everyday life—with the necessary specialized knowledge, notably agriculture, architecture, and medicine (which in the eyes of these sedentary people is the essence of civilization), mixed with certain miraculous powers without which there can be no sainthood.[19] In addition to these qualities, however, he had a political vision, a plan to organize the community which the village was compelled to recognize. He was thus very much the man for those troubled times.

It is not out of a kind of intellectual populism that reserves its favors for the lesser saints—a sort of hagiography of the poor—that I have taken such pains to recreate the personality of Si Lhachemi. The fact is that he was one of the notable figures of the end of the nineteenth century in the Aurès. Only a few others merit inclusion in this list: Si Saddok bel Hadj, who died in exile between 1850 and 1870; Muhammad ibn 'Abdallah, the leader of the 1879 rebellion, and perhaps Si Muhammad bin 'Abbas, the ex-Ottoman local official who shamefully agreed to serve as *qaid* on behalf of France. If there are others, their names are not known to us. If all of them were men of religion, it may be, as Masqueray said, that the Aurès knows no other great men.[20] Their kind disappeared with the nineteenth century. Nonetheless, their legacy was continued by the Salafiya reformists, as well as in today's Algeria.

"It was the *zawiya* that made possible our survival," said an informant. Although other factors and social forces deriving from the peasantry contributed to maintaining the permanent state of sedition which was the normal situation in the Aurès for over 130 years, still we cannot deny the emblematic role of men like Si Lhachemi for the villagers.

THE MEANING OF A HISTORICAL DISJUNCTURE

Just before his death Si Lhachemi was described by French informants as being rich and alone. At about the same time, according to oral tradition, the F. came into great wealth. Newly favorable conditions were at work: the sequestration by the colonial authorities of the property of their arch-rivals, the Banu A., in the southern part of the valley; their purchase from French authorities "by a settler" who had an Arab or Jewish name, Ben Driss; and their progressive sale, no doubt with much speculation. The property involved was vast in extent and dispersed from the south to the north of the Oued Abdi, together with other parcels in the parallel valley of the Oued Ahmar, in Oued Taga, and in the little high valley of Laarba. Thus dispersed, they permitted the owners to benefit from the climatic diversity of the Aurès, a major advantage. They were the lands of the lords. The F. acquired a good amount of this land, all north of Chir.[21]

The oral tradition can still name these estates, describe their boundaries, and estimate their value. It also describes what happened after the death of Si Lhachemi. It mentions the names of the European settlers who, unlucky or frightened, rapidly withdrew upon the outbreak of war in 1914. On balance, the process of accumulation more than made up for the bloodshed which accompanied the confiscation of the domain of Oued Taga in 1859. Finally, the fact that the expansion of the patrimony of the group continued and diversified into the 1930s must be underscored. The installation of modern flour-milling machinery, which was an extremely profitable investment in the period, is only one example. The mills were judiciously situated at a distance from the villages of origin of the lineage. The period from 1900 to 1950 witnessed the continued extension of the economic sphere of influence of the F. through purchase and the establishment of business associations, to the north as well as to the west in the direction of Tazoult, and to the east toward Khenchela. The F. invested all the way up to the northern piedmont, most likely including the city of Batna. This mechanism is entirely symmetrical with the one by which important religious families like the Lahmar Khaddou to the south of the Aurès have bought property and water rights extending into the Sahara, as well as part of the city of Biskra. The Awlad Sidi Saddok bin Hadj of Tibermacine, for example, whose fortunes will be discussed in greater detail a bit further on, operated in just this fashion. Most remarkable, perhaps, is that the process described is by no means a new one. Nor was it directly connected to the possibilities opened up by French property laws, like that of 1873. For example, there is the case discussed in the Procès verbal du Senatus Consulte du douar Tajmout of 1894, which includes the transcription of a deed prepared before a *qadi* in 1639 in which "the members of the tribe of Awlad Abderrahman" represented by nine of their *imgharen*, or leaders, all of whom are named, purchased "for the sum of one thousand *rials*... a property called *meziraa*, located in the Sahara." [22] The land involved was grain-farming land in a flood-plain which was for a long time the spring home of the Awlad Abderrahman and which today is a rather sad-looking sedentary habitat.[23]

Who can say whether or not, as Germaine Tillion notes judiciously, in 1639 the people of Lhamar Khaddou "had enough money and confidence in the future to buy out the Hilalian [Arab] conquerors [who by this period had so thoroughly taken over the piedmont that the toponyms of this otherwise completely Berber zone are today wholly of Arabic origin] of these difficult to defend Saharan lands?" [24]

It should be noted that the process of the acquisition of property and social mobility in the more recent period with which we are concerned is not confined to the Aurès. It is the same one described by Augustin Berque when he speaks of the emergence of local saints.[25] It is also the one underlined often by Gilbert Meynier in his description of Algerian society around the time of World War I.[26] In certain regions (Batna, Setif, Bone) from 1915 on, land transactions increased steadily. Finally, it is the same process as that Ahmad Henni has examined in his study of the statistics on the circulation of property between 1917 and 1954. He notes that only 1 percent of the landholdings farmed in 1930 by Muslim Algerians were larger than 100 hectares, while the lineage we have studied—evidently a number of families—probably held several times 100 hectares.[27] Not entirely coincidentally, perhaps, the Salafiya reformist movement developed in just this rural setting. The same fact has been observed by Michel Launay further to the west, in the fertile region around Ain Temouchent.[28]

THE DUST OF WANDERING

The K. acquired land, then, for almost a century. Still more obviously, they accumulated charisma—that is, the lineage became known for its sanctity among the other tribes, since the attributes of charisma, or its intertribal existence, were present according to tradition from the time the H. first set foot on this site.

What was unique about Si Lhachemi's project was the preaching of a message so oriented to the times, so focused on the political and economic organization of the community. Elsewhere in the Aurès the bearers of charisma, while they were interested in accumulating wealth, continued to speak to their followers exclusively of heaven. Si Lhachemi's preaching differed from theirs in ways that suggest the cumulative influence of his years of wandering.

Si Lhachemi's modernity can be seen in the tenacity of his program, which was directed on the one hand toward the diffusion of knowledge, and on the other hand toward the sort of political realism that turns its back on suicidal impulses. Seen from this point of view, his connection to the *sharif* of the Twaba pastoralists and to the activities leading to the insurrection of 1879 take on a different meaning. While the H. doubtless had little penchant for warfare— though they must have remembered the sack of Haidous in 1847—their sedentary way of life (especially the vulnerability of their fruit trees) delivered them bound hand and foot to the French repression. No doubt, then, that because of his considerable experience in the world Si Lhachemi could see the extent to which the traditional logic of refusal—insurrection, as had been tried already in 1849 at Zaatcha and again in 1859—was by that time obsolete. Compared to him, Si Muhammad Jarallah (the leader of the 1879 rebellion) seems quite rustic.

However, his political realism was not a simple concession to the reality of superior French force, as seems to have been the case in numerous *zawaya* in the region. It is clear that Si Lhachemi's strategy was not just aimed at survival, but that he elaborated a veritable religious program, whose fruits only gradually became clearer. Most important, his religious program drew on his long experience outside the mountains, including the period of his captivity in Corsica. It is this that gave the shaykh, his entourage, and his descendants the capacity "to understand," to comprehend what was going on outside the mountains. Most of his contemporaries were content to endure; others sought to enrich themselves. Only a few groups sought to transform themselves in ways that would yield a variety of results. The entire tribe of the F. is one of these groups.

THE DEMANDS OF THE LAITY

The F. are a tribe from the Aurès who over the centuries were able to conquer a territory and to accumulate symbolic power and wealth. Their confrontation with the French authorities is marked by two religious innovations: the establishment of the Derduriya in the 1870s by Si Lhachemi, and that of the Islamic reformist Islah movement by his grandnephew in the 1930s. In this chapter, and in a previous essay,[29] I have sought to uncover the social conditions of their development.

But what about those on the receiving end, that is, the villagers? What happened to "the laymen's interest," as Weber would say? In the jumble of details unearthed by our research, interesting anecdotes can be found that speak about those who were till then but numbers—tribesmen, disciples, members. These *ikhwan*, these militant reformers, who had been tribesmen and rebels in the nineteenth century, emerge in the sources on the 1920s as under the jurisdiction of the *code de l'indigénat*, or as peasants, or even in some cases as emigrants to France.

How did this occur in concrete terms? What links were there between this change and the other more radical one they experienced in the mode of religious control and the form of mobilization against the occupier (both of whom were in fact carried out by the same saintly lineage)? How did these forms of social structuring adapt themselves to new social forms of production and of exchange in the market of goods and labor (in a broad sense the *code de l'indigénat* which was to shape the trajectory of the people of the Aurès between 1880 and 1930)? In a future work I hope to give more complete answers to these questions.

Suffice it to say that while the grandnephew and the greatuncle grew up in different times and places and had different ideologies and aims, each responded to similar changes. The real subject of a history of the politicization of the Algerian peasantry is perhaps to be sought in the equivalence and articulation between these changes, which took place in distinct and not necessarily synchronous spheres as a result of independent influences (some, such as money and emigration, coming from Europe, and others, such as Islah, from the East). There is no doubt that rather different social relations developed among the K. than what we find, for example, at Tibermacine: "when the *chergiin* came to see us, they were servile, we sensed that they were used to obeying." It was not only because the spring of the most remotely situated village in the mountains became fouled that the F. moved to K at the beginning of the century; the very remoteness of the village was especially auspicious for the gradual development of political power. It was also, I believe, because K is more easily reached from the valley and more open to the circuits of exchange. Thus, the goal was to stay in touch with happenings outside the mountains, while maintaining control within.

It seems relevant to this debate seriously to reexamine the decades at the end of the nineteenth century and the beginning of the twentieth century, which are the blank spots in our understanding of Algerian society, especially its peasant society.[30] I am not recommending here that we simply change our chronology because "everything began much earlier," both modernity and its very heavy social price.[31] This would be to fall into the trap of historical naiveté. Rather, I am calling for the reexamination of the periodization of Algerian history, whose very language (*Nahda, Islah*) designates the obscure period (between 'Abd al-Qadir and Ibn Badis) and the renaissances that precede and follow it. To return to the more limited case analyzed here, the social experience of Si Lhachemi appears to me to have been much more radical in its social and political creativity, and much more original and personal than that of the generations that followed (especially that of the 1930s), which were part of a movement common not only to Algeria but to the entire Arab world.

Seen in the light of the foregoing, local history can help us to understand that the nineteenth century was not only the century of rebellions (at its beginning against the Turks, at its end against the French), but also the century of a social, religious, and poetic work having its own raison d'être. Here we have examined these Berber creators (though there were others), which a certain type of history, content faithfully to reproduce the colonial perception, has accustomed us to view as merely the apocalyptic upheaval of a defeated society.[32]

NOTES

1. Fanny Colonna, "L'Islah chez les paysans," *Revue Algérienne de Sciences Juridiques* (June 1977): 277–87.

2. The events on which this essay focuses took place to the north of the valley of Oued Abdi in three villages on the left bank, perched on the mountain. Today, taken together, they form a commune of 12,000 individuals. At the end of the nineteenth century they must have had fewer than 1,000 inhabitants each. One village, which I'll call A, still cannot be reached by automobile. A. second one, Z., furnishes more emigrants to Europe than any other village in the Aurès. Village K. has a lovely spring—about which more soon—which occasioned many conflicts with Z. Irrigated farming on small parcels of land has always been the only form of employment in the area. Today both Z. and A. are partially depopulated. Only K. retains some vitality, stubbornly defending its water and land against all comers.

3. Si Muhammad bin 'Abd al-Rahman bin Qobrin, its founder, died in 1793. In the colonial archives see especially Archives Nationales (Aix-en-Provence) (hereafter cited as AN-Aix), 16HB, "Confréries et notables—enquête de 1898."

4. It is important to mention that it is an open question whether a "Derduriya *tariqa*," in the positivistic sense in which the term is employed in the colonial literature, ever existed. That there were rivalries between individuals, families, strategies (spiritual and other) is undoubted. We should not permit ourselves to be led astray by such spurious questions as the facticity of the Derduriya, however. What counts here are the patient efforts of Si Lhachemi, his family, and his group to devise a distinctive strategy of survival in a new context, that of late-nineteenth-century Algeria. "Derduriya" is the name that has been given to that enterprise.

5. AN-Aix, Algérie, 16H2, deposition of the Shaykh of Medrouna.

6. On the question of customary law vs. Quranic law in the Aurès, see G. H. Bousquet, "La persistance des coutumes berbères dans l'Aurès," *Revue Algérienne de Législation* (1952): 109–15, which includes a good bibliography.

7. AN-Aix, Algérie, 16H2, deposition of the Shaykh of Haidous.

8. AN-Aix, Algérie, 16H2, deposition of the Shaykh of Hallaoua.

9. There is a large literature on the insurrection of 1879. See especially Charles-Robert Ageron, *Les Algériens musulmans et la France*, 2 vols. (Paris: Presses Universitaires de France, 1968), vol.1, pp.59–62; Emile Masqueray, *Note concernant les Aoulad Daoud* (Algiers: Jourdan, 1879); and Capt. Noellat, *L'Algérie en 1882* (Paris: J. Dumaine, 1882). The last-named was written by an officer of the Arab Bureau who commanded French troops during the insurrection. More recently, see Abdelhamid Zouzou, *Al-thawra 1879 bil-Auras* (forthcoming).

10. AN-Aix, Algérie, 16H2, deposition of the Shaykh of Teniet el Abed.

11. AN-Aix, Algérie, 16H2, Rapport du général commandant la subdivision de Batna, 2 janvier, 1880.

12. Cited in Lartigue, *Monographie de l'Aurès* (Constantine, 1904).

13. Cf. on this point Malek Bennabi, *Mémoires d'un témoin du siècle* (Algiers: Editions Nationales Algériennes, 1967), p.95.

14. On the Djerid, see Abdelhamid Henia's thesis, *Le Jrid, ses rapports avec le Beylik de Tunis (1676–1840)* (Tunis: University of Tunis, 1980). Also see the unpublished thesis by Moncer Rouissi, "Une oasis du sud tunisien, le Jarid (essai d'histoire sociale)," 2 vols., Ecole Pratique des Hautes Etudes, Paris, 1973.

15. On the Zitouna mosque university and the student milieu of Tunis at the end of the nineteenth century see the fine article by Mohamed Ferid Ghazi, "Le milieu zitounien de 1920 à 1933 et la formation d'Abu l-Qacim ach-Chabbi, poète tunisien (1909–1934)," *Cahiers de Tunisie* (1959): 437–74. According to Ghazi, at the beginning of the century the Zitouna was still what it had been in the nineteenth century.

16. AN-Aix, Algérie, 16H2.

17. An opposition which lies behind the work of Emile Masqueray. See the new edition of his *La formation des cités* (Paris: CNRS, 1983), with an introduction by Fanny Colonna.

18. The historiographical tradition claims that the tribes of the Aurès never paid taxes. However, a slightly skeptical reading of the sources presents a much more complex and changeable situation. It is worth remembering that according to ibn Khaldun, "to pay taxes is shameful." Thus whenever they could the tribes attempted to hide the fact that they paid taxes. For a study of tribal relationships with the state, see Henia, *Le Jrid*, which is very suggestive for the Aurès.

19. On the representation of civilization as connected to sedentarization and irrigation in the Oued Abdi see F. Colonna, "Discours sur le nom: identité, altérité," *Peuples Méditerranéens* 18 (1982): 59–65.

20. Cf. F. Colonna, "Saints furieux et saints studieux ou, dans l'Aurès, comment la religion vient aux tribus," *Annales ESC* 35 (1980): 642–62.

21. Algérie, Service du Cadastre, Wilaya de Constantine Procès Verbal no. 5, p. 159.

22. See Thérèse Rivière, "L'habitation chez les O. Abderrahman, Chaouia de l'Aurès," *Africa* (1938): 294–311.

23. On Mziraa see the photojournal prepared by the Ministry of Agriculture and Agrarian Reform and the documentary film *Les Sourciers* by Abdelhalim Nauf (of ONCIC), scenario by François Chevaldonne, 1967 (it is, however, a dated treatment of peasants, particularly remotely situated ones).

24. Germaine Tillion, "Le partage annuel de la terre chez les transhumants du sud de l'Aurès," unpublished report, CHEAM, July 1939.

25. Augustin Berque, "Esquisse d'une histoire de la seigneurie algérienne," *Revue de la Mediterranée*, 19 (1949): 18-34, and vol. 30, 168–80. "The lesser marabouts in the fief of the Djouads are taking their revenge," notes Berque. But our "modest saint" is not included in Berque's analysis. Although he founded a family dynasty, Si Lhachemi did not seek to become a *qaid* and did not become associated with the conservative forces of Muslim society.

26. Gilbert Meynier, *L'Algérie révélée* (Geneva: Droz, 1981), especially pp. 653–72. Meynier emphasizes that in about 1914 in the arrondissement of Batna, that is, the zone in which the lands of the F. are situated, included 25 percent of the 7,035 Algerian Muslim landowners holding more than 100 hectares. "Even taking account of the growing French acquisition of land," Meynier writes, "it is certain that a rural petite bourgeoisie of landholders increased its holdings at the expense of the vanishing settler smallholders and Muslim smallholders."

27. Ahmad Henni, *La colonisation agraire et le sous-développement en Algérie* (Algiers; SNED, 1982), p. 52.

28. Michel Launay, *Paysans algériens* (Paris: Editions du Seuil, 1963), especially pp. 144ff., where he discusses the religious renewal in the countryside. The Awlad O. Messaoud, "descendants of a maraboutic tribe," had their lands expropriated in 1879. In 1880 they went back to work, clearing the mountain lands they had been given in compensation for their expropriated property. Between the two wars they planted grapevines and "became the wealthiest fellahs in the region"; later on, "they joined the reformist movement." This history resembles that of the F. so closely that one wishes to know more.

29. Unpublished research survey on the oral history of emigration, done in the town of Pompey (Lorraine) in 1975 and 1976, in collaboration with Marguerite Gilles. In our findings, emigration from the Aurès (chiefly from the Oued Abdi and, especially, Teniet el Abed) dates from around 1920. See also Colette Berthin, "Activité, chômage et émigration dans l'Est algérien," thèse de 3ème cycle, Université Louis Pasteur, Strasbourg, 1970, pp. 140–46; and her "La monographie de la commune de Teniet el Abed," in *Manuel de géographie de 6ème année secondaire, l'Algérie* (Algiers: IPN, n.d.), p. 213.

30. There are other such blank spots, for example, the decade 1940–50. Because of the inaccessibility of the archives, but also because of the proximity of the period and its continued relevance to contemporary disputes, the history of this decade is singularly opaque.

31. See Pierre Bourdieu, "Le mort saisit le vif," *Actes de Recherches en Sciences Sociales* 32/33 (1980): 3–14. One must be constantly vigilant in an effort, like this one, seeking to discern the continuities, premises, and historical ruptures and to struggle against the conventional periodization. This process of continual questioning can only be accomplished fully in a more thorough study—on which I am currently engaged.

32. See, for example, the articles of Joseph Desparmet, which for all their valuable insights can, through an overly hasty reading, induce just such an erroneous understanding.

SIX

Abu Jummayza:
The Mahdi's Musaylima?

John O. Voll

Abu Jummayza was a religious figure in western Dar Fur who emerged into prominence in 1888, three years after the death of the Mahdi. The historical context of Abu Jummayza's movement can best be understood within the framework of regional and local opposition to outside control. The traditional sultanate of Dar Fur had been annexed to the Egyptian Sudan in 1874 following a major defeat of the Sultan Ibrahim's forces. On a number of occasions, claimants to the Fur throne revolted against Egyptian control, and opposition to that regime provided support for the Mahdist cause in Dar Fur after 1881. However, it was not long before attempts to reestablish the old sultanate were again made. After the Mahdi's death the Mahdist governor, Muhammad Khalid, became involved in the political struggles for succession to power in the Mahdist state itself and marched toward Omdurman with a large portion of the Mahdist forces that had been in Dar Fur. Muhammad Khalid left Dar Fur in the hands of Yusuf, the son of Sultan Ibrahim. Yusuf soon took the title of sultan and worked to reestablish an independent state. Early in 1888 he was defeated by Mahdist forces and 'Uthman Adam, a relative of the Khalifa 'Abdallah and already the Mahdist commander in Kordofan, took control of Dar Fur. In this way, it can be seen that regional separatism was still active though a defeated force in Dar Fur at the time of the rise of Abu Jummayza.

In addition to the movements of Fur restorationism, there were many other currents of local politics. Between the old sultanates of Dar Fur and Waddai, in the areas of the eastern part of modern Chad and the far western sections of the Sudanese Republic, existed a number of smaller groups. These peoples, among whom are the Qimr, Masalit, and Tama, had their own traditions of defending their lands against outsiders. They were often in conflict with the sultans of Dar Fur and Waddai. They were sometimes independent and sometimes controlled by one of the larger states. Even when under outside control, these groups usually preserved some measure of autonomy and had their own sultans.[1] At the time of Gustav Nachtigal's travels, in the decade before the Mahdiya, this border region was unstable, with the local groups fiercely guarding their own special rights. Nachtigal reported, for example, that the Tuma sultan was willing to pay tribute to Waddai regularly, thus "avoiding any chance of allowing his neighbor a glimpse of the scrupulously secluded country."[2] Military expeditions sent by the sultans of Waddai against the Tama had failed regularly. Tribal and local loyalties were strong throughout the region and frequently obstructed the dynastic leaders attempting to create larger states.

A third aspect of the historical context of Abu Jummayza is the status of Islam in the region. In a number of ways the area was and is a "frontier." In the first, Dar Fur in general is part of the great boundary region between the world of Islam and the non-Islamic areas that stretches across Africa just south of the Sahara. The interaction between Muslim and non-Muslim societies is an important feature of the history of the region. None of the Islamic areas of Dar Fur and the surrounding *dars* had been a part of the world of Islam for more than three centuries, and for many the period was even shorter.

A second way the region was a frontier area is in terms of interactions within the Islamic world. Islamic influences came to Dar Fur from a number of different directions. "Dar Fur became the meeting ground of several different African Islamic traditions, from Egypt, from the Nilotic Sudan and from North Africa via West Africa."[3] Islamic practice was strongly influenced by wandering holy men and teachers who came from a variety of areas and helped to give the Islamic dimension of society a special character. The teachers were encouraged by the Fur sultans and were granted land and other privileges. At the level of scholars and the state, it seems clear that the formal commitment to Islam "spread in Dar Fur from the ruling institutions outwards and downwards. If the key external factor was the coming of the holy men, the crucial internal commitment came from the rulers."[4]

The major Islamic figures are the rulers themselves and the teachers/holy men whom they supported. Religious orders, which played an important role in other parts of the Islamic world, were not a vital part of Muslim life in the Dar Fur area. There are indications, however, that below the level of the landowning and teaching holy men who were clients of the sultans, a less formal and more popular style of Islamic life brought together a wide range of religio-cultural elements. The *faqih* or local religious figure was too solidly a part of local life in the early twentieth century to have been the product of less than a decade of history.

The local *faqih* performed a variety of roles that ranged from mediating disputes to writing amulets and performing cures. Most *faqihs* were not grand figures supported by the sultan of Dar Fur. They were, rather, struggling minor figures working among the tribes and villages. They, too, were frontier figures, working at the point of intersection in the daily life of the people between Islamic and local ideals and customs. Such men were of greatest importance in the areas beyond the control of the major sultans in areas like Dar Tama and Dar Masalit. It seems likely that Abu Jummayza originally was a member of this Islamic leadership group. Sources do not mention special relations with polit-ical leadership before the beginning of his call, but they do speak of his popularity as a writer of amulets and charms for the common people.

Little is known about Abu Jummayza, and most of that is filtered through the eyes of his enemies. Much of what is known about him comes from the re-ports of the Mahdist commander in Dar Fur, 'Uthman Adam, who attempted to find out as much as he could about this man.[5] In general terms, it seems clear that Abu Jummayza began his career as a minor religious teacher and writer of amulets in the western section of modern Dar Fur. 'Uthman Adam heard reports that he had lived among the Mahriya for a time and had gained respect for his effectiveness in writing charms. These reports indicated that he had fled to Dar Tama when the Ansar (followers of the Mahdi) moved into the area. Then, when Mahdist forces defeated the local sultan in Dar Tama, Abu Jummayza began to organize resistance.

'Uthman Adam describes Abu Jummayza as a young man with some eloquence who was originally named Muhammad al-Zayn. The Mahdist commander noted that some of his followers believed that he had emerged out of a *jummayza* (sycamore fig) tree. This emphasized the element of miracle-belief among his followers.[6] A more simple explanation of his name was also current at the time: this was that it was the teacher's custom to speak to his followers while sitting in the shade of a *jummayza* tree.[7]

Reginald Wingate, writing as a contemporary of Abu Jummayza's whose sources of information were less direct than 'Uthman Adam's, describes Abu Jummayza as a shaykh of the Masalit tribe in western Dar Fur. Wingate says that Abu Jummayza organized a major tribal confederation in opposition to the Mahdists and that he also possessed considerable religious influence among the people.[8] While none of the other sources mentions his being a tribal shaykh, all agree that Abu Jummayza was able to attract the support of the major tribes in the region and that he had real spiritual influence. On this basis, it seems likely that he was a *faqih* in origin rather than a tribal shaykh.

The history of Abu Jummayza's movement in this context is relatively simple. Mahdist forces had defeated the attempt by Yusuf ibn Ibrahim to restore the Fur sultanate, and they continued their expansion to the west. Fur loyalists gathered around Abu al-Khayrat, a brother of Yusuf's, but these forces appeared weak and disheartened. Local leadership in the smaller sultanates seems to have been unsure about how to deal with the continuing Mahdist expansion. It was at this point that Abu Jummayza made his appearance. In a report to the Khalifa 'Abdallah, 'Uthman Adam describes his emergence. He noted that Abu Jummayza had gone to Dar Tama: "When the Ansar came thither and arrested the sultan ... he came to the sultan's sons in their perplexity and said that he was sent from the son of al-Sanusi to kill the Ansar. He told them to take their weapons and said that ... if they went against [the Ansar] they would slay them all and [the Ansar] would never prevail against them. He said, 'The winds have driven me to you,' and began to work enchantments for them." [9]

This message provided a catalyst for opposition to the advancing Mahdist forces. The young *faqih* soon gathered a large force. This included tribesmen from the smaller western groups, especially the Tama and Maslit. He also attracted the attention of Abu al-Khayrat, who joined the new movement and brought with him the remaining Fur forces. In a short time this new army inflicted two major defeats on the Mahdists, who were forced to withdraw from most of the region. 'Uthman Adam concentrated his remaining troops in al-Fashir and waited for reinforcements. Abu Jummayza's advance to the east was relatively slow, giving the Mahdists time to rebuild strength. Then, suddenly, Abu Jummayza died of smallpox, and command of his army passed to his brother, Saghah. In February 1889, the two armies fought near al-Fashir; after a difficult struggle, the Mahdists won. Saghah was killed in the battle, Abu al-Khayrat fled to a mountain refuge where he was later killed, and the followers scattered. In this way the movement came to a sudden end.

A comparison of this movement with that of Musaylima in the first Islamic century helps to clarify some aspects of Abu Jummayza's career. [10] Musaylima is described in traditional Islamic accounts as one of the false prophets of the period of the Ridda wars, the wars of the apostasy. Following Muhammad's death, the new Islamic community under the leadership of Abu Bakr clashed with a number of groups in the Arabian peninsula. These groups had had some ties with the Muslims during Muhammad's lifetime, and Abu Bakr set out to restore or establish Islamic dominance over these groups.

In a number of cases, the challenge to the Muslim community was raised by movements led by individuals claiming prophetic powers or special religious authority. Musaylima was one such leader, [11] claiming a prophetic role among the Banu Hanifa in Yamama. Under his leadership, the Banu Hanifa refused to recognize the authority of Abu Bakr and the new Muslim community. There are traditional reports that Musaylima had been in contact with Muhammad, but it appears that he did not emerge into a prominent position until after the death of Hawdha, a major tribal leader of the Banu Hanifa. There are suggestions that first Hawdha and then Musaylima offered to share authority or divide territory between themselves and the Muslims. This was rejected by the Islamic leaders. Musaylima then, acting as a religious and political leader claiming prophetic authority, led the opposition to the expansion of Islamic control in Yamama. In 634, the Islamic army under the leadership of Khalid ibn al-Walid attacked and defeated the "false prophet," and the movement of Musaylima came to an end.

The general similarity of the positions of Musaylima and Abu Jummayza make comparisons appealing. Muhammad Ahmad, the Sudanese Mahdi, called on his followers to follow the path of the Prophet Muhammad and consciously tried to follow it himself. This was both natural in theological terms and, often, practical in terms of the development of the Mahdist movement at the end of the nineteenth century. Clearly, a leader whose proclaimed mission was to purify the practice of Muslims and create a society in accord with the Quran and the *sunna* of the Prophet would view the example of Muhammad and the early community as being of great importance.

The Sudanese Mahdiya, however, had experiences that parallel those of the Prophet Muhammad and go beyond conscious actions taken by Muhammad Ahmad al-Mahdi. It appears that the Prophet's successor, Abu Bakr, and the Mahdi's *khalifa*, 'Abdallah, faced similar problems when they attempted to continue the mission of their original leader. In both cases, soon after the death of the first leader, revolts against the authority of the *khalifa*s broke out which challenged the newly created states. In the first century of the Islamic era, this opposition included men who claimed special religious authority as a basis for their opposition to the new state. One of the leading figures in this was Musaylima. In the Sudan, the successor to the Mahdi faced a number of similar opponents, including Abu Jummayza.

It is clear that the Mahdi and his successor would have preferred not to have had opposition of the kind raised by Abu Jummayza. This parallel with the Prophet's experience was not consciously desired. However, in looking at the figures of Abu Jummayza and Musaylima, it is logical to ask whether or not Abu Jummayza was "the Mahdi's Musaylima." It is a comparison that is worth examining in its Sudanese dimension because it can provide a perspective for a further understanding of the significance and nature of religious revolts in nineteenth- and twentieth-century Sudan. It may also provide some useful observations in the broader area of the study of Islamic renewal in particular and renewal in religious traditions in general.

The suggestion made by Eickelman that Musaylima's movement can be regarded as "a case study of a 'religious revitalization movement' which failed" [12] provides a number of grounds for instructive comparisons with Abu Jummayza. The first comparison is that both movements were not isolated phenomena. They were among a number of similar contemporary groups. Musaylima's contemporaries who based their movements on claims of special religious authority included, among others, al-Aswad in Yemen, Tulayha among the Banu Asad, and Sajah, the prophetess of the Banu Tamin.[13] Because of the general interest in the formative years of the Islamic community, these "false prophets" are better known than Abu Jummayza's contemporaries. However, a number of charismatic religious leaders raised their banners in the same period as Abu Jummayza. Among these was Adam Muhammad, who announced his mission as the Prophet 'Isa in the eastern Sudan in 1887–88.[14] The expectation of such leaders was widespread: rumors of new prophets frequently swept through Mahdist lands. One such case is that of Mazil al-Mahn in 1893. Stories of his military successes circulated in Omdurman and Dar Fur, and even caused British intelligence in Cairo to believe that the end of the Mahdist state was at hand. However, as Mahmud Ahmad reported to the *khalifa* after a diligent search for the man throughout Jabal Nuba, where he was reported to be active, the rumors had no basis in fact.[15]

The phenomenon of a number of movements arising at the same general time is not uncommon in revitalization movements. Whether or not Musaylima was imitating the Prophet Muhammad and whether or not Abu Jummayza was directly inspired by Mahdist teachings, it seems clear that in both cases there were many people in both social contexts who were ready to follow religious charismatic leadership. In such a situation there can be many claimants to the position of leader of the social transformation. In circumstances where traditional structures of authority are being challenged by charismatic leadership, numerous "prophets" can emerge. In the terminology of modern social science, it is possible to say that the "spread of independent movements is particularly contagious when the basis for claims to leadership is revelation, as any number of leaders and prophets can claim divine inspiration."[16]

Traditional Islamic scholars have also noted the phenomenon of the contagiousness of prophetic leadership. Ibn Khaldun, for example, made a distinction between prophets and soothsayers. However, in his analysis, soothsayers who live in the time of a prophet are aware of the power of the prophet and try to capture it for themselves. "Soothsayers who are a prophet's contemporaries are aware of the prophet's truthfulness and the significance of his miracles. . . . What prevents soothsayers from acknowledging the truthfulness of the prophet, and causes them to deny [him], is simply their misguided desire to be prophets themselves. This leads them to spiteful opposition. This happened to . . . Musaylima."[17] The multiplicity of prophetic claimants in times of stress is recognized also in a tradition in which the Prophet Muhammad is reported to have said, "The hour will not come until thirty antichrists come forth, each of them claiming to be a prophet."[18]

The believer knows that the prophets ultimately succeed because their message is true and that false prophets ultimately fail. One does not have to reject this position to examine the question of how the call of one charismatic leader was more effective than another. In this general area, the comparison of Musaylima and Abu Jummayza is again helpful. Both were part of a situation in which there were competing religious claims. While the visible decision between the Muslims and Musaylima and between the Ansar and Abu Jummayza was made on the battlefield, there are broader factors involved.

In the two cases, the winning and losing sides were similar in the style of their mission. Eickelman suggests that Musaylima's "claim to authority was based upon the traditional ties of tribe and kin, as opposed to the innovatory, non-kin rationale (innovatory at least in emphasis) which buttressed the Muslim claim." [19] This tribal orientation made it possible for Musaylima to mobilize considerable tribal support within his region. He could appeal to the natural desire of many not to be assimilated into a relatively "non-tribal" movement, thereby losing touch with kin traditions. However, even though there was stress on the religious element in his message, this meant that in Musaylima the "concept of prophet seems to be fused with that of the more traditional chief of a tribe." [20] In this framework, Musaylima had little basis for appeal beyond the Banu Hanifa and, in the last analysis, could not compete effectively with the more dramatic, supratribal message of Islam.

The experience of Musaylima raises the question of whether or not Abu Jummayza had a similar problem. Clearly, the Mahdist message was a continuation of the supratribal call of Islam. While Khalifa 'Abdallah was accused of bringing his own tribe into positions of dominance and diluting the more universalistic aspects of the Madhiya, Mahdism under 'Abdallah continued to be significantly broad in its orientation. In contrast to this, Abu Jummayza seems to be more clearly regional and tribal in orientation. His initial support came from tribes who were consistently active in opposing outside intervention in their internal affairs. Many of his soldiers were drawn from the Tama and Masalit. It was said that one reason why Abu Jummayza delayed so long in advancing toward al-Fashir and why, as a result, his army did not fight the major Mahdist force until after it had been significantly reinforced was that many of his troops were reluctant to fight outside their own areas.[21] The other major component in Abu Jummayza's army was the Fur led by Abu al-Khayrat. This element was committed to the restoration of the Fur sultanate and thus was also committed to a localist rather than a more universalist goal. It may be that there were broader dimensions of Abu Jummayza's call which were cut off by his sudden death. As it stands, however, Abu Jummayza's experience is similar to that of Musaylima. Purely in terms of power, even, the more nearly universal appeals of the early Islamic message and the Mahdist call were able to mobilize a greater array of forces than the relatively localized movements of Musaylima and Abu Jummayza.

Traditional accounts of the claims to authority of the two men indicate that in addition to being less broad in scope, they were also less absolutely held. In both cases it is reported that the leaders were willing to give at least some recognition to their opponents' claims to authority. Musaylima recognized the prophethood of Muhammad even as he was preaching his own, and the Banu Hanifa agreed with him.[22] Musaylima emphasized the tribal and regional orientation of his mission by expressing a willingness to divide the land between the two leaders. In one form, Musaylima is reported to have written to Muhammad that "I have been made partner with you in authority. To us belongs half the land and to Quraysh half." [23] In another form of the sharing offer, Musaylima attempts to gain recognition as Muhammad's successor. The offer was: "If it be thy will, we will have all authority in thy hand and swear allegiance to thee, with the understanding that after thee, all will return to us." [24] Such offers were vehemently rejected by Muhammad.

Abu Jummayza, too, appears to have made his acceptance of the mission of the Mahdi quite clear. Rather than rejecting the Mahdiya, he tried to integrate himself into the framework of the emerging Mahdist state and at the same time to ensure the separate position of his people. His claim, in relation to Mahdism, was that he had the seat of succession to 'Uthman. This reflects the fact that Muhammad Ahmad the Mahdi had named his major followers as *khalifas* or successors to the early leading companions of the Prophet Muhammad. In this way, 'Abdallah was named the successor of Abu Bakr, and others were named successors of 'Umar and 'Ali. The Mahdi wrote to Muhammad al-Mahdi al-Sanusi in Libya, telling him that in a vision the Prophet Muhammad said that the position of successor of 'Uthman was for the son of al-Sanusi, "whenever he comes to you, whether it be soon or in a long time." [25] Muhammad al-Sanusi had rejected the claims of Muhammad Ahmad, and so the position of the successor of 'Uthman remained vacant. It was this post within the ideological framework of Mahdism that was claimed by Abu Jummayza.

Abu Jummayza's religious claims were thus not for independent authority. He informed Khalifa 'Abdallah that he was a follower of the Quran and the *sunna* of the Prophet, that he accepted the path of the Mahdi, and that he announced his allegiance to Khalifa 'Abdallah. At the same time, however, the soldiers of Abu Jummayza had opposed the Ansar troops that had moved into the territories of the far western Sudan. As a result, Khalifa 'Abdallah's reply to Abu Jummayza was a vigorous denunciation. The *khalifa* stated that to make such claims while opposing the Ansar was "a lie, falsehood, and slander against God," and as for the claim to be the successor of 'Uthman: "If some one were to have the sign of the Succession of 'Uthman he would, in reality, not be in a position [of causing discord], but would be following his example and pursuing his programs. Have you ever heard that 'Uthman drew his sword against Muslims or spread evil or fought against any of the Companions of the Messenger of God in the time of Abu Bakr?" [26]

It is possible that the experiences of Musaylima and Abu Jummayza show that regionally oriented rather than universal claims and partial rather than absolute positions of authority are less effective when confronted by a vigorous universalist and uncompromising claim to authority. In concrete terms, these two movements were unable to mobilize large-scale forces as effectively as their absolute and universalist opponents. Under other conditions, the more tribally oriented and compromising position may have been more effective, but it does not appear to have been as effective in a period of proliferation of religious charismatic leaders.

The conditions at the time of these two leaders appear to have been conducive to the emergence of charismatic claims and messianic expectations. It is worth noting, at the same time, that the success of the larger movements did not mean that the other style of groups disappeared: small religious revolutionary groups continued to arise to combat both the mainline Islamic community of the seventh century and the centralized regimes in the nineteenth- and twentieth-century Sudan. This becomes an additional area for comparison between Abu Jummayza and Musaylima. The initial comparison, which recognized the fact that the two movements were not isolated or unique in their time, can be expanded: both appear to have been part of a longer series of movements that continued to excite at least some people for a period of time after the defeat of Musaylima and of Abu Jummayza.

In the case of Musaylima, the subject is part of the controversial and difficult topic of the diverse movements within the early Islamic community. Since the focus of this paper is on the Sudanese dimension of the comparison, it is important here simply to note that a comparison with Musaylima raises the issue of continuity of religious revolutionary traditions, and the place of the movements under study within those traditions. In examining Musaylima it has been noted that even after his defeat and death, at least some of his tribe and people in his region continued to be involved in religiously defined revolutionary movements. W. Montgomery Watt, for example, states that "there would seem to be a special connection between the Kharijite movement and certain northern Arab tribes, notably Tamim, Hanifa and Shayban." [27] An analysis by M. A. Shaban that emphasizes the economic and political rather than the religious dimension of early Islamic history describes the conflict within the Islamic community around 65/685 as being "virtually a repeat performance of the *ridda* wars." [28] Shaban notes the critical role of the Hanifa, stating that the "so-called Kharijite movement" of that time "was in fact a major revolt in Arabia itself, led by a tribe [Banu Hanifa] with a long tradition of independence." [29] In this way, again, the local and tribal loyalties are a critical factor in the definition of a revolt in the name of a religious cause.

It is also clear that Abu Jummayza's movement was not an isolated case. In his area in the far west, a number of religious leaders raised the standard of religious opposition. In discussing religious revolts against the Mahdiya during the time of Khalifa 'Abdallah, one author of a general study states that, given the number of prophetic claimants in Dar Tama, the *dar* might be called a "factory for the production of false prophets." [30] The phenomenon of leaders claiming to be the Prophet of God, 'Isa, or some other eschatological figure was not limited to western Dar Fur. Many such people appeared during the Mahdiya and also in the early twentieth century, in many different areas of the Sudan.

This general feature makes it important to place Abu Jummayza in the broader development of Sudanese history. In so doing, it is possible to add some elements to the understanding of that history. In particular, it can provide a different orientation for evaluating the Mahdiya itself, both in relationship to the Egyptian government of the nineteenth century and in relationship to the developments taking place during the Condominium era. Abu Jummayza's movement is an example of small-scale, regionally or tribally oriented revolts whose mission was proclaimed in messianic or eschatological terms.

These revolts were part of a broader pattern of development within the Sudan in the past two centuries. Early in the nineteenth century, movements of concentration of power and authority began to gain strength in the northern Sudan. These came into direct and indirect conflict with small-scale and local organizations and institutions. In the political dimension this can be seen especially as a consequence of the Egyptian conquest of the Sudan in 1820–21. A state structure was established that had available to it physical power on a much greater scale than any of the tribes or regional sultanates. There was a constant interaction between the forces of centralizing power and control on the one hand and local opposition on the other. Many of the earlier revolts did not take on a religious tone and, as a result, were never able to mobilize more than locally influential movements that could be defeated by the central government on an individual basis.

In the northern Sudan, the only impetus that could transcend the limitations of localized power was religious. However, even within the Islamic framework, the traditional Sudanese institutions tended to be organized through local, often tribally oriented, religious organizations. The characteristic religious figure was the local miracle-working teacher and preacher. The basic organizational style was what J. S. Trimingham has called "cellular."[31] In this, the local teacher might be associated with some broader religious brotherhood, but there would be few direct organizational ties. "The school-*tariqa* units tended to be separate and autonomous, with a limited area of influence and only informal ties with other units."[32]

This situation was beginning to change early in the nineteenth century when ideas of more carefully organized brotherhoods or *turuq* began to arrive in the Sudan. Revivalist Sufi orders with a greater sense of translocal organization and reformist mission were brought to the Sudan at that time. The best-known of these were the Sammaniya *tariqa* and the Khatmiya *tariqa*. In addition, a more traditional Sudanese order, the Majdhubiya, was reorganized along the newer lines early in the century. In this way, less localized religious organizational concepts were emerging at the same time as a relative centralization of political power was taking place. The two trends appear to have been parallel and mutually reinforcing in northern Sudanese society. As a result, it is not surprising that the *tariqa* that built up and maintained the largest and most centralized organization, the Khatmiya, became a close ally of the centralizing Egyptian administration. In addition to cooperating with the Khatmiya, the Egyptian regime began to create a more official learned religious establishment that could act as a counterweight to the influence of the local religious leaders.

It has been noted by many scholars that this brought increasing pressure upon the local religious figures, and their resentment grew.[33] Tribal revolts against the Egyptian rulers had regularly failed. However, the growing local religious resentment could provide a vehicle that could unite the disparate opposition groups. This religious expression of opposition came to a climax with the Mahdist movement that brought an end to the Egyptian regime. Although the origins of the Mahdiya are complex, as P. M. Holt has said, "in one respect it was the vehicle of a protest by the indigenous and traditional Islamic leadership against the regime which had diminished their status. From this point of view, it was a revolt of the *faqihs*, and very appropriately its leader was a holy man who had undergone the traditional education of the Sudan."[34] From this perspective, one can say that the revolt of the Mahdi was a revolt of people like Abu Jummayza, and it is possible to see the foundations for Abu Jummayza's adherence to the Mahdiya.

The case of Abu Jummayza, however, makes it necessary to go beyond the generalization that Mahdiya was a "revolt of the *faqihs*," because Abu Jummayza's and other similar anti-Mahdist revolts might also be described as revolts of the *faqihs*. In some ways, at least, it is possible to say that the original socio-religious impetus of the *faqih* revolt was more directly carried on by people like Abu Jummayza than by Khalifa 'Abdallah. This appears to be the case, at least in the sense that the result of the overthrow of the Egyptian regime was not a creation of social structures in which the local *faqih* could remain autonomous and in control of his own immediate area. The Mahdist victory, instead, confirmed the centralizing tendencies of the previous decades. The state that Muhammad Ahmad established and Khalifa 'Abdallah organized and expanded was in many ways more directly a successor state to the centralized Egyptian regime with a stronger sense of Islamic mission than it was the creation of a state which would meet with the full approval of the local religious teacher.

Neither the Mahdi nor Khalifa 'Abdallah was willing to tolerate the "normal" religious practices of the village *faqih*. Regulations were made by both leaders prohibiting a number of local customs in which the *faqihs* participated and from which they often benefitted. The Mahdi opposed, for example, the wearing of amulets although the making of amulets was a major activity of the local *faqih*. The local autonomy of the *faqih* was to be replaced by submission to the central leadership of the Mahdiya. In this way, although the movement of Muhammad Ahmad may have been a revolt of the *faqihs* against the Egyptian regime, the continuation of that spirit of revolt is to be found in movements like that of Abu Jummayza rather than in the centralizing policies of Khalifa 'Abdallah. This may help to explain why the revolt of Abu Jummayza was not an isolated incident. As long as local *faqihs* had the ability to collect even a small number of followers through the preaching of eschatological messages, there would continue to be revolts inspired by the same motivations that had to some extent inspired the Mahdiya itself.

These conditions continued even after the defeat of the Mahdist state. In the

early years of the twentieth century, there were a number of religious movements led by local religious teachers making prophetic claims. These revolts are
usually discussed as being the result of the defeat of the Mahdiya, and they are
seen as a type of primary resistance to the establishment of imperialist rule. It
has been said, for example, that outside of the south and the Nuba Mountain
areas, opposition to the new administration was tied to religion and the cult of
Nabi 'Isa. "Although Mahdism was defeated on the battlefields and outlawed,
its ideology remained, and outbursts of neo-Mahdist movements continued for
a long time." [35] It is clear that some of the rationale for the religious revolts of
the early twentieth century was based on the conditions created by the defeat
of the Mahdiya. The British could be identified as the Anti-Christ, and the
traditional belief was that after the appearance and initial defeat of the Mahdi,
the Prophet of God, 'Isa, would come. This opened the way for a number of
religious enthusiasts, and "a dedicated Mahdist minority tried to topple the
'infidel' government by force. With the exception of the war years, hardly a
year passed during the first generation of Condominium rule without a Mahdist
rising." [36]

The case of Abu Jummayza, however, provides a reminder that these revolts
did not begin with the defeat of the Mahdist state in 1898. It is possible that
the Nabi 'Isa revolts are a continuation of a longer tradition of which Abu
Jummayza was a part. The twentieth-century movements, like many of the
earlier ones, were relatively closely tied to localist issues and were less uncompromising in the presentation of their claims. At heart, their struggle was a
continuation of the earlier opposition by local *faqih*s to more centralized and
universalistic control.

British fears of a Mahdist revival in the early years of the Condominium may
have masked the longer-term continuity of the style of local revolts and the
diversity within the Mahdist experience of the time. Every "Mahdist" revolt
after 1900 was suspected of being in some way connected with the mainline
Ansar leadership and the emerging role of Sayyid 'Abd al-Rahman, a son of the
Mahdi. However, it gradually became apparent to some people, such as C. A.
Willis, the director of British intelligence in Khartoum, that this Mahdist
"establishment" was not directly involved in local movements and may even
have opposed them.

The double level of "Mahdist" activity is illustrated in a number of incidents. One situation discussed in some detail by Willis provides a good example
of the general context. During 1923 there was considerable "suspicious" religious activity in western Dar Fur. It was felt that rumors of international wars
helped to revive eschatological ideas. However, Willis was clearly persuaded
that Sayyid 'Abd al-Rahman and the Ansar establishment had little to do with
these excitements. "Whilst the Sudan Government is aware of the inflammable
elements in Dar Fur and to a certain degree the Kordofan Baggara, and the
possibility of local disturbances through the machinations of fanatical fikis, it is

confident that Sayyed Abd el Rahmad el Mahdi is himself loyal to the Government and does his best to lead his followers in the right way. Unfortunately however many of these are beyond his reach and are influenced by local or itinerant fikis who either from ignorance or malice incite the native to fanaticism and disloyalty." [37]

It seems possible that the "fanatical local fikis" of this report are the reflection of the continuing tradition of which Abu Jummayza was a part. Parallel to this, the support of Sayyid 'Abd al-Rahman al-Mahdi for a more centralized and less anarchic system reflects at least some of the spirit of Khalifa 'Abdallah and other rulers who tried to control the local *faqihs*. In this framework, Sayyid 'Abd al-Rahman stated that all the Nabi 'Isa claimants were unbelievers, and he worked in a number of ways with the government to bring these anarchic Mahdist elements under control.[38] To do this, Sayyid 'Abd al-Rahman created a general organization of his own agents in as much of the country as he could. While the British administrators often expressed reservations about this structure, it represented a different type of phenomenon than that of the scattered local enthusiastic *faqihs* who claimed a new prophetic mission.[39] The gradual disappearance of local resistance led by such figures indicates a significant change in the social context. In a process that lasted for more than a century, the traditional "cellular," organized and popular *faqih* was finally suppressed as an independent unit in Sudanese society.

The suppression of this tradition involves many factors beyond the scope of this essay. The growing strength of centralizing forces in Sudanese society and the gradual transformation of the role of local religious leaders in the context of modernization are a part of this. In addition, the transformation of basic messianic ideology into the more staid forms of Islamic fundamentalism and then of Sudanese nationalism is also a factor. It is clear, however, that Abu Jummayza was part of a long-term evolution of Islamic society in the Sudan.

The comparison of Musaylima with Abu Jummayza helps to identify a number of critical areas in understanding the modern history of the Sudan. While the two leaders arose in two widely separated eras of Islamic history, a number of significant similarities appear. In the analysis of those similarities, it emerges that Abu Jummayza reflected a broader dynamic of Sudanese history. His was not a unique movement. Rather, it can be seen as part of the long-term interaction between the local *faqih* traditions and the emerging forces of large-scale organization and centralization. As a result, one form of opposition to the Mahdiya was from that local *faqih* class whose interests Muhammad Ahmad may have originally represented. Similarly, the case of Abu Jummayza helps to show that the local *faqih* revolts that took place early in the twentieth century may not have been simply reactions to the defeat of the Mahdiya. They may also have been part of this longer tradition.

Both Abu Jummayza and Musaylima can be viewed as case studies in religious revitalization movements that failed. However, in examining their histories, it becomes possible to identify larger dynamics of socio-religious history. By representing a more localist orientation in opposition to a more comprehensive one, Abu Jummayza probably was the "Mahdi's Musaylima."

NOTES

1. H. A. MacMichael, *A History of the Arabs in the Sudan* (1922; reprint ed. London: Frank Cass, 1967), part 1, pp. 84–89.

2. Gustav Nachtigal, *Sahara and Sudan*, trans. Allan G. B. Fisher and Humphrey J. Fisher (Berkeley and Los Angeles: University of California Press, 1971), part 4, p. 158.

3. R. S. O'Fahey, "Saints and Sultans: The Role of Muslim Holy Men in the Keira Sultanate of Dar Fur," in *Northern Africa: Islam and Modernization*, ed. Michael Brett (London: Frank Cass, 1973), p. 51.

4. R. S. O'Fahey, *State and Society in Dar Fur* (New York: St. Martin's Press, 1980), p. 122.

5. Musa al-Mubarak al-Hasan, *Tarikh Dar Fur al-Siyasi 1882–1898* (Khartoum: Khartoum University Press, n.d.), pp. 147–61, provides an excellent history of Abu Jummayza's movement based on 'Uthman Adam's correspondence.

6. Ibid., p. 148.

7. Na'um Shuqayr, *Tarikh al-Sudan al-Qadim wa al-Hadith wa Jughrafiyatuh* (Cairo: n.p., 1903), p. 462. See also F. R. Wingate, *Mahdiism and the Egyptian Sudan* (2d ed. London: Frank Cass, 1968), p. 375, and F. R. Wingate and Joseph Ohrwalder, *Ten Year's Captivity in the Mahdi's Camp, 1882–1892* (London: Sampson Low, Marston, 1892), p. 237. The Wingate and Ohrwalder account adds a miraculous dimension to this by reporting that, at the time, it was said that the shade of a *jummayza* tree followed him wherever he went.

8. Wingate, *Mahdiism*, pp. 374–76.

9. Quoted in P. M. Holt, *The Mahdist State in the Sudan, 1881–1898* (2d ed. Oxford: Clarendon Press, 1970), pp. 157–58.

10. Dale F. Eickelman, "Musaylima: An Approach to the Social Anthropology of Seventh Century Arabia," *Journal of the Economic and Social History of the Orient* 10 (1967): 52.

11. For more detailed analyses of his career and his role in the Riddah period, see Eickelman, "Musaylima"; Elias Shoufani, *Al-Riddah and the Muslim Conquest of Arabia* (Toronto: University of Toronto Press, 1973); and the sources cited by these scholars.

12. Ibid., p. 18.

13. Brief summaries of the careers of these people can be found in the following articles in the *Shorter Encyclopaedia of Islam*, ed. H. A. R. Gibb and J. H. Kramers (Ithaca: Cornell University Press, 1965); F. Buhl, "Al-Aswad," p. 49; V. Vacca, "Sadjah," pp. 485–86; V. Vacca, "Tulaiha," pp. 595–96. See also W. Montgomery Watt, "Al-Aswad," in *The Encyclopaedia of Islam* (new edition), vol. 1, p. 728.

14. Muhammad Sa'id al-Qaddal, *Al-Mahdiyyah wa al-Habashah* (Khartoum: Khartoum University Press, 1973), pp. 79–81.

15. Shuqayr, *Tarikh al-Sudan*, vol. 3, p. 547.

16. Eickelman, "Musaylima," p. 50.

17. Ibn Khaldun, *The Muqaddimah*, trans. Franz Rosenthal (New York: Pantheon Books), part 1, pp. 206–7.

18. 'Abdal-Malik ibn Hisham, *The Life of Muhammad: A Translation of Ibn Ishaq's Sirat Rasul Allah*, trans. A. Guillaume (London: Oxford University Press, 1955), p. 648.

19. Eickelman, "Musaylima," p. 48.

20. Ibid., p. 49.

21. Al-Hasan, *Tarikh Dar Fur*, pp. 160–61, and Holt, *Mahdist State*, p. 159.

22. Ibn Hisham, *Life*, p. 637.

23. Ibid., p. 649; cf. Ahwad ibn Yahya al-Baladhuri, *The Origins of the Islamic State*, trans. Philip Khuri Hitti (1916; reprint ed. Beirut: Khayats, 1966), p. 133.

24. Al-Baladhuri, Origins, p. 132.

25. *Manshurat Sayyidna al-Imam al-Mahdi* (Khartoum: Sudan Government—Central Archives, 1963–64), vol. 2, p. 71.

26. Shuqayr, *Tarikh al-Sudan*, vol. 3, pp. 460–61.

27. W. Montgomery Watt, *The Formative Period of Islamic Thought* (Edinburgh: Edinburgh University Press, 1973), p. 37.

28. M. A. Shaban, *Islamic History, a New Interpretation. Vol. 1: A.D. 600–750 (A.H. 132)* (Cambridge, England: Cambridge University Press, 1971), p. 96.

29. Ibid., p. 97.

30. Bashir Kawkaw Hamaydah, *Safahat min al-Turkiyyah wa al-Mahdiyyah* (Khartoum: Dar al-Irshad, n.d.), p. 209.

31. J. Spencer Trimingham, *Islam in the Sudan* (1949: reprint ed. London: Frank Cass, 1965), p. 197.

32. John Voll, "Effects of Islamic Structures on Modern Islamic Expansion in the Eastern Sudan," *IJAHS* 7 (1974): 90.

33. See, for example, the comments in Richard Hill, *Egypt in the Sudan, 1820–1881* (London: Oxford University Press, 1959), pp. 126–27.

34. P. M. Holt, *Studies in the History of the Near East* (London: Frank Cass, 1973), p. 129.

35. Mohamed Omer Beshir, *Revolution and Nationalism in the Sudan* (London: Rex Collings, 1974), p. 52.

36. Hassan Ahmed Ibrahim, "Mahdist Uprisings against the Condominium Government in the Sudan, 1900–1927," *IJAHS* 12 (1979): 440.

37. Director of Intelligence, Sudan Government to Chief Secretary to the Nigerian Government (Lagos), 3 December 1923 (no. D.I./X/25767), Public Record Office, London, FO 371–10065, pp. 53–59.

38. Ibrahim, "Mahdist Uprisings," p. 466. See also Hassan Ahmed Ibrahim, "Imperialism and Neo-Mahdism in the Sudan: A Study of British Policy towards Neo-Mahdism, 1924–1927," *IJAHS* 13 (1980): 214–39.

39. For descriptions of this organization and British evaluations of it, see the various reports included in the following: Public Record Office, London, FO 371–10065, pp. 194–95, 222–25; FO 371–11613, R. Davies, "A Note on the Recent History of Mahdism," 17 April 1926; FO 371–11614, S. Hilleson, "Mahdism," 4 November 1926 (in SSIR no. 8); FO 371–12374, R. Davies, "Memorandum on the Policy of the Sudan Government towards the Mahdist Cult," 11 December 1926; FO 371–19096; Public Security Intelligence, Khartoum (no. P.S./65222), "Mahdism and El Sayed Abdel Rahman El Mahdi, K.B.E., C.V.O.," enclosure in Sir G. Symes to Sir M. Lampson, Khartoum, 13 May 1935, secret despatch no. 74.

PART THREE

Islam and Nationalism:
Secular or Communal?

SEVEN

The Roots of Muslim Separatism in South Asia: Personal Practice and Public Structures in Kanpur and Bombay

Sandria B. Freitag

One of the main themes of twentieth-century South Asian history has been seen as the growth of an inexorable movement for separatism among Indian Muslims, culminating in the 1947 partition of British India into the independent states of India and Pakistan.[1] The standard interpretation has described a process leading from nineteenth-century fragmentation among Muslims to the development of a militant national consciousness by the mid-twentieth century. However, as a dying Muhammad 'Ali made clear in a speech to the 1930 London Round Table Conference, the drive toward separatism was neither inevitable nor monolithic.

> Where God commands ... I am a Muslim first, a Muslim second and Muslim last and nothing but a Muslim.... But where India is concerned, where the welfare of India is concerned, I am an Indian first, an Indian second, and an Indian last and nothing but an Indian.... I belong to two circles of equal size but which are not concentric. One is India and the other is the Muslim world ... we belong to these circles ... and we can leave neither.[2]

Only in certain areas and in certain quite specific historic contexts did Muslim sentiments coalesce into "communalism," in which one's religion took precedence over all other loyalties, and the related demand that religious identity receive political expression.[3]

The formation of an Indian Muslim identity was thus not a monolithic process at all, but one full of variety in its very localized expressions. To illustrate the significance of local events and experiences in shaping Muslim identity and separatism, this chapter compares similar periods in two industrialized urban centers: Bombay city on the west coast, and Kanpur, the premier industrial city of the heartland area known as the United Provinces (now Uttar

Pradesh).[4] It contrasts important events in each place, looking first at the turn of the century (1913 in Kanpur and 1911 in Bombay) and then at episodes two decades later (1931 in Kanpur and 1929 in Bombay). In each case attention is focused on the circumstances and experiences both that fostered and that prevented development of a vocabulary of community and its expression in a public structure for Islam.

THE UNITED PROVINCES

In the nineteenth century, Muslims in the Kanpur area of the United Provinces made up about 14 percent of the population, and they could be divided into two main groupings: the *ashraf* and the "lower-caste" Muslim groups. The *ashraf* constituted the Muslim elite. Enjoying superior status based on being "well-born," these constituent groups shared an Indo-Persian culture fostered by the Mughal court (based in Delhi for the previous two centuries) and exported to the *qasba* urban centers that developed throughout northern India during the seventeenth and eighteenth centuries. Despite the nineteenth-century decline in the fortunes of those espousing *sharif* status, this culture continued to thrive in *qasba* centers, emphasizing education, literary and other artistic accomplishments, the holding of administrative positions in Muslim states, study of Islamic law, and Muslim reformist activities. Although long shared by non-Muslims, this elite way of life was perceived by the Muslims who embraced it as "Islamic." This identification would prove a significant bridge to the concerns held by Muslims of lower status.

Alongside this *ashraf* elite group was a cluster of lower-class groups, designated by their traditional occupations as butchers, weavers, etc. These groups were characterized by strong corporate identities (measured by the presence of effective group *panchayat*s, or caste councils), capable of enforcing appropriate codes of behavior and, often, mobilizing for collective action.[5] Although not always punctilious about observing Shari'a injunctions, these groups had begun placing great emphasis on maintenance of certain Islamic activities, particularly those occurring in public spaces, such as the parading of *tazia*s (replicas of the tombs of 'Ali and Husayn) during *muharram*,[6] sacrifice of cattle on the 'Id, or prevention of music-playing in front of mosques. Indeed, the foremost group—Julahas, or weavers—was consistently characterized in late nineteenth- and early twentieth-century official documents as "bigoted" or "fanatic," volatile in their defense of Islamic practices.

Despite the class gulf, on a number of occasions and in many contexts Muslims would cooperate, albeit in a very localized way.[7] Significantly, these occasions preeminently were those occurring in public spaces—on the city's streets and lanes, or within its mosques and 'Idgas.[8] Moreover, though perceptions of the significant issues within Indian Islamic culture were not identical across the class divide, they did overlap. Perceptions came to be expressed by a shared vocabulary emphasizing symbols such as the mosque, prayer, the Quran, and Urdu literature (as expressed in both poetry and newly emerging newspaper journalism). These symbols, shared even by those with widely differing notions of how they should be used, provided an effective way to give a single identity to groups that might disagree on substantive issues.

The decades surrounding the turn of the century were a period of experimentation in shared identity. Muslims in this region were faced with a new situation, created first by the decline of the Mughal empire and imposition of colonial rule, then by the impetus of Islamic reformist movements and the development under the British of self-governing institutions.

It must be emphasized that no single Islamic style or definition of community could have emerged from this experimentation; but the end result was to reinforce the sense of community by drawing on the same tradition and using the same vocabulary. These experiments addressed several issues crucial to the well-being of Muslims, including the extent to which the community should be demarcated within the larger Indian culture; the relationship of Muslims to the government; the extent to which reformist (high Islamic) standards should prevail over objectionable customary practices; and the methods that could be used to mobilize the community to protect its interests.[9] These experiments simultaneously addressed issues of community definition and of the personal practice of Islam.

PERSONAL PRACTICE AND PUBLIC STRUCTURES

Relating the practice of Islam to the evolving definition of community was a crucial issue. There were at least two possible paradigms for the relationship. In one, emphasis was placed on a Muslim ruler. He employed men learned in Islamic law in service to the state as judges (*qadis*) and legal scholars (*muftis*); he patronized religious education, supervised religious charities, and in general provided a symbolic focus for Muslims. Thus he provided the public setting in which the free exercise of Islam could occur; in this setting it was less necessary to pay close attention to particular personal practices.

When, later, it proved impossible to provide this public setting, attention was shifted to the second pattern—the reformation of personal religious practice. In this pattern, a structure drawing on the Quran and *hadith* (sayings, actions of the Prophet) provided a model of personal behavior to substitute for the public structure previously provided by the state. The resulting shift in emphasis profoundly affected the context in which Islam was perceived and the style of its practice in India, for it demanded a new attention to the details of living and provided a new role for the ulama, one that focused on guiding ordinary Muslims in their everyday lives. Not all Muslims were drawn to this new emphasis on personal practice, but the number exposed to the reformist arguments expanded rapidly in the late nineteenth century. The emphasis on personal practice brought home to Muslims of the United Provinces that their religious practices set them apart from other Indians, and it provided a method and a rationale for mobilizing collective action.

How were personal practice and public structures to be combined? If there was to be no Islamic state, Muslims in north India had to find an alternate public framework for the practice of their religion. "Public" activities could be defined in several different ways. A new political structure could be devised, where leaders of Muslims represented an Islamic framework within which Indians who were Muslims could be effective and exercise power. It was also possible to see as "public" those Islamic exercises expressed through powerful public ceremonials. Finally, collective action taken in the name of Islam could be seen as "public" activity on behalf of an increasingly self-conscious Muslim community. Over the turn of the century all three of these arenas proved central to the evolving definition of community, with greatest emphasis on participation by Muslims in public observances.

Leaders effectively tied together the constituent parts of the Muslim "community" either by working through networks of ulama or by making public efforts on behalf of the community. Self-styled leaders interested in this latter type of activity ranged from professionals and educators to publicists active in the newly emerging Muslim press. To see these groups as representing opposing philosophies and approaches, however, would be inaccurate; rather, they represent important points on a continuum of leadership based in *sharif* culture.

The lines of debate among the ulama could be drawn clearly, for these religious leaders shared certain experiences as well as a common vocabulary of dispute.[10] Yet the very exercise of debate among these styles and their proponents led to an increased awareness of a common tradition. Significantly, most of these activities took place in public forums. In debates over proper personal principles, leaders utilized such innovations as printing presses and newspapers to publicize and propagate their points of view. Their appeals easily reached their fellow *ashraf*, and new and conscious efforts were made to reach lower-class Muslims as well. New forms of organization and structures for education were adopted, and additional ulama were trained in their respective values. Existing mechanisms, such as Friday prayers and the issuance of *fatawa* (Ar. sing. *fatwa*) (pronouncements on the Law applied to everyday problems) were also employed. From traditional networks of kinship, *biradari* (patrilineal brotherhoods) and Sufism, and through the spiritual and emotional connections that developed in the schools where ulama were trained, a sense of shared community emerged.

Always more interested in the public issues of Islam, publicists and professionals used similar forums to emphasize their perceptions of shared community. The press presented issues their editors deemed significant to Muslims, both within and outside India. Educators (particularly those connected to the "Westernized" Aligarh University) focused on making Muslims competitive in the professions and government bureaucracy. All these issues were interpreted through the cultural framework of Indo-Persian *qasba* culture and thus shared much of the language and cultural values being invoked by the ulama. It is not surprising, then, that in the twentieth century this kind of atmosphere fostered an increased sensitivity to symbols and practices in the believer's life, and made north Indian Muslims more receptive to calls from beyond their locality.

THE KANPUR MOSQUE AFFAIR OF 1913

The study of Kanpur demonstrates a two-part process occurring in many urban centers in the United Provinces: first, the development of a language of shared symbols serving an abstract concept of community, and, second, the difficulties encountered when leaders attempted to create a concrete program implementing this shared concept. Kanpur stood in dramatic contrast to the older urban centers of north India, for it was a British creation. In the words of one inhabitant, "Cawnpore is neither a cultural nor a historical place. It is an industrial town with shifting population... without much regard for their neighbors."[11] Nevertheless it existed in the heart of the region of Mughal rule and Indo-Persian culture and could therefore draw on the older *qasba* centers.

Significantly, its recent creation meant that those in powerful political positions owed their unfluence more to factional alignments than to ties with an established commercial or landed elite. These factions were based on personal relationships that shifted frequently, unrelated to ideological, class, or religious issues.[12] Yet, in a society with large numbers of laborers and a commercial atmosphere encouraging entrepreneurial success, class and even religious differences were real and important, even though they were never expressed through the factional alignments in the political structure. Increasingly in the twentieth century, these divisions instead sought outlets in violent action. Kanpur is noteworthy as the site in 1900 of a coalition of millworkers—leatherworkers joined by those in the cotton, wool, and jute mills—who rioted against plague control measures imposed by civil authorities. Moreover, there were riots in both 1913 and 1931 over religious issues. By the later 1930s, an effective labor movement emerged in Kanpur, only to be sapped eventually by its connections to the factionalized political structure. All these characteristics made Kanpur a unique place for an event that would dramatically express the fusion of the public and the personal aspects of Indian Islam.

In 1913 the washing place of the mosque of Macchli Bazaar stood in the path of a new road being constructed by British city planners.[13] Determined to remove it, the administration accepted assurances by "trustworthy and good Muhammedans" that the bathing place need not form an integral part of the mosque. Since a group of Muslims had walked with shoes on through the washing place, the area did seem "less sacred." No doubt the administration expected little trouble from the peddlers, principal worshippers at the mosque, who chose informally from among themselves the manager (*mutawalli*) of their mosque. Yet the last decision, made in 1906, had designated two such managers who were prompt in protesting the demolition.

Public opinion supported their protests. When the washing place was removed, "large crowds of julahas [weavers at the mills] left their work and went to the spot . . . and [then] went off to see their moulvis." Other Muslims soon joined in: at a meeting attended by some 125 Muslims from all quarters of the city, a body of eleven new managers was chosen for the mosque. Though the two original managers were included among this number, it is clear that this new body was a radical departure from traditional practice. It is also clear that, despite Lieutenant-Governor Meston's protests, it was more than a political ploy by out-of-towners: this new method of selection suggested to every Muslim of Kanpur that he had a potential stake in any mosque, regardless of location.

The move meant, too, that when the demand arose, traditional positions of leadership could be infused with new purpose—for the new body of managers began immediately to act as the corporate representatives of the mosque. They first addressed the Municipal Board chairman, to find out who had worn shoes through the bathing place.[14] And when Meston issued a press communiqué to "counteract misrepresentations" printed in the newspapers, the eleven published a rejoinder. They then called two public meetings to discuss Muslim reaction to the demolition.

The second meeting at the 'Idga on 3 August was elaborately planned. Placards urged "all Mohammedan gentlemen whose hearts [were] upset and agitated by the martyrdom of part of the mosque" to "postpone their urgent duties and take part in the assemblage." Muslim neighborhoods were canvassed door-to-door. Mourning symbolism was invoked: "large groups of Muslims from every quarter of the city were seen proceeding towards the 'Idga bare-footed and carrying black flags . . . some of the groups used to halt at intervals during their march . . . and at every halt a man recited an elegy on the demolished portion."[15] Early speeches evoked a shared culture by reciting Persian poetry; a sense of affront to Muslim values was expressed as the rhetoric became increasingly heated. The crowd, although not initially violent, ended by showering police (and then a nearby temple) with debris from surrounding, demolished houses.

The cause had also rallied Muslim opinion outside Kanpur on an unprecedented scale. Heavy coverage in the press stated the case plainly. The washing place had been demolished because "Muslims are loyal and they obey all the just as well as the unjust orders of the authorities"—another in a long line of laments filling the newspapers over the reunification of Bengal.[16] Moreover, "when hundreds of mosques have been destroyed in Macedonia, when the tomb of Imam Raza has been desecrated in Meshed, it is no wonder that a mosque is being demolished in India"—a reflection of the anguish felt by Indian Muslims for the international condition of Islam.[17] Newspaper editors and prominent Muslims from other areas of India came to Kanpur to see the site for themselves and passionately urged local Muslims to express their concern. "Every day," admitted Meston, "brought news of meetings and telegrams [sent from] different parts of India."

A revealing indication of the wide range of Muslims affected by the Kanpur affair was the juxtaposition of the roster of rioting millhands and other lower-class Muslims with that of the leaders forming a delegation to Meston. All fourteen of the *ashraf* signatories to a memorial presented by the Raja of Mahmudabad were from outside Kanpur (generally Delhi- or Lucknow-based) and had been active in province- or India-wide Muslim causes.[18] They were certainly living proof of their memorial's contention that "the feelings of our community on this question as a whole are neither individual, local nor manufactured." Indeed, by this time they could speak as well for the rioting Pathan and Julaha weavers when they insisted "these feelings are genuine, real and founded upon the bedrock of religious faith."

Thus a number of important symbols and examples of Islamic vocabulary were brought to bear on the issue. The invocation of a shared literary heritage, the concept of martyrdom, and the replication of mourning practices were now applied to a mosque, the preeminent symbol of Muslim sacred space. The institution of mosque management was reshaped to fulfill new purposes. Face-to-face contact (through neighborhood canvassing to publicize the protest meeting) was used to reinforce and personalize the sense of shared community among Muslims. These techniques and Islamic symbols successfully bridged the gap, at least temporarily, between *sharif* Indo-Persian culture and the combative sense of community felt by lower-class Muslims. The result was an unprecedented level of protest against the government's actions.

Such public protest was important because it expressed a new reality. A sense of community was emerging through protests aimed not against Hindus but against the government: an indication that Muslims were concerned about creating a viable public structure for the practice of Islam and the protection of Islamic symbols. In the vocabulary used that day, its success could be measured by the amount of "zeal" exhibited by Muslims. "There are 47,000 Muslims in the city [of Kanpur] and only women are left in our houses; cannot our zeal now be called real?... Can Government have any objection to recognizing our zeal now?" Indeed, it was the government's misfortune to have been caught unsuspecting in the changing perceptions of community that broadened the focus from personal practices to the public sphere, and that united behind one cause the usually bifurcated *ashraf* and lower-class Muslims. In the event, the government had to capitulate to public opinion.

Though played out in public arenas, these developments reflected the success of the ulama in proselytizing their visions of the personal practice of Islam. Yet this very success presented a paradox of immense importance in the coming decades, for the transfer of symbolic language from personal practice to public arenas carried with it the potential for a divorce of the symbols from the meaning the ulama had intended them to have. Because issues of practice divided Muslim from Muslim—whereas symbolic language had the potential to unite them—practice became secondary to the language of community. In turn, activity in the public arena on behalf of the community became an important way of identifying who was a Muslim.[19] Moreover, the expectations raised by success in 1913 presented more problems than solutions, for there remained a basic disjuncture between the perception of community as a symbol —an abstract, emotive identity—and the attempted expression of that community in a concrete political program. The dilemma was masked for a time by the shared symbolic language. In the riots of 1931, Muslims in Kanpur were finally brought face to face with this disjuncture.

KANPUR, 1931

The story of Kanpur in 1931 begins, appropriately enough, with public collective activity. The riot was prompted by a protest strike called by the Indian National Congress.[20] By 1931 few Muslims willingly observed these congress-initiated protests, as the congress, particularly in Kanpur, had become identified with the majority "Hindu" community. To achieve strict observance of the strike meant that youthful congress volunteers had to coerce Muslims (as well as the British and some Hindus) into cooperation. These volunteers initiated the violence, but it spread immediately and continued for several days, moving from commercial to residential areas. Crowds used hit-and-run tactics, attacking people hiding in a house and then looting and/or setting fire to the house afterward. Though evidence shows that neither of the most turbulent elements of Kanpur—the millworkers and the large *badmash* ("bad character" or gangster) population—initiated the riot, its scale worsened dramatically when they became involved.

The attacks ran along established lines of cleavage, and their targets were frequently (especially in the early days of the rioting) those that had figured in earlier experiences. Thus Macchli Bazaar mosque and its neighboring temple were attacked almost immediately. So too was a Muslim cap merchant who had figured in a 1927 riot. At least 300 people were killed,[21] a huge number of houses were burnt and looted, and a substantial number of temples and mosques were desecrated or destroyed.

The riot tells us much about the nature of leadership in Kanpur and the difficulties it encountered in linking factional politics and the symbolic rhetoric used in public arenas. As befitted the nature of Kanpur civic life, power was exercised primarily by the commercial interests. They ran the municipality; much of their control stemmed from their participation as municipal commissioners and members of the District Board, the Kanpur Improvement Trust, and the Provincial Legislative Council.[22] They also joined the congress.[23]

Through the Kanpur congress these same leaders then ran a number of programs, not all of which were fostered by the provincial or all-India congress committees. These included neighborhood-level congress committees, *prabhat pheris* (nationalist processions each morning), and the Shuddhi and Sangathan movements as well.[24]

The evidence strongly suggests, then, that people in positions of power moved to control each new arena of public participation and to shut out all those without preexisting power bases in the city. This scramble for control was prompted by a deep but distinctly personal pattern of factionalism among those with influence, but since those shut out were consistently, though not solely, Muslims, this process was perceived as communally inspired.[25] That competition for control centered on personal animosities rather than on ideological or class differences meant that the very real problems of Kanpur were neither reflected in nor provided an outlet through the political structures of the city.

In addition, like other cities in north India, in the late 1920s Kanpur had experienced a spate of religious reformist, mass-oriented programs. As one witness put it:

> There is not much of real religious animosity among the people here, but mutual rivalry and jealousy between Hindus and Muslims have always been in existence here. Both communities have been vying with each other in Mohurram and Dasehra celebrations, and Ryabbi Sharif and Arya Samaj processions. The Shuddhi and Sangathan and Tabliqh movements touched Cawnpore too.... For some time almost daily [Tanzim] processions were organized, and the weekly Sunday procession, in which the mill hands could also join, were much more elaborate and attracted a bigger crowd.[26]

Yet, for all these public-arena activities, leadership was divided between very localized leaders, such as the managers of the Macchli Bazaar mosque, and traditionally and newly prestigious powerholders from outside the city, like the landholder Raja of Mahmudabad and the publicist Muhammad 'Ali. Few of those who came from inside Kanpur had the stature to command widespread cooperation without factional backing. The few Muslims who did manage to find places of power among the municipal leadership were there not as Muslim voices but as members of one or another faction.

The fact that most Muslims were shut out of power took on increasing importance in the decades before 1931 because this was a period of escalating commercial competition as well. Most of the competing Muslims dealt in foreign goods and had little sympathy with the Civil Disobedience movement launched in 1930. At the same time, other Muslim merchants were being forced out of certain professions and locations by successful "Hindu" entrepreneurs, including dyers, wealthy timber merchants, and vegetable and fruit sellers.[27] Prolonged litigation was used against wealthy and influential timber merchants, and then against vegetable and fruit sellers. Internal evidence suggests that, again, these actions were not directed against Muslims per se but that the men in question, like others in the city, fell prey to those who could manipulate municipal connections to their own economic advantage.[28]

In a similar way the patronage distributed by municipal commissioners found its way to few Muslims, as they were seldom in a position to be useful to the competing factions on the board.[29] The statements given to the commission made it clear that all Muslims testifying were aware of these slights and perceived them as a sign that Muslims were both powerless and systematically discriminated against.

It is small wonder, then, that when an occasion for violence was finally presented, those who had been excluded from power responded with a violent resistance to the "martyrdom" of their community. This should not have come as a surprise; the connection between the martyrdom motif, community defense, and violent action had been underscored by a reinvigorated Tanzim (activist preaching) movement in the two years preceding the riot. Tanzim demonstrated that success was possible in two public arenas, those of public ceremonial and collective action. This raised expectations for a public structure, even as events made it ever more unlikely they could be satisfied in the one critical arena—the political structure.

AN ELUSIVE PUBLIC STRUCTURE: KANPUR, 1913-31

As we have seen, crucial to all three arenas was the structure in Muslim community life provided by leadership exercised in a variety of settings. Yet the most significant changes in the early twentieth century were those that affected the very process by which leadership in urban India was legitimated.

Though many aspects of Muslim life were not directly connected to the British government, it was only after the turn of the century that the legitimation of authority ceased to be the virtual monopoly of the government. Up until that time, even those whom the British saw as natural leaders had required official recognition to ensure their status in society, and the British had been anxious to cooperate with them by naming them honorary magistrates, appointing them to municipal boards, allowing them to sponsor religious festivals and parades, and the like.

But the expansion of the franchise, and reliance on the psychological pressure of mass protest, meant that leadership status now had to come from popular support. At the same time, retention by the British administration of final authority meant that to be effective, leaders were required to move back and forth between appeals to the populace and participation in the practical politics engendered by government-created institutions.

By the early 1920s, then, a series of political and economic changes had dramatically increased the number of Indians participating in agitational politics; these changes proved especially significant because they meant that the old-style patron-client networks had to be supplemented by ideological appeals.[30] The use of such appeals had been especially encouraged in the late 1920s by movements aimed at conversion (the Arya Samaj's Shuddhi and Muslim retaliatory Tabliqh) and community defense (Hindu Sangathan and Muslim Tanzim). Tabliqh was an effort to thwart Hindu appeals to particular groups of converts: Muslim reformists aimed at removing a number of Hindu practices retained by these groups after conversion, as well as protecting the groups' "Muslimness" from the proselytizing advances of the Arya Samaj. We will examine the Tanzim (self-defense) movement in more detail below; here it will suffice to note that it too focused on particular Islamic practices and symbols, such as prayer and martyrdom, to foster a sense of protectiveness for community interests. These were joined to training in physical fitness to encourage Muslims to defend their community. The implications of these for the use of violence in the interest of the community are apparent.

Efforts to harness religious identities were accompanied by similar attempts to tap the basic class identities present in an industrial center. The 1920s were marked by efforts in many urban areas to develop a labor movement. These efforts were initially successful in Kanpur but were soon short-circuited. Leaders concerned to maintain their dominance took over the labor union, amalgamating that control with their other political activities. Thus class identities, too, were subsumed under factional alignments in the pattern typical of Kanpur.

By 1929, then, there were several developments encouraging the creation of an Islamically defined program, including the creation of an Islamic language stressing martyrdom and defense of the community, and a strong neighborhood-based Tanzim movement. Together these two meant that a public framework based on collective activities or public ceremonies was certainly possible. Much more problematic was transference of this kind of public structure to the political arena; yet in the heightened expectations of the 1930s, this is what Kanpur Muslims wanted. The riot of 1931 resulted from the frustration of community expectations by the structural realities of colonial Kanpur's political arena.

THE TANZIM MOVEMENT

The late 1920s were marked particularly by experiences that reinforced a communal identity. Hindu *prabhat pheris*, for instance, were introduced in Kanpur in 1929–30 by the local congress committee. Hindu in style, and designed to appeal to youthful supporters, they were a "sort of morning prayer in which young men and students [made] a round in [the] city . . . singing national songs on the way."[31] These processions were "small parties of people, about 10 or 12, [who] used to go to the Ganges for their morning bath and in returning they used to form themselves into groups, one leading singing and the

others following.... They were singing Congress songs." [32] Adorned with flags
and employing nationalist rhetoric, such *prabhat pheris* were soon incorporated
into the congress's special "Sunday Programmes" as well, thus providing the
youthful activists with special recognition before the entire city. [33]

These localized processions joined other distinctly Hindu activities meant to
be anti-British at the same time, such as the picketing of toddy shops (whose
clientele was estimated to be about 60 percent lower-class Hindu and 40
percent Muslim), [34] and introduction of physical fitness groups to teach "the art
of warfare" (Muslims felt that only Hindus were permitted to attend these
municipally sponsored activities). [35] In each of these experiments the organizers
deliberately evoked the same sense of identity, the use of a symbolic vocabulary,
and the incorporation of certain quasi-religious practices for emulation.

Among Kanpur Muslims the Tanzim movement enjoyed a resurgence in
direct response to the organization of the *prabhat pheris*. Neighborhood groups
were utilized to improve the religious and social practices of the Muslim lower
classes, of whom the mills had attracted a substantial number to the city. One
witness saw "some youngsters coming both morning and evening and persuad-
ing people to offer prayers and observe Ramzan etc." [36] Another said that "the
slogans shouted by the processionists were 'say your prayers regularly' and
during the last Divali 'do not gamble.'" [37] That is, these Tanzim organizations
became a way of turning personal religious practice into a public, collective
activity.

Moreover, by giving processionists green flags and banners and as much of
a special uniform as they could afford, they fostered feelings of group identity
and solidarity in much the same way as the *prabhat pheris* had done. The values
being inculcated emerge in the verses sung by one such Tanzim procession
(translated by a witness):

> Wake up now, sleeping Muslims: get ready to support Islam. Time is coming for
> you to sacrifice yourself [when time comes]. Losing your life [getting beheaded]
> become the Leader [*sardar*] of your community.
>
> Even the skeptics [denyers] acknowledge your sensitiveness and courage. It is a
> mere trifle for you to get ready for fighting. Those who ridicule your Shar'iat and
> worship, such unpious persons should be consigned to flames.
>
> We shall wake up the world; we shall shake the world when, united, we shall raise
> the monotheistic cry. With the light [splendor] of Monotheism, we shall light a
> fire and shall obliterate, O Infidelity, thy existence out of the world.
>
> We shall place our throats on swords, on spear heads. Where religion is involved,
> we shall get beheaded. [38]

Though the verses support Hindu testimony that many of the actions of the
Tanzim committees were aimed against them, it is also clear that the perception
of Islam as endangered and Muslims as an abused minority was central to the
movement. Tanzim became an ostensible remedy for the martyrdom imagery

now so familiar to Muslims of the United Provinces. Seen in this light, the efforts by some branches of the movement to teach the "use of *lathi, ballam* and sword, *pharik gadka* and wrestling" may be construed as defensive, not offensive.[39]

In such a movement as this lay the greatest potential for uniting a reformist program, focusing on personal religious practices, with a public structure to protect Islam. Yet the Kanpur Tanzim movement failed to develop a structure that integrated the few prominent Muslim leaders of the city and the neighborhood branches of the organization. Indeed, the assorted Tanzim committees were emphatically rooted in their various neighborhoods. No citywide network united them, nor was there any ongoing connection with a similar organization in Allahabad. More than one observer bemoaned the fact that the neighborhood *anjuman*s,

> instead of concentrating their attention to the main work before them drifted into rivalry one against the other: who had the largest number of members, who had the largest number of volunteers, whose flag was highest; who looked smarter, who resembled this high personage or that high functionary, were some of the matters that riveted attention in the spirit of rivalry.[40]

Thus, though united by the values and symbols of Tanzim, they were fragmented by neighborhood identities within the Tanzim structure. Certainly organization within the *anjuman*s was a very localized affair.

> There was a Tanzim-ul Salat in Ghoolwali Gali [neighborhood]. I was its vice-chairman.... The Anjuman is closed since the riots.... This Anjuman had twelve members.... There were thirty-five volunteers.... The Anjuman of Tanzim was started ten or eleven months ago. It was started by all the [neighborhood] people. It was started to keep up Som and Salahat. These people used to induce those who did not say prayers, to say prayers, give charity and do good deeds. They used to request people. They also used to boycott them socially and did not join their funerals.... The meetings were held in the evening on Sundays. No record was kept of the proceedings. There were no written rules in connection with these Anjumans. No servants were engaged for the work of the Anjuman.... Subscriptions used to be paid by office bearers and members. Volunteers paid no subscriptions and even if they did pay it was nominal.[41]

Yet their unifying potential was demonstrated when these neighborhood committees were amalgamated in Sunday processions, "which the millhands could also join" and which were "more elaborate and attracted bigger crowds" than the smaller, localized exercises.[42] For some of these Sunday processions, speakers with all-India stature were brought to Kanpur; then the various neighborhood Tanzim organizations marched to the mass meetings as groups.

Thus, by 1931, even urban north Indian neighborhoods recognized the need for a public structure for Islam and turned to a highly developed symbolic language to express it. For all this promising potential, however, it proved impossible to bridge the gap between reform of personal practices and the organizational infrastructure needed for a political program.

Even had Muslims been able to agree on a public structure to protect the practice of religion, this would have been difficult to achieve in the colonial context. As David Gilmartin has shown,[43] it was a matter of deliberate British policy that the state system operated without reference to religious ideology. In such a system political effectiveness was judged not by a leader's ability to integrate an ideology with day-to-day political machinations, but by his ability to move from one arena to another. The very exclusivity of each arena made more inexorable the recourse to violence, the only public structure that continued to prove its (at least temporary) efficacy in protecting community identity. In U.P. the prolonged period in which this process developed created a long-lasting way of looking at the world from a Muslim perspective. For a very different pattern, we turn now to Bombay.

BOMBAY CITY

Although it, too, was a creation of the British, Bombay city had been founded much earlier than Kanpur: control of Bombay had been transferred to the East India Company in 1668.[44] Long-existent trading activity made the area an attractive entrepôt not only for the EIC but also for Indian and foreign merchants. By the 1850s these merchants had begun to invest in industrial activities, particularly cotton mills, and within three decades a "distinct industrial-capitalist group had emerged out of the old trading and banking group which had hitherto dominated Bombay's public life."[45] Late nineteenth- and twentieth-century Bombay was an intensely industrialized city.

Certain other characteristic features of life in Bombay also shaped the distinct pattern of interaction among resident Muslims. These included highly fragmented clusters of groups of Muslims; a dramatic disjuncture between those exercising leadership at the citywide and those at the localized, neighborhood level; and a lack of preconditions, such as experience of a Muslim ruler and a shared Islamicate culture, favoring expectations for a public structure.

The population of Bombay city reflected its complex urban development; the city grew from an estimated 156,987 in 1816 to 773,196 by 1881. Muslims constituted a fairly constant 20 percent of the population throughout this period,[46] but their distribution among subcategories changed significantly over the nineteenth century. Sunni Muslims from Konkan were predominant in the early years of the century. By the end of the century, Muslim migrants had arrived in large numbers from other parts of India; the most notable were U.P. Julahas, working as weavers in the rapidly growing mill industry. The complexity of the Muslim population is indicated, for instance, in the 1901 census, which identified fourteen categories (Arab, Bohra, Baluchi, Egyptian, Julhai [Julaha], Khatri, Khoja, Memon Mughal, Pathan, Sayad, Shaik, Sidi, Turk, and Unspecified); these in turn could be grouped on linguistic (Marathi, Gujarati and Sindhi/Cutchi, Urdu/Hindi) or occupational lines (traders and

merchants, weavers, service groups), as well as across the doctrinal divide of
Sunni and Shi'i.[47] The regional or foreign origin of each group was of some
significance as well.

Unlike the debate among Muslims of the United Provinces over appropriate
Islamic style, in Bombay myriad definitions were isolated within their respective boundaries, jostling one another uncomfortably in Bombay's public spaces.
This isolation was expressed spatially as each group established distinct neighborhoods (muhallas) throughout the city. As noted by Masselos, the changes in
Bombay's population composition had important ramifications for the public
ceremonial aspects of Islam there, and particularly for the preeminent observance of muharram.[48] The changing shape of the public rituals of muharram gives
graphic expression to the diversity and intracommunal rivalry: from at least the
1830s there were innovations, protests about them, then competing innovations
and British administrative reactions to control the competition.

CONFLICTING PUBLIC STRUCTURES

Lacking a traditional princely or ruling Muslim elite and its concomitant
courtly culture, the myriad Islamic groups in Bombay had difficulty finding
common bonds. The felt need for a public structure in which to practice Islam,
created by the historical precedent of local Muslim rulers in the United
Provinces, was lacking here. Moreover, without a shared Indo-Persian cultural
base, no literary, artistic, and cultural norms could evolve. Indeed, even the
seemingly standard symbols of Islam could not be used integratively in
Bombay.

The class, caste/ethnic, sectarian, regional, and linguistic divisions of
Bombay Muslims were reflected as well in their differing conceptions and
practices of Islam. A brief comparison of three such groups, especially in terms
of their participation in muharram, will demonstrate the diversity of Islam as
practiced in this city.[49]

Dominant, imposing their mark on the shape of muharram throughout the
nineteenth century, were the most numerous of the early migrants, the Sunni
Muslims from the Konkan. "Konkanis were to be found in virtually the whole
gamut of class roles then accessible to Indians," including laborers, sailors and
service categories, as well as wealthy merchants and traders, and the occasional
western-educated clerk.[50] Equally important, Konkanis controlled the major
mosques and provided the personnel for the position of qadi of Bombay (the
city's most important "administrative" religious post). Muharram as shaped
by the Konkanis emphasized the public, processional aspects of the observance
and focused on the symbolism of the tabut (replicas of the tomb of Husayn).
Neighborhood-sponsored tabuts were paraded throughout the ten days of
muharram and then "immersed" on the last day.

The first to provide a challenge to this muharram style were the Mughals, a term applied to Muslims from West Asia generally and in particular to Persian Shi'is. In the early nineteenth century these Shi'is had built an *imambara* and then created a "procession of the horse"; during this parade typically Shi'i mourning rituals were invoked. Because this public mourning included calling down imprecations on Sunni-recognized successors to Muhammad, resentment soon led the British to limit the horse procession to the *imambara* compound itself. The result of this first challenge was that the Sunni Konkani style emerged as the only approved public processional, supported by the authority of the British raj.

Another group of Shi'is was also active in attempts to redefine the public practice of Islam. The Khojas, a convert group of Sindhi and Gujarati traders, gained prominence in the mid-nineteenth century, when the Aga Khan's arrival in Bombay touched off a battle over his right to exercise control over the community. How the Khojas observed *muharram* was an important aspect of this power struggle. For our purposes it is sufficient to note that as the Aga Khan emerged triumphant he first bound the Shi'is to one faction of Mughals in their observance (thereby including them as targets of Sunni hostility), and then added a special nightly enactment of a Persian passion play about Karbala. Because it was limited to space occupied by the Khojas—the Husaynabad tomb of the first Aga Khan—it did not compete or conflict directly with the Konkani style of *muharram*. Nevertheless, it must be seen as distinct from other public observances.

Thus *muharram* could not function in the integrative fashion typical of many public ceremonials in India.[51] Indeed, the parading of *tabuts* was used as an occasion for expressing deeply felt and frequently violent competition between neighborhoods. (This was compounded by the practice of organizing huge neighborhood-based crowds, called *tolis*, to follow each *tabut*.) In both 1904 and 1908, for instance, *muharram* riots were prompted by the parading of one neighborhood's *tabut* in another, antagonistic *muhalla*. These neighborhood antagonisms were of long standing, based as much on economic rivalries as on competition between leaders or on regional and ethnic competition. The traditional lines of schism are further indicated by the development of these riots along sectarian (Sunni versus Shi'i) lines.

There was, then, by the early twentieth century, an established pattern among Muslims of competition and conflict surrounding the observance of *muharram*. This was exacerbated, first by changes occurring within the community—including challenges to the upper-level leadership and impulses toward religious reform—and, second, by a century-long tradition of interference by the British raj.

Muharram provides a useful focal point for us in analyzing changes within the community, especially the development of challenges to the upper-class Muslim leadership. The evolution of Bombay as an industrial center had led to a situation in which "natural leaders" were not necessarily those with the most influence on the large number of lower-class laborers residing in the city.[52] Instead, these leaders were interested in different kinds of public structures: those related to the raj and to citywide commercial and political worlds. There was no particular role for them to play in any of the more localized arenas in which Bombay identity was expressed, be it religious, neighborhood (including regional, ethnic, and caste), or class identity.

Within the neighborhoods, however, leadership was exercised as well by "an alternate structure of power ... derived from the strength of patronage, influence, or physical might ... [by] teashop owners, or controllers of gymnasiums and wrestlers, or jobbers in mills, or [the heads] of gangs of petty criminals or the out-of-work." [53] In disgust, the Bombay police commissioner attested to the influence of this alternate leadership, noting that the level of *muharram* violence in 1910 "would never have reached the pitch of insolence ... had not [the "Sunni hooligans"] felt assured that they had the support of the leading Sunnis residing in the *muhalla*s, many of whom, though comparatively wealthy, were almost illiterate and totally uncultured." [54] As noted earlier in discussing such groups in the United Provinces, lower castes/classes—such as butchers or weavers—generally had the strongest internal organizations and mechanisms for enforcing group solidarity. Edwardes complained of the (immigrant U.P.) Julahas in Bombay that they were "an extremely illiterate and fanatical population. When once an individual gets influence over them, they will do anything that he asks." [55] A recent study of the relationship between these alternative leaders and their supporters has characterized it as "the political culture of the working-class neighborhoods." [56]

The public observances of *muharram* offered an ideal opportunity for this alternate leadership both to exercise its control (by supporting its retainers with the funds collected—often extorted—from wealthy members of a *muhalla*) and to demonstrate its influence through the massing of huge numbers in the *toli*s (crowds that followed the *tabut*s). The *toli*, perhaps derived from Gujarati Hindu examples, was "originally a small band of youths who symbolically frightened evil spirits away from Husayn's tomb by mimic warfare and beating sticks." [57] By the end of the century, however,

> these *toli*s had been gradually allowed to assume a gigantic size, as for example that of the Julhai weavers of Ripon road, which comprised from two to three thousand men, all armed with *lathi*s [wooden clubs] tipped with brass or lead. Similarly [several other "notorious" *muhalla*s] could count upon turning out several thousand followers, armed with sticks and staves, who could be trusted to render a good account of themselves if there was a breach of the public peace.[58]

The *toli* crowd was "working class and lumpenproletariat in character, predominantly Muslim but with numerous, usually poor and low caste, Hindus." [59] For these followers, the *toli*s offered opportunities over several nights for unrestrained festival behavior, neighborhood chauvinism, and—if in protest the *tabut*s were "laid down" and leaders refused to parade them—free-for-all carousing through the streets and byways of the city. It is not surprising, then, that the public nature of *muharram* caused both the police and upper-class leaders to complain that "the lowest and most turbulent portion of the population was permitted to take charge of the central portion of the city" during *muharram*.[60] This underscores the huge gap between citywide and alternate leaders, a gap which had been bridged, at least partially, in the United Provinces by shared Islamic symbols.

There were other complaints as well. Some Sunni and Shi'i leaders argued uneasily that the predominant style of public procession had little to do with Islamic precepts or the original point of the Karbala story. For reformist Sunnis the proper observance was that which occurred within the mosques in evening *waaz*, during which "sermons and homilies" were presented drawing lessons from "Husayn's final sufferings," Shi'is had similar sessions called *majalis*, with an added ritual lamentation (*matam*) based on the style of self-punishment and self-mortification associated with Shi'i funerary rites. Upper-class Muslims seem to have attended only these evening congregations; until the turn of the century, lower-class participants may have gone first to the *waaz* and then to the *tabut* processions.[61] Reformist Muslim leaders eagerly substituted these nightly congregational meetings for popular processions: Sirdar Saheb Sulayman Cassum Haji Mitha in the *muharram*s after 1911 "led the way ... in popularizing the *waaz* ... and in spending upon them, and upon illuminations and charitable distribution of food to the poorer classes, the money which was formerly wasted on irreverent and turbulent processions."[62]

These British-fostered attempts to turn Muslim attention to localized nightly discourses were consistent with a larger effort to contain *muharram* observances within specific neighborhoods. Reorienting the *muharram* observances to neighborhood congregational gatherings also made it possible for reformers within each constituent community to emphasize the doctrinal and ritual characteristics that marked each one; no one could object, since these localized practices did not infringe on the rights or sensibilities of other groups.

Much more than reformist standards of Islam were at issue in this substitution, however. At its most basic, this turning inward to the neighborhood marked an emphasis on the personal, rather than the public, framework required by Muslims in their adherence to Islam. In this concentration on the personal sphere, and in the concomitant fragmentation among Bombay Muslims, lay the important differences between developments in the United Provinces and in Bombay.

It may have been easier to emphasize the personal over the public framework because the raj had always played such an obtrusive public role in Bombay religious life. There was nothing in Bombay to match the uneasy reticence of the United Provinces government, which for so many years had tried to confine itself to an evenhanded maintenance of "time-honored custom." [63] Instead, the Bombay city police frequently took a leading role, introducing many innovations into the observance, such as their 1836 denial to the "horse procession" of permission to circle the city, confining it to the *imambara*. Perhaps more startling was their action three years later in prohibiting Hindus from sponsoring *tabuts*, despite protests from some Muslims over this interference with "custom." [64]

The pace of interference stepped up after 1870, as did *muharram*-related violence. The connection between the two was not accidental; incidents of violence produced administratively imposed changes that led, in turn, to more violence. Indeed, violence was virtually assured, since the favored form of protest was to refuse to parade by "laying down" the *tabuts*; this let loose upon the city the large numbers of lower-class participants enrolled in the *tolis*. Even without this refusal, violence frequently resulted from the combination of intense neighborhood rivalries and differing *muharram* observances.

Riots in 1904 and 1908 set the stage for a new and final round of heavy-handed interference by the police. In both of these cases the rivalry between neighborhoods was augmented by Sunni attacks on Shi'is (particularly on Bohras of the Doctor Street area); the interneighborhood conflicts prompted complex alliances, animated by antagonisms previously established among the *muhallas*. "Critical in bringing the crisis [of 1908] to a head was the refusal of some tabutwallas to lift the tabuts on the ninth night, and their confrontation with police who insisted they do so. Large and angry crowds gathered, the police lost control of parts of the Muslim quarter and did not regain it until they fired upon the crowds." [65] By 1911 this inter-*muhalla* and sectarian violence provided the material for change to be instituted by the new and energetic police commissioner. In effecting a changed shape for *muharram*, the British permanently cut off access to an Islamic public structure for Bombay, ensuring that only the raj—and reference to its institutions—could hold the city together.

MUHARRAM, 1911

Police Commissioner S. M. Edwardes approached his first *muharram* in 1910 determined to exercise firm control. [66] In protest against his numerous stipulations on how they should be paraded, the *tabuts* were not lifted at all that year; Edwardes responded by banning the final immersion ceremony. Sensing that popular frustrations over the observance would explode in 1911, Edwardes issued even more stringent regulations, denying processions "access to the side-alleys and the crowded narrow streets of the Muslim quarter. He [also] forbade Hindus from joining any *toli* and threatened that if *muharram* was disturbed he would not permit any processions at all the following year." [67] In the event, he deputed the majority of the police force to form a cordon around the Bohra section of Doctor Street, denying entry to any *tabuts* wishing to parade there.

If the principle of official interference had long been established, this level was unprecedented. Edwardes himself was aware of the impact of his policies. Though he was largely responsible for remaking the city police along the lines of the London model and creating a new and efficient C.I.D. to gather information, he said of himself: "It is possible that long after the details of the reorganization of the police force have passed into oblivion, Mr. Edwardes' tenure of office will be remembered for the abolition of the dangerous and rowdy side of the annual *muharram* celebration." [68] Indeed, in the complex maneuverings carried on over the 1911 *tabut* processions, there is evidence that the alternate leaders perceived as their antagonists both the other *muhalla*-leaders and the raj, personified by Edwardes himself. In the riot report written after the 1911 *muharram*, Rangari *muhalla* (one of the most recalcitrant neighborhoods, and the chief Sunni antagonist of the Bohras) was characterized as having "passed the word around that though Doctor Street had been closed by the Police, it had found a new Doctor Street and had checkmated the Commissioner." [69] In the face of police interference, several neighborhoods united, hoping to resist police manipulation of the observances.

But this style of alliance guaranteed the end of the old *tabut*-centered *muharram*. Recalcitrance on the part of these leaders, their indecision, and sometimes their refusal to parade their *tabut*s, the insistence by some on using different routes: all led to a situation in which rioting was inevitable. Edwardes's use of the military to fire upon the most violent of the crowds gave him the final word. "Like Napoleon's famous 'whiff of grapeshot,' the firing of the Warwicks may be said to have blown the old *muharram* into the limbo of oblivion, its blackmail, its terrorism and its obscenities, ceased to exist and has not ... been revived." [70] This control was reinforced through widespread arrests of those "who were identified as having played a prominent part in the disturbances." No doubt those arrested suffered more from the questionable nature of their lifestyle than from eyewitness accounts of riot-related behavior. Edwardes observed with amusement that "the bad characters of a particular type, who signalize their mode of life by wearing their hair long in front and curled, have had their locks cropped by the barber for fear of being arrested by the police as participants in the *toli* disturbances." [71]

The commissioner quickly followed up his "whiff of grapeshot," framing new rules that required of *tabut*-license holders a humiliating security deposit for good behavior; completely remapped the processional routes for each *tabut*; and banned the *toli*s completely. By 1913 he had essentially banned the *tabut* processions as well: they might still be erected but could not be moved outside their *muhalla*s. The tenth day's "immersion" in the sea had now to be symbolically enacted within the neighborhood by sprinkling water. Though large numbers of *tabut*s continued to be built, these limitations on their use effectively defused their appeal for the alternate structure of leadership: no longer were they useful in representing either the leadership's influence or the neighborhood's prestige.

Without question, then, the public structure of religious observance in Bombay city had been completely undermined by the police. This was made possible in part because there were many within the Muslim population who encouraged the move. Masselos notes that "educated Muslims in general approved of the changes as increasingly did the traditional leaders.... Certainly the bulk of the Muslim press accepted [Edwardes's] views and characterized the processions as 'irreligious' and without any real Islamic precedent, whatever the force of local custom."[72] Reformist Muslims in particular could be pleased, for the banning of the *tabut* processions drew ever-larger numbers to the *waaz* and *waaz* congregational meetings.[73]

Thereafter, issues identified as Islamic were interpreted within each neighborhood in differing ways. The inherent fragmentation among Muslims was now expressed concretely. What had been the most visible public symbol of Islam in Bombay had been rendered less public, more localized. In this localization, the new form of *muharram* expressed the existing antagonisms between Muslim neighborhoods organized on ethnic, regional, linguistic, and sectarian lines within Indian Islam. The format focused on the personal practice of religion, thus accentuating those aspects that separated, rather than united, Muslims. It became impossible to abstract from Bombay city–style Islam unifying symbols on which to base a sense of community identity. That the interests and causes of many Muslim leaders coincided with those of the British administrators made it extremely difficult to define a Muslim community as one declining in status vis-à-vis the raj.

Even without a common identity, however, certain characteristics of Bombay Muslims continued to be significant in the ensuing decades. These included the facts that Muslims were still an important and sizable portion of a population much moved by the nationalist struggle, and that there was an alternate structure of leadership which, though excluded from active control of Islamic public structures, still had influence and power in the *muhalla*s. Indeed, by this time a distinctive pattern had emerged in Bombay. The citywide and alternate (or neighborhood) levels of leadership generally worked at cross-purposes, moved by different values and perceptions. Mass-based movements tended to emerge from a localized milieu, embraced by the neighborhood leadership. When such movements became large or pervasive enough to disturb the operations of citywide control networks, however, citywide leaders moved in to either circumscribe or co-opt the issues, often with the assistance of British administrators. We have seen how this worked before 1911 in the case of *muharram*; thereafter a similar pattern emerged concerning both the labor movement and Muslim separatism.

THE RIOTS OF 1929 AND THEIR AFTERMATH

The set of events most comparable to the Kanpur Riot of 1931 were clusters of riots in Bombay in February and April 1929. Like the Kanpur riot, these events were treated as a watershed by the committee of inquiry: the degree of Hindu-Muslim communal dissent was noteworthy, and the amount of damage and number of deaths were significantly higher than in previous events. At the time, observers saw the events of 1929 as anomalous. Instead, it was an important transition point from one style of community interaction to another.

The years between 1911 and 1929 had been eventful ones, though not in terms of the development of communalism or Muslim separatism. The Rowlatt Satyagraha of 1919, for instance, had commanded a relatively high level of participation throughout the Bombay population.[74] Similarly, the combined Khilafat/Non-Cooperation Movement in the early 1920s was widely supported in the city and did not lead (as it had in some parts of India) to increased tension between Hindus and Muslims.[75] Where Bombay began to differ from other areas with substantial Muslim populations (and particularly from the United Provinces) was in its reaction to the successor movements to Khilafat, especially Tanzim and Tabliqh.

Given the success at the neighborhood level of Tanzim in Kanpur, its lukewarm reception in Bombay *muhallas* is particularly noteworthy. Moreover, the neighborhood institutions that might, by this time, have been used to convey political or separatist propaganda—the now heavily attended *waaz* congregations that made up the *muharram* observances—seem to have been signally unsuccessful in this role.[76]

Contemporary explanations advanced for the lack of development of communalism, for instance by the committee of inquiry convened after the second set of riots in April, concentrated on the lack of historical precedent in Bombay City.

> In respect of the Hindu-Muslim tension a considerable amount of evidence has been given on both sides. It may be hoped that this evidence has helped to "clear the air," and to show both communities that there is a good deal to be said on the other side.... The evidence goes to show that [such tension] does not normally exist here to any appreciable extent ... so far as there is any in Bombay, [it] is not a repercussion of tension outside Bombay.... ["We are disposed to agree" with the contention] that though in other parts of India the Arya Samaj and Maha-sabha movements may be ultra-communal, this is not so in Bombay city, where the movements are under the control of moderate leaders.... The tension is also attributed to the Shuddhi, Sangathan, Tanzim and Tabliqh movements, to [the playing of] music before mosques and to parading cows intended for sacrifice. This latter reason however has not arisen in Bombay. The other movements also have only an inappreciable effect in Bombay.[77]

Communally inspired movements, then, had not received noteworthy levels of support in Bombay; what activity did occur was controlled by a "moderate leadership." Indeed, the style of citywide political leadership that had evolved was predominantly nationalist,[78] composed of such industrialist and mercantile leaders as those who were victorious in 1911. Given the turbulent immigrant millworking population which predominated in the city, it is not surprising that these moderate leaders were not drawn to mass-based movements, particularly those appealing to neighborhood leadership.

What, then, did prompt the riots in 1929? The committee answered firmly: "the recent riots were not primarily communal. They were in our opinion primarily communist vs. Pathan, and only developed later into communal riots."[79] In the parlance of the day, "communist" meant those involved in the burgeoning labor movement, while "Pathans" had functioned as strikebreakers.

The February riots had been prompted by a strike in the oil installations of Bombay city. Strikers were replaced by "new men especially Pathans who couldn't be intimidated," and the result was serious clashes between the Pathans and the strikers, which then spread to the mills: "Millworkers agreed to support the strikers [and the protest] turned into a Pathan-hunt."[80] Referring primarily to those from the Northwest Frontier and beyond, "Pathan" conveyed a type of man volatile and physically powerful, quick to defend his honor. In Bombay he was also often perceived as a moneylender ("who is known to be taking 150% or more, is not really affected by [debtor-protection] acts, as he usually does not resort to the Courts, but uses a big stick to recover his dues"),[81] and, as we have seen, as a strikebreaker.

Similar causes had carried over to the April riots. To a now general communal mistrust was added the problem that a second mill strike was observed primarily by Hindu millworkers and not by the Muslims employed there.

The role played by labor strikes was extremely central to the Bombay of the 1920s. The labor movement had been singularly successful among the large population of immigrant poor working in the city's mills. Critical to its success was the support of many of the alternate leaders, especially the jobbers who acted as middlemen in recruitment and negotiation between the immigrant workers and the millowners. For them, and probably for many of the workers as well, it mattered little whether the leaders and organizations agitating on their behalf were "Nationalist" (some followed the ostensible guidance of the Congress Party) or "Communist."

What did matter was the economic dislocation produced in the aftermath of World War I. The mills had done well during the war, and so had millworkers. But the inefficiencies in mill production, absorbed during these good times, had to be removed during the economic downturn of the 1920s. The millowners' first solution—to reduce wages radically—prompted a series of strikes in the early 1920s. Their second solution—to introduce job-related efficiency measures—led to widespread layoffs and more strikes. A general strike, staged in 1928, lasted six months and was only called off pending a final settlement to be based on the findings of a government-appointed committee. One of the results of this last strike was to swell the membership ranks of the Girni Kamgar (Labor) Union from 324 to 54,000. Another was to attract at least the nominal support of the workers for the Communist movement.

The Royal Commission on Labor, reporting on labor conditions in India at the time, stated that the absence of a strong organization of cotton mill workers, combined with the mood generated by prolonged strike, allowed a few communist leaders "by an intense effort to capture the imagination of the workers and eventually to sweep over 50,000 of them into a communist organization." In Bombay, communist influence also spread among municipal, oil installation, transport and dock workers. As a result of the influx of membership in the communist dominated unions, trade-union membership in Bombay increased seventy percent in the four-month period preceding December 1, 1928.[82]

By 1929, then, Bombay workers were militant and at least nominally radicalized. Under these circumstances the influence of the moderate, citywide style of leadership was bound to be limited and that of the neighborhood-focused alternate leadership enhanced. Once again, there was a kind of "public structure" in which the alternate leaders had complete legitimacy and a recognized role. In this case, however, the focal point of these energies was neither the neighborhood nor communal identity, but class interests.

This was not to last. Two separate forces sounded the death knell of the labor movement in Bombay, as elsewhere in India. The first was the arrest and conviction of most of the top Communist/labor movement leaders in the Meerut Conspiracy Case of 1929; the second was the reshaping of Bombay unrest into a communal form. Crucial to this process was the interplay between externally created values and expectations (and the symbolic expression of these), and the circumstances internal to Bombay. This second process is significant enough to demand more attention.

Widespread antipathy to "Pathans" initiated much of the second development. They were viewed as aliens because of their moneylending and strike-breaking activity, as had been expressed before the February riots in widespread rumors sweeping Bombay that "Pathans" were kidnapping children for use in sacrifices. Their own violent codes of honor did not help their cause once they had been attacked. The police surgeon, swept along in one of their avenging missions, noted: "I would say that the body of Pathans who I accompanied ... could not be classed as hooligans. They were a grim, determined crowd, lusting for blood to avenge their dead. They discussed matters with me in a most friendly manner, saying they were going to even matters up a bit. As they could find or catch no Hindus in the streets, they broke in the shop fronts methodically, as they proceeded along."[83]

These events were reinterpreted, for Muslims outside Bombay, in terms of the martyrdom motif so much elaborated in the north. This prompted Bombay Muslims to look differently at their experiences, developing a new sensitivity to "slights" and "insults" to their religion. Thus the fact that the Pathans were Muslims who had been victims of attacks by Hindu workers attracted all India Muslim leaders to their cause. Many of the witnesses before the commission of inquiry considered highly inflammatory the "interviews" given by the nationally influential brothers Shaukat and Muhammad 'Ali as they entered the hospital to check on riot victims.

> Asked what he thought bout the present situation Mohamed Ali excitedly exclaimed, "What are the Police and the Government doing? What are the newly elected members of the Corporation and the leaders of the Youth Movement doing? ... [He then made a vehement attack on the labor leaders, with endorsements from his brothers.] ... It is now more than a week that this rumor has been going around and no leader has yet denied it. If Miss Mayo came to India and wrote a chapter about children being kidnapped for sacrificial purposes would we not deny it as a wicked libel? Why do the leaders not deny this wicked libel?" Is it likely that the situation will develop into a Hindu-Muslim conflict seeing that most of the victims are Muslims? he was asked. "Of course it will" he said. [Here Shaukat 'Ali interjected:] "I am going to organise the Muslims for purposes of self-defense."[84]

Though Muhammad 'Ali "specially asked" the reporter not to publish the interview and proved very active in helping to quell the disturbances, the damage was done when this exchange was printed in the principal newspaper, the *Times of India*. As in the Kanpur mosque affair, it was possible—particularly outside Bombay—to present the situation as an attack on Muslims. The irony is that in Bombay there were certainly more Muslims to be counted among the millworkers affected by the strike than among the Pathans brought in as strikebreakers. Once a public cause had been made of the attacks, however, this was of little import. Certainly once the riots had turned from strike-oriented to communal attacks, religion proved of more significance than occupation.

This new communal orientation was attested to by the pattern of rioting in the April outbursts. To begin with, Muslim workers tended not to honor the strike called that month and were attacked for this reason. Reflecting the impact of an externally created language of martyrdom, Muslims throughout the city protested against actions they now saw as insulting. As was noted by the commission, Muslims were on the "lookout," taking offense on occasions not previously perceived as objectionable. The playing of music before mosques during Hindu processions, for instance, suddenly became a visible gauge of this new sensitivity. Administrators were puzzled, for the rules governing such occasions had been effective since 1902; now outbursts testified to the new inclination among Muslims to view themselves as an embattled minority community.

Nevertheless, though communal sensitivity had been raised, it was impossible in the context of fragmented Bombay to express it through a shared symbolic vocabulary. The pattern of outbursts suggests this: the attacks were sporadic and isolated, limited to a particular Muslim neighborhood or group. No coherent worldview or set of symbolic values connected the incidences of violence. With no prior experiences to build on, the riots of 1929 were just what the commission said they were: an anomaly in a city with no established tradition of Muslim separatism or pronounced communal bitterness.

However, after 1929 Bombay Muslims would never again return to the pattern of relationships that had earlier prevailed. The following decade brought to Bombay, as to many other cities, a new way of reckoning and expressing an identity rooted in an Islamic idiom. What had seemed an anomaly in 1929 became a pronounced and persistent perception of identity in the years following. Indeed, after three months of rioting in 1932, the commissioner of police commented that "the mutual feelings of suspicion and distrust are more bitter today than at any time in my 30 years' service."[85] Of necessity, the vocabulary expressing this identity had to be brought from outside Bombay, where longer and more integrative experiences had created and refined it. Yet it is not explanation enough to attribute the emerging Muslim separatism of Bombay to experiences occurring outside the city.

On the contrary, the events of 1929 are useful precisely because they point to plausible reasons why these outside influences should have taken hold in Bombay. The attenuation of the labor movement at this point proved crucial to the process of defining community identity, for it effectively removed common class-oriented experiences in the mills as a basis for formulating definitions of identity, but not before it had demonstrated the effectiveness of collective action.

Leadership was affected as well. After prosecution stemming from the Meerut Conspiracy Case, and related repressive activities by the government, leadership of any existing mass-based movements had to go by default to the more moderate, citywide style of leader who had so often prevailed in Bombay in the past. Where, then, were the alternate leaders to find an outlet for the exercise of their influence? Though evidence is scanty, it can be plausibly argued that the movement for Muslim separatism provided an almost ideal opportunity for such alternate leaders. The appeals of the movement had often proved most effective at the neighborhood level.[86] And the legitimacy of a subcontinentwide movement could be appropriated by these leaders, bypassing the existing moderate leadership.

We may infer the appeal and effectiveness of such a movement by using the incidences of collective (often violent) activity as indicators of mass support. In the 1920s these had preeminently expressed support for the labor movement; widespread strikes and related violence had occurred in 1920, 1921, 1925, continuously for six months in 1928, and twice in 1929.[87] By contrast, the significant incidents involving mass violence during 1932, 1933, 1936, 1937, and 1938 were all related to conflict between those maintaining communal identities and boundaries.[88] On each of these latter occasions the symbols invoked were those which—though previously little attended to in Bombay—had been treated elsewhere in India as important and evocative, such as mosques and their surrounding sacred space, cows, and processional music.

CONCLUSION

This new emphasis on Islamic symbols is noteworthy. It did not emerge naturally from the reservoir of common Islamic experiences in Bombay, for, as we have seen, these were isolated within the boundaries of specific subsets of Muslims; even reformist influences were internally focused and concentrated more on the personal practice of religion than on the public structure required to be a Muslim. Instead, modern communications and publicity in a period of high sensitivity to nationalist and religious issues had provided access to those with a tradition of shared Islamic activism developed elsewhere. In this respect, at least, Muslim separatism in Bombay was greatly dependent on outside influence and was very much a product of the highly charged atmosphere of the 1930s.

But only changes within the city itself could have rendered Bombay Muslims receptive to this Islamic vocabulary. Once again, it was the juxtaposition of a felt need for a public structure (felt, this time, by the alternate leadership and the lower-class Muslims of Bombay) and the lack of access to it that made Bombay Muslims receptive.

By the 1930s, then, the fragmented and localized perceptions of Muslims in Bombay had been harnessed to a subcontinentwide movement to protect Muslim interests. Violence, previously used to protect neighborhood interests or to make class-oriented protests, now expressed the existence of a community. Though antithetical in their initial experiences, Muslims of Bombay and Kanpur came to share an important new identity: they were all Muslims, a minority in the Indian subcontinent, suffering from the lack of a public structure in which to practice Islam.

Arguably it was the simultaneous success of "public" activities in the realms of collective violence and public ceremonials and failure to find an adequate political structure to express the resulting community identity that led eventually to the demand for Pakistan. In this respect the experiences of Muslims in Kanpur and Bombay end by being similar. Nevertheless, the very substantial differences in timing and context make even the demand for Pakistan distinctive in each place: by 1935, for instance, advocates of Muslim separatism in the United Provinces became increasingly preoccupied with the issue of Pakistan, while this did not appear as a plausible solution to Bombay Muslims until early in the 1940s. Moreover, the legacy of these experiences has figured very differently in the two places since independence and partition: while in the United Provinces the problems created by Hindu-Muslim and Sunni-Shi'i conflict continue to erupt periodically, the current problems in Bombay have much more to do with these regional, linguistic, class, and ethnic identities that had proved so problematic before Muslim separatism was embraced there.

NOTES

1. I would like to thank David Gilmartin, Barbara Daly Metcalf, Jim Masselos, and, above all, Ira Lapidus for very helpful comments on earlier drafts of this chapter.

2. Quoted in P. Hardy, *The Muslims of British India* (Cambridge, England: Cambridge University Press, 1972), p. 218.

3. This argues directly against the usual position taken; see, for instance, Francis Robinson, "Islam and Muslim Separatism," in *Political Identity in South Asia*, ed. David Taylor and Malcolm Yapp (London: Curzon Press, 1979), pp. 78–112.

4. Both these areas were Muslim "minority" areas; the problems of mobilization among Muslims in areas where they constituted the majority of the population are somewhat different. For a discussion of these areas, see David Gilmartin, "Tribe, Land and Religion in the Punjab: Muslim Politics and the Making of Pakistan," Ph.D. dissertation, University of California at Berkeley, 1979; and Rafiuddin Ahmad, *The Bengal Muslims 1871–1906* (Delhi: Oxford University Press, 1981).

5. Cf. Imtiaz Ahmad, "Caste and Kinship in a Muslim Village of Eastern Uttar Pradesh," in *Family, Kinship and Marriage among Muslims in India*, ed. Imtiaz Ahmad (Delhi: Manohar, 1976), pp. 319–46.

6. Ostensibly a Shi'i observance, *muhurram* was widely popular, particularly in the nineteenth century, among many urban Muslim populations.

7. For a more detailed discussion of this localized activity and the styles of leadership associated with it, see my "Religious Rites and Riots: From Community Identity to Communalism in North India, 1870–1940," Ph.D. dissertation, University of California at Berkeley, 1980.

8. *'Idgas* are enclosed public grounds used for sacrifices and other observances for 'Id celebrations.

9. See Barbara D. Metcalf, *Islamic Revival in British India: Deoband 1860–1900* (Princeton: Princeton University Press, 1982), for a detailed discussion of these issues.

10. Ibid.

11. India Office Records (hereafter abbreviated as IOR), L/P and J/7/775 for 1931, "Evidence on the Cawnpore Riot of 1931."

12. Paul R. Brass, *Factional Politics in an Indian State* (Berkeley and Los Angeles: University of California Press, 1965).

13. Narrative based on "Minute by the Lt. Governor [Meston] on the Cawnpore Mosque and Riot," dated 21 August 1913. The account is corroborated (except as noted) by stories in the vernacular press in 1912 and 1913: see United Provinces Government, *Selections from the Vernacular Press* (hereafter *SVN*) (Allahabad: U. P. Gov't Press) volumes for those years. For a fuller analysis of this event, see my "Religious Rites and Riots."

14. Though this information was refused to them, they must have discovered at least some of the culprits. One told Meston that "he dared hardly stir out of his house on account of the fury of his co-religionists" ("Minute," p. 13).

15. *Muslim Gazette*, 6 August 1913, in *SVN* 1913.

16. The province of Bengal had originally been divided, the government claimed, to provide Muslims with more administrative jobs. During the six years' division, however, Hindu activists and terrorists made the price of government consideration of Muslim sensitivities too high. When the British reversed their decision, Muslims saw it as a public statement that their previous policy of government support did not pay.

17. *Muslim Gazette*, 2 June 1913, in *SVN* 1913.

18. List of signatories for "Address by Muhammadan Delegation and Lt. Governor's Reply" (n.d.), Appendix 11 to "Minute," p. 4. Biographical information on signatories from F. C. R. Robinson, *Separatism among Indian Muslims* (Cambridge, England: Cambridge University Press, 1974).

19. For a more detailed discussion of this development, see my "Religious Rites and Riots."

20. This riot is extraordinarily well documented. A government-appointed commission of inquiry was ordered on 13 April 1931, and richly detailed evidence filling over 600 pages was collected. It is available in IOR, L/P and J/7/775 for 1931. The official report published by the commission (which does not, in fact, adequately reflect the insights provided by the evidence) was printed as Command Paper 3891, British Parliamentary Papers, 1930–31, vol. 12, pp. 3–66, "Report of the Commission of Inquiry and Resolution of the Government of U.P." (hereafter BPP). Congress conducted its own investigation and then issued a massive report which attempted to put this riot in a general historical context. This has been recently edited and published, see N. Gerald Barrier, ed., *Roots of Communal Politics* (Columbia, Missouri: South Asia Books, n.d.). Because the congress did not identify any of its witnesses, I have instead used the testimony to the commission to express the general complaints, which the congress committee also heard.

21. That was the offical death count. Even the government report admits that probably 2,000 more people were killed (BPP, p. 4).

22. See "Evidence" for the various positions held by those testifying.

23. Brass, *Factional Politics*, chapter 3.

24. "Evidence," testimony of Sabu Narain Nigam on 22 April 1931, pp. 89–93; testimony of L. Diwan Chand, p. 254. *Shuddhi* was a conversion/purification movement; *Sangathan* involved community defense training.

25. See Brass, *Factional Politics*, chapter 3, for a detailed discussion of this factionalism, which dictated power alignments in Kanpur for at least forty years. Both of the faction leaders discussed by Brass were politically active in 1931: see discussions of the Municipal board activities in "Evidence."

26. Written statement of Daya Narain Niyam, 25 April 1931: "Evidence," p. 242.

27. See, for instance, testimony by Syed Zakir Ali, 4 May 1931: "Evidence," p. 427.

28. See machinations among Municipal Board members, in ibid., pp. 303–13: "Proceedings of the 37th Meeting of the Cawnpore Municipal Board, 5 March 1930."

29. Ibid., p. 592. For instance, between 1926 and 1929 only six of fifty-three municipal clerk positions were filled by Muslims.

30. For a more detailed discussion of these changes, see my "Religious Rites and Riots."

31. "Evidence," p. 92.

32. Ibid., p. 258.

33. Gyanendra Pandey, *The Ascendancy of the Congress in Uttar Pradesh, 1926–34* (Delhi: Oxford University Press, 1978), p. 81.

34. "Evidence," p. 92.

35. Ibid., p. 105, testimony of Khaliluddin.

36. Ibid., p. 76.

37. Ibid., p. 116.

38. Ibid., p. 249, statement of L. Diwan Chand, who translated the verses.

39. Ibid., pp. 390–91, statement of Azizuddin in court of Additional Sessions judge, included in the collection of evidence.

40. Ibid., pp. 589–95, statement of H. H. Hosain, MLC, representative to the first Round Table Conference.

41. This evidence was tendered not to the commission, but for a court case prosecuted earlier: ibid., pp. 390–91.

42. "Evidence," p. 241.

43. David Gilmartin, "Customary Law and Shariat in British Punjab," in Katherine Ewing, ed., *Shariat and Alternative Codes of Behavior in South Asian Islam* (Berkeley and Los Angeles: University of California Press, forthcoming).

44. This discussion of Bombay, unlike that of U.P., is based in large part on secondary sources. Though I have analyzed a number of primary documents—particularly riot reports—for Bombay and nearby cities in the nineteenth and twentieth centuries, I have not studied as closely as I have

for the United Provinces the general historical context of the area. Thus there are limitations in the conclusions put forward here. The nineteenth century is less problematical, as the work of Masselos is particularly helpful and apt. Unfortunately the only studies made of the city for the following decades have been preoccupied with nationalist political history. It has therefore been necessary rather sketchily to infer conclusions for the period after 1920.

45. Jim Masselos, *Nationalism on the Indian Subcontinent: An Introductory History* (Melbourne: Thomas Nelson, 1972), pp. 30–31.

46. This dropped to 15 percent after independence: Jim Masselos, "Change and Custom—The Format of the Bombay Mohurram during the Nineteenth and Twentieth Centuries," draft paper, spring 1982, p. 4. This article has recently been published as "Change and Custom in the Format of the Bombay Mohurrad," *South Asia* n.s. 5, no. 2 (1982): 47–67. (Page numbers refer to draft version.)

47. See Masselos, "Power in the Bombay 'Mohalla,'" *South Asia* 6 (1976): 76–95.

48. For a fascinating study of the evolution of *muharram* over more than one hundred years, see Masselos, "Change and Custom."

49. Based on ibid.

50. Ibid., p. 6.

51. For a detailed discussion of this function, see chapter three of my "Religious Rites and Riots."

52. The phrase "natural leaders" was used frequently by British administrators to refer to those men—such as bankers and mill owners—who exercised citywide authority based on their cultural, religious, and economic preeminence.

53. Masselos, "Change and Custom," pp. 23–24. For a more detailed discussion of this leadership struggle, see his "Power in the Bombay 'Mohalla.'" The terms *citywide* and *alternate* leadership are used hereafter to remind the reader of the source of authority legitimating each level of leadership.

54. S. M. Edwardes, *The Bombay City Police: A Historical Sketch, 1672–1916* (London: Oxford University Press, 1923). Edwardes was commissioner of police there from 1909 to 1916.

55. "Report on the Final Moharram Riot of 1911 and the Bombay Government's Order Thereon," included as an appendix to *Bombay City Police.*

56. Raj Chandavarkar, "Workers' Politics and the Mill in Bombay Between the Wars," *Modern Asian Studies* 15 (1981): 603–47.

57. Masselos, "Change and Custom," p. 23.

58. Edwardes, *Bombay City Police*, p. 182.

59. Masselos, "Change and Custom," p. 23; cf. sources listed in n. 70 there.

60. Masselos, "Change and Custom," p. 187. See Chandavarkar, "Workers' Politics," p. 606, on the public quality of neighborhood social life.

61. Masselos, "Change and Custom," pp. 20–21.

62. Edwardes, *Bombay City Police*, p. 186.

63. For a full discussion of the provincial government's changing role and attitudes in the United Provinces, see chapter two of my "Religious Rites and Riots."

64. Masselos, "Change and Custom," p. 22. Hindus still participated in Muharram informally, joining in the crowds surrounding the *tolis* and having their children dress up and beg from door to door.

65. Ibid., p. 25.

66. In fact he had experienced numerous Bombay city *muharram* observances in other official capacities. He was the first Indian Civil Service officer to be made commissioner of police; his predecessors had all been members of the police force. Nevertheless, he began with a solid understanding of the department, as he had been one of the three-member review commission that had designed the police reorganization plan in the city.

67. Masselos, "Change and Custom," pp. 25–26.

68. Edwardes, *Bombay City Police*, p. 181.

69. "Report on the Final Moharram," included as appendix in ibid., p. 200.

70. Ibid., p. 186.

71. "Report," in ibid., p. 210.

72. Masselos, "Change and Custom," p. 28.

73. Edwardes, *Bombay City Police*, p. 187, and sources cited in Masselos, "Change and Custom," n. 83, referring to the nightly gatherings in 1916, 1924, and 1926.

74. Ravindar Kumar, ed., *Essays on Gandhian Politics: The Rowlatt Satyagraha of 1919* (Oxford, 1971).

75. An exception may have been the Daudi Bohra population. See their 1921 petition to the Prince of Wales: IOR, L/P and J/6/1730.

76. See Masselos, "Change and Custom," p. 29.

77. Paragraphs 44, 46, 49 (pp. 17–19) of "Report of Bombay Riots Enquiry Committee," dated September 1929: IOR, L/P and J/1974, file 3899 for 1929.

78. See work in progress by K. E. Dickson on Bombay city businessmen; and Masselos, "Some Aspects of Bombay City Politics in 1919," in Kumar, ed., *Essays on Gandhian Politics*.

79. Paragraph 44 of "Report of Bombay Riots."

80. IOR, L/P and J/1974, file 3899 for 1929, paragraphs 13 and 14, p. 4.

81. Ibid., paragraph 86, p. 31.

82. J. P. Haithcox, *Communism and Nationalism in India* (Princeton: Princeton University Press, 1971), p. 105. See also Chandavarkar, "Workers' Politics."

83. IOR, L/P and J/1974, file 3899 for 1929, paragraph 21, p. 7.

84. Ibid., paragraph 41, pp. 15–16.

85. IOR, L/P and J/7, file 371 of 1932: copy of confidential letter to the secretary to the government of Bombay, dated 29 September 1932.

86. See, for instance, the argument that the pattern of rioting in 1936 followed lines established in the preceding years of the decade, concentrating in mixed neighborhoods of Hindus and Muslims: Richard Lambert, "Hindu-Muslim Riots," (Ph.D. dissertation, University of Pennsylvania, 1951, pp. 112–14. We may also assume, as in the past, that when the authorities talked about the pronounced participation of "hooligans," they were referring both to "bad characters" (*badmashes*) and to those recruited by the alternate structure of leadership within the neighborhoods: IOR, L/P and J/7, file 1132 for 1936.

87. Haithcox, *Communism*, p. 100.

88. See riot reports for each of these years in IOR, L/P and J/7 series. As Masselos notes in a personal communication, there *were* riots on religious issues earlier than this, but "the riots were not large, and *muharram*—and all that implies—were the dominant element in Bombay and amongst Muslims."

EIGHT

The Shahidganj Mosque Incident: A Prelude to Pakistan

David Gilmartin

Musulmans never hesitate to make any sacrifice in the path of preserving the emblems of religion and God—MAULANA ZAFAR 'ALI

The power of Islamic symbols to mobilize Indian Muslims in the twentieth century was strikingly demonstrated by the outbreak of an agitation in 1935 to defend an obscure mosque located outside the walls of the old city of Lahore.[1] In the face of the mosque's threatened destruction, Muslims of Lahore rallied, through the press and the courts, through public demonstrations, and ultimately through threatened civil disobedience, to protect the mosque from its enemies. But although the mosque—appropriately named Shahidganj, "treasure of martyrs"—became a symbol of the unity and commitment of an "Islamic community" in Lahore and in the Punjab, the course of the agitation demonstrated the dilemmas faced by Muslims who attempted to define the political existence of an Islamic community within the context of colonial rule.

The search for a political definition of *Islamic community* in British India has been the subject of a good deal of recent scholarly attention. Scholars such as David Lelyveld in his history of Aligarh College,[2] Barbara Metcalf in her study of the *madrasa* at Deoband,[3] and Gail Minault in her account of the Indian Khilafat movement,[4] have stressed the roles of education and of symbols in defining the continuing presence of an Islamic community in colonial India. Others have attempted to analyze the structure of politics among Muslims within the British colonial situation. But the difficulties in analyzing the relationship between politics and religion in British India remain considerable.

The research for this paper was conducted with the assistance of a Fulbright-Hays grant for research in Pakistan and India. I would like to thank the staffs of the Punjab Civil Secretariat Archives in Lahore, Pakistan, and the National Archives of India, New Delhi, for allowing me access to their files. I would also like to thank Sandria Freitag for her many suggestions and ideas on the development of community identity in north India, without which it would have been very difficult for me to write this paper.

These difficulties are evident in a recent scholarly exchange between Paul Brass and Francis Robinson. In analyzing the political role of Islamic symbols in British India, Brass has argued that one must first understand the structural position of the Muslim elites who made use of them. In Brass's view, different Islamic symbols were used by different Muslim elites—by landlords, government servants, ulama, and politicians—in order to enhance their own fortunes in Indian politics. Brass does not deny that these elites were "limited" and "constrained" by the cultures of the groups they represented, but he argues that it was the process of "symbol selection and symbol manipulation" that defined for these leaders the political shape of the community.[5] Francis Robinson has in turn argued that such a view fails to take account of the emotive power of the Islamic tradition itself—a tradition which by the nineteenth and twentieth centuries had deeply influenced Muslim masses and elites alike. The charisma of the "ideal religio-political community," Robinson argues, defined in the classical Muslim tradition, exercised a powerful influence not only in guiding the political positions taken by nearly all Muslim elites, but also in shaping the development of Muslim separatist politics in the twentieth century.[6]

Neither of these views can be ignored in analyzing a movement such as the agitation in defense of the Shahidganj mosque. On must begin an account of the Shahidganj agitation by acknowledging the pervasive power of the classical tradition of Islamic community among Lahore's Muslims, for the role of the Shahidganj mosque as a political symbol is inexplicable except in this context. But to acknowledge this is only to begin to understand the agitation. As Brass argues, different groups not only had different definitions of the political meaning of *Islamic community* but, at times, different definitions of *politics* and of *Islam* as well. An understanding of the political context in which the agitation occurred is thus critical for an understanding of the mosque's symbolic significance.

In this paper I will attempt to demonstrate how certain leaders of Lahore focused their attention on the defense of a mosque in the 1930s in an attempt to reconcile their ideas about the symbolic meaning of Islamic community with the political realities they were facing. It was this that gave the Shahidganj agitation significance. But the ultimate failure of the Shahidganj mosque agitation also dramatized the severe problems facing Punjabi Muslims in the search for an effective symbolic and political definition of Islamic community in colonial India. The failure of the agitation pointed the way for many Punjabi Muslims toward ultimate support of another, more powerful political symbol of Islamic community—the concept of an independent Islamic state.

LAHORE AND THE SHAHIDGANJ MOSQUE

The Shahidganj mosque itself was the product of an era when Muslims ruled in Lahore. The mosque had been constructed during the first half of the eigh-

teenth century, during a period when Lahore was the provincial capital of the
Punjab under the Mughals and was a center of Muslim culture and administration. As a result of bitter conflict among Mughals, Afghans, and Sikhs during
the eighteenth century, however, Lahore had suffered repeated occupations
and eventually fell into Sikh hands. As a result of these conflicts, the Shahidganj
site came to have important symbolic associations. For the Sikhs, the site had
gained notoriety in the mid-eighteenth century as the scene of brutal executions
conducted by the Mughal governor, and it was thus for them associated with
martyrs for their faith—hence the name Shahidganj. When a Sikh army
occupied the city in 1762, the mosque was seized and closed off permanently to
Muslim prayer—a situation which remained unchanged in the nineteenth
century even after the arrival of the British.[7]

For many Muslims, the period after the collapse of Mughal authority had
been a difficult one. Under Sikh rule, despite Maharaja Ranjit Singh's continued holding of court in the city, Lahore had in many respects been surpassed
in importance by the nearby city of Amritsar, which was the religious capital of
the Sikhs and the most important commercial center of the Punjab. The first
census after the British occupation of the Punjab showed that Lahore's population had dropped to fewer than 100,000 persons, three-quarters the population
of Amritsar. Many of its leading Muslim families had fallen on very hard times.
But with the British annexation of the Punjab in 1849 and the reestablishment
of Lahore as provincial capital within a new empire, the fortunes of the city
began to revive. As a center of administration, culture, and education, Lahore
grew rapidly under the British, attaining by 1931 a population of 430,000,
almost double that of Amritsar. In part this reflected the increasing importance
of the city as an agricultural market and rail center, but much of this growth
came in the new sections of Lahore outside the city walls, which were dominated by the educated elites associated with the new colonial administration.[8]

For Lahore's Muslims, the growth of these elites had proved a mixed
blessing. Though Muslims made up about 58 percent of the population of the
city in 1931—a percentage comparable to their proportion in the population of
Punjab as a whole—they comprised only a relatively small part of the educated
elite associated culturally with the new imperial power. They were also sparsely
represented among the new, largely Hindu, financial and professional elites
who had taken advantage of the opportunities offered by colonial rule. With
little modern industrial development in the city aside from the big Northwestern Railway workshops at Mughalpura, the Muslims of Lahore were
concentrated in traditional manual and commercial occupations, their numbers swollen to a degree by agriculturalists from the surrounding, predominantly Muslim countryside.[9]

The structure of Muslim leadership in these circumstances was shaped
strongly by the system of administration that the British had established in the
Punjab as a whole. In the rural areas, where the political foundations of colonial

power lay, the British had developed in the second half of the nineteenth century an administration that was tied to the power of landed, often tribally based intermediaries, who had thrown their support to the British early on in return for important places in the colonial administration. With relatively weak representation among the educated elite in the city, political leadership among Muslims in Lahore also tended to be dominated by landed "notables." Families such as the Qazilbash Nawabs, an old Shi'i family with substantial property in Lahore Tehsil and in the United Provinces, were favored recipients of British patronage in the nineteenth century.[10] Politically more important in the twentieth century were many of the landed families of Lahore's suburbs— Baghbanpura, Mughalpura, Mianmir, Mozang—who in the nineteenth century under British patronage had "consolidated their social and political position even as their land gradually became more urbanized,"[11] and who had thus emerged in the twentieth century with growing political influence. Using the ties of *biradari* (kin group) and faction to cement links with Muslim *muhalla* leaders in other parts of the city, some of these men emerged among the city's most powerful bosses (*rais*). Some also played important roles in commerce and began, in the twentieth century, to enter the new professions.[12]

The influence of such urban *rais* was enhanced by their role in the structure of religious organization in colonial Lahore. The role of Muslim notables in the structure of Lahore's religious organization had, in fact, long been institutionalized in the support provided to mosques and shrines through endowments (*waqf*) which were administered by Mirza Sir Zafir 'Ali, scion of an old Mughal family and *mutawalli* of the important Wazir Khan mosque. With the establishment of colonial control, the British had attempted to bolster this pattern of influence by encouraging the formation of a committee of Muslim notables to administer the city's most important mosque, the Badshahi mosque of the Emperor Aurangzeb, which had fallen into the hands of the British after the annexation of the city. Formed in 1869 under the leadership of a former British Tehsildar, Khan Barkat 'Ali Khan, the Anjuman Islamia eventually assumed control of several other important mosques in Lahore as well.[13] Though professing a commitment to the promotion of Muslim culture and to the administration of these mosques in the name of the "community," the Anjuman Islamia in fact reflected the emerging structure of British authority among the Muslim *rais* of the city. It sought both to encourage loyalty to the administration and to carry the views of the "Muslim community" to the government.[14]

This structure of authority provided the backdrop for the emergence of conflict in the twentieth century over control of the Shahidganj mosque, which remained in the hands of the Sikhs. Though a Muslim claiming hereditary rights as a descendant of the *mutawallis* of the mosque had filed a personal appeal for the return of the mosque in the 1850s,[15] the first serious claim for control of the Shahidganj mosque on behalf of the "Muslim community" was lodged by the Anjuman Islamia in the 1920s. Ironically, this claim was lodged in a context that called into question not only the right of the Sikhs to control the site but also the political foundations of the authority of the Anjuman Islamia itself. The appeal of the Anjuman was precipitated by passage in the Punjab legislature in the 1920s of an act that threatened to revolutionize the administration of religious places in the Punjab. After a long and bitter struggle among the Sikhs, the passage of the Sikh Gurdwaras and Shrines Act of 1925 had officially removed Sikh *gurdwaras* (temples) from the control of hereditary pro-British custodians and placed them under the control of popularly elected Sikh committees—an effort which had at first been strongly resisted by the British. This act had grown out of the concerns of Sikh leaders to develop an institutionalized popular Sikh identity in British Punjab that was independent of the structure of power under the colonial regime.[16] Though the act applied only to the Sikhs, it had important implications for the organization of religious authority within all the Punjab's religious communities. In fact, although it provided the Anjuman Islamia with an opening to press for the return of the Shahidganj mosque, it had also raised important questions about the character of community leadership, not only among the Sikhs but among Muslims as well.

For the Anjuman Islamia, the most critical feature of the act in the short run was its establishment of a Gurdwaras Tribunal which was now given the power to rule on the validity of Sikh property claims. In the case of the Shahidganj mosque, the Anjuman entered an appeal arguing that in spite of long Sikh occupation and sacred association with the site, the Shahidganj mosque was still a mosque and was thus not the property of the Sikhs at all but of the "Muslim community." But the plea of the Anjuman highlighted a question that would be central throughout the Shahidganj affair: who could now speak in the name of the "Muslim community"? Though the Anjuman Islamia itself was the most prominent organization in Lahore in the administration of mosques, it had changed little in its basic structure or orientation since its founding, remaining closely tied to the influence of urban notables and to the British administration. The conflict with the newly created Sikh Central Gurdwaras Committee (S.G.P.C.) had provided clear evidence of the degree to which the basic foundations for the political expression of community solidarity were changing in twentieth-century Punjab. For most Muslims in Lahore, the Anjuman Islamia, with a nonelected membership of little over 300, seemed a poor excuse in 1930 for a Muslim counterpart to the S.G.P.C.[17]

THE POLITICAL DEFINITION OF MUSLIM COMMUNITY

The various answers to the question of a voice for the Muslim community reflected the emergence of sharply divergent ideas in the twentieth century as to what defined a Muslim community's political existence in the Punjab. The strongest claim to Muslim political leadership in the first decades of the twentieth century had come from a newly emergent class of Muslim men who had sought, with a command over the English constitutional idiom, to speak in the name of the Muslim community in the new institutions of representative government created by the British. These men—lawyers like Sir Fazl-i-Husayn and Sir Muhammad Shafi—exercised a stronger influence than that of the local *muhalla* patrons. Their political conceptions of the Muslim community were in fact forged largely out of competition with Hindu and Sikh professional men for places in the services and in the courts in the late nineteenth and early twentieth centuries. The political character of the Muslim community had been defined for them largely by the requirements of the competition for places within the institutions of authority established by the British, and they had thus stressed the importance of public education as a preparation for it. Not only was education a prerequisite to these men for effective participation in the public services, but—even more important, from their perspective—it helped to instill in Muslim youth a distinctive cultural identity, an awareness of the Muslim community as a distinctive entity in competition with those outside it. In contrast with the Anjuman Islamia, in the late nineteenth and early twentieth centuries they had thus tended to support the more socially and educationally activist Anjuman-i Himayat-i Islam, which had established a network of Islamic schools in Lahore emphasizing a combination of English education and Islamic culture.[18] For them, leadership of the Muslim community required an aggressive expression of both Muslim interests and Muslim culture.

Unlike the Sikhs who had established the S.G.P.C., however, these leaders in no way sought to challenge the power of the local patrons who provided the backbone of the British administration. Their ideas of Muslim community were not shaped by any desire to change the basic structure of political authority among the Muslims; they had instead sought to define a community identity that would allow Muslims to compete more effectively within the British system. This strategy was perhaps most dramatically epitomized by the career of Sir Fazl-i-Husayn, who in the early 1920s rallied the primarily rural Muslims who dominated the provincial legislature in support of a program that guaranteed Muslims larger shares of power in the Punjab's municipal committees and greater access to the province's educational institutions, yet that was, at the same time, a defense of the existing power structure in the countryside.[19] For men like Sir Fazl-i-Husayn, the leadership of the community, whether in competition for places in the services or in defending a mosque, was defined by the requirements of effective political action within the British political system.

Such a view contrasted sharply with views about the meaning of community within another important group in Lahore—the ulama. Unlike the professional class among the Muslims, the ulama of Lahore tended in the late nineteenth and early twentieth centuries to be neither well organized nor politically active, their activities revolving around the city's numerous mosques and *madrasas*. But they were by no means immune to the currents of religious reform that in the late nineteenth century influenced the ulama of the subcontinent generally—currents that had pushed them toward a view of community defined not by political competition but by popular adherence to personal Islamic religious norms. The establishment in particular of the *dar al-ulum* (college) at Deoband in the United Provinces had produced a stress on popular religious education among the ulama, which had led to the crystallization of an ideal of Muslim community in which the instruction of the individual Muslim in the Shari'a was primary. Such an ideal had become increasingly important in the Punjab in the early twentieth century not only to those influenced directly by Deoband, but to the Deobandis' theological opponents among the more radically scripturalist Ahl-i Hadith and among the more custom-oriented Barelvi ulama as well. The result was an increasingly widespread conception of the meaning of Islamic community among the ulama which diverged sharply from the conceptions of men like Sir Fazl-i-Husayn, for it was an ideal defined, in its essence, independently of the structure of political authority and based on the spread of correct Islamic practice.[20]

The political implications of the ulama's view of community in twentieth-century British India were, however, ambiguous. With their focus primarily on religious education, the ulama of Deoband had been largely apolitical in the late nineteenth century, turning to politics only during and after World War I, when they had sought to mobilize support for the Turkish Khilafat. This had led to the foundation at Amritsar in 1919 of the Jamiat-i Ulama-i Hind, an association that had sought to express the increasingly pro-Khilafat and anti-British views of the ulama in Indian politics.[21] But defining the political position of the Muslim community in the context of British India proved no easy task for these ulama. In the 1920s, in rallying support for the Khilafat in opposition to the British government and in seeking the cooperation of the largely Hindu Indian National Congress in the task, the Jamiat-i Ulama-i Hind had begun to define the Muslim community as a self-regulating *millat* within the larger Indian polity, a community defined internally both by the diffusion of religious education and by the religious leadership provided by the ulama. It had even looked forward to an independent India in which the community would, in spite of the existence of a predominantly non-Muslim government, regulate its own internal affairs according to the Shari'a.[22] Still, the immediate political implications of such a view remained largely ill-defined. Like the Sikhs who had established the S.G.P.C., the ulama of the Jamiat-i Ulama-i Hind had sought to establish a structure for community identity independent of the structure of political patronage and control under the British administration. But unlike the S.G.P.C., theirs was a structure rooted in the spread of personal standards of Islamic behavior, and it thus offered little as an organizational alternative for the community's political expression.

Such views were by no means held by all Lahore's ulama, however. The most important supporter of the political views of the Jamiat-i Ulama-i Hind in

Lahore was probably Maulana Ahmad 'Ali, the leading Deobandi *'alim* in the city, who had gained a wide reputation in Lahore in the 1920s by teaching daily public Quran classes and who, by the mid-1920s, had organized his following into an influential *anjuman*, the Anjuman Khuddam al-Din.[23] But not all the ulama followed his example. Many of the reformist ulama, in spite of sympathy for the Jamiat-i Ulama-i Hind, sought to provide themselves with a more direct vehicle for political activity in the Majlis-i Ahrar, a radically anti-British party formed in 1929 in cooperation with other urban political leaders.[24] Others, particularly among the Barelvi ulama, rejected the Jamiat-i Ulama-i Hind altogether and organized their own independent *anjuman* under the leadership of the *khatib* (preacher) of the Wazir Khan mosque, the Anjuman Hizb al-Ahnaf.[25] Like the Deobandis, this *anjuman* focused its attention primarily on religious education and thus stressed individual adherence to the Shari'a as a foundation of Muslim community. But its political position seems to have been far more sympathetic to the British administration; indeed, many of these ulama continued to be influenced by their close connections with traditional *muhalla* patrons in the urban localities and with Sufi *pirs* in the countryside.

In fact, popular ideas about the political shape of the Muslim community in Lahore were probably most deeply influenced in the twentieth century by neither the politicians nor the ulama, but by another newly emergent class of leaders associated with the rapidly expanding Muslim press. The press itself had become an important political force in Lahore only in the late nineteenth century after the launching of the *Paisa Akhbar* (Penny Paper) in the 1880s, the first mass-circulation Urdu daily in the city.[26] But the importance of the press in the definition of Muslim community identity derived not just from the increasing political influence wielded in the city by the leading newspaper editors in the twentieth century, but from the particular character of the ideal of community they expounded—an ideal that transcended in some respects the contradiction between the politicians' and the ulama's conceptions of community. Unlike Sir Fazl-i-Husayn, whose political view of Muslim community was grounded in the imperial political culture of the British, or the ulama of the Jamiat-i Ulama-i Hind, whose view was grounded in the spread of adherence to the Shari'a, the conception of community popularized in the twentieth-century press tended not to be grounded in any particular form of organization or code of conduct, but, rather, in the special inheritance—symbolized by the Prophet, the Quran, and the mosque—that every Muslim could claim as his birthright.

To understand this view of the community and its popular influence in Lahore, one can do no better than to turn to the writings of the poet Allama Muhammad Iqbal who, though not himself a journalist, crystallized many of the ideas that found less literary expression in the popular press. The key to Iqbal's thought in this regard was his stress on *tawhid* (the unity of God) as the basic foundation for Muslim identity and community. "Islam," he wrote, "as a polity is only a practical means of making this principle [*tawhid*] a living factor in the intellectual and emotional life of mankind." [27] In emphasizing *tawhid* as a foundation for Islamic faith, Iqbal was only stating a position that most ulama and serious Muslims would have fully accepted. The key to Iqbal's ideas on the character of Muslim community was his emphasis on *tawhid* not as the direct foundation for a particular form of organization, but as an ideal which pointed the Muslim individual toward a realization of his own "ideal nature"—the "ideal nature" which bound him to God's larger community. [28] The definition of the community, in Iqbal's view, was thus not tied to the overlordship of monarch or priest, of politician or *'alim,* but to the awareness by individual Muslims of their own special heritage and identity [29]—an identity symbolized by nothing more complicated than the confession of faith:

> There is no god but God: this is the soul
> And body of our pure Community,
> The pitch that keeps our instrument in tune,
> The very substance of our mysteries,
> The knotted thread that binds our scattered thoughts. [30]

For Iqbal it was more than anything else the common realization by Muslims of the meaning of the confession of faith, and thus of their own "Muslimness," that brought the community into being:

> When several hearts put on a single hue
> That is Community. [31]

Such a view of community was an extremely simple one, and yet it was one with political implications far different from those of the views of community held by the Anjuman Islamia, by men like Sir Fazl-i Husayn, or even by the leaders of the Jamiat-i Ulama-i Hind. In Iqbal's view, community was defined not only independently of the structure of authority under the colonial administration but also independently of the primary stress on outward standards of Islamic conduct maintained by many of the ulama. No doubt both of these, and particularly the Shari'a, were critically important to Iqbal, but the community itself was defined in its essence only by the awareness of individual Muslims of their own Islamic identity—an identity which, even without the guidance of the ulama, gave them a special place in history as the inheritors of the Prophet's revelation. The charismatic character of the community in this context was perhaps nowhere more clearly exemplified than in the first line of Iqbal's dedication of *The Mysteries of Selflessness* to the Muslim community, that community which had inherited the revelation of the Seal of the Prophets:

> You, who were made by God to be the Seal
> Of all the peoples dwelling on the earth. [32]

It was in large part such a view of Muslim community that was translated into popular terms and carried into the public arena in the twentieth century by the leading editors of Lahore's Urdu press—men like Maulana Zafar 'Ali Khan, editor of the daily *Zamindar*. Zafar 'Ali Khan, the son of a post office inspector and a graduate of Aligarh, rose rapidly to prominence in the years after 1911, when he moved his father's newspaper, the *Zamindar,* to Lahore and established it as a daily.[33] In the years before World War I, Zafar 'Ali Khan gained a reputation as one of the leading public spokesmen for the Muslim community, largely as a result of his championing of pan-Islam, and his defense, in language both passionate and sentimental, of the Muslims of the Ottoman empire against the onslaught of the "devouring wolves of the cross." [34] Subsequently he supported a wide variety of Islamic causes, including the defense of the Kanpur mosque in 1913,[35] the Khilafat movement in 1920,[36] and the defense of the honor of the Prophet in the 1927 *Rangila Rasul* agitation[37]—many of which brought him into sharp conflict with the British and led to the repeated forfeiture of the security of the *Zamindar* under the British press laws.[38]

In spite of his clashes with the British, Zafar 'Ali Khan's prime concern throughout his career was the public focus of Muslim politics on Islamic symbols. For Zafar 'Ali Khan it was, in fact, this focus on symbols that was central to the public dramatization of the conception of community which men like Iqbal had offered. Like Iqbal, Zafar 'Ali Khan was a poet, and through the press he transformed Urdu poetry—a symbol of Muslim greatness and elite dominance in India—into an idiom of everyday political expression. Though he was by no means blind to the immediate political realities facing the Muslims within British India or, for that matter, to the Shari'a-based concerns of the ulama, he stressed public action in the name of Islamic symbols as a means of dramatizing the community's power and charisma. The Khilafat, the Prophet, a mosque—these were the causes that Zafar 'Ali Khan defended most passionately, and his popular influence in championing such causes was indicated by the *Zamindar*'s attainment by 1915 of a circulation of over 15,000, unprecedented for an Urdu newspaper at that time.[39]

For many of those who sought a twentieth-century voice for the community in Lahore, newspapers like the *Zamindar* proved irresistible. The idiom of the *Zamindar* in fact came to dominate much of the popular discourse in Lahore on the subject of community in the 1920s and 1930s—a discourse in which not only the Muslim press but also public orators, poets, pamphleteers, and even many of the ulama took a prominent part. But although this discourse carried with it a strong call to individual action, it was a call to action which, perhaps as much as the call of the Jamiat-i Ulama-i Hind, was politically unorganized and rarely focused on concrete political goals. Perhaps no one captured the highly emotional, essentially individualistic character of this appeal better than the fiery Muslim orator Sayyid Ayatullah Shah Bokhari, the outstanding public orator of his generation.[40] "Even if a person offers prayers all night and fasts during the day and even if he recites the Namaz at midnight," Bokhari declared in 1935, "his piety and prayers are useless if he does not cherish in his heart the desire of launching a crusade to vindicate the honour of the Prophet.... A man may be a sinner, a liar, a thief and a *dacoit*, but if he is prepared to lay down his life when the question of defending the honour of the Prophet comes up, then he is truly pious." Ultimately, the key to finding the voice of the Muslim community thus lay in the active, disinterested sacrifice of the individual in such a symbolic Islamic cause. "I would fain allow myself to be thrown before fierce lions as a punishment for my love of the Prophet," Bokhari declared. "I would deem myself fortunate if those lions were to chew my bones in their jaws and I were conscious enough to hear them cracking." [41]

THE SHAHIDGANJ AGITATION:
"A TREASURE OF MARTYRS"

When the Anjuman Islamia appealed to the Gurdwaras Tribunal to restore the Shahidganj mosque to the Muslim community, it was thus attempting to speak for a community whose voices were various and whose perspectives on the political meaning of community were radically different. In fact, this did not prevent these groups from expressing in the early 1930s their common concern about the fate of the Shahidganj mosque. When the Gurdwaras Tribunal initially rejected the appeal of the Anjuman Islamia, a variety of Muslim leaders, including lawyers, ulama, and newspapermen, joined together in an ad hoc committee, the Anjuman-i Tahaffuz-i Masjid Shahidganj, to negotiate with the Sikhs and with the government for the mosque's preservation. [42] But when the Sikhs, ignoring the efforts of the government to mediate, demolished the mosque during the night of 7 July 1935, it caused a sensation among Muslims in the city. In the eyes of a large number of Muslims, the Shahidganj mosque had itself now become a symbol of the community, a *shahid* itself in the community's defense.

The history of the subsequent agitation in fact demonstrated dramatically the power in the 1930s of such a symbolic cause in mobilizing Muslim opinion in the city. The destruction of the mosque triggered a series of events that culminated in massive demonstrations in Lahore on 19, 20, and 21 July and, ultimately, in police shootings that left over a dozen Muslims dead. Zafar 'Ali Khan and others rallied Muslims to action in the days after the mosque's destruction, forming a political organization, the Majlis Ittihad-i Millat, to fight for the mosque and calling for the mobilization of "blue shirt" volunteers to carry on the agitation. [43] It was not primarily Zafar 'Ali Khan's position as a newspaper editor that provided the drive behind the agitation; it was, rather, his effective rhetorical use of the mosque as a dramatic symbol of community identity. The "blue shirt" movement produced, in the words of the government, "comparatively few active followers," but, far more important, it gained "the active sympathy of a large number of Muslims in Lahore itself." [44] When the British attempted to control the situation by exiling four leaders of the agitation, including Zafar 'Ali Khan, from Lahore, they discovered to their cost that it was not any particular leader but the fate of the mosque itself that had galvanized support among Lahore's Muslims. When a large crowd gathered outside the Delhi Gate on the morning of 20 July, attempting to reach the site of the Shahidganj mosque to offer prayers, no Muslim leaders could control it—"all [are] ready to die," one pro-government Muslim reported; "they don't listen to anyone"—and only police bullets finally brought the situation under government control.[45]

The martyrdom of more than a dozen Muslims thus provided dramatic proof of the existence of an aroused Muslim community in Lahore, defined by their sacrifice in the community's name. But in the aftermath of the police firing, Muslims who identified with that community still had to wrestle with the contradictions in organization and political expression that the community faced. The British themselves of course strongly encouraged the efforts of men like Malik Firoz Khan Noon, a minister in the government and a protégé of Fazl-i-Husayn's, in their attempts to rally the traditional community leaders associated with the British administration, the "city gentlemen," rais, and municipal commissioners, in order to reassert administrative control over the Muslims of the city.[46] But such an effort was extremely difficult, as even the British realized, for in the volatile atmosphere prevailing in the city these leaders could hardly be counted on politically to "deliver the goods."[47] Perhaps even more important, however, the British also attempted to encourage strongly the position of the Anjuman Islamia, in spite of its failure before the Gurdwaras Tribunal, as a continuing focus for community control of religious places in the city—a politically malleable embodiment of community identity. The British could hardly now overturn the decision of the Gurdwaras Tribunal and themselves give control of the Shahidganj mosque site to the Anjuman Islamia. Nevertheless, they publicly demonstrated their continuing confidence in the anjuman's position as a community representative by announcing the transfer of another Lahore mosque which had long been in government possession, the Shah Chiragh mosque, into the Anjuman Islamia's hands—a gift, as a government communiqué declared, "to the Muslim community through the Anjuman Islamia."[48]

If nothing else, the agitation over the mosque had dramatized the degree to which, by 1935, popular conceptions of community had bypassed the Anjuman Islamia. Perhaps nothing demonstrated this better than the launching of a new court case by a group of Lahore Muslims who sought now to regain the site of the Shahidganj mosque through the regular British courts, with arguments which challenged the basic claim of the Anjuman Islamia before the Gurdwaras Tribunal to have represented the Muslim community at all. To punctuate this point, Lahore Muslims instituted their own case not in the name of the Anjuman, or any other Muslim organization, but in the name of the

Shahidganj mosque itself, which, in the role of a juristic person, was now made
to sue the S.G.P.C. on its own behalf for the restoration of its rights as a
mosque.[49] This was an ingenious approach, in effect transforming the mosque
from a symbol of the community to being the actual representative of the
community in court, a reflection with a vengeance of the charismatic conception of the community that had largely inspired the agitation. But at the same
time, the pleading of the mosque itself in court, particularly in opposition to the
powerful and well-organized Sikh Central Gurdwaras Committee, provided
dramatic evidence, if any were needed, of the complete lack of a comparable
organized political alternative among the Muslims—a body on which the
community in the Punjab could rely for the expression of its political interests.

The organizational problems of the community were demonstrated in far
more concrete terms by the course of the agitation outside the courts. In spite
of the formation by Zafar 'Ali Khan of the Majlis Ittihad-i Millat, the Urdu
press in the month following the police firings continued to be primarily
responsible for keeping public interest in the agitation at a high level. In spite
of the externment of Zafar 'Ali Khan and the editor of the daily *Siyasat*, Sayyid
Habib, from Lahore, the *Zamindar* and the *Siyasat* continued to take the lead in
their support of the agitation, joined by innumerable news-sheets which
emerged during the course of the agitation, "sell [ing] for one *pice* and cater
[ing] to the taste of the sensation-loving half-educated public." Such publications, as the government put it, exploited "the disturbed communal situation
through trained news-hawkers who read aloud the numerous bold headlines
which cover the entire pages of these news-sheets." [50] More important, much of
the writing in the press attacked sharply those Muslim leaders who, in the eyes
of the press, had failed to provide the sort of leadership the community now
required. As the *Siyasat* wrote in attacking those Muslims whose foremost
concern was their place in the colonial administration, "You do not know what
sacrifice means.... You fear the lords of the Government. You are strangers to
love for the Prophet. You love the Prophet of the English." [51] Much of the
bitterest criticism was directed at those members of the ulama who had refused
to give direction to the agitation. This criticism was directed in part at the
ulama of the Jamiat-i Ulama-i Hind, but far more pointedly at the ulama
associated with the Ahrar Party, who, as a result of strategic political alliances,
had refused to support the agitation.[52] As the *Siyasat* demanded, what place
could such political alliances have in a cause such as the defense of the Shahidganj
mosque, when the very existence of the community was at stake? "Of course,
you had differences with Zafar 'Ali and Sayyid Habib," the newspaper declared, "but what differences had you with youths who in a state of excitement
tore their collars and received bullets in their chests.... You are responsible for
the blood shed outside the Delhi Gate on the 20th and 21st of July and you will
have to give account for each drop of blood." [53] Though some ulama issued
fatawa to support the agitation, the *Zamindar* bemoaned the failure of the ulama

in general to provide organized leadership of the agitation. "A prominent but sad feature of the Shahidganj Mosque affair is that the local 'ulema' have not published any statement from the religious point of view." While the uninstructed youths of Lahore "sacrificed themselves like moths on the lamp of Islam," the *Zamindar* declared, the ulama, who were once fighters for Islam, remained silent.[54]

A month after the shootings of July 1935, the agitation thus remained, in spite of the enthusiasm that had been aroused, in a state of disorganization. Seemingly, the very emotional character of the call to action in the name of the mosque had precluded effective political organization. In early September 1935, however, several leaders decided on a bold new stroke to try to give the Shahidganj movement, in spite of its symbolic definition, an organized political foundation. At a special conference held at Rawalpindi in the first week of September, they turned not to the ulama but to one of the most prominent of Punjab's rural *pirs*: Sayyid Jamaat 'Ali Shah of Alipur Sayyidan in Sialkot District was called upon to assume the title of *amir-i millat* and take over the leadership of the agitation. This move may at first seem a strange one, for although such *pirs*, far more than ulama, were the dominant religious figures in rural Punjab, they had not, by and large, previously taken a prominent role in affairs of community.[55] Unlike the ulama, most *pirs* were tied to a structure of religious authority in the rural areas which centered on local Sufi shrines, their influence diffuse and based largely on inherited powers of spiritual mediation in the villages. Structurally speaking, the religious influence of many *pirs* thus tended to mirror the mediatory political authority of the rural landlords and "tribal" intermediaries who formed the backbone of the British administration. Pir Jamaat 'Ali Shah thus seemed an unlikely leader for a "community" agitation.

But in spite of all this, for many of the urban supporters of the Shahidganj agitation the selection of Pir Jamaat 'Ali Shah as *amir-i millat* was an effort to come to terms with the contradictions the movement was facing. On the most basic level, the selection represented a calculated gamble aimed at reinvigorating the agitation, in spite of divisions in the community, by focusing authority in a single leader. The political influence of Pir Jamaat 'Ali Shah was in fact substantial, far wider than that of any single *'alim*, a result not only of the large number of his *murid*s in the Punjab but also of his ties to many of the powerful Muslim administrative intermediaries in the countryside. Though educated at several well-known *madrasa*s in the Punjab and U.P., Pir Jamaat 'Ali Shah, like many rural *pirs*, numbered among his followers both officials and prominent Muslim political leaders.[56] Unlike most of the ulama, he could thus claim an influence that cut into the basic foundations of government political power in the province, and the organizers of the agitation were quick to try to take full advantage of this. Calling not only on Jamaat 'Ali Shah, but on "all Pirs and other religious leaders to openly identify themselves with the struggle to regain possession of the Shahid Ganj mosque," the Rawalpindi conference sanctioned the launching of a movement of civil disobedience to regain the mosque site, a movement to be initiated at Pir Jamaat 'Ali Shah's discretion.[57] Some even hoped that by naming Pir Jamaat 'Ali Shah as head of the agitation they might be able to embarrass the government by enlisting the thousands of the *pir*'s followers who were serving in the army.[58]

But it was not simply the *pir*'s potential political influence that accounted for his selection at Rawalpindi as *amir-i millat*. For all his connections, the *pir* was in fact a very aged man, "easily accessible to influence, and prone to listen to the last person who talks to him."[59] But as the *sajjada nashin* of a Sufi shrine and a descendant of the Prophet, the *pir* also represented a particular style of Islamic leadership—a style of leadership that, ironically, in spite of the *pir*'s practical ties to the structure of the British administration, embodied to an important degree the charismatic conception of the Muslim community which had largely inspired the agitation. Though the *pir* himself was a man learned in the Shari'a, with important contacts among the ulama at Lahore,[60] the force of his moral authority derived not from his learning in Shari'a, as was the case with the ulama, or, for that matter, from his influence in the colonial political system, but from his charisma, the special inheritance that, as a *sayyid* and a *pir*, he could claim from the Prophet and from his own saintly ancestors. This was the foundation of his religious influence among those predominantly rural Muslims who sought his spiritual mediation. Perhaps even more important, it was also the foundation for his recognition now by many as a community leader whose intrinsic charisma, based on his descent, seemed to transcend the organizational contradictions in the Shahidganj movement.[61]

In fact, his assumption of the leadership of the Shahidganj agitation almost immediately revitalized the movement and led to pledges of support from many of the influential rural *pir*s, including the Chishti *pir*s of Golra and Jalalpur Sharif.[62] Pir Jamaat 'Ali Shah himself announced plans to recruit a million volunteers for the Majlis Ittihad-i Millat and to raise money for the establishment of a community *bait al-mal* (treasury),[63] and he organized a national day of mourning on 20 September for the mosque, which included huge processions and a call for Muslims from all sections of Lahore to meet for united *juma* prayers at the Badshahi mosque.[64] But in spite of the enthusiasm which the *pir*'s selection as *amir-i millat* generated, he soon found himself subjected as head of the agitation to diverse political pressures which were practically impossible for him to control. Perhaps most important, in spite of his wide rural connections— in fact, largely because of them—the *pir* was easily accessible to the political pressures brought to bear by the British administration, and he was quickly forced to back away from the call issued at Rawalpindi for the launching of civil disobedience. "Deeply as he may have appeared to have committed himself," the chief secretary wrote immediately after the Rawalpindi conference, "there is some reason to think that he is not altogether comfortable about his position, and he may retreat from it." Most important, he added, "influences are being brought to bear to this end."[65] The *pir*, in fact, bowing to such pressure, announced at the end of September that he would postpone any announcement of a political program for the agitation until he had had a chance to tour the Punjab and other parts of north India in order to consult with political leaders and leading ulama. But after returning from a tour which included consultations at the *urs* (shrine festival) in Ajmer and meetings with important ulama in Budaun and Bareilly in the United Provinces, the *pir* took few concrete steps to organize the agitation. Though he briefly proposed, and then repudiated, a program of economic boycott of the Hindus, the *pir* found himself largely unable to propose any independent program or to free himself politically from the influence of his wealthy rural *murids* and advisers, who bound him to the British administration. "All of the gaddi holders," one Hindu newspaper wrote in analyzing his situation, "whether Hindu or Muslim, cannot rise against the Government."[66]

It was not only government influences on the *pir* that made his position an awkward one. The very character of the *pir*'s leadership, with its roots in the tradition of *piri-muridi* in the rural areas, generated almost immediate misgivings among a large section of Muslims themselves, who were mistrustful of the blind faith with which the *pir* was regarded by much of his rural following—a faith so strong that, it was rumored, his *ta'wiz* (protective amulet) had been accepted during the army recruiting campaigns during World War I as a guarantee against enemy bullets. The *pir* was no stranger to sectarian controversy, but in the enthusiasm of the Rawalpindi conference he had pledged to rise above such controversy and had accordingly been accepted by all those who supported the liberation of the site of the mosque. "What affords the Faqir the greatest pleasure," the *pir* had declared after the conference, "is that all the Islamic sects have heartily accepted the Faqir's services as a servant of Islam."[67]

But almost immediately some questioned the oath of allegiance to the *pir* that had been taken at the conference, suggesting that it resembled far too closely the traditional oath of fealty to a Sufi *pir (bay'a)*.[68] Such criticisms came particularly from those influenced by the reformist schools among the ulama, and this was at least in part responsible for an uproarious scene when Pir Jamaat 'Ali Shah attempted to deliver an address after Friday prayers at the Jama Masjid in Delhi to a congregation which consisted largely of students from several Delhi *madrasas*.[69] As one Delhi Muslim wrote to a Lahore newspaper, "In the opinion of Pir Jamaat 'Ali Shah I am a 'great infidel,'" for differing with the *pir* on the question as to whether the Prophet was to be considered as something more than just a human being—long a point of theological controversy between the reformist ulama and many of the Sufi *pirs*. Such differences, he stressed, did not alone prevent his supporting Jamaat 'Ali

Shah's efforts to regain the site of the Shahidganj mosque, but they did certainly prevent his accepting the *pir* as *amir-i millat*.[70] For his own part, Jamaat 'Ali Shah was quick to label those who opposed his leadership as outside the pale of Islam. "I request the Muslims to arrive at the definite decision," he declared, "that they will not say the funeral prayers of [any] one who does not participate in this auspicious movement, nor will they allow his dead body to be buried in their graveyards."[71]

For all the promise in Pir Jamaat 'Ali Shah's leadership as an expression of the community's inherent charisma, therefore, in the end the leadership of the *pir* could not overcome the divisions within the community; indeed, by the end of 1935 the movement was fast moving toward a state of complete collapse. Thrust into a position of political leadership, Pir Jamaat 'Ali Shah increasingly found it impossible to deal with both the sectarian and the political pressures facing him, and could only, as one government officer reported, "change his views from day to day."[72] For the leaders of the urban press, the almost pathetic indecisiveness of the *pir* soon seemed nothing less than betrayal. In October, one Lahore daily which had strongly supported the *pir*'s assumption of leadership in the agitation implored him "to show some regard for the promises made and the speeches delivered at the Rawalpindi conference."[73] But by January, it admitted the truth, that "the Musalmans are still in a state of disintegration.... Not to speak of 10 lakh volunteers, the Majlis Ittihad-i Millat had not been able to collect even 10 volunteers and its coffers do not contain even 10 rupees today."[74]

The *pir* himself attempted to organize a conference at Amritsar in January 1936 to try to revive the agitation, but this only produced bitter conflict between the more radical urban agitators and some of the *pir*'s wealthy, pro-government *murid*s. As a result the *pir* himself, apparently in order to salvage his personal prestige, departed on *hajj*. As one newspaper noted in frustration, far from demonstrating the vitality of an aroused Muslim community in Punjab, the agitation over the mosque had in the end only demonstrated once again the community's disorganization. Indeed, so much had God's chosen community failed in the symbolic task given to it that, as one daily declared, "a divine visitation is likely to fall upon them."[75]

CONCLUSION: THE COMMUNITY AND
THE COMING OF PAKISTAN

The failure of the Shahidganj agitation in 1935 and 1936 provided dramatic evidence of the depth of the political contradictions facing Muslims as they sought to define a community identity within the colonial context. The *pir*'s departure did not end the agitation, for the emotional concern to regain the mosque's site surfaced repeatedly during the succeeding years.[76] But the *pir*'s failure had demonstrated clearly the essential difficulties the Muslims faced. Split by differing conceptions of the meaning of Muslim community, a large number of Lahore Muslims had focused in 1935 on the Shahidganj mosque, destroyed by the Sikhs, as a symbol of the inherent charisma of the community, a symbol of the community's special inheritance from God and the Prophet, which it was the duty of every Muslim to protect. Beyond politics, beyond the ulama, and even beyond the Law, this was a conception of the community that stressed the symbolic commitment of the individual—a conception which had been expressed most eloquently in the poetry of Iqbal and which, in the early twentieth century, the Urdu press of Lahore had taken the lead in popularizing among Lahore's Muslims. But as the course of the agitation had shown, such a view of community was one which, by its very nature, left the community with little political organization. To attempt to organize the community politically for concrete goals was in fact almost to risk denying the primacy of the basic, disinterested, individual commitment to Islamic symbols that defined the community's existence.

The selection of Pir Jamaat 'Ali Shah as *amir-i millat* represented one effort to resolve this dilemma. The *pir*'s position highlighted the potential political significance leadership based on descent had for Punjab Muslims. Since the *pir*'s legitimacy as a leader of the community was derived from sources wholly outside the political structure of Punjab society, he was well placed to transcend the political divisions of Muslim Punjab in order to act in the name of a symbolically defined community. The hope of his supporters was that he would be able to lead a community defined in symbolic terms and yet capable of incorporating the most powerful elements in rural society. But in practice the *pir* found himself a prisoner of his own background as a rural religious leader—a tool in the hands of rural magnates and a focus for sectarian controversy. In spite of its symbolic promise, the leadership of the *pir* thus proved politically ineffective.

In spite of its failure, however, the Shahidganj mosque agitation was historically significant from another perspective. In highlighting the contradictions between the symbolic definition of community identity and the organization of political power within the British system, the Shahidganj agitation pointed the way toward the emergence in the 1940s of another symbol of the Muslim community: the concept of the Islamic state of Pakistan. Support for the concept of Pakistan in fact developed initially in the Punjab among many of those same groups that had supported the Shahidganj mosque agitation, including the leading editors of the Muslim press in the cities and, somewhat later, the Sufi *pir*s of the countryside. The concept also eventually gained the support of many of the rural magnates who had dominated politics in the Punjab under the British.[77] But the success of the Pakistan idea resulted not just from the political support of these groups but from the symbolic resolution the idea offered to the long-standing contradictions of Muslim community politics under the British. Like the Shahidganj mosque, the Pakistan concept offered to the individual a symbolic focus for the active, public expression of Islamic identity. At the same time, it provided a powerful institutional base for the expression of the community's political solidarity and for the competing interests of the Muslim elites who composed it.

But the creation of Pakistan also evoked considerable controversy. For many of the ulama in particular, the popular dissemination of the substance of Islamic law and practice had long been more important than the commitment to what were often viewed as hollow symbols. Many of the ulama of Jamiat-i Ulama-i Hind and the Ahrar, who had initially opposed the Shahidganj mosque agitation, also opposed the creation of Pakistan as a perversion of their own view of community and their own concern with personal Islamic reform. Islamic symbols, as many saw it, could easily be divorced from the substance of Islamic life—a fact which was perhaps nowhere more poignantly illustrated than in the fate of the Shahidganj site itself. In spite of its significance as a symbol of community identity in British India, after partition the Shahidganj site took on a different symbolic connotation. As a symbol of the government's commitment to the protection of minorities, the Shahidganj site was not reconverted after partition into a mosque but was maintained officially as a *gurdwara* by the Pakistan government, in a country now with virtually no Sikh population. Clearly, Islamic symbols could have uncertain political lives, and to guarantee that the symbolic Pakistan state did not come to a similar fate, the ulama fought hard in independent Pakistan for the establishment of a state that would enforce the Shari'a in the workings of society itself.

But although the influence of the ulama after partition was substantial and led to increasing pressure for the creation of a true Islamic community as the ulama defined it, the Pakistan state nevertheless retained for the majority of Pakistanis its own intrinsic symbolic significance in defining the community. Like the Shahidganj mosque, the Pakistan state remained first and foremost a symbol of the community's charisma bequeathed to it by the revelation of the Prophet. As supporters of Pakistan thus argued in 1947, the creation of Pakistan stood, at base, for nothing more complicated than the political realization of the concept of *tawhid,* which Iqbal himself had defined as the foundation of Muslim community. Transcending everyday politics, and yet at the same time defining the Islamic nature of the political system, the meaning of Pakistan in this context, like that of the Shahidganj mosque, could be summed up in a single, popular couplet:

Pakistan ka matlab kya
La ilaha illa allah

(What is the meaning of Pakistan?
There is no God but Allah.)

NOTES

1. *Zamindar* (Lahore), 2 July 1935, Punjab Civil Secretariat Archives, Lahore (henceforth P.C.S.A.), Press Branch, file 8331, vol. IA.

2. David Lelyveld, *Aligarh's First Generation: Muslim Solidarity in British India* (Princeton: Princeton University Press, 1978).

3. Barbara Metcalf, *Islamic Revival in British India: Deoband, 1860–1900* (Princeton: Princeton University Press, 1982).

4. Gail Minault, *The Khilafat Movement: Religious Symbolism and Political Mobilization in India* (New York: Columbia University Press, 1982).

5. Paul Brass, "Elite Groups, Symbol Manipulation and Ethnic Identity among the Muslims of South Asia," in David Taylor and Malcolm Yapp, eds., *Political Identity in South Asia* (London: Curzon Press, 1979), pp. 35–77.

6. Francis Robinson, "Islam and Muslim Separatism," in ibid., pp. 78–112.

7. The history of the Shahidganj mosque was a matter of some dispute. The basic facts here are taken from the court judgment in the case of Masjid Shahid Ganj and others versus Shromani Gurdwara Prabandhak Committee, Amritsar (First Appeal no. 244 of 1936), *All India Reporter* (Lahore) (1938), p. 372, and from Ganda Singh, *History of the Gurdwara Shahidganj, Lahore* (1935), pp. 1–42. Ganda Singh argued that there was no evidence that the Shahidganj building, though shaped like a mosque, had ever been used for Muslim prayer.

8. The census figures here are taken from *Census of India*, 1931, vol. 17 (Punjab), pt. I—Report, pp. 93–95.

9. There is no readily available history of Lahore during the British period. See, however, Ravinder Kumar, "The Rowlatt Satyagraha in Lahore," in R. Kumar, *Essays on Gandhian Politics* (Oxford: Clarendon Press, 1971), pp. 236–97, for general background on the social composition of the city.

10. R. Kumar, "Rowlatt Satyagraha," pp. 260–61. For the family history of the Qazilbash Nawabs, see L. Griffin and C. F. Massey, *Chiefs and Families of Note in the Punjab* (Lahore: Civil and Military Gazette Press, 1910), vol. 1, pp. 253–59.

11. Shahid Javed Burki, "Migration, Urbanization and Politics in Pakistan," in W. Howard Wriggins and James F. Guyot, eds., *Population, Politics and the Future of Southern Asia* (New York: Columbia University Press, 1973), p. 155.

12. The outstanding example of such a family is the Mian family of Baghbanpura. See Mian Bashir Ahmad, *Justice Shah Din: His Life and Writings* (Lahore: Mian Bashir Ahmad, 1962) and Jahanara Shah Nawaz, *Father and Daughter* (Lahore: Nigarishat, 1971).

13. The founding of the Anjuman Islamia is discussed in S. M. Ikram, *Modern Muslim India and the Birth of Pakistan* (Lahore: Sh. Muhammad Ashraf, 1970), p. 195.

14. The purposes and goals of the Anjuman included explicitly the fostering of loyalty to the government: *Anjuman Islamiya-yi Punjab Lahaur ka sirmahi risala*, 1926, p. b.

15. Singh, pp. 41–57.

16. An account of the *gurdwara* reform movement, which produced the Sikh *gurdwara* legislation of the 1920s, is Mohinder Singh, *The Akali Movement* (Delhi: Macmillan, 1978).

17. The initials stand for Shiromani Gurdwara Prabandhak Committee. See judgment of District Judge, S. L. Sale, 25 May 1936; Lahore High Court, First Appeal no. 244 of 1936; Masjid Shahid Ganj and others vs. Shiromani Gurdwara Prabandhak Committee, Amritsar. Sale reviewed the arguments against the representative character of the Anjuman Islamia which were produced in court.

18. Ikram, *Modern Muslim India,* pp. 198–200.

19. Mian Fazl-i-Husayn's career, and his organization of the Unionist Party in the Punjab Council, is detailed in the biography by his son, Azim Husain, *Fazl-i-Husain* (Bombay: Longman's, Green, 1946).

20. The history of the Deobandi ulama in the nineteenth century and the development of their ideas are detailed in Barbara D. Metcalf, *Islamic Revival in British India: Deoband, 1860–1900* (Princeton: Princeton University Press, 1982).

21. Peter Hardy, *The Muslims of British India* (Cambridge, England: Cambridge University Press, 1972), p. 189.

22. For the political ideas of the ulama in the twentieth century, see Peter Hardy, *Partners in Freedom—and True Muslims: The Political Thought of Some Muslim Scholars in British India* (Scandinavian Institute of Asian Studies, 1971).

23. Abdul Hamid Khan, *Mard-i Momin* (Lahore: Ferozesons, 1962), pp. 59–71.

24. Wilfred Cantwell Smith, *Modern Islam in India* (Lahore: Sh. Muhammad Ashraf, 1969), pp. 270–75.

25. Iqbal Ahmad Faruqi, *Tazkirah-yi Ulama-yi Ahl-i Sunnat o Jamaat, Lahaur* (Lahore: Maktabah Nabviya, 1975), pp. 320–21.

26. S. M. A. Feroze, *Press in Pakistan* (Lahore: National Publications, 1957), pp. 69–72. "Mass circulation" is of course used in a relative sense, for its circulation was still quite small by present-day standards.

27. Allama Muhammad Iqbal, *The Reconstruction of Religious Thought in Islam* (Lahore: Sh. Muhammad Ashraf, 1971), p. 147.

28. Ibid.: "[Islam] demands loyalty to God, not to thrones. And since God is the ultimate spiritual basis of all life, loyalty to God virtually amounts to man's loyalty to his own ideal nature."

29. Riffat Burki, "Iqbal and Tauhid," *Iqbal Review* 14, no. 3 (1973): 12.

30. Sir Muhammad Iqbal, *The Mysteries of Selflessness* (Rumuz-i Bekhudi), trans. A. J. Arberry (London: John Murray, 1953), p. 12.

31. Ibid.

32. Ibid., p. 1. This concept is developed in W. Montgomery Watt, "The Conception of the Charismatic Community in Islam," *Numen* 7, no. 1 (1960).

33. Kumar, "Rowlatt Satyagraha," pp. 269–71; Data on Zafar 'Ali Khan and *Zamindar*, corrected up to 1940, P.C.S.A., Press Branch, file 1918, vol. XIVA. See also Ghulam Husain Zulfiqar, *Zafar 'Ali Khan: Adib o Sha'ir* (Lahore: Maktabah Khayaban-i Abad, 1967).

34. Data on Zafar 'Ali Khan and *Zamindar*, corrected up to 1940, P.C.S.A., Press Branch, file 1918, vol. XIVA.

35. The removal of a portion of a small mosque in Kanpur in 1913 led to local riots and an all-India agitation to protect the mosque. For an account of the episode see Sandria B. Freitag, Chapter 7 in this volume. For an example of Zafar 'Ali Khan's rhetoric on this issue, see Kumar, "Rowlatt Satyagraha," p. 271.

36. For a history of the Indian Khilafat movement, see Minault, *Khilafat Movement*. Zafar 'Ali Khan was for a time secretary of the Punjab Khilafat Committee and in October 1920 was prosecuted and imprisoned for seditious speeches. In 1920 the *Zamindar* also forfeited its security to government. P.C.S.A., Press Branch, file 1918, vol. XIVA.

37. *Rangila Rasul* was a Hindu-authored pamphlet ridiculing the Prophet which was published in Lahore in 1924. The publisher was prosecuted, but after long court proceedings, he was acquitted in 1927. For a discussion of the case see G. R. Thursby, *Hindu-Muslim Relations in British India* (Leiden: E. J. Brill, 1975), pp. 40–47. The publisher's acquittal led to a Muslim agitation and, among other things, his assassination. Zafar 'Ali Khan was also arrested once again during the course of the agitation: Letter, H. D. Craik (Chief Secretary, Punjab) to Government of India, 5 July 1927, National Archives of India, Home Political, file 132/III/1927.

38. For an account of the history of British press laws in India, see N. Gerald Barrier, *Banned: Controversial Literature and Political Control in British India, 1907–1947* (Columbia: University of Missouri Press, 1974). The security forfeitures of the *Zamindar* are discussed in a letter from H. D. Craik (Chief Secretary, Punjab) to Secretary of Home Dept., Government of India, 6 August 1927, P.C.S.A., Press Branch, file 5950. Zafar 'Ali Khan was able to avoid prosecution in connection with most of these articles by employing "dummy" editors.

39. Feroze, *Press in Pakistan*, pp. 74–81.

40. Shorish Kashmiri, _Sayyid 'Ataullah Shah Bukhari (Sawanih o Afkar)_ (Lahore: Chatan Press, 1973); Janbaz Mirza, _Hayat-i Amir-i Shari 'at_ (Lahore: Maktabah Tabsirah, 1969). For most of his later career, Sayyid Ataullah Shah Bokhari was a leader of the Ahrar Party.

41. Translation of speech delivered by Ataullah Shah Bokhari at Muslim Tabliqh Conference, Saharanpur, 19 May 1935, National Archives of India, Home Political, file 36/5/35 Poll.

42. Letter, F. H. Puckle (Chief Secretary, Punjab) to all Deputy Commissioners, 19 July 1935, National Archives of India, Home Political, file 5/14/35. There is also an untitled, typed report by Mian Abdul Aziz, a former chairman of the Lahore Municipal Committee, in the Mian Abdul Aziz Papers, Lahore, which details the activities of the Anjuman-i Tahaffuz-i Masjid Shahidganj during this period.

43. Punjab Fortnightly Report for the first half of July 1935, National Archives of India, Home Political, file 18/7/35; Singh, _Gurdwara Shahidganj_, pp. 80–81.

44. Letter, Sir Herbert Emerson (Governor, Punjab) to Viceroy, 18 July 1935, National Archives of India, Home Political, file 5/14/35 Poll.

45. The description is from a letter from Malik Firoz Khan Noon to Sir Fazl-i Husayn, 20 July 1935, in Waheed Ahmad, ed., _Letters of Mian Fazl-i-Husain_ (Lahore: Research Society of Pakistan, 1976), p. 411.

46. Letter, Malik Firoz Khan Noon Sir Fazl-i Husayn, 26 July 1935, in Ahmad, ed., _Letters of Mian Fazl-i Husain_, pp. 418–19.

47. Sir Herbert Emerson was referring in particular here to the members of the Legislative Council; letter, Emerson to Viceroy, 18 July 1935, National Archives of India, Home Political, file 5/14/35 Poll.

48. Government communiqué of 13 July 1935, quoted in Singh, _Gurdwara Shahid-ganj_, p. 79.

49. The case, Mosque known as Masjid Shahid Ganj and others vs. Shromani Gurdwara Parbandhak Committee, Amritsar, First Appeal no. 244 of 1936, is reported in _All India Reporter_ (Lahore) (1938), pp. 369–425.

50. Press branch note, 6 November 1935, P.C.S.A., Press Branch, file 4311.

51. _Siyasat_ (Lahore), 30 August 1935, P.C.S.A., Press Branch, file 8331, vol. VA.

52. The Ahrar Party was attempting to maneuver into an alliance with the Sikhs, with hopes of gaining representation in the ministry after the upcoming elections. The attitude of the Ahrar Party to the Shahidganj agitation, at least in its early weeks, is discussed in _Punjab Fortnightly Report_ for the second half of July, in National Archives of India, Home Political, file 18/7/35.

53. _Siyasat_ (Lahore), 13 August 1935; P.C.S.A., Press Branch, file 8331, vol. IIIA.

54. _Zamindar_ (Lahore), 24 August 1935, P.C.S.A., Press Branch, file 8331, vol. IVA.

55. There were, however, an increasingly large number of _pirs_ in the twentieth century with important contacts among the urban ulama and an interest in the controversies that had grown out of the reformist religious movements of the nineteenth century. Pir Jamaat 'Ali Shah was among these. An account of the careers of some of these _pirs_ is in David Gilmartin, "Tribe, Land and Religion in the Punjab: Muslim politics and the Making of Pakistan," Ph.D. dissertation, University of California, at Berkeley, 1979, chapter 2.

56. Among Pir Jamaat 'Ali Shah's prominent _murids_ was Mir Maqbul Mahmud, the brother-in-law of Sir Sikander Hyat Khan, who succeeded Sir Fazl-i Husayn in 1936 as the leader of the Unionist Party. For a biography of Pir Jamaat 'Ali Shah, see Pir Sayyid Akhtar Husain Shah, _Sirat-i Amir-i Millat_ (Alipur Sayyidan, 1974).

57. CID diary, report on Shahidganj conference, 3 September 1935, National Archives of India, Home Political, file 5/21/35 Poll.

58. Ibid.

59. Appreciation of the Shahidganj Situation, F. H. Puckle, 6 September 1935, National Archives of India, Home Political, file 5/21/35 Poll.

60. Pir Jamaat 'Ali Shah's contacts were apparently, in particular, with the Barelvi ulama, and he had donated money to the Anjuman Hizb al-Ahnaf: Haider Husain Shah, _Shah-yi Jamaat_ (Lahore: Maktabah Shah-yi Jamaat, 1973), p. 116; Faruqi, _Tazkirah-yi Ulama-yi Ahl-i Sunnat o Jamaat_, p. 321.

61. The potential political significance of such inherited charisma, including descent from the Prophet, is discussed for a somewhat different setting (Morocco), but in comparative perspective in Clifford Geertz, *Islam Observed* (Chicago: University of Chicago Press, 1971).

62. *Zamindar* (Lahore), 8 September 1935, P.C.S.A., Press Branch, file 8331, vol. VA. Pir Fazl Shah of Jalalpur announced after the Rawalpindi conference that he would attempt to form a Jami'at al-Mashaikh to organize the support of the *pirs*: Siyasat (Lahore), 10 September 1935, P.C.S.A., Press Branch, file 8331, vol. VA.

63. *Ihsan* (Lahore), 23 September 1935, P.C.S.A., Press Branch, file 8331, vol. VIIA.

64. Punjab Fortnightly Report for the second half of September 1935, National Archives of India, Home Political, file 18/9/35.

65. Appreciation of the Shahidganj Situation, F. H. Puckle, 6 September 1935, National Archives of India, Home Political, file 5/21/35 Poll.

66. *Pratap* (Lahore), 23 September 1935, P.C.S.A., Press Branch, file 8331, vol. IIIB.

67. *Inquilab* (Lahore), 15 September 1935, P.C.S.A., Press Branch, file 8331, vol. VIIA.

68. *Inquilab* (Lahore), 28 November 1935, P.C.S.A., Press Branch, file 4285. One of Pir Jamaat 'Ali Shah's lieutenants, Sufi Inayat Muhammad of Pasrur, claimed that in Rawalpindi 50,000 Muslims took an "oath of fealty at the hands of Pir Jamaat 'Ali Shah" to carry on this "purely religious struggle": *Zamindar* (Lahore), 13 September 1935, P.C.S.A., Press Branch, file 8331, vol. VIA.

69. Delhi Fortnightly Report for the first half of October 1935, National Archives of India, Home Political, file 18/10/35.

70. Letter from Abdul Ghaffar of Delhi, *Inquilab* (Lahore), 29 October 1935, P.C.S.A., Press Branch, file 4285. The *Inquilab* urged the *pir* to try to avoid such issues of religious controversy. "Ever since Pir Jamaat 'Ali Shah has been appointed the Amir of the Muslims for securing the Shahidganj mosque we have been expecting that he will devote his sole attention to the real object, viz. the release of the Shahidganj mosque and will not refer to questions about which the Muslims are not one; but different sections of Muslims make complaints about the Pir at different places": *Inquilab* (Lahore), 22 October 1935, P.C.S.A., Press Branch, file 4285.

71. *Siyasat* (Lahore), 11 September 1935, P.C.S.A., Press Branch, file 8331, vol. VIA.

72. Punjab Fortnightly Report for second half of December 1935, National Archives of India, Home Political, file 18/12/35.

73. *Ihsan* (Lahore), 25 October 1935, P.C.S.A., Press Branch, file 8331, vol. IXA.

74. *Ihsan* (Lahore), 12 January 1935, P.C.S.A., Press Branch, file 8331, vol. XIA.

75. *Ihsan* (Lahore), 12 January 1936, P.C.S.A., Press Branch, file 8331, vol. XIA.

76. The Shahidganj mosque agitation went through numerous stages after the *pir*'s departure in 1936 and ended in 1940 only after a final decision by the Privy Council confirmed the site in the hands of the Sikhs. In early 1936, after the failure of the Amritsar conference, the Shahidganj mosque itself became the focus of a small civil disobedience campaign in which groups of Muslims courted arrest while trying to march to the mosque. Later, Muhammad 'Ali Jinnah came to Lahore as leader of the All-India Muslim League to try to mediate a settlement, but met with little success. In 1937, after the passage of an All-India Muslim League resolution demanding restoration of the site to the Muslims, the Ahrar Party and the Majlis Ittihad-i Millat challenged each other to start civil disobedience to prove their commitment to the cause of the mosque. In 1938, the Muslim League tried to force the passage of a bill in the Unionist-controlled Punjab Legislative Assembly that would have restored the site to the "Muslim community," a move intended to embarrass the Unionist ministry. Though this move was unsuccessful, it indicated the strongly emotional symbolic appeal the mosque still held. The eventual disappearance of the issue was really a result largely of its suppression after 1940 by the demand for Pakistan.

77. For an account of the triumph of the Pakistan idea in the 1946 election campaign, see David Gilmartin, "Religious Leadership and the Pakistan Movement in the Punjab," *Modern Asian Studies* 13 (July 1979); and I. A. Talbot, "The 1946 Punjab Elections," *Modern Asian Studies* 14 (January 1980).

NINE

The Role of the Palestinian Peasantry in the Great Revolt (1936–1939)

Ted Swedenburg

Between 1936 and 1939, a major anti-colonial rebellion known among Arabs as the Great Revolt shook the mandate territory of Palestine. The struggle pitted a poorly armed peasant movement against the might of the world's preeminent colonial power, Great Britain. Despite the militancy and duration of the revolt, scholarly work on this period tends to emphasize the shortcomings of the insurgent movement and, in particular, to discount the role of the peasantry. Dominant accounts generally define the fellahin as "traditional, backward, and conservative," as "activated by tribal and religious loyalties,"[1] and as "too isolated, ignorant and poor" to play a significant role in the national movement.[2] Because they consider the peasants to be completely dominated by the local ruling class, these scholars view them as incapable of political initiative. Moreover, they attribute the disintegration of the revolt to the traditional clannish, factional, and regional divisions among fellahin that prevented them from maintaining a unified movement. The rebellion's demise is thus seen as due to the peasantry's accession to leadership in the vacuum left by the urban elites. A parallel argument, which imposes a model derived from industrial capitalism upon an agrarian society, attributes the uprising's defeat to its failure to develop a strong leadership. Since only a revolutionary party could have provided the command structure and social program necessary for victory, the peasantry as a class is considered incapable of providing guidance. Such analyses not only dismiss the crucial role of the peasants, who made up 75 percent of the population of Palestine,[3] but also ignore their legitimate social and political demands.

I propose, as an alternative, to read existing historical accounts "against the grain" so as to bring the marginalized Palestinian peasantry to the center of my analysis.[4] I will argue that the peasantry's relation to the ruling notables was never simply one of complete subservience. As Gramsci notes, a dominant class's hegemony is never "total or exclusive"; it is, rather, a process, a relation of dominance that has, as Raymond Williams says, "continually to be renewed, recreated, defended and modified. It is also continually resisted, limited, altered, challenged by pressures not all its own."[5] The Palestinian peasantry, therefore, while subordinated to the rule of the notables, nonetheless possessed a long tradition of opposition to their hegemony. It also possessed a history of challenging capitalist penetration and state formation. Such traditions of resistance were kept alive in popular memory and could be drawn upon as powerful tools of mobilization in moments of rupture. These "folk" traditions were not isolated, however, from other influences. They did not exist in a state of pristine purity, but were affected and transformed both by the dominant ideologies of the notables, who led the nationalist movement, and by alternative discourses emanating from more radical factions of the educated middle class. Also the fellahin's "common sense" notions[6] and their forms of political mobilization were jolted by the rapidly changing material conditions of the British mandate period. The Palestine peasantry, in short, was not simply an unchanging, backward social category.

During the course of the revolt, the rebels, who represented a broad alliance of peasants, workers, and radical elements of the middle class, developed an effective military force and began to implement social and political programs that challenged *a'yan* (notable) leadership of the nationalist movement and threatened the bases of mercantile-landlord dominance. The threat of a counter-hegemonic peasant leadership with a class-based program caused large numbers of wealthy urban Palestinians to flee the country. The movement also posed a serious threat to British strategy in the region and forced them to expend considerable military energies to crush the rebellion, which they succeeded in doing only after more than three years of struggle.

In order to recuperate and to assess the Palestinian peasants' historical achievements and traditions of resistance, I will trace the historical evolution of Palestinian society and its prevailing ideologies prior to the rebellion, going back to the period before capitalism was imposed as the dominant mode of production in Palestine. This will lay the foundation for a revised understanding of the pivotal role of the struggles of the Palestinian peasantry against the expansion of the Ottoman state, Zionist colonization, and British occupation that culminated in the Great Revolt.[7]

PALESTINE IN THE PRE-CAPITALIST ERA

In the period immediately prior to its occupation by Egypt's ruler Muhammad 'Ali in 1831, Palestine was only loosely controlled and integrated into the Ottoman empire.[8] At best, Ottoman sway extended to Palestine's towns and their immediate environs. But even the towns, dominated by notables whose authority was based on religious or genealogically claimed "noble" status, enjoyed substantial autonomy and frequently rebelled against Ottoman authority.[9] Towns along the coast had suffered a decline in the late eighteenth century due to the demise of the cotton trade with France and the ravages inflicted by the successive invasions of coastal Palestine by Egypt's 'Ali Bey (1770–71) and France's Napoleon Bonaparte (1799).[10] By the early nineteenth century the center of gravity had shifted to the towns of the interior highlands. While these urban centers in no way rivaled the great commercial emporia and textile-producing cities of northern Syria (Damascus, Homs, Hama), they were important centers of local and regional trade and artisanal production (particularly the olive oil of Nablus). In an era of weak imperial authority, these towns were generally dominated by the countryside. The population of the rural areas was concentrated in the central highlands of the Galilee, Jabal Nablus (Samaria), and Jabal al-Khalil (Judea). Here, clan-based coalitions organized along highly fluid "tribal" lines (Qays and Yemen) competed over local resources and political power. A rudimentary class structure separated the shaykhs of the leading patrilineages (*hamulas*) and the district tax collectors (*shuyukh al-nawahi*)from the mass of peasant producers.[11] The shaykhs' obligations to the Ottoman state were to maintain security and to collect taxes, a portion of which they retained. In practice they only sporadically remitted taxes to the state; more frequently they defended their autonomy by raising rural confederations to fend off tax-foraging expeditions sent out by the Ottoman governors of Damascus and Sidon.[12] Local class antagonisms were thus somewhat mitigated by the benefits that the peasantry gained in supporting their local chieftains against direct Ottoman rule.

The lowlands of Palestine—the plains of the coast and the Jordan and Esdraelon valleys—functioned as a hinterland for the highlands. But they were not merely an empty zone. The plains were cultivated but sparsely populated. Villagers who resided permanently in the more secure and salubrious hills and foothills went down to the lowlands to work the nearby plains on a seasonal basis. In contrast to the highlands, where individual ownership (*mulk*) by the head of the extended family predominated and where orchard and vine cultivation was typical, the peasants of the plains participated in *musha* or "communal" tenure and practiced extensive grain cultivation.

Unlike the highlands, in the lowlands agricultural practices interpenetrated with pastoralism, for both villagers and nomads used marginal and fallow lands to pasture their herds. The relation between peasants and nomads, usually represented as implacably hostile, was actually one of complexity and fluidity, characterized by moments both of cooperation and of struggle. Commentators who have described conditions on the plain as "anarchic" and have singled out the Bedouin as the chief cause of desolation merely reproduce the viewpoint of the Ottoman state. In fact the lowlands were simply a zone where peasants, nomads, bandits (both of peasant and of nomadic stock), and the forces of the state vied for control, with no group able to take decisive command. Bedouin chiefs commonly ruled over certain areas and "protected" peasants against the forces of the state (and against thieves and other nomadic tribes), in return for protection fees paid as a form of rent.

PRE-CAPITALIST IDEOLOGIES

Although the peasants of Palestine recognized the Ottoman sultans as successors to the Prophet and thus as legitimate rulers, in practice they exercised a great deal of independence from the state; Ottoman authority may have been legitimate but it scarcely intervened in everyday life. The local shaykhs served as mediators between the peasants and the state, but, given the balance of forces, they enjoyed virtual autonomy. Their own authority rested upon their imputed "noble" descent. As is typical in pre-capitalist societies,[13] relations between the "noble" shaykhs and their inferiors appeared highly personalized and intimate. This appearance in fact served to refract the underlying relations of exploitation, recasting them in terms consonant with the constitution of amicable interpersonal relations. Class antagonisms were also softened by the shared interests of shaykhs and peasants in defending highland villages from state intervention and in struggling against competing rural confederations. In addition, peasants were positioned in their productive relations through idioms of kinship,[14] while other relations based on village, regional, and "tribal" ties also served to divide peasants internally.[15] These vertical cleavages were not insuperable, for the various confederations (including Bedouin) were able to unite under the leadership of the shaykhs to resist foreign invaders, as in the broad-based 1834 rebellion against Egyptian occupation.[16] The principles of these dynamics of division and unity are expressed in the famous proverb, "I and my brother [unite to fight] against my cousin, but I and my cousin [unite to fight] against the stranger."[17]

Lack of state control over rural areas was also reflected in the distinctly "folk" character of peasant Islam. Mosques were virtually unknown in the villages, for rural religious practice centered instead on the worship of saints (*walis*) whose shrines (*maqams*) dotted the countryside. Nearly every village possessed at least one *maqam* where peasants went to plead for the *wali*'s intercession on their behalf.[18] A proliferation of shrines underlined the localized, particularistic nature of Palestinian folk Islam. However, other aspects of popular religion point equally to its socially unifying effects. For one thing, it was not *strictly* Islamic, for Muslim peasants visited many Christian churches and respected them as holy shrines.[19] Feasts (*mawsim*) celebrated in honor of various prophets also enhanced popular unity. For example, the *mawsim* of Nabi Rubin (Reuben), held south of Jaffa, attracted pilgrims from all the nearby towns and villages and lasted for a full lunar month.[20] The *mawsim* of

Nabi Musa (Moses), celebrated near Jericho, was an even bigger event, attended by peasants, city-dwellers, and Bedouin from all over southern Palestine and Jabal Nablus.[21] Such feasts, joining peasants from a wide area together with town-dwellers, were important rituals of popular solidarity.

Despite localized folk practices, the peasants of Palestine remained part of the wider Ottoman Islamic community which owed its loyalty to the sultan in Istanbul. In theory at least, their broader sense of belonging involved diffuse notions of duties and obligations to the Ottoman state, including the duty to pay taxes. Although the prevailing balance of forces in practice diminished the effects of such sentiments of loyalty to imperial authority, they held the potential to override localized interests. As the Ottoman authorities increased their hold over the provinces, they could draw on such sentiments to impose their hegemony.

PALESTINE'S INTEGRATION INTO THE WORLD MARKET

During the course of the nineteenth century, Palestine, like most of the non-Western world, was integrated into the capitalist world market, which dramatically transformed its social structure. These changes were not a "natural" evolutionary process, but required the sharp intervention of the Ottoman state under pressure from the European powers. Such developments began with the Egyptian invasion of Palestine and the rest of Syria, and Ibrahim Pasha's vigorous efforts to secure order there between 1831 and 1840. After the Egyptian exodus, the transformation proceeded more slowly as the Ottomans gradually subdued the towns and pacified the countryside, making the atmosphere safe for export agriculture and commerce.

The process involved a major shift in the local balance of forces. Ottoman authorities broke the power of the rural confederations and shifted control over local administration and tax collection from the independent-minded rural shaykhs to an emerging class of urban *a'yan* or notables, the Porte's local partners in its project of "reform." Their local power eroded, many rural shaykhs subsequently shifted their base of operations to the towns and merged with the urban notable class.

The *a'yan* took command over much of agricultural production, besides seizing political control over rural areas. Notable families and an emerging commercial bourgeoisie acquired vast properties in the wake of a series of new land laws beginning with the Ottoman Land Code of 1858. These new laws required individual registration of title to what was considered state or *miri* land and facilitated a massive land grab. The *a'yan*, who controlled the state apparatus administering the laws, were best positioned to profit from the situation. Many peasants failed to register their properties, some to avoid paying the registration fee, others to keep their names off government rolls and so escape conscription into the Ottoman army. Still others, rather than simply lose their lands in this fashion, registered their properties (sometimes a whole village) in the name of a powerful notable, who then served as their "patron" in their relations with the state. Other forms of alienation occurred when the Ottoman government decreed that specific tracts of land, especially in the northern plains, were "not permanently cultivated" or when it confiscated particular domains for "security" reasons. Such properties were put up for sale, and the largest of them were often purchased by absentee owners residing in Beirut. Peasants who had customarily farmed these lands were transformed into share-croppers working for large landowners; a similar change occurred among those who "voluntarily" registered their lands in the names of notables. As cash gained in importance in the regional economy and as the Ottomans began to demand taxes in cash, numbers of fellahin fell into debt to usurers, either notables or commercial bourgeois members of the local ruling bloc. Many peasants foreclosed on their loans, lost title to their lands, and became share-croppers. Others, who remained "independent" small or middle peasants, often became deeply dependent on their creditors.

The effects of these transformations were uneven. Land alienation was concentrated in the central and northern plains of the coast and the Esdraelon valley, where Ottoman authorities were most concerned to establish permanent settlements and where the most profitable crops for export to Europe could be grown. The highlands, however, generally remained a stronghold of small-holdings, but even there many peasants were forced to take out loans and thereby became dependent on moneylending notable "patrons."

The subordination of the local economy to the needs of the capitalist world economy paralleled the subjugation of the peasantry. Pacification of the coun-tryside and the onset of landlord-merchant control over agrarian production created a dramatic rise in agricultural exports. As a cash economy gradually developed, peasants were increasingly forced to sell part of their product on the market. Already by the 1870s, Palestine exported significant amounts of wheat, barley, sesame, olive oil, and citrus to Europe and to regional markets.[22]

Such transformations were not motivated simply by external factors but were integrally linked to the rise of leading classes composed of two sectors: first, the notables, predominantly Muslim, who owned large tracts of land, engaged in moneylending, and dominated the increasingly centralized government and religious apparatuses; and, second, the commercial bourgeoisie, composed chiefly of Palestinian and Lebanese Christians, Jews, Europeans, and European protégés, who were representatives of banking and merchant capital but who also owned large tracts of land.[23] Muslim notables, allied with Christian merchants, constituted the dominant sector, whose hegemony was organized under the form of what social scientists have termed "patron-client" relations, or pyramid-shaped networks of notables and their peasant client-clans.

IDEOLOGIES OF NOTABLE DOMINANCE:
PATRONS AND CLIENTS

Notable patrons used their power and influence to assist their peasant clients in dealing both with the state and with other groups (such as peasants belonging to other patronage networks and Bedouin). In return, peasants supported their patrons in political struggles. The notables also provided sharecroppers with their subsistence needs during the year and made regular advances to them on holidays. In addition, they carried over the sharecroppers' debts in case of a series of poor harvests.[24] Similar favors were accorded to their smallholding "clients" as well as to farm laborers who worked for landlords on a seasonal basis. The hierarchical relation between notable and peasant appeared to involve a high degree of mutuality and reciprocity. On the basis of an empirical description of this system many observers have concluded that it is wrong to conceive of Palestinian society during this era in terms of social classes.[25]

What most observers have done is to accept, at face value, native conceptions (with a notable bias) about how politics and economics "worked." In fact, the patron-client system was simply the form that class relations assumed as Palestine was integrated into the capitalist world market as a dependency of the industrialized European powers. During this period landlords and usurers seized control over the countryside and manipulated existing precapitalist means of domination for their own interests.[26] The form that the relations between the fundamental classes took—"paternalism" in the sphere of production (cash advances by patrons to peasants) and "patronage" in the sociopolitical sphere (an "exchange" of favors)—tended to refract the fundamentally exploitative relations between landlord-usurers and peasants.[27] Politico-economic relations between them were represented as "exchanges" between individuals unequal in status—notables whose superior birth and noble lineage qualified them to rule and to manage property, and peasants who had internalized their position of inferiority and who behaved deferentially toward their superiors. On the other hand, "politics" in the larger sense of the "affairs of state" appeared as a struggle among the notables themselves, in which peasant clients played only a supporting role. The notables acted as "their" peasants' representatives to the government, a role acquired not through democratic elections but by ascribed superior status. The literature that characterizes political struggle in this period as "factionalism" in fact disguises a high degree of class unity at the upper level. But on the lower levels, patron-client ideology largely reinforced and rigidified preexisting vertical cleavages based on idioms of clan, village, and regional distinctions. The patron-client system did not assume the form of exchanges between "free" individuals, as under full-blown capitalism. Instead, the system of exploitation required an extra-economic element, the force of status hierarchy, to justify the "exchange" between persons of unequal position. Economic relations between patron and client were always expressed in such terms as "honor," gift-giving, kinship.

Although paternalism and patronage provided the ideological basis for rule by the notables, their hegemony did not go unchallenged by the fellahin. There was room for struggle even on the basis of such an ideology. From the peasants' point of view, the system was designed to guarantee them the rights to a "fair" and "just" exchange. A notable could not charge too much rent without appearing to break his end of the bargain, without seeming to fail in his duty to uphold a standard of noblesse oblige. This meant that a landlord-usurer who charged peasants high interest on loans was simultaneously forced to advance them additional credit to maintain his labor force. In addition, the patron had to provide his client with the culturally regulated "just" minimum of subsistence in order to neutralize potential class antagonisms. This level of subsistence was determined through similar struggles of a distinctly class character, for the peasant was able to use the notable's dependence on his labor as a wedge to demand adherence to the notion of "fair" exchange. In the political realm, peasants (primarily the smallholder) could shift their allegiance if they received insufficient benefits from their patron. The patron-client alliances were thus far more fluid in composition than the model of a solid pyramidal structure purveyed by social scientists would suggest.[28]

Subordination of the political economy of Palestine to nineteenth-century Western industrial capitalism entailed, paradoxically, the reinforcement of precapitalist or "feudal" ideologies. While peasants increasingly worked for capital, they did so under transformed pre-capitalist forms of productive relations and ideologies. In order to make these transformations, the notables had to "work on" pre-capitalist ideologies of hierarchy, so as to reinforce the peasants' attitude of deference and to reproduce their sensibility of mutuality and exchange. The conditions of peripheral capitalism required a much more active ruling-class hegemony than had been needed in the pre-capitalist era. Ruling-class ideologies now had to penetrate deeply the cultural life of the peasantry,[29] including their religious "common sense." As a consequence folk practices were substantially transformed by notables in this period.

The organization of the feast of Nabi Musa exemplifies this process. In the latter half of the century, the Ottomans appointed the Husaynis—a rising notable clan from Jerusalem—as hosts of the Nabi Musa feast and custodians of the shrine.[30] Festivities were now launched at Jerusalem with a procession in which the banner of Nabi Musa was brought from the Husayni-owned Dar al-Kabira where it was housed. Notables led the procession, followed by crowds from the city and the villages. At the site of the feast itself (near Jericho), the Husaynis and the Yunises, another Jerusalem notable family, served two public meals a day to all visitors.[31] Such rituals demonstrated notable generosity and claims to supremacy in powerful ways.

At the same time as unifying folk practices were subsumed under notable control, saint worship came under increasing attack by religious reformers, particularly from the Salafiya movement. Mosques, where state-backed Islamic orthodoxy was preached, replaced the *maqam*s as village centers of worship. The chief reason for the suppression of saint worship was the localism it expressed.[32] Though such folk practices were not immediately wiped out, they were forced into regression as more and more peasants were "educated" and came to regard such activities as "un-Islamic."

THE EMERGENCE OF ORGANIZED OPPOSITION

The piecemeal implementation of notable domination confined resistance against land transfers and growing state control to a localized, sporadic, and manageable level. No large-scale eruptions or even jacqueries occurred. However, opposition was still significant. For instance, many peasants demonstrated their opposition to the changing state of affairs by leaving their villages to settle as farmers in Transjordan or by migrating overseas. Others chose to join gangs of bandits, which continued to operate in the hills despite increasing pressure from security forces. Young men sought refuge with Bedouin tribes or even resorted to self-mutilation to avoid conscription into the army. Perhaps the major form of resistance in this period took place at the point of production. Palestinian peasants, particularly in the plains where sharecropping predominated, were often described at the time as "lazy, thriftless and sullen."[33] As James Scott has observed, "footdragging and dissimulation" are a common form of resistance under unequal power relations.[34] While such resistance may not have posed a grave danger to the new system, it at least slowed the process of accumulation.

Peasant opposition to the colonization of Palestine by foreigners in fact presented the greatest threat to the hegemony of local notables. In 1878, Jewish settlers from Europe, with the backing of powerful capitalist financial interests, began to take advantage of the general land-grab in Palestine by acquiring lands and establishing agricultural colonies in the fertile coastal plains and the Esdraelon valley. By 1914, 12,000 Jews lived in such colonies, which produced valuable citrus and wine exports and encompassed over 162,500 acres of land concentrated in the richest agricultural regions. Most estates were purchased from absentee landowners in Beirut who had only recently acquired them. As new colonies were set up, large numbers of peasant sharecroppers were forcibly removed from the lands they considered their birthright, although they may never have formally "owned" them. Jewish settlers who established colonies even on "marginal" lands were able to improve them due to their access to capital and advanced scientific techniques, and so denied nomads and peasants their customary-use rights to these common lands for grazing and gathering.

Palestinian notables were not at this stage implicated in any great degree in land sales to Jewish settlers. They protested Jewish immigration and land purchases as early as 1891, but their efforts were largely "sporadic and non-systematic" and limited to sending formal petitions of protest to Istanbul.[35] The advances made by urban Jews in commerce and industry were perceived as a greater threat to the interests of the Arab upper classes, particularly the commercial bourgeois sector, than were their purchases of agricultural properties.

In contrast, peasants whose livelihoods were directly threatened by Jewish colonies—especially those who cultivated and who pastured their herds in the northern and central plains—reacted in militant fashion. By 1883, displaced peasants and Bedouin were already attacking, raiding, robbing, and generally harassing the new Jewish settlements. Although spontaneous and fragmented, this violent opposition meant that the government was routinely forced to call out troops to drive fellahin off lands purchased by Jewish colonists. These activities eventually prompted the notables to protest the Zionist influx, albeit feebly.

The *a'yan*'s ineffectiveness in confronting the external threat began to undermine their own legitimacy (and that of the Ottoman state in general) in the eyes of many Palestinians. The disastrous experiences that befell dispossessed peasant sharecroppers in particular prompted them to question the usefulness of the patron-client system. Arab nationalism, emerging at the same moment, was able to tap these sentiments. As a nascent movement that advocated in its different versions either complete Arab independence from the Ottoman empire or greater autonomy, it became a significant social force in the wake of the ferment aroused by the Young Turk revolution (1908). Although the nationalist movement was less important in Southern Syria (Palestine) than in Lebanon and Northern Syria, and though it was dominated by notables and the commercial bourgeoisie, nonetheless there arose within it a radical wing composed of elements of the educated middle class. Opposition to Zionism was one of the Palestinian radical nationalists' chief themes, which they advanced through a new means of communication that had sprung up in this era of enhanced political freedom, namely, newspapers. Although the early Arab nationalist movement is usually characterized as a strictly urban phenomenon, beginning in 1909 the political activities of its militant wing included helping to organize peasant attacks on Jewish settlements.[36] These raids increased in tempo in the years immediately preceding World War I, but this militant sector of the developing Arab national movement and its peasant connections assumed real prominence only during the years following the war.

THE BRITISH OCCUPATION OF PALESTINE
AND THE MANDATE, 1918–29

Expectations for national independence rose sharply in Greater Syria as World War I and the privations it caused came to a close. These hopes intensified in

1918 with the establishment of an Arab government at Damascus under Prince Faysal. Many young Palestinian radicals from the educated middle class held prominent positions in the new Sharifian government. At the same time, their influence in Palestine began to outstrip that of the more moderate notables. Through organizations such as al-Nadi al-'Arabi (the Arab Club) and al-Muntada al-Adabi (the Literary Club), the radicals pushed for a program of complete independence of Palestine from Britain and for its political unity with the rest of Syria. By contrast, the Palestinian notables who had organized Muslim-Christian Associations in all the towns favored a separate political autonomy for Palestine under British protection. The euphoria that followed the end of the war was dampened by the Balfour Declaration, which announced Britain's intention of establishing a "national home for the Jewish people" in Palestine. This tarnished Britain's local reputation and helped win broad popular support for the militant nationalist program. Popular radicalism in turn pressured the notable *zu'ama* or "chiefs" to adopt more combative positions themselves. The militants capitalized on the moment by pushing through a resolution advocating Palestine's political unity with Syria at the notable-dominated First Palestine Arab Congress.[37]

In this period the radicals not only organized effectively in the public arena but also secretly purchased arms and prepared for armed revolt in favor of Faysal.[38] So effective was the radicals' work among the peasantry that in December 1919, British Naval Intelligence reported with concern that fellahin were listening with keen interest to both Damascus and local newspapers advocating pan-Arabism and discussed the possibility of anti-Zionist actions.[39] Despite widespread illiteracy, "advanced" pan-Arab and anti-Zionist ideas circulated among the peasantry and helped to mobilize them. At least one organized act of violence against the British occurred. In April 1920, Palestinian radicals (connected to the Arab government at Damascus) organized over 2,000 armed Bedouin from the Hawran (Syria) and the Baysan valley of Palestine in an attack on British military forces.[40] The countrywide anti-British upsurge that the radicals expected to ensue did not, however, come to fruition.

In the same month, soon after Faysal was crowned as king of Syria, radicals intervened in the Nabi Musa procession at Jerusalem. In 1919 the practice of delaying the procession for speeches had been introduced;[41] this year Musa Kazim al-Husayni, Jerusalem's mayor and a leading notable, praised Faysal in his speech, while young activists made "inflammatory" declamations from the balcony of the Arab Club. The crowds, including peasants from the surrounding villages, responded by roaming the streets of the Old City, attacking Jewish residents.[42] This event transformed the *mawsim* of Nabi Musa from a folk festival into an annual nationalist demonstration.[43]

In May 1921, clashes between Arabs and Jews at Jaffa led to generalized fighting and attacks on Jewish settlements throughout the country. The British military quickly and violently restored order. Two months later King Faysal's troops at Damascus were defeated by the French, who dismantled the Arab government. The moment of crisis had ended. Great Britain, which now held a mandate to govern Palestine under the auspices of the League of Nations, strengthened its control. The threat of pan-Arab militants to *a'yan* hegemony and their ability to mobilize the peasantry subsided. The notables, who favored a policy of peaceful negotiations with the British authorities rather than mass mobilization as the means of achieving the nationalist goals, reemerged as the dominant force within the national movement.

During the 1920s, the notables reasserted their hegemony over the Arab population of Palestine through a consolidation of their role as "natural" leaders of the national movement. British authorities in turn absorbed members of notable families into important administrative positions in the mandate government.[44] As chief agents of state rule in the late Ottoman and mandate periods, they expected to emerge as the country's rulers once Great Britain granted Palestine its independence. Their principal means of organization, the Muslim-Christian Associations, were not mass-membership bodies but were composed of religious leaders, property owners, those who held positions in the Ottoman administration, and "noble" families of rural origin—in short, the *a'yan* class. These associations periodically met in Palestine Arab Congresses and in 1920 set up an Arab Executive, chaired by Musa Kazim al-Husayni, to tend to the daily affairs of the national movement. At the same time, mandate authorities co-opted a young militant from a prominent notable family, Hajj Amin al-Husayni, making him first Grand Mufti (1921) and then president of the Supreme Muslim Council (S.M.C.) in 1922. As "Head of Islam in Palestine," Hajj Amin gradually consolidated all Islamic affairs under his administration and began to compete with the more cautious Arab Executive for leadership of the nationalist movement.[45]

The notables continued to lead the Arab population of Palestine in the mandate period under the ideology of patronage. *A'yan* served as mediators between the people and the British authorities. Politics was strictly reserved for organizations (the Muslim-Christian Associations, the S.M.C.) "qualified" to lead. Once the radical pan-Arab threat had passed and Palestine was established as a territorial unit, notables were able to co-opt the growing popular self-awareness of "Palestinian Arabness" that arose in response to the Zionist threat and to alien rule.[46] Furthermore, the British bolstered the *a'yan* position by ruling through their agency and by upholding their control over rural areas.[47]

In spite of the fact that the legitimacy of notable leadership was constructed on "national-popular" sentiments, the notables themselves were caught in a fundamentally contradictory position, for while the *a'yan* posed as leaders of nationalist aspirations, they served as officials in the British mandate administration. Rifaat Abou-el-Haj sums up the predicament of Palestinian notables (characteristic of all Mashriq elites):

[As the nationalist elite] actually began to collaborate with the new ruling powers, the [elite] cadre managed to portray itself in the "vanguard" of resistance against outside domination—in some instances even taking a revolutionary posture. The other role it adopted for itself was that of realist-pragmatist mediator with which it defended its compatriots against the direct and therefore presumed odious rule of the foreigner.[48]

The British in Palestine depended in particular on erstwhile "radical" Amin al-Husayni to act as such a mediator. The Mufti worked hard to prevent outbursts and to pacify the Muslim community, channeling nationalist energies (including those of his former comrades) into legal activities.[49]

The contradictory position of the Palestinian notables—at once servants of the British mandate and leaders of "the nation"—was rendered even more unstable than that of Arab elites elsewhere, due to the competition of the Zionist movement. Since Zionists opposed the establishment of any legislative body in Palestine that would relegate the Jews to a minority position, they effectively blocked the development of national Palestinian institutions of self-rule. Had not the threat of Jewish immigration appeared somewhat limited due to internal problems of the Zionist movement, conditions might have been more unstable in the 1920s. But meanwhile, the Zionists were quietly building an infrastructure that served as the basis for expansion of the Jewish community in the 1930s and made the Yishuv virtually self-governing.[50]

The lack of progress in the creation of Palestinian institutions of self-rule began to undermine even the notables' own liberal self-image. Steeped in Western liberal ideas,[51] the *a'yan* expected the British to behave toward them according to the standards of justice that Great Britain preached. As it gradually became clear that the British authorities did not adhere in practice to the standards that the two groups supposedly shared, Palestinian liberal notables became disillusioned. Both notables and liberal intellectuals developed an ambivalent attitude toward the West and, in particular, Britain.[52] Although the notables never entirely abandoned their affection for Britain since service in the mandate administration was still profitable, disaffection for British policies slowly undermined their confidence in diplomatic discussions between "gentlemen" as the best means of resolving the national question.

Rapidly changing agrarian conditions during the 1920s were potentially more unsettling to *a'yan* hegemony. Land purchases by the Zionists continued apace, resulting in the dispossession of increasing numbers of peasants. The notables' appeals that the government halt the process were ineffectual. Moreover, by 1928, land sales to the Zionists by Palestinian landowners had eclipsed those by non-Palestinians.[53] A section of the notable class was thus enriching itself through land sales to Zionists and contributing directly to peasant landlessness, especially in the northern and central plains. This portion of the *a'yan*, clustered around the leadership of the Nashashibi clan, which opposed the Husayni dominance in the national movement, generally comprised its wealthier and commercial elements, who used their profits for urban construction and expansion of citrus production.

Small but growing numbers of peasant holders also sold their lands to Zionist developers, usually not for profit but to pay off debts. Peasant indebtedness to usurers who charged high rates of interest was exacerbated by the mandate government's rationalization of rural property taxes, now set at a fixed percentage based on the net productivity of the soil (that is, minus the cost of production). This meant that the capital-intensive Jewish agricultural enterprises paid lower rates because of higher "labor costs." Regressive indirect taxes added to the peasants' financial burden. The weight of taxation therefore fell disproportionately on poor Palestinian fellahin, whose contributions helped to finance industrial and agricultural development in the Jewish sector and to pay Britain's expenses in defending the Jewish "national home." [54] The British administration also ensured that taxes were more efficiently collected by enlisting the services of the village *mukhtars* (headmen) to maintain rural security and to pass on taxes and information to the government.[55]

As a consequence of such pressures, by 1930 some 30 percent of all Palestinian villagers were totally landless, while as many as 75 to 80 percent held insufficient land to meet their subsistence needs.[56] Some peasants made up this imbalance by renting additional farmlands, but most now depended on outside sources of income for survival. During peak periods of economic activity in the mandate, about one-half of the male fellahin workforce (over 100,000 persons) engaged in seasonal wage employment outside the village (on road or construction projects, in citrus harvesting and packing, and so forth). Often the entire male population of a village was recruited to work as a team on short-term construction projects.[57] Thus Palestinian rural villagers no longer filled a purely "peasant" position in the economic structure; increasingly they assumed a dual economic role as peasants and as casual laborers. So while notable landowners and moneylenders maintained economic dominance over the villages, particularly through client networks, the new experiences of peasants in the wider labor market altered their "traditional" fellahin subjectivities and provided alternate sources of income.

Indebtedness and expropriation at the hands of Zionist colonies forced a significant sector of the peasantry to emigrate permanently to the rapidly growing metropolises of Haifa, Jaffa, and Jerusalem. There they worked mainly as casual laborers and as a "scuffling petty bourgeoisie" in petty trading and services, a class situation typical of urban centers in underdeveloped colonial social formations.[58] Permanent wage work was difficult to come by in the face of competition from Jewish workers who monopolized positions in the more advanced Jewish economic sector. The work that Arab workers did obtain was extremely low-paying, due to an abundant labor supply and the difficulties inherent in organizing casual workers. As a consequence, the costs of Arab labor were never fully met by wages but were subsidized by the workers' access to subsistence agriculture and support networks at home in the village.[59]

These rural-to-urban migrants did not remain passive in the face of such conditions. On the contrary, they set up various associations based on village of origin which ignored the *hamula* distinctions that were so divisive at home.[60] They also joined semi-political organizations headed by artisans, enlisted in trade unions whenever possible, and came in contact with militant religious reformers like Shaykh 'Izz al-Din al-Qassam. Their entry into the urban wage workforce helped to weaken clan, village, and regional divisions; these new experiences also had an impact on the home villages, with which migrants maintained close contact. Thus the old cleavages that buttressed patron-client networks were slowly breaking down under the impact of capitalist development. The nationalist leadership tried to reverse the process by making frequent appeals to the British on behalf of the impoverished peasantry, but this had little effect on British policies or on economic conditions.[61] Furthermore, the fellahin were increasingly skeptical of the *a'yan*'s sincerity. By 1927, according to a British official, the notables were apprehensive that the peasantry "show[ed] a growing tendency to distinguish between national and Effendi [notable] class interest."[62]

The brewing crisis in agriculture, closely tied to steady Zionist progress in the 1920s (between 1919 and 1929 the Jewish population of Palestine had doubled, reaching 156,000 persons),[63] was a major factor in igniting the violence that erupted over expanded Zionist claims to the Wailing Wall at Jerusalem (known by Arabs as the Buraq, the western wall of the Haram al-Sharif, third holiest shrine in Islam). The Mufti as usual tried to settle the problem through the good offices of the British, at the same time attempting to allay the anger of the populace, who saw in Zionist "religious" expansionism a condensed form of the general danger Zionism posed to Palestinian Arab sovereignty.[64] A series of provocative demonstrations at the wall by Zionist extremists took place during 1929. Finally, on 23 August, peasant villagers influenced by the propaganda work of nationalist militants arrived in Jerusalem for Friday prayers armed with knives and clubs. Hajj Amin made every effort to calm the crowds, but radical religious shaykhs made speeches inciting them to action.[65] Violence broke out against Jews in Jerusalem and quickly spread throughout the country; British forces restored order in brutal fashion.

The widespread nature of the violence demonstrated that the mass of the population was ready to take direct action against the Zionist threat, independently of the cautious notable leadership. Unfortunately they could also be incited to ugly sectarian violence, which assumed the dimensions of a pogrom at Hebron and Safad. One of the most important forms of organization to emerge from this outbreak was the guerrilla band known as the Green Hand Gang established by Ahmad Tafish in the Galilee hills in October 1929. Composed of men associated with radical circles who had taken part in the August uprising, the band launched several attacks on Zionist colonies and British forces in the north.[66] The band's organization probably resembled that of the gangs of peasant bandits that traditionally operated in the Palestine hills and were a growing security problem in the 1920s.[67] But unlike them, Ahmad Tafish's band had an overt political purpose. Although quickly subdued, the Green Hand Gang aroused considerable sympathy among the peasantry who, the Shaw Commission concluded in 1930, were "probably more politically minded than many of the people of Europe."[68] This atmosphere of popular agitation provided new opportunities for alternative political forces within the national movement to challenge notable hegemony.

HARBINGERS OF REVOLT, 1930–35

The early 1930s were characterized by extremely unstable conditions, which the Palestinian *zu'ama* were incapable of controlling. Contradictions piled one on top of another, ushering in a series of crises that, by fits and starts, led to the explosion of 1936.

One major destabilizing factor was the global depression. Due chiefly to forces released by the worldwide economic downturn, Jewish immigration to Palestine jumped sharply in the early 1930s. Between 1931 and 1935 the Jewish community grew from 175,000 to 400,000 persons, or from 17 to 31 percent of the total population of Palestine. The advance of anti-Semitism in Poland, the tightening of the U.S. quota system in 1929, and the triumph of Nazism in Germany all contributed to the floodtide of immigration to Palestine.[69]

The effects of Jewish immigration upon Palestinian Arab society were uneven. Between the late 1920s and 1932, the country suffered a recession and a steep rise in Arab unemployment. But with the refugee influx, the economy expanded in the 1933–36 period, while the rest of the world (except the Soviet Union) languished in deep depression. As a result of an agreement, known as the Ha'avara, between the World Zionist Organization and the Nazis, Jews leaving Germany were able to import large amounts of capital into Palestine. Nearly 60 percent of all capital invested in Palestine between August 1933 and September 1939 entered by means of the Ha'avara.[70] This capital inflow permitted wealthy Jews greatly to increase their investments in industry, building, and citriculture. In addition, rapid British development of Haifa as a strategic eastern Mediterranean port meant the construction of a new harbor, an oil pipeline (which began pumping oil from Iraq in 1935), refineries, and a railroad during the same period.[71] As a consequence, job opportunities for Arab workers expanded. The greatest share of jobs, however, went to Jewish workers, as Zionist leaders and especially the Histadrut (the Zionist labor federation) made sure that the burgeoning Jewish economic sector provided for the new Jewish immigrants. This caused resentment among Arab workers and led to clashes with Jews over access to jobs.[72] The economy suffered another recession from 1936 to 1939, which affected semi-proletarianized Arab workers much more deeply than largely unionized Jewish labor.

The capital influx accompanying Jewish immigration increased the pace of land purchases as well. Zionist acquisitions from large Palestinian owners and small peasants now assumed greater importance than in the 1920s.[73] An increasingly desperate economic situation constrained peasants to sell their lands, for by 1936 the average debt of a peasant family—25 to 35 pounds per year—equaled or surpassed their average annual income of 27 pounds.[74] The money peasants earned from land sales usually did little more than release them from debt and propel them toward the urban slums. Due to inflated real-estate prices, large Palestinian landowners, on the other hand, could make huge profits by selling their estates to the Zionists. Some owners arbitrarily raised rents to force their tenants off the land prior to concluding such a sale, in order to avoid paying compensation to the peasants.[75] A law, decreed in 1933, extending greater rights to tenants contributed to a noticeable increase in disputes between landlords and peasants over tenancy rights. Militant nationalists were involved in encouraging such conflicts.[76] By the mid-1930s the government was routinely forced to call out large numbers of police in order to evict sharecroppers from sold properties as, more and more frequently, peasants resisted dispossession through violent means.[77]

The bankruptcy of the notables' policies was therefore increasingly apparent: they had made no progress toward achieving national independence and were incapable of stemming the Zionist tide of increasing population, land settlement, and economic development. The a'yan's inability to achieve successes threatened their hold over the national movement and made it difficult for them to claim the discourses of nationalism or even Islam as their exclusive property. Moreover, the notable front had splintered over disagreements on national strategy. Opposition to Husayni leadership crystallized around the Nashashibi clan, which represented the richest landowners, citrus growers, and entrepreneurs. More heavily involved than other notables in land sales to the Zionists, and the greatest beneficiaries of citrus exports to England, the Nashashibi-led groups of the notable-mercantile class opposed pan-Arab unity and was ready to accept less than total independence from Britain.[78] This group, which established the National Defense Party in 1934, had a certain base of support through its patron-client networks.[79]

The radical nationalists took advantage of the openings provided by the series of crises and by the swelling of their ranks with a new contingent of young men educated in mandate institutions. As Göran Therborn notes, the training of an intellectual stratum in colonial situations often generates revolutionary ideologies, due to the disparity between the nature of the training they receive, suitable for an advanced capitalist society, and the colonial form of subjection.[80] The mandate educational system in Palestine produced young men whose qualifications were not commensurate with the holy roles assigned to them, and so their discontent generated new and critical forms of subjectivity.

The 1930s witnessed an upsurge in Palestine of independent political organizing by the educated middle class, just as in the rest of the Arab world, where a new generation of radical nationalists were raising slogans of socioeconomic justice and Arab unity and developing novel forms of political organization.[81] Palestinian radicals set up a variety of bodies such as the Young Men's Muslim Association, the Arab Youth Conferences, and the Arab Boy Scouts (independent of the international Baden-Powell movement). The most important organization was the Istiqlal (Independence) Party, established in 1932, whose roots lay in the old Istiqlal movement associated with the Sharifian government at Damascus.[82] Led by elements of the educated middle class and the disaffected offspring of notable families, it appealed to educated professionals and salaried officials: lawyers, doctors, teachers, government employees.[83] Unlike other Palestinian parties founded in the 1930s, it was organized not on the basis of family or clan loyalties but around a political program, and thus it was the first (excluding the Communist) to appeal to and construct a new and modern form of subjectivity. It also distinguished itself by centering its political actions on opposition to the British mandate government rather than aiming them at the Jewish community alone.

The Istiqlal took a "populist" political stance representative of an aspiring national bourgeoisie.[84] Its adherents criticized the chronic unemployment besetting Arab workers, and the high taxes, rising prices, and unjust government treatment that the peasants suffered under. The Istiqlal advocated the establishment of a nationalist parliament and the abolition of "feudal" titles, such as *pasha, bey,* and *effendi,* that were common among the notables. In 1933, Istiqlalists began to attack the notable leadership, asserting that because it had remained abject in the face of Zionism and imperialism, Palestinian nationalism was not the cause of the *zu'ama* but, rather, that of the poor.[85] The Istiqlalists therefore attempted to mobilize the popular classes along the faultlines of class antagonisms by constructing a popular-democratic discourse that took advantage of fellahin disaffection from the notables and used it for "national" purposes.[86]

In 1934, however, only a year and a half after its founding, the Istiqlal Party ceased to function effectively. Aided by the party's division into pro-Hashemite and pro-Saudi factions, Hajj Amin al-Husayni was able to sabotage it. Many Istiqlalists subsequently joined the Mufti's Palestine Arab Party, which, paradoxically, made it into something more than simply a clan-based grouping.[87] In addition, their entry pushed Hajj Amin to take a more militant stance. But even after their party's demise, Istiqlalists continued to be active as individuals, while other independent groupings stepped up their organizing efforts. The Arab Youth Congress attempted to prevent illegal Jewish immigration by organizing units to patrol the coasts.[88] Arab labor garrisons were set up at Jerusalem, Haifa, and Jaffa to defend Arab workers against attacks by Jewish workers trying to prevent Jewish capitalists from hiring Arabs.[89]

Efforts to mobilize the peasantry were even more consequential. Educated young men from the villages, who returned home to serve as teachers, spread radical nationalist notions among the fellahin, particularly in the northern foothills of Jabal Nablus (the region known as the Triangle, comprising the environs of Nablus, Janin, and Tulkarm) where villages had lost land to Zionist colonies on the coastal and Esdraelon plains.[90] Poetry was an especially significant vehicle for this dissemination of nationalist ideas and sentiments in the countryside. Written in simple language and style, nationalist poetry frequently criticized the notable leadership.[91] According to Ghassan Kanafani, it often took the form of "almost direct political preaching."[92] Poems and songs by artists like Ibrahim Tuqan, 'Abd al-Karim al-Karmi, and 'Abd al-Rahim Mahmud were well known in the countryside and recited at festive and public occasions. Peasants had access to newspapers (which began to appear daily after the 1929 riots) and magazines that printed nationalist poetry; the anthropologist Hilma Granqvist reports that fellahin from the village of Artas who went to Bethlehem for market heard newspapers read aloud in the coffee shops there.[93] Probably most villages had similar access to the printed word. Al-Baquri claims that the poetry of the nationalist bards "rang out on the lips of the fighters and popular masses" during the 1936–39 revolt.[94]

The Palestine Communist Party should be mentioned in this context, even though its impact on events was minimal. Founded in 1922, the P.C.P. remained primarily a Jewish organization until 1929, when the Comintern ordered it to undergo "Arabization."[95] At its Seventh Congress in 1930, it began to orient itself programmatically toward the peasantry. Asserting that in an agricultural country like Palestine it was "the peasant revolution" that was "the most significant," it called for the confiscation of estates held by big Arab landowners, religious institutions, and Jewish colonies, and for their distribution to landless and land-poor peasants. The P.C.P. urged peasants to refuse to pay taxes and debts and advocated armed rebellion. It also proposed conducting propaganda at the mosques on Fridays and at popular festivals like Nabi Musa, for "it is during such mass celebrations that the fighting capacity of the fellahin is appreciably aroused."[96] In addition, the P.C.P. campaigned vigorously on behalf of Bedouin and peasants dispossessed by Zionist colonization.[97] But due to its paucity of Arab members, the fact that no cadre lived in villages, and widespread perceptions that it was chiefly a Jewish organization, the party's influence in the Palestinian Arab community remained circumscribed. In any case, after the onset of the Comintern's Popular Front strategy, the P.C.P. dropped its call for agrarian revolution (typical of the world Communist movement's ultra-left "Third Period") and began trying to build closer ties with middle-class nationalists. 'Abd al-Qadir Yasin asserts that the party's social demands were influential among workers and peasants by the mid-1930s,[98] but such claims are difficult to verify, since the P.C.P.'s ideas were not backed up by practices. At best, Communist notions may have influenced radical nationalist individuals with whom the party maintained contact.

A wave of renewed violence in 1933 further demonstrated the notables' tenuous hold over the nationalist movement. Violence rapidly spread through the urban centers (and some villages) of the country after an anti-British demonstration at Jaffa in October led to clashes with police. Unlike the situation in 1929, this violence was aimed specifically at the British mandate administration, which represented a significant shift in the movement's strategy and political awareness. The British leaned harder than ever on the Mufti to keep these disturbances from getting out of hand. In return for preventing the fellahin from following the "extremists" and for restraining demonstrations, the British granted the Supreme Muslim Council complete control over *waqf* (religious endowment) finances.[99] But as tensions mounted, Hajj Amin's position as mediator became more precarious. He moved in two directions at once, trying both to maintain good relations with the British by reining in the national movement and to retain credibility with the populace by adopting a militant posture.

Hajj Amin's primary activities concerned land sales, a significant issue of public concern. The Palestinian Arab press frequently editorialized against land traffic with the Zionists, and in the early 1930s the Muslim-Christian Associations and the Arab Executive had sent agents out to the villages, urging peasants not to sell their land.[100] In the fall of 1934 the Mufti and the S.M.C. initiated a more vigorous campaign, mobilizing the ideology and institutions of Islam to fight land sales (and to maintain Hajj Amin's influence with the peasantry). The Mufti toured areas where transactions were occurring, to explain the dangers they posed to the nation and condemn them as acts of sin and high treason.[101] In January 1935, he issued a *fatwa* (legal opinion) on the matter that forbade traffic in land with the Zionists and branded *simsars* (real estate brokers) as heretics (*mariq*).[102] But religious propaganda alone could not reverse the economic forces that led the peasants into indebtedness and forced them off the land. The dire agrarian situation was exacerbated by a series of crop failures between 1929 and 1936 and by competition from cheap agricultural imports, their prices depressed by the global economic downturn.[103] The Mufti recognized, in theory, the need for structural changes, and he called for (1) measures to protect peasants from big landowners; (2) the establishment of national industries; (3) aid to small farmers; and (4) a campaign of purchasing notional products.[104] But the S.M.C.'s only concrete action was to put some tracts of land under *waqf* (mortmain) protection.

By the mid-1930s the political impasse in Palestine forced even the Mufti to realize that more drastic measures might be called for. Accordingly, in late 1933 a young associate of Hajj Amin's, 'Abd al-Qadir al-Husayni, organized a secret military group known as Munazzamat al-Jihad al-Muqaddas (Organization for Holy Struggle).[105] At the same time, various groupings of radicals were also preparing for military struggle. And in 1934, according to Palestine Communist Party propaganda, a popular bandit known as Abu Jilda was carrying out significant armed activity in the countryside. Abu Jilda's "partisan detachments," claimed the Communists, were pulling the country toward disorder and toward armed revolt against the colonial authorities.[106]

THE REVOLT OF AL-QASSAM

The spark that ignited the explosion came from an independent organization intimately connected to the peasantry and semi-proletariat created by the agrarian crisis. That organization was founded by radical Islamic reformer Shaykh 'Izz al-Din al-Qassam. A native of Jabla, Syria, and a key figure in the 1921 revolt aginst the French, al-Qassam took refuge in Haifa after fleeing Syria under sentence of death. A man of great religious learning who had studied at Cairo's al-Azhar, al-Qassam was associated with the Islamic reform (Salafiya) movement,[107] as well as with certain Sufi *turuq*.[108] He quickly achieved prominence in Haifa as a preacher and teacher. Unlike other political activists in Palestine, al-Qassam concentrated his efforts exclusively on the lower classes with whom he lived.[109] He set up a night school to combat illiteracy among the casual laborers (recent migrants from rural areas) of Haifa shantytowns and was a prominent member of the Young Men's Muslim Association. In 1929 al-Qassam was appointed marriage registrar of Haifa's Shari'a court. The duties of this office, which required that he tour northern villages, permitted him to extend his efforts to the peasantry, whom he encouraged to set up growing and distribution cooperatives.[110]

Using his religious position, al-Qassam began to recruit followers from among the fellahin and the laborers of Haifa, organizing them into clandestine cells of not more than five persons. By 1935 he had enlisted 200, perhaps even 800, men.[111] Many received military training, carried out after dark; all were imbued with al-Qassam's message of strict piety, of struggle and sacrifice, of patriotism, the necessity for unity, and the need to emulate early Islamic heroes.[112] In the 1920s, al-Qassam made a name for himself by attacking as un-Islamic certain folk religious practices still common in the Haifa area.[113] Such censure accorded with al-Qassam's Salafiya leanings and recalled the actions of 'Abd al-Karim, leader of the 1924–27 anti-Spanish rebellion in the Moroccan Rif. A Salafiya advocate like al-Qassam, 'Abd al-Karim had banned a number of traditional folk religious practices in the interests of promoting unity among the Rif rebels.[114] Al-Qassam's political activities also paralleled those of Hasan al-Banna, founder of the Muslim Brothers (al-Ikhwan al-Muslimin) in Egypt. Just as al-Banna recruited his first followers in the new towns of the Canal Zone, so al-Qassam recruited in the newly developing city of Haifa. But while al-Banna attracted the new Egyptian petty bourgeoisie, al-Qassam focused on the recently dispossessed peasants working as casual laborers in the slums.[115]

Al-Qassam's appeal to religious values was not simply a return to tradition or a retreat into the past, but instead represented a real transformation of traditional forms for revolutionary use in the present.[116] He seized on popular memories of the Assassins and the wars against the Crusaders by invoking the tradition of the *fida'iyin,* the notion of struggle that involved sacrifice. His clandestine organization resembled that of a Sufi order: his followers grew their beards "wild" and called themselves shaykhs.[117] This was not as incongruous as it might seem, for, as Thomas Hodgkin argues, the Islamic worldview contains elements that can be articulated together to constitute a revolutionary tradition.[118] Al-Qassam's efforts represent just such an articulation and condensation of nationalist, religious "revivalist" and class-conscious components in a movement of anti-colonial struggle.

Although his followers may have begun carrying out small armed attacks on Zionist settlements as early as 1931,[119] it was not until November 1935 that al-Qassam decided the moment was ripe for launching a full-scale revolt. Accompanied by a small detachment of followers, he set out from Haifa with the aim of raising the peasantry in rebellion. An accidental encounter with the police led to a premature battle with the British military, however, and al-Qassam died before his rebellion could get off the ground.

Nonetheless, his example electrified the country. Independent radical organizations eulogized al-Qassam and gained new inspiration from his revolutionary project. Al-Qassam rapidly achieved the status of a popular hero, and his gravesite became a place of pilgrimage.[120] His legacy also included the many Qassamites still at large and prepared for action, as well as militant nationalists who set up fresh political groupings in the towns and organized armed bands on the Qassam model. Urban radicals also redoubled their organizing in the villages in preparation for a new anti-British outbreak.[121] In such a highly charged atmosphere, only a small event was needed to trigger an explosion.

THE GREAT REVOLT (AL-THAWRA AL-KUBRA)

That incident occurred on 13 April 1936, when two Jews were murdered in the Nablus Mountains, perhaps by Qassamites. Following a wave of brutal reprisals and counter-reprisals, the government declared a state of emergency. In response, "national committees" led by various militant organizations sprang up in the towns and declared a general strike. The notables followed along, trying to retake control of the unruly movement. On 25 April all the Palestinian parties (including the Nashashibi's National Defense Party) met with the national committees and set up a coordinating body known as the Higher Arab Committee (H.A.C.), with Amin al-Husayni as its president. Although the H.A.C. grew out of the notables' move to regain their dominant position, nonetheless, as a merging of the independent radical groupings with the traditional leadership it was more representative than the old Arab Executive had been.[122] The H.A.C. quickly declared that the general strike would continue until the British government put an end to Jewish immigration to Palestine, and it restated the other basic national demands—the banning of land sales and the establishment of an independent national government.

Though it initially sprang up in the towns, the revolt's focus rapidly shifted to the countryside. A conference of rural national committees convened in May and elaborated a specific peasant agenda, including a call for nonpayment of taxes and the denunciation of the establishment of police stations in villages at fellahin expense.[123] In addition, Istiqlalists (still active as individuals) toured the countryside of the Triangle to mobilize support for the general strike, while both Qassamites and S.M.C. preachers spread propaganda and attempted to organize among peasants.[124]

In mid-May, armed peasant bands in which Qassamites featured prominently appeared in the highlands. They were assisted by armed commandos in the towns and by peasant auxiliaries who fought part-time. Though connected to the urban national committees, in general these bands operated independently of the Mufti and the H.A.C.[125] From mountain hideouts they harassed British communications, attacked Zionist settlements, and even sabotaged the Iraq Petroleum Company oil pipelines to Haifa. This last activity posed a particular threat to British global hegemony, for in the 1930s Great Britain still controlled the bulk of Middle East oil, and the Haifa pipeline was crucial to imperial naval strategy in the Mediterranean.

The towns, in a state of semi-insurrection, were finally brought under control by the British in July, which left the countryside as the undisputed center of revolt.[126] In the following month Fawzi al-Qawuqji, hero of the Syrian Druzed rebellion of 1925, resigned his commission in the Iraqi army and entered Palestine with an armed detachment of pan-Arab volunteers, declaring himself commander-in-chief of the revolt.[127] Although the military effectiveness of the rebel movement was improved and al-Qawuqji was hailed as a popular hero throughout the country, he never managed to unite all the diverse bands under his command.

While popular forces fought the British in the countryside, the notables of the H.A.C.—only one of whom had been arrested—were negotiating with the enemy for a compromise to end the conflict. British authorities increased the pressure in late September by launching tough countermeasures—boosting their military force to 20,000, declaring martial law, and going on a new defensive. The H.A.C. was also constrained by the onset of the agricultural season: peasants wanted to resume work, but, more important, harvest season started in September on the plantations of wealthy citrus-growers.[128] The H.A.C., preferring negotiations to mass mobilization, which threatened notable leadership, called off the six-month-old general strike on 10 October, with the understanding that the Arab kings (of Iraq, Jordan, and Saudi Arabia) would intercede with the British government on the Palestinians' behalf and that the government would act in good faith to work out new solutions. A long interim period ensued. While notables pinned their hopes on a Royal Commission of Inquiry, activists and rebel band leaders toured the villages and purchased weapons in preparation for a new round of fighting.

In July 1937, the British Peel Commission published its recommendations for the partition of Palestine into Arab and Jewish states. Arab reaction was universally hostile; even the Nashashibi faction which had defected from the H.A.C. condemned the partition proposal. Feelings ran especially high in the Galilee, a highland region with few Jewish residents, which the plan of partition included in the proposed Jewish state.[129] In September, following the assassination of the British district commissioner for Galilee (possibly by Qassamites), the second phase of the revolt erupted. British authorities responded by banning the H.A.C. and deporting or arresting hundreds of activists. The Mufti managed to evade arrest by escaping to Lebanon in October. Shortly thereafter, fierce fighting broke out. With the notable leadership in exile or imprisoned, command now shifted decisively to the partisans in the countryside.

Rebel bands were most active in the Nablus and Galilee highlands, the areas of greatest popular resistance. The Jerusalem-Hebron region, where the Munazzamat al-Jihad al-Muqaddas operated, was also an important center. In these districts the various bands set up their own court system, administrative offices, and intelligence networks. While peasants and ex-peasant migrants to the towns composed the vast majority of band leaders and fighters, young urban militants played important roles as commanders, advisers, arms transporters, instructors, and judges.[130] Qassamites were particularly well represented at the leadership level. By taxing the peasantry, levying volunteers, and acquiring arms through the agency of experienced smugglers,[131] the bands were able to operate autonomously from the rebel headquarters-in-exile set up by the notable leadership at Damascus. A network of militants in the towns, particularly from among the semi-proletariat, collected contributions, gathered intelligence, and carried out acts of terror against the British, the Zionists, and Arab *simsars* and collaborators.[132]

In the summer and fall of 1938 the rebellion reached its peak. Some 10,000 persons had joined the insurgent bands, now sufficiently well organized for a handbook of instructions to be issued for their members.[133] Commanders of the largest bands established a Higher Council of Command to enhance military coordination. Most of the Palestinian highlands were in rebel hands, and by September government control over the urban areas had virtually ceased.

Once rebels gained the upper hand in the towns, the peasant character of the revolt expressed itself even more clearly. Rebel commanders ordered all townsmen to take off the urban headgear, the fez, and to don the peasant headcloth, the *kafiya;* urban women were commanded to veil. This action was both practical, in that it protected rebels from arrest by the British when they entered the towns, and symbolic, in that it signified the countryside's hegemony over the city. Insurgents also instructed urban residents not to use electric power, which was produced by an Anglo-Jewish company. Few dared disobey these orders. Large sums of money were extracted from wealthy city-dwellers as contributions to the revolt, and particularly large "contributions" were demanded from the big orange-growers and merchants at Jaffa who supported the Nashashibi opposition.[134]

On 1 September, the joint rebel command issued a declaration that directly challenged the leading classes' dominance over the countryside. Although limited in scope, the declaration represented a social program which went beyond the merely "national" goals of the a'yan. In it the commanders declared a moratorium on all debts (which had so impoverished the peasantry and by means of which notables controlled agricultural production) and warned both debt collectors and land agents not to visit the villages. Arab contractors, who hired work teams for the construction of police posts in the villages and roads to facilitate access to rebel strongholds, were also ordered to cease operations. In addition, the statement declared the cancellation of rents on urban apartments, which had risen to scandalously high levels. This item was particularly significant in that, by linking the needs of peasants and urban workers, it revealed the new class alliance underpinning the revolt.[135]

The rebels' interference with landlord-usurer control over the countryside and their demands for contributions from the wealthy constituted a "revenge of the countryside," which prompted thousands of wealthy Palestinians to abandon their homes for other Arab countries. Well-off Palestinians tended to view the rebels as little better than bandits. In part this charge was justified, for there were serious discipline problems within the rebel camp, despite the considerable advances the bands achieved in coordination and unity of purpose. For instance, clan or family loyalties occasionally interfered with the class or national interests of certain rebel commanders, who carried out petty blood-feuds under cover of nationalist activity.[136] Some peasants were alienated by the coercive manner employed by particular leaders to collect taxes and by their favoritism toward certain clans. Moreover, although class divisions among the peasants were not well developed, villagers were by no means homogeneous in their class interests. The assassination of a mukhtar who collaborated with the British, for example, was likely to alienate those members of his hamula who benefited from the mukhtar's ties to outside forces.

Most accounts of the revolt stress the internal problems faced by the rebels. Although such criticisms are exaggerated and detract from the rebel's positive accomplishments, they cannot simply be dismissed. The British and the Nashashibis were able to exploit the contradictions within the rebel movement through such means as the formation of "peace bands" in late 1938 to do battle with the rebels. Although representative primarily of the interests of landlords and rural notables, the "peace bands" were manned by disaffected peasants.[137]

More important for British strategy than the "peace bands" was the signing of the Munich Agreement on 30 September 1938. This allowed Britain to free one more army division for service in Palestine and to launch a military counteroffensive. Is it possible that British Prime Minister Chamberlain signed the Munich Agreement not merely to appease Hitler momentarily but also to protect Britain's oil supply in the Mediterranean from "backward" but dangerous bands of peasants? It would be difficult to chart a clear cause-effect relation, but it is evident at least that for the British chiefs of staff, Palestine was a crucial strategic buffer between the Suez Canal and potential enemies to the north (Germany, Soviet Union) and was an indispensable link in land communications. With war looming on the horizon in Europe, Britain was seeking desperately to end the disturbances in Palestine.[138]

In any event, the Munich Agreement had disastrous consequences not just for Czechoslovakia but for the rebellion in Palestine as well. By 1939 the rebels were fighting a British military force of 20,000 men as well as the R.A.F. In addition, Orde Wingate, a British officer, organized a counterinsurgency force of Jewish fighters known as the Special Night Squads to terrorize villagers and to guard the oil pipeline.[139] The British counteroffensive increased pressure on the rebels and prompted further internal problems, such as abuses in collecting taxes and contributions and an upsurge in political assassinations.

However, the intensified military offensive was still not enough to finish off the rebellion, so the British launched a diplomatic one as well. In March 1939 the government issued a White Paper declaring that it was opposed to Palestine becoming a Jewish state, that Jewish immigration would be limited to 75,000 over the next five years, that land sales would be strictly regulated, and that an independent Palestinian state would be set up in ten years with self-governing institutions to be established in the interim. Although both the notables and the rebels rejected the White Paper, the Palestinian populace responded to it more favorably.[140] Clearly, while it did not satisfy the maximum national demands, the White Paper represented a concession wrung from the British by armed resistance. Zionist reaction against the White Paper, by contrast, was much more virulent.

The revolt was gradually crushed by extreme external pressures and the resultant internal fracturing of the movement. After over three years of fighting, the intervention of substantial British military forces aided by the Zionists, and nearly 20,000 Arab casualties (5,032 dead, 14,760 wounded),[141] the rebellion was finally subdued. In July the last major rebel commander was captured; once the war with Germany began in September 1939, fighting ended altogether. An entirely new set of circumstances on the international scene were to determine subsequent events in Palestine.

CONCLUSION

I have tried to propose an alternative to the prevailing analyses of the Great Revolt in Palestine, which represent Palestinian society as so fractured by vertical cleavages that neither the class or national unity necessary for success in the anti-colonial, anti-Zionist struggle could emerge. Given the prevailing social structure, so the argument goes, once the Palestinian peasantry took leadership of the revolt it could only act true to its inherently "backward" character. Arnon-Ohanna's assessment is typical: "The absence of cooperation and mutual responsibility, the deep-seated divisiveness of a society based on patriarchal lines and *hamula*s, the ancient inter-village and inter-*hamula* wrangles over stretches of land and water sources, over blood feuds, family honor and marital problems—these were simply transferred to the [guerrilla] bands movement." [142] According to many of those who make such an argument, only one force could have ensured victory: a modern, revolutionary party.[143]

I have argued that the model of vertical cleavages was essentially ideological, in that it was the form through which the Palestinian ruling class maintained its political and economic hegemony. As an ideology of rule, it worked by refracting the underlying class structure of the society, making relations of exploitation appear as amicable "exchanges" between persons of unequal status. In an effort to show that class antagonisms overdetermined this relation, I argue that peasants manipulated the dominant ideology in their struggle for a better life. Although peasants lived in a state of subordination, landlord-notable domination was never total but was resisted on the basis of the very *terms* of the dominant ideology, that is, the struggle for a "just" exchange.

What is more, peasants possessed traditions of resistance, which they could call on in moments of crisis to forge a movement of opposition. I have charted a genealogy of these traditions of resistance prior to 1936. Despite its weak and often broken lines of descent, its vague and hidden traces, there are strong indications of such a tradition: a semi-autonomous existence prior to 1831, banditry and unorthodox religious practices, resistance to the expansion of the Ottoman state and to land registration in the late nineteenth century, and spontaneous struggles against new colonies of European Jews. Buried deeper within popular consciousness, moreover, were memories of earlier struggles, such as that of Salah al-Din's (Saladin) against those earlier European invaders, the Crusaders. Such traditions do not necessarily imply practices of a conservative or retrograde nature, for, as Raymond Williams has argued, the "residual" can be an important source for progressive political practices even in advanced industrial societies.[144]

I have stressed too that the fellahin's folk heritage was not a pure, unblemished one. Their "common sense" was penetrated and altered over time by dominant ideologies of the state during the resurgence of Ottoman power in the second half of the nineteenth century, and by the nationalist idioms of the notables in the mandate period. Peasant consciousness was influenced as well by radical ideas emanating from militants of the middle class. Older traditional notions came to be articulated with the newer discourses of the nation, democracy and reformist Islam. In some cases, as with al-Qassam's attack on folk Islamic practices, popular traditions were modified in order to enhance the unity of the popular movement. In other instances, traditional practices such as banditry were transformed into powerful modern vehicles of struggle.

My aim has also been to demonstrate that the Palestinian peasantry was not an unchanging "backward" component of Palestinian society, but that it underwent constant change in the period under study. During the nineteenth century it was transformed from a class of relatively independent producers to one dominated by landowners and usurers, producing to a growing extent for the capitalist world market. A substantial number of peasants were displaced by Zionist colonization and indebtedness, forced out of agriculture altogether, and made into casual laborers. The fellahin were transformed further in the twentieth century, assuming a dual character as peasants and as casual workers. The partial integration of peasants into the wage circuit of "free" labor socialized peasant-workers in new ways and contributed to the dissolution of the pre-capitalist institutions in the village. Although the notables and the British tried mightily to uphold the hierarchies of patron-client networks, the grounds on which they were established were destabilized by the advances of Zionism and the notables' own failure to achieve "national" goals. Peasants totally abandoned by the system—dispossessed of their lands by Zionist colonies and driven into the towns as a subproletariat—eagerly embraced new ideas and practices that challenged notable dominance.

All these forces came into play during the Great Revolt. The peasant-led movement represented a congealing of nationalism, religious revivalism, and class consciousness, no element of which can be neatly disentangled from the others. Here I have underscored the emergence within the rebel movement of specific demands and practices of the peasantry as a class, in part because in other accounts this aspect is so underplayed. The refusal to pay taxes, the moratorium on debts, the heavy contributions levied against the wealthy: all these rebel practices aimed at addressing the needs of the peasants. In addition, the declared moratorium on rental payments for apartments indicates the movement's close linkage with the urban semi-proletariat. The campaign of terror launched against collaborators, land agents, mukhtars, and Arab police officers represented a serious attempt to deal with traitors whose activities had hurt peasants, even though by all accounts it was carried to unnecessary extremes. While such demands and actions on the part of the rebels did not, strictly speaking, constitute "revolutionary" practice, they nonetheless posed a considerable threat to the political and economic hegemony of the notables. They also show that to claim that the rebels had *no* discernible, coherent social or political program is to oversimplify the issue considerably.[145]

We have seen how the rebels were able partially to overcome "traditional" social divisions based on region and clan. The establishment of a council of command by the leading commanders was an important political step in this direction, as were the efforts of Qassamites who organized on the basis of an Islamic discourse colored by the interests of the popular classes. Such factors made crucial contributions to the remarkable degree of coherence that the rebellion was able to achieve.

Much has been made, in accounts of the rebellion, of the internal problems besetting the rebel forces. Indeed, misguided practice—such as regional, familial, and lineage loyalties which overrode fidelity to the movement, and the resort to assassination, brutality, and heavy-handed methods in extracting "contributions" from peasants—posed real problems for the movement and undermined its ability to sustain broad popular support. It is difficult here to achieve a "correct" analytical balance. But we should remember that throughout the world, unsavory practices have been common during moments of social upheaval. We should not therefore focus on them exclusively in order to discount an entire movement. Such problems would not necessarily have magically been transcended under the guidance of a "revolutionary" party and leadership, for a party is no guarantee of a successful outcome for social struggle. To focus attention on the absence of a party, as many have done, is to belittle the militant, honest leadership and forms of organization that the peasantry and semi-proletariat were able to muster. While some commanders were given to self-aggrandizement and petty feuding, many others (most of whom remain anonymous) deserve to be remembered. Qassamites, who played a key leadership role, were particularly noted for their devoutness and honesty, and 'Abd al-Rahim al-Hajj Muhammad, the most respected commander, was renowned for his nationalist convictions, for his opposition to political assassination, and for his tirelessness as a fighter.[146]

If anything, it was the formidable strength of the enemy that was more crucial to the peasant rebels' defeat than their purported "backwardness." The British, determined to maintain control over this area of major strategic importance (particularly the harbor at Haifa, the oil pipeline, and communication routes to India) mustered a substantial military force to fight the rebels. In addition, the powerful Jewish community was enlisted to assist the British efforts. Jews were enrolled in the police and the constabulary; Jewish fighters were organized into special counterinsurgency squads by Orde Wingate. Zionist revisionists, without British approval, launched terrorist attacks against the Arab community. Moreover, the rebellion gave the Zionists the opportunity to build up their military capabilities. While by the end of the revolt the Arab community was substantially disarmed, the Zionists in the meantime had put 14,500 men, with advanced training and weaponry, under arms.[147] This military imbalance between the two communities, enhanced during World War II, was an extremely important factor in the disaster that befell the Palestinian Arabs in 1948.

I have tried, then, to develop a counterargument to the dominant analysis of the Great Revolt. The "master narrative" of the rebellion tends to proceed by defining (and thereby diminishing) the peasants and casual laborers as "traditional," "backward," "fanatical," or even "terrorists." By presenting the peasantry as essentially unchanging, this approach also permits scholars to ignore the very real history of peasant resistance which preceded the rebellion. Other writers sympathetic to the revolt often disparage it for lacking a revolutionary party at its helm. Such arguments allow analysis to trivialize or ignore the accomplishments of the revolt and to concentrate on other questions, such as the role of the middle class, the treachery of the notables, or the Palestine Communist Party (which in fact was largely irrelevant to this affair).[148] What is at stake in such a dismissal is that the legitimate social and political desires of subaltern popular social movements have gone unheeded by the "progressive" as well as the dominant commentaries. Scholarly work that would constitute a social history of the revolt, including an investigation of the cultural life of the peasantry, the economic organization of the countryside, traditions of resistance, and ideologies of domination and opposition, has therefore scarcely begun.[149]

For this reason, I have stressed in polemical fashion the positive accomplishments of the peasantry in the course of the Great Revolt—achievements which have so often been minimized. This should be seen, then, only as a tentative step toward the development of a complete analysis, which requires the investigation of both structures of dominance and movements of opposition in their complex historical relation.

NOTES

1. Musa Budeiri, *The Palestine Communist Party, 1919–1948: Arab and Jew in the Struggle for Internationalism* (London: Ithaca Press, 1979), pp. 46–47.

2. Ann Mosely Lesch, *Arab Politics in Palestine, 1917–1939: The Frustration of a Nationalist Movement* (Ithaca: Cornell University Press, 1979), p. 17.

3. Ibrahim Abu-Lughod, "The Pitfalls of Palestineology: A Review Essay," *Arab Studies Quarterly* 3 (1981): 403–11.

4. Methodologically this requires a strategy of reading from the margins of existing works on the history of Palestine. This chapter does not pretend to be an exhaustive survey but is meant to suggest further avenues of research. A major problem is that the role of peasant women cannot be recovered through such a reading strategy; other means are required to develop an analysis of this important question.

5. Gramsci's notion of hegemony is summarized by Raymond Williams, *Marxism and Literature* (Oxford: Oxford University Press, 1977), pp. 112–13.

6. Antonio Gramsci, *Selections from the Prison Notebooks*, ed. and trans. Quintin Hoare and Geoffrey Nowell Smith (New York: International Publishers, 1971), pp. 323–26, 419–25.

7. The conclusions of the following four sections are based in part on my M.A. thesis: Theodore Swedenburg, "The Development of Capitalism in Greater Syria, 1830–1914: An Historico-Geographical Approach," University of Texas at Austin, 1980.

8. Palestine was only united as an administrative entity under the British mandate. In the Ottoman period, it was ruled from various cities such as Damascus, Sidon, Beirut, and Jerusalem. I am treating it here as a geographical unit.

9. Aref el-Aref, "The Closing Phase of Ottoman Rule in Jerusalem," Moshe Ma'oz, ed., *Studies on Palestine during the Ottoman Period* (Jerusalem: Magnes Press, 1975).

10. Constantin F. Volney, *Travels throughout Syria and Egypt in the Years 1783, 1784, and 1785*, vol. 2 (England: Gregg International Publishers, 1973).

11. This class structure is comparable to what Rey terms a "hierarchical society": Pierre-Philippe Rey, "Les formes de la décomposition des sociétés précapitalistes au Nord-Togo et le mécanisme des migrations vers les zones de capitalisme agraire," in Emile le Bris et al., eds., *Capitalisme négrier* (Paris: Maspero, 1976), pp. 195–209.

12. Volney, *Travels*, pp. 252–53. A similar relationship among peasants, their overlords, and the state characterized conditions in Southeast Asia during the same period: Michael Adas, "From Avoidance to Confrontation: Peasant Protest in Precolonial and Colonial Southeast Asia," *Comparative Studies in Society and History* 23 (1981): 217–47.

13. Karl Marx, *Grundrisse*, trans. Martin Nicolaus (New York: Vintage Books, 1973).

14. Maurice Godelier, "Infrastructures, Societies and History," *Current Anthropology* 19 (1978): 63–68. Empires based on a tributary mode of production typically left economic systems based on kinship intact, only modifying them to ensure that tribute was rendered. See also Samir Amin, *The Arab Nation* (London: Zed Press, 1978), pp. 87–102.

15. The situation in Palestine resembled that of the Kabyle Mountains of Algeria, where during the same era "league feuds channeled or drained off the energies of the peasants and diverted them from the social struggle.... Even though the leagues and alliances ... veiled social tensions and disjunctures, these were nonetheless manifest": René Gallissot, "Pre-Colonial Algeria," *Economy and Society* 4 (1975): 424–25.

16. Mordechai Abir, "Local Leadership and Early Reforms in Palestine, 1800–1834," in Ma'oz, ed., *Studies on Palestine*, pp. 284–310.

17. Taufik Canaan, *Mohammedan Saints and Sanctuaries in Palestine* (London: Luzac, 1927), p. 251. Such proverbs are typical of mountain peasants of the Arab world and of "segmentary" Bedouin societies. (For Morocco, see David M. Hart, *The Aith Waryaghar of the Moroccan Rif* [Tucson: University of Arizona Press, 1976].) My own reading of this proverb diverges from the usual interpretation given by anthropologists, who see it exclusively in terms of kinship and alliance. I suggest a broader political interpretation.

18. Canaan, *Mohammedan Saints*.

19. Ibid., p. 98.

20. Ibid., pp. 215–16.

21. Ibid., p. 193.

22. Alexander Scholch, "The Economic Development of Palestine, 1856–1882," *Journal of Palestine Studies* 39 (1981): 35–58.

23. Alexander Scholch, "European Penetration and the Economic Development of Palestine, 1956–82," in Roger Owen, ed., *Studies in the Economic and Social History of Palestine in the Nineteenth and Twentieth Centuries* (Carbondale: Southern Illinois Press, 1982), pp. 10–87.

24. Ya'akov Firestone, "Crop-sharing Economics in Mandatory Palestine," *Middle Eastern Studies* 11 (1975): 10.

25. Lesch, *Arab Politics*, p. 89.

26. For criticisms by anthropologists of the patron-client model as applied to Mediterranean societies, see Michael Gilsenan, "Against Patron-Client Relations," in Ernest Gellner and John Waterbury, eds., *Patrons and Clients* (London: Duckworth, 1977), pp. 167–83; Luciano Li Causi, "Anthropology and Ideology: The Case of 'Patronage,'" *Critique of Anthropology* 4/5 (1975): 90–109; and Paul Littlewood, "Patronage, Ideology and Reproduction," *Critique of Anthropology* 15 (1980): 29–45.

27. Littlewood, "Patronage," pp. 37–38.

28. See David Seddon, *Moroccan Peasants* (Folkestone, Ky.: Dawson, 1981), p. 92, and Göran Therborn, *The Ideology of Power and the Power of Ideology* (London: New Left Books, 1980), pp. 56–57, 61–62, for discussions which support this line of argument.

29. Gramsci, *Selections*, p. 54.

30. J. C. Hurewitz, *The Struggle for Palestine* (New York: W. W. Norton, 1950), p. 54.

31. Canaan, *Mohammedan Saints*, pp. 197, 204–5.

32. Gilsenan, "Against Patron-Client Relations," pp. 53, 151–52; see also Albert Hourani, *Arabic Thought in the Liberal Age, 1798–1939* (London: Oxford University Press, 1962), p. 150.

33. Claude Regnier Conder, *Tent Work in Palestine* (New York: D. Appleton, 1878), p. 267.

34. James Scott, "Hegemony and the Peasantry," *Politics and Society* 7 (1977): 284.

35. Yehoshuah Porath, *The Emergence of the Palestinian-Arab National Movement, 1918–1929* (London: Frank Cass, 1974); Neville Mandel, *The Arabs and Zionism before World War I* (Berkeley and Los Angeles: University of California Press, 1975), pp. 70, 214–22.

36. Mandel, *Arabs and Zionism*, pp. 70, 214–22.

37. Porath, *Emergence*, pp. 7–8.

38. Abdul-Wahhab Kayyali, *Palestine: A Modern History* (London: Croom Helm, 1978), pp. 71–72; Porath, *Emergence*, pp. 129–30.

39. Kayyali, *Palestine*, p. 73.

40. Nathan Weinstock, *Le Sionisme contre Israel* (Paris: Maspero, 1969), p. 169.

41. Kayyali, *Palestine*, p. 75.

42. Lesch, *Arab Politics*, p. 89.

43. Hurewitz, *Struggle*, p. 54.

44. Ylana M. Miller, *Government and Society in Rural Palestine 1920–1948* (Austin: University of Texas Press, 1985), pp. 16–18.

45. Hurewitz, *Struggle*, pp. 52–53.

46. Miller, *Government*, pp. 27, 54–62.

47. Ibid.

48. Rifaat Abou-el-Haj, "The Social Uses of the Past: Recent Arab Historiography of Ottoman Rule," *IJMES* 14 (1982): 187.

49. Porath, *Emergence*, pp. 200–202.

50. Miller, *Government*, pp. 24–25, 47.

51. Hourani, *Arabic Thought*, passim. For an example of a liberal Palestinian mode of argument, see George Antonius, *The Arab Awakening* (London: Hamish Hamilton, 1938).

52. Walid Khalidi, ed., *From Haven to Conquest* (Beirut: Institute for Palestine Studies, 1961), p. 72.

53. Yehoshuah Porath, *The Palestinian Arab National Movement: From Riots to Rebellion, 1929–1939* (London: Frank Cass, 1977), pp. 83–84.

54. Talal Asad, "Anthropological Texts and Ideological Problems: An Analysis of Cohen on Arab Villages in Israel," *Review of Middle East Studies* 1 (1975): 1–40.

55. Gabriel Baer, "The Office and Functions of the Village Mukhtar," in J. S. Migdal, ed., *Palestinian Society and Politics* (Princeton: Princeton University Press, 1980), pp. 103–23.

56. Shulamit Carmi and Henry Rosenfeld, "The Origins of the Process of Proletarianization and Urbanization of Arab Peasants in Palestine," *Annals of the New York Academy of Sciences* 220 (1974): 470.

57. Ibid., pp. 481–82.

58. Ken Post, *Arise Ye Starvelings: The Jamaican Labour Rebellion of 1938 and Its Aftermath* (The Hague: Martinus Nijhoff, 1978), pp. 133–36.

59. Sarah Graham-Brown, *Palestinians and Their Society, 1880–1946: A Photographic Essay* (London: Quartet Books, 1980), p. 150. For a theoretical analysis of this phenomenon in South Africa see Harold Wolpe, "The Theory of Internal Colonialism: The South African Case," in Ivar Oxall et al., eds., *Beyond the Sociology of Development* (London: Routledge and Kegan Paul, 1975), pp. 229–52.

60. Rachel Taqqu, "Peasants into Workmen: Internal Labor Migration and the Arab Village Community under the Mandate," in Migdal, *Palestinian Society*, p. 271.

61. Miller, *Government*, pp. 79–89.

62. Nels Johnson, *Islam and the Politics of Meaning in Palestinian Nationalism* (London: Routledge and Kegan Paul, 1982), p. 37.

63. David Hirst, *The Gun and the Olive Branch* (New York: D. Appleton, 1977), vol. 2, p. 63.

64. Philip Mattar, "The Role of the Mufti of Jerusalem in the Political Struggle over the Western Wall, 1928–29," *Middle Eastern Studies* 19 (1983): 104–18.

65. Ibid., p. 114; Lesch, *Arab Politics*, pp. 210–11.

66. Kayyali, *Palestine*, p. 156; Shai Lachman, "Arab Rebellion and Terrorism in Palestine 1929–1939: The Case of Sheikh Izz al-Din al-Qassam and His Movement," in Elie Kedourie and Sylvia G. Haim, eds., *Zionism and Arabism in Palestine and Israel* (London: Frank Cass, 1982), p. 56.

67. Ivar Spector, *The Soviet Union and the Muslim World, 1917–1956* (Seattle: University of Washington Press, 1956), p. 100.

68. Ibid., p. 156. The Shaw Commission's statement reflects an ethnocentric and classist bias that assumes that the non-Western peasantry was inherently apolitical. In fact, movements of peasants have posed the greatest threat to imperialist rule in the underdeveloped world.

69. Porath, Palestinian Arab, p. 40.

70. Lenni Brenner, *Zionism in the Age of Dictators* (Highland Park, N.J.: Lawrence Hill, 1983), p. 65; Weinstock, *Sionisme*, pp. 135–36.

71. Carmi and Rosenfeld, "Origins," p. 476.

72. Porath, *Palestinian Arab*, pp. 129–30.

73. Ibid., pp. 182–84.

74. Weinstock, *Sionisme*, p. 64.

75. Porath, *Palestinian Arab*, pp. 103, 105.

76. Kenneth Stein, "Legal Protection and Circumvention of Rights for Cultivators in Mandatory Palestine," in Migdal, ed., *Palestinian Society*, pp. 250–54.

77. Kayyali, *Palestine*, p. 179.

78. Porath, *Palestinian Arab*, p. 67.

79. Lesch, *Arab Politics*, pp. 110–11.

80. Therborn, *Ideology*, pp. 17, 46.

81. Philip S. Khoury, "Islamic Revivalism and the Crisis of the Secular State in the Arab World: An Historical Reappraisal," in I. Ibrahim, ed., *Arab Resources: The Transformation of a Society* (London: Croom Helm, 1983), pp. 219–20. Women's organizations emerged in Palestine as a new form of mobilization in this period, but those discussed in the literature were led by the wives of the notable leaders (Mrs. Matiel E. T. Mogannam, *The Arab Woman and the Palestine Problem* [London: Herbert Joseph, 1937]) and were similar in form to the Muslim-Christian Associations. It is possible that their example inspired mobilization by women of the educated middle classes, but for now we can only conjecture.

82. Kayyali, *Palestine*, pp. 167–68.

83. 'Abd al-Qadir Yasin, *Kifah al-Sha'b al-Fisastini gabl al-'am 1948* (Beirut: PLO Research Center, 1975), pp. 125–26; Hurewitz, *Struggle*, p. 63.

84. Yasin, *Kifah al-Sha'b*, pp. 125–26. This national bourgeoisie existed, however, in embryo only.

85. Ibid., pp. 125–26; Kayyali, *Palestine*, pp. 167–68, 172.

86. For a discussion of populism see Ernesto Laclau, *Politics and Ideology in Marxist Theory* (London: New Left Books, 1977), especially p. 109.

87. Kayyali, *Palestine*, p. 187; Porath, *Palestinian Arab*, pp. 16–17.

88. Zvi Elpeleg, "The 1936–39 Disturbances: Riot or Rebellion?" *Wiener Library Bulletin* 29 (1976): 41.

89. Kayyali, *Palestine*, p. 177.

90. Porath, *Palestinian Arab*, p. 181.

91. Adnan Abu-Ghazaleh, "Arab Cultural Nationalism in Palestine during the British Mandate," *Journal of Palestine Studies* 3 (1972): 48–49.

92. Ghassan Kanafani, *The 1936–39 Revolt in Palestine* (Committee for a Democratic Palestine, n.d.), p. 17.

93. Abu-Ghazaleh, "Arab Cultural Nationalism," p. 87; Hilma Granqvist, *Marriage Conditions in a Palestinian Village* (Helsingfors: Societas Scientarium Fennica, 1931), p. 99.

94. Abd al-'Al, al-Baquri, "Al-thawra bayn barakat al-jamahir wa tadahun al-giyadat," *Tali'ah* 7, no. 4, p. 95.

95. Joel Beinin, "The Palestine Communist Party, 1919–1948," *MERIP Reports* 55 (1977): 8–9.

96. The resolutions of the Seventh Congress are reproduced in Spector, *Soviet Union*, pp. 91–104.

97. Beinin, "Palestine Communist Party," p. 12; Budeiri, *Palestine Communist Party*.

98. Yasin, *Kifah al-Shab*, p. 143.

99. Kayyali, *Palestine*, p. 175.

100. Porath, *Palestinian Arab*, pp. 92–93.

101. Ibid., pp. 96–97.

102. Yasin, *Kifah al-Shab*, pp. 147–48.

103. Firestone, "Crop-sharing," pp. 17–18.

104. Yasin, *Kifah al-Shab*, pp. 146–48.

105. Kayyali, *Palestine*, pp. 179–80.

106. Budeiri, *Palestine Communist Party*, p. 77.

107. It has been claimed that al-Qassam was a student of Muhammad 'Abduh's, but S. 'Abdullah Schleifer, in "The Life and Thought of 'Izz-al-Din al-Qassam," *Islamic Quarterly* 23 (1979): 61–81, asserts that 'Abduh's influence on al-Qassam was very limited.

108. Al-Qassam's grandfather and granduncle were prominent shaykhs of the Qadari order in his hometown of Jabla, and al-Qassam taught for a time in a school maintained by that *tariqa*. Al-Qassam is said to have belonged to the Tijaniyya and Naqshbandi *turuq*, the latter of which was involved in anti-colonial struggles in Syria during the nineteenth century: Schleifer, "Life and Thought," pp. 62–63, 69.

109. Lachman, "Arab Rebellion," p. 77.

110. Porath, *Palestinian Arab*, pp. 133–34; Kayyali, *Palestine*, p. 180; Schleifer, "Life and Thought," p. 47.

111. Kayyali, *Palestine*, p. 180; Porath, *Palestinian Arab*, p. 137.

112. Hirst, *Gun and Olive Branch*, p. 76.

113. Schleifer, "Life and Thought," p. 68; Lachman, "Arab Rebellion," p. 62.

114. Hart, *Aith Waryaghar*, pp. 170ff., 377ff.

115. Gilsenan, "Against Patron-Client Relations," pp. 217–28.

116. Laclau, *Politics and Ideology*, p. 157. Al-Qassam's practices recall Walter Benjamin's notion of the "dialectical image," a reconstellation of materials from the past in the revolutionary present: Susan Buck-Morss, "Walter Benjamin—Revolutionary Writer (1)," *New Left Review* 128 (1981): 50–75. See also Williams's category of the "residual": *Marxism*, pp. 121–27.

117. Lachman, "Arab Rebellion," p. 64.

118. Thomas Hodgkin, "The Revolutionary Tradition in Islam," *History Workshop* 10 (1980): 148–49.

119. Lachman, "Arab Rebellion," p. 65; Yasin, *Kifah al-Shab*, p. 154, maintains that armed action began only in 1933.

120. Lachman, "Arab Rebellion," p. 72.

121. Ibid., p. 74; Kayyali, *Palestine*, pp. 182–83.

122. James J. Zogby, "The Palestinian Revolt of the 1930's," in I. Abu-Lughod and B. Abu-Laban, eds., *Settler Regimes in Africa and the Arab World* (Wilmette, Ill.: Medina U.P.I., 1974), pp. 182–83.

123. Kayyali, *Palestine*, p. 192.

124. Lachman, "Arab Rebellion," p. 78; Porath, *Palestinian Arab*, pp. 179–82.

125. Porath, *Palestinian Arab*, pp. 192–93.

126. Ibid., pp. 179–82.

127. The Palestinians had shown solidarity with the rebellion of 1925, when the Mufti had headed an emergency committee to aid the Druze: Michael Assaf, *The Arab Movement in Palestine* (New York: Masada Youth Organization of America, 1937), p. 39.

128. Porath, *Palestinian Arab*, pp. 211–21; Kayyali, *Palestine*, p. 201.

129. Lesch, *Arab Politics*, p. 122.

130. Porath, *Palestinian Arab*, p. 261.

131. Tom Bowden, *The Breakdown of Public Security: The Case of Ireland 1916–1921 and Palestine 1936–1939* (Beverly Hills: Sage, 1977). Among the usual items the smugglers trafficked in was hashish.

132. Kayyali, *Palestine*, p. 212; Porath, *Palestinian Arab*, pp. 249–50; Lachman, "Arab Rebellion," p. 80.

133. Porath, *Palestinian Arab*, p. 247; Yuval Arnon-Ohanna, "The Bands in the Palestinian Arab Revolt, 1936–39: Structure and Organization," *Asian and African Studies* (Jerusalem) 15 (1981): 232. According to Arnon-Ohanna (p. 233), band membership was between 6,000 and 15,000.

134. Porath, *Palestinian Arab*, pp. 267–69.

135. Ibid., pp. 267–68; Kayyali, *Palestine*, p. 214.

136. Porath, *Palestinian Arab*, p. 269.

137. Ibid., pp. 251, 262, 269.

138. Gabriel Sheffer, "Appeasement and the Problem of Palestine," *IJMES* (1980): 377–99.

139. Christopher Sykes, *Cross Roads to Israel* (London: New English Library, 1967), p. 193.

140. Porath, *Palestinian Arab*, p. 293.

141. Walid Khalidi, ed., *From Haven to Conquest* (Beirut: Institute for Palestine Studies, 1971), pp. 848–49.

142. Arnon-Ohanna, "Bands," p. 247.

143. Those who advance the "solution" of the revolutionary party are of various political persuasions and include Porath, *Palestinian Arab*, p. 269; Yasin, *Kifah al-Shab*, pp. 195–96; Budeiri, *Palestine Communist Party*, p. 107; Weinstock, *Sionisme*, p. 178; Tom Bowden, "The Politics of Arab Rebellion in Palestine, 1936–39," *Middle Eastern Studies* 11 (1975): 147–74; Kayyali, *Palestine*, p. 231.

144. Williams, *Marxism*, pp. 121–27.

145. This claim is made by, for instance, Graham-Brown, *Palestinians*, p. 171.

146. Porath, *Palestinian Arab*, p. 183; Elpeleg, "1936–39, Disturbances," pp. 48–49; Lesch, *Arab Politics*, p. 223.

147. Hirst, *Gun and Olive Branch*, p. 104.

148. For instance, Samih Samara Samih, *Al-'amal al-shuyu 'i fi filastin: al-tabaqa wa-al-sha'b fi mawajaha al-kuluniyaliya* (Beirut: Dar al-Farabi, 1979). Budeiri, *Palestine Communist Party*; Alain Greilsammer, *Les communistes israéliens* (Paris: Presses de la Fondation Nationale des Sciences Politiques, 1978). For a review of this growing body of literature, see Alexander Flores, "The Palestine Communist Party during the Mandatory Period: An Account of Sources and Recent Research," *Peuples méditerranéens* 11 (1987): 3–23, 175–94. Such studies touch only lightly on the 1936–39 rebellion and contain little socioeconomic analysis of the Palestinian social formation.

149. The work of Sarah Graham-Brown is a noteworthy exception. On this point, see Ibrahim Abu-Lughod, "The Pitfalls of Palestiniology: A Review Essay," *Arab Studies Quarterly* 3 (1981): 403–11.

PART FOUR

The Working Class between Nationalism, Communism, and Islam

TEN

Islam, Marxism, and the Shubra al-Khayma Textile Workers: Muslim Brothers and Communists in the Egyptian Trade Union Movement

Joel Beinin

From 1919 until 1936 the hegemonic tendency in Egyptian mass politics was the liberal secular nationalism embodied by the Wafd. The influence of the Wafd began to erode after the party concluded a treaty of alliance with Great Britain in 1936 which failed to achieve the evacuation of British troops and full Egyptian national independence. But it was not only this political-diplomatic failure that brought an end to Wafdist hegemony. During the 1930s, elements of the social impasse that brought an end to the monarchy in 1952 became sharper and more persistent: increasing unemployment among the urban intelligentsia, continuing agrarian crisis due to concentration of agricultural land in the hands of a small number of large landowners and increasing population pressure on the land, rapid urbanization, accelerated growth of an industrial working class, and intensification of the industrial conflict that had appeared in the first decade of the twentieth century. The socially conservative Wafd proved as incapable of resolving these issues as it was of achieving Egyptian national liberation.

In response to the failures of the Wafd, more radical political forces began to assert themselves and to articulate alternative frameworks for the resolution of Egypt's problems. The mid-1930s heralded the establishment of the Fascist-influenced Young Egypt, the reorganization of the Egyptian communist movement, and the reassertion of Islamic politics as the Society of Muslim Brothers outgrew its provincial origins to become a national political factor. In retrospect it is now clear that despite the dominance of secular liberal nationalist politics in the post–World War I period, the majority of Egyptians never abandoned their Islamic religious commitment or cultural orientation. It therefore should not surprise us that the decline of the Wafd and the intensification of political struggle among competing Egyptian political forces led to the emergence of Islamic politics as a significant contender for mass allegiance. We should also not be surprised to find that against the background of the bankruptcy of political liberalism in Egypt and the rise of fascism in Europe, sectors of the Egyptian intelligentsia and working class turned to Marxism as an explanation of Egypt's political and economic conditions and a guide to achieving national and social liberation.

The trade union movement was one of the focal points for the struggle between contending political forces from the late 1930s until 1952. Workers constitute a relatively easily mobilized group concentrated in politically critical urban centers. For this reason in the 1920s and 1930s the Wafd had sought to organize the trade union movement, working through lawyers who established a patron-client system of political leadership over the unions. The Wafd and its principal rival for trade union leadership in the 1930s, Prince 'Abbas Halim, a renegade of the royal family, shared a corporatist vision of Egyptian society which denied the existence of social classes with contradictory interests in Egypt. They viewed the trade union movement as part of the broader nationalist movement, not as a manifestation of the independent interests of an emergent working class. This view was adopted by the communists, whereas the Muslim Brothers were close to the Wafd and Prince 'Abbas Halim.

From the late 1930s on, contention for leadership of the trade union movement intensified, and by 1944 the Wafd and 'Abbas Halim had lost much of their earlier support. This was in part a reflection of broader national political trends, but it was also due to the rapid growth of large-scale, mass-production industry during the 1930s and especially during World War II. This development dramatically changed the conditions and relations of production for a large number of Egyptian workers who, although they by no means comprised the majority of the urban working class, played a critical role in setting the more militant tone and independent political direction of the post–World War II workers' movement. The success of the Muslim Brothers and the communists, the most significant rivals to the Wafd and Prince 'Abbas Halim for trade union leadership, varied in accordance with the particular conditions in each workplace or industry where they attempted to organize. In general, however, the Muslim Brothers were relatively unsuccessful and the communists relatively successful in the leading sector of Egypt's industrial economy—the textile industry.

In 1945, textile workers comprised 37 percent of Egypt's officially enumerated industrial workforce of 316,144 persons.[1] Nearly half of the textile workers labored in large enterprises employing 2,000 to over 20,000 wage earners. In the postwar period, textile workers were the leading force in the Egyptian trade union movement and the most important base for the development of militant, politically independent trade unionism. In 1950 over one-quarter of all the unionized workers in Egypt were textile workers, and 32 percent of all workers in the textile industry were union members.[2] Strike action was highly concentrated in the textile industry. Of the 137 officially recorded strikes in 1947, 88 (66 percent) were in the textile industry.[3] In 1950, 33 of the 49 officially recorded strikes (67 percent) were in the textile industry.[4] Although statistics for other years are not available, the absolute number of strikes as well as the proportion of strikes in the textile industry was undoubtedly even higher in 1945 and 1946.

The textile industry was widely recognized as both an economic asset and a social problem of major importance in Egypt. Therefore it became a major arena of struggle between the Muslim Brothers and the fragmented but rapidly developing communist movement for leadership of the postwar workers' movement. In this struggle the Muslim Brothers advanced an Islamic alternative to both the secular liberal nationalism of the Wafd and Marxism. The central question in this struggle was whether or not workers constituted a social class with specific interests fundamentally antagonistic to those of both foreign and Muslim Egyptian capitalists. However, the highly concentrated character of the textile industry and the militancy of many textile workers' struggles put the Muslim Brothers at a serious disadvantage. In the textile industry, more than in any other sector of the Egyptian economy, class struggle was a readily observable reality which might impinge on even the strongest commitment to an Islamic vision of social solidarity. The Muslim Brothers' failure to organize workers in the textile industry did not prevent them from organizing other workers in circumstances where the appeal of the Brothers was less clearly at odds with social reality. However, the clash between the Muslim Brothers and the communists in the textile industry, and in particular in the industrial suburb of Shubra al-Khayma north of Cairo, had far-reaching ramifications for the wider struggle between these two opposing forces to determine the leadership and content of the postwar nationalist movement in Egypt in the wake of widespread disillusionment with the Wafd.

In the late 1930s Shubra al-Khayma developed rapidly as an industrial center. By 1937 there were ten industrial enterprises in the town, mainly textile mills, and at the end of the war there were twenty to twenty-five textile mills in Shubra al-Khayma and its environs, employing 15,000 to 20,000 workers. The population of Shubra al-Khayma grew rapidly from several tens of thousands in the early 1930s to over 250,000 on the eve of the war. Shubra al-Khayma and its textile industry represented for Egypt in the 1940s and 1950s the quintessence of modern capitalism with all its attendant opportunities and problems. The mills of the Misr Spinning and Weaving Company in al-Mahalla al-Kubra employed a larger number of textile workers than all of the mills of Shubra al-Khayma combined. But the Misr Company, because it was an Egyptian-owned firm, was widely perceived as a national institution, and until 1947 the level of industrial struggle there was kept relatively low by extremely harsh and repressive management tactics. Therefore, Shubra al-Khayma figured much more prominently in the public consciousness as the classical locus of the postwar "workers' question" (*mushkilat al-'ummal*). Most of the mills in Shubra al-Khayma were medium-sized, inadequately capitalized enterprises unable to afford many concessions to trade union demands. A large proportion of the owners were non-Egyptians—either Europeans or Levantines. Labor struggles against foreign-owned enterprises tended to assume the character of nationalist struggles, and this enhanced their national political impact.

In some respects Shubra al-Khayma and its workers were exceptional in Egypt. Nowhere else was the working class so concentrated, so militant, and so politically visible. No other group of workers in Egypt developed the same high level of sustained independent organization as the Shubra al-Khayma textile workers. And nowhere else was the struggle between competing ideological trends inside the Egyptian labor movement so sharp and so fully documented. But because the issues raised in struggles at Shubra al-Khayma found their way quickly to Cairo and the national political stage, they were generally perceived and debated as questions of concern to the entire nation. In this respect Shubra al-Khayma represents a more highly concentrated and sharply delineated version of tendencies present in other industrial centers. Analytically, Shubra al-Khayma can be viewed as a vanguard region where contradictions less fully developed in other industrial centers received their fullest expression.

The first clear indication of the existence of a trade union among Shubra al-Khayma textile workers is in November 1937, when the embryonic trade union federation, the Commission to Organize the Workers' Movement (C.O.W.M), granted recognition to the Shubra al-Khayma Mechanized Textile Workers' Union.[5]

Although the C.O.W.M. was nominally under the leadership of Prince 'Abbas Halim, the driving force in the organization was Yusuf al-Mudarrik, a veteran trade union organizer committed to the principle of the independence of the trade union movement from all nonworker elements. Yusuf al-Mudarrik was soon to become one of the most prominent communist leaders in the workers' movement. Mahmud al-'Askari, the General Secretary of the SKMTWU and its representative to the C.O.W.M. Executive Committee, was a supporter of al-Mudarrik within that organization. Thus, from the very earliest period of its formation, the SKMTWU was closely associated with independent and socialist tendencies in the workers' movement.

In the same period, the weekly newspaper *Shubra* reported that a "group of educated workers" met in the headquarters of the Society of Muslim Brothers and decided to hold a workers' conference on 22 August 1938 to discuss the poor condition of the workers' movement and the possible formation of a workers' party.[6] Such a party apparently was formed, although it was not very significant, and its offices were located at the headquarters of the Muslim Brothers.[7] This is the earliest record of the Brothers' association with labor-organizing in the Cairo metropolitan area. According to Muhammad Sharif, the former head of the Workers' Section of the Society of Muslim Brothers, the society formed a workers' committee in the Shubra al-Khayma area in the late 1930s.[8] This appears to be the activity he was referring to.

A much more important source of Muslim Brothers' influence among the Shubra al-Khayma textile workers in this period was Taha Sa'd 'Uthman, who became one of the principal leaders of the Shubra al-Khayma textile workers. Many aspects of his career are typical of textile union activities, not only in Shubra al-Khayma but elsewhere in Egypt.[9] From 1935 to 1938, 'Uthman was a member of the Society of Muslim Brothers. He was a prominent and capable organizer for the society and a close personal friend of its founder and Supreme Guide, Hasan al-Banna. In January 1938, after training in a tuition-free technical secondary school in Bani Suwayf, 'Uthman and four other technical-school graduates became the first Egyptians to be employed as foremen at the Henri Pierre mill (Masna' Nasij al-Aqmisha al-Haditha) in Shubra al-Khayma. As a result of a dispute with the management over failure to pay promised wage increases, they became active in the SKMTWU. By the end of the year, Taha Sa'd 'Uthman became president of the union, a post he held until 1943; he subsequently served as treasurer and sergeant-at-arms.

The presence of educated and highly skilled workers like 'Uthman and the other technical school graduates made a great contribution to the development of the textile workers' unions throughout the industry. Many of the leading members of these unions had received some basic education but could not finish it because their families were not able to bear the expense. Some went to free technical schools and entered the mills as skilled workers or foremen. Others were chosen for advanced training after employment because of their basic literacy. These skilled workers and foremen formed the backbone of the independent trend within the trade union movement. The relatively large number of educated workers in the textile industry was an important factor in building the leadership of the textile workers in the entire trade union movement. In Shubra al-Khayma, discrimination against Egyptian foremen and skilled workers, who were not accorded the pay or the status granted to foreigners in similar positions, was a major motivation for their high level of union participation. The Egyptian foremen thought of themselves as workers and were accepted as such by other workers. This is one of the many ways Egyptian national sentiment became an important component of textile workers' consciousness.

When Taha Sa'd 'Uthman became active in the SKMTWU, Hasan al-Banna released him from his organizational responsibilities to the Muslim Brothers in order to free him to carry out his trade union duties.[10] But 'Uthman continued to share the world outlook of the Brothers, at least until early 1945, and he maintained close personal relations with Hasan al-Banna until 1946. According to Mahmud al-'Askari:

This good relationship helped us to build a firm bridge between ourselves and the Society of Muslim Brothers represented in the person of its great leader. He [Hasan al-Banna] became completely convinced that trade union organization is a humanitarian organization first and foremost, which defends the subjugated wretched of the earth without regard to their religion.[11]

This account and the reports of Muslim Brothers' activity in Shubra al-Khayma cited earlier make it clear that the Brothers were an active factor among the forces that contributed to the formation and early leadership of the SKMTWU. They cooperated with trade union radicals such as al-Mudarrik and al-'Askari, whose guiding principle was the creation of a trade union independent of nonworker patrons. There is no evidence of any friction between these two tendencies at this time. This may be due to an actual congruence of views about the nature and purpose of trade unions, as Mahmud al-'Askari's account cited above suggests. But it is more likely the result of the fact that at this time the Muslim Brothers had not yet developed clearly articulated views about these issues. In the late 1930s and early 1940s, the Brothers and trade union radicals could therefore cooperate in building an organization to defend "the subjugated wretched of the earth" within the context of the broad nationalist sentiment which provided the basic political outlook of the SKMTWU leadership at this time.

During World War II the SKMTWU developed into one of the strongest, best organized, and politically most independent trade unions in all of Egypt. The union established a tradition of militant direct action as its basic method of achieving its demands. A successful hunger strike at the Henri Pierre mill in September 1939, protesting the layoff of an entire shift because of a shortage of raw materials, resulted in a government ban on mass layoffs and the subsequent rapid growth of the union.[12] The SKMTWU employed the tactic of the hunger strike again in early 1942 when it launched a campaign to win a 10 percent cost-of-living allowance for Shubra al-Khayma textile workers. The hunger strike began as a result of a lockout at the Beso mill, a Greek-owned enterprise employing some 500 workers.[13] During this hunger strike, the Wafd was returned to power. Despite the strong nationalist sentiment in the union and the generally pro-Wafd feelings of the majority of the members, the union avoided any organization or patronage relationship to the Wafd. The dialectic of unity and struggle that characterized the SKMTWU's relationship with the Wafd during its tenure in office in 1942–44 was established only a week after the Wafd government assumed office. On 11 February 1942 the Committee of Hunger Strikers organized a march on the Wafd headquarters in Cairo to present to the Wafd leadership the demand for a cost-of-living allowance. Textile workers from Shubra al-Khayma and several other suburban Cairo textile centers participated.[14] When the march reached its goal, the workers occupied the meeting room of the Wafd Executive Committee and demanded to meet with the new prime minister, Mustafa al-Nahhas. After his representatives had negotiated with the workers, al-Nahhas issued an order to reopen the Beso mill, and all the workers arrested in the course of this struggle were released. All the workers returned to their jobs and received forty-five days' worth of back pay for the time of the lockout, and the 10 percent cost-of-living allowance was implemented.[15]

This impressive victory enabled the SKMTWU to expand its activities and membership. A regional branch of 150 members was established in the town of Mit Halfa, and the number of mills with elected union stewards grew to at least 16.[16] This growth was reflected in the change of the name of the union to the General Union of Mechanized Textile Workers in Shubra al-Khayma and Cairo (GUMTWSKC).

The GUMTWSKC continued to guard its organizational independence from the Wafd by declining to participate in the publication of *Al-Yara'*, a weekly workers' newspaper which the Wafd established as an organizing tool in its attempt to assert its hegemony over the Egyptian trade union movement in 1942–44. Instead of joining in this effort, the GUMTWSKC began to publish its own weekly newspaper, *Shubra*. Mahmud al-'Askari became the paper's managing editor, and Taha Sa'd 'Uthman served as secretary of the Editorial Board. The first issue of *Shubra* published under GUMTWSKC appeared on 30 April 1942.

This development laid the basis for a new stage in the union's organizational and political development. *Shubra* provided a stable legal means of expression for the union and served not only as an organizational tool for the union's internal affairs but also as a means to broaden its political vision and extend its influence to other sectors of the working class. This broader political perspective was indicated on the masthead of *Shubra* which, after 7 May 1942, carried the subtitle "a weekly workers' political newspaper." The control of an independent newspaper enabled the union to express not only its general support for the Wafd, but also its reservations, which would not have been possible to declare openly in the pages of *Al-Yara'*.

The most important point of difference between the GUMTWSKC and the Wafd was on the crucial trade union question of the right to strike. *Shubra* published a "warning" for workers to beware of being misled by those who said that the strike weapon should not be employed so long as the Wafd was in power.[17] The willingness to publish this statement, which stood in sharp contradiction with official Wafd policy banning strikes for the duration of the war, is a clear indication that the union's support for the Wafd was conditional and limited. This support was not to be permitted to obstruct the union's pursuit of its own interests as defined by its leadership in the light of their experience. The Wafd did not have the power to determine GUMTWSKC policy in the same way that it (and Prince 'Abbas Halim) had been able to manipulate the various trade union federations of the 1920s and 1930s. This point was further underscored when the GUMTWSKC openly challenged the

Wafd leadership by calling a general strike of textile workers to protest the removal of 'Abd al-Hamid 'Abd al-Haqq, who was considered a pro-labor figure, as minister of social affairs and his replacement by the more conservative Fuad Siraj al-Din.[18]

The militancy of the GUMTWSKC and its outstanding success in winning its demands enabled it to assume a leading role among Egyptian textile workers and throughout the entire trade union movement. After the victory at Beso in the struggle for the 10 percent cost-of-living allowance, delegations representing textile unions from all the major centers of the industry in Egypt came to Shubra al-Khayma to consult with the leadership of the GUMTWSKC.[19] The union's leading role in the trade union movement was further enhanced because it possessed in *Shubra* an organizing tool unmatched by any other trade union.

Shubra also provided a platform for intellectual development and cultural expression. Many worker-intellectuals gained experience and confidence by writing in the pages of *Shubra*. Mahmud al-'Askari and Taha Sa'd 'Uthman are the most important figures in this group, but there were several others who, though their long-term influence may have been less, are nonetheless representative of the political ferment among Shubra al-Khayma textile workers at this time.

One of the best examples of the emerging working-class pride and self-consciousness for which *Shubra* served as a platform is the *zajal* poetry of Fathi al-Maghribi. Al-Maghribi began his career as a worker at the Misr Spinning and Weaving Company. Subsequently he moved to Cairo and became a leading exponent of workers' popular culture. He was a member of *Shubra*'s editorial board and participated actively in the affairs of the GUMTWSKC, reciting his verses at union meetings and composing poems memorializing the struggles of the union.[20] The following are translated excerpts from one of his poems, celebrating the national feeling of Egyptian workers and their pride in their role as the makers of Egyptian civilization.

In All Pride We Are the Workers

We are the Egyptian workers, we are the brave,
A thousand salutes O Egypt, mother of all.

Workers are the secret of the beauty of cities,
The arts of manufacture are the secrets of heroes.

We are the builders of your pyramids, O Sphinx,
Workers, all of us your servants, as we all know.

We are builders of the Pharaoh's fleets
And all that is beautiful in this world.[21]

Another of the worker-intellectuals who made an important contribution to shaping and expressing the consciousness of Shubra al-Khayma textile workers was Iskandar Sulayman Salib, social affairs editor of *Shubra*. His articles on economic and social issues show some familiarity with general Marxist concepts and a definite tendency toward socialism. For example, in an article on "Egyptian Industry after the War" he demanded that industry be developed, not for private gain, but for the benefit of the general public. Salib's argument hinted at public ownership of industry, but this was posed as a nationalist demand, not as a call for socialism. "Egypt demands nationalism in the economic and social arena," he wrote.[22]

The GUMTWSKC continued to grow and to expand its activities and moved into a new and better headquarters.[23] But pressure from the textile mill owners resulted in the cancellation of the union's license to publish *Shubra*. The mill owners were concerned about the union's contacts with textile workers in other areas and its attempts to create a federation of textile unions.[24] The last issue of *Shubra* to be published by the union appeared on 21 January 1943.

The activities of the GUMTWSKC in 1942 and the tone of many of the articles in *Shubra* indicate that the union leadership was becoming increasingly radicalized and class-conscious during this period. This was fundamentally the result of the union leadership's own experience in waging and winning economic struggles. This process was an expression of what one Egyptian political activist has termed the "self-directed bursting forth" (*al-inbithaq al-dhati*) of the Egyptian working class.[25] The four component elements of the emerging class consciousness and radicalization of the union leadership were, first, independence of the union from domination by nonworker political elements; second, nationalism rooted in the struggle against the foreign mill owners and particularly against discrimination directed against Egyptian skilled workers and foremen; third, reliance on militant direct action rather than intercession of patrons to achieve demands; and, fourth, a conscious pride in being workers, as expressed by the *zajal* of Fathi al-Maghribi.

The worker radicalism of the GUMTWSKC leadership began to develop into a systematic Marxist worldview largely as a result of the efforts of Yusuf Darwish. Darwish was a member of a small circle of communist intellectuals who began to organize among workers in the middle of World War II. What Darwish and his comrades proposed to the GUMTWSKC was a coherent analysis that offered to explain the structural relationships and deeper causes for perceptions the union leaders already substantially grasped. In 1942 Yusuf Darwish became the union's legal counsel. Subsequently he and his comrades helped the union to establish a school where English, French, and general social studies were taught.[26] Eventually secret Marxist study circles were established, in which Mahmud al-'Askari, Taha Sa'd 'Uthman, and others participated.[27]

The Marxist influence in the union was clearly apparent in the decision to nominate the union's president, Faddali 'Abd al-Jayyid, as an independent candidate for the office of representative of the Shubra al-Khayma district in the parliamentary elections of January 1945. A broad-based election campaign involving three different textile workers' unions in the Shubra al-Khayma area

was organized and managed by a committee of thirty workers.[28] A comprehensive program of political demands was developed dealing with all the major
political questions facing Egypt. Among the program's demands were: (1) an
end to the British occupation of Egypt; (2) Arab unity; (3) nationalization of
monopolies and Egyptianization of all major economic and cultural institutions; (4) free and compulsory primary education; (5) redistribution of re-
claimed agricultural land to landless peasants; and (6) extension of labor
legislation to agricultural workers and institution of a minimum wage, maximum hours, a collective contrast law, and comprehensive social insurance.[29]

   This program reflects the development of a broad political vision among the
textile workers' leadership. Its concerns clearly extend far beyond the local
arena of Shubra al-Khayma and even beyond the boundaries of the industrial
working class. National political and economic questions as well as rural issues
are treated in a manner that indicates a fair degree of political sophistication
among those who adopted this platform. Yusuf Darwish undoubtedly played a
major role in the formulation of this program, and it corresponds, in its broad
outlines, to the immediate demands of the communist movement in this period.
However, it contains no explicit call for socialism, although many of its elements
lean in that direction. The most prominent aspect of the program is its nationalist demand for full political and economic independence for Egypt. And it
should be noted that nothing in it is in the least critical of religion, nor is there
anything a devout Muslim could not, in principle, support.

   Faddali 'Abd al-Jayyid failed in his election bid. But this cannot be taken as
an expression of popular sentiment in Shubra al-Khayma because these elections were among the least honest conducted in Egypt under the constitution of
1923. Their results were fixed in advance by negotiations between the competing parties except the Wafd, which boycotted them entirely.[30]

   Despite this electoral defeat the union continued to grow, and the activities
of the communist elements in its leadership became bolder. The expansion of
the union's activity is reflected in another change in its official name: it now
became the General Union of Mechanized Textile and Preparatory Workers in
Greater Cairo (GUMTPWGC). The British Embassy in Cairo considered the
GUMTPWGC to be one of the six most important unions in the Cairo area at
this time.[31]

   The period of January to April 1945 was marked by an extraordinary strike
wave among the Shubra al-Khayma textile workers. The GUMTPWGC was
accused by the Egyptian government of inciting and participating in over fifty
strikes during this period.[32] The strike wave was motivated by the collapse of the
industrial boom which had been based on the requirements of the Allied war
effort in the Middle East. The military production effort had drawn over a
quarter of a million mainly unskilled former peasants into the urban working
class.[33] Toward the end of the war, when military requirements began to fall off,
these new workers were fired from their jobs and the Egyptian economy proved

unable to absorb them in civilian production. Postwar unemployment was very high, particularly in the textile industry, and it was a major factor shaping the demands and the tone of the Egyptian workers' movement in this period. No reliable official unemployment statistics are available, but several unofficial estimates indicate that the number of workers unemployed as a result of the closure of the allied military production facilities and the withdrawal of military orders from civilian managed enterprises was about 250,000.[34]

During this period of intense strike activity by the Shubra al-Khayma textile workers, Yusuf Darwish and three other intellectuals formally established the New Dawn communist group. Mahmud al-'Askari and Yusuf al-Mudarrik joined this group and assumed responsibility for conducting political activity among workers.[35] They began to issue leaflets to workers under the signature "Workers' Vanguard" (*Tali'at al-'ummal*).[36] Workers' Vanguard actively supported the textile workers' strike movement, urging the formation of strike committees and the establishment of strike funds. Workers' Vanguard also called for the public celebration of May Day 1945.

Because of strike activity, the Egyptian government officially dissolved the GUMTPWGC on 28 April 1945. The stated reasons for the dissolution were the union's strike activity and its attempts to establish a federation of textile workers' unions. But the strong influence of communists in the union was in all likelihood an important contributing factor to the government's decision. The official dissolution of the union did not critically affect its activities, which continued to be carried on under the leadership of its elected Stewards Committee.

Following the dissolution of the GUMTPWGC its leadership became increasingly more involved in working-class political action led by the New Dawn communist group. Mahmud al-'Askari and Taha Sa'd 'Uthman were key figures in the Preparatory Committee for an Egyptian Trade Union Representative to the World Federation of Trade Unions Congress. This committee chose and dispatched Yusuf al-Mudarrik as its delegate to the September 1945 World Federation of Trade Unions Congress held in Paris. Al-'Askari, 'Uthman, and Mahmud Qutb, a member of the Stewards Committee, participated in the establishment of Workers' Committee for National Liberation (W.C.N.L.) and its weekly newspaper *Al-Damir* in October 1945. The Shubra al-Khayma steamboat workers and rubber-shoe workers, whose unions had been formed with the help of the GUMTPWGC and Yusuf Darwish, and the textile workers provided the main base of support for the W.C.N.L.

The increased activity of communist elements among the Shubra al-Khayma textile workers provoked a sharp response from the Society of Muslim Brothers. It has already been noted that the Brothers had been active among the Shubra al-Khayma textile workers from the earliest days of the union's existence. But in the late 1930s and early 1940s their activity appears to have been confined to providing a social solidarity framework and financial mutual aid. According to Taha Sa'd 'Uthman, these activities, as well as the Brothers' general nationalist perspectives, were the main attractions for their adherents among the Shubra al-Khayma textile workers in this period.[37] At this time the Brothers had no distinctive views on specific questions of tactics and strategy within the union.

In late 1942 and 1943, Taha Sa'd 'Uthman belonged to the Shari'a Co-operative Society, which was subsequently absorbed by the Muslim Brothers, and he still shared the basic world outlook of the Muslim Brothers. His series of articles in *Shubra* on "Work and Workers in Islam" is indicative of the views of the Brothers and their supporters within the union at this time.[38] These articles argue that the Quran confers an honored status upon manual labor and that Islam respects workers and requires that people work diligently and not be lazy. These themes are central elements of the Brothers' views on the role of labor in society as they subsequently became more explicit. The didactic and abstract character of these articles corresponds closely to the tone and content of the articles on "social reform" that began to appear in the Brothers' maga-zine, *Al-Ikhwan al-Muslimun*, during 1942 and 1943.[39]

Taha Sa'd 'Uthman's presidential address to the 1 November 1942 General Assembly of the textile workers' union had the same didactic tone, but it differed in several important respects. It was much more concrete than the articles in *Al-Ikhwan al-Muslimun*. It not only stressed the importance of main-taining brotherly relations between union members, but it offered a way to operationalize this by urging the prompt payment of monthly dues. Most important, it argued that there existed a distinction between the interests of the union and those of management.[40] This concept was diametrically opposed to the Muslim Brothers' theory on labor-management relations as it was later articulated. It was his perception of the existence of antagonistic class interests and his ultimate identification with the interests of the working class that eventually led 'Uthman away from the worldview of the Muslim Brothers and into the ranks of the communist movement.

To the Marxist view of society as divided into contending classes with mutually contradictory interests the Muslim Brothers counterposed the ideal of an organically interdependent social unity. Relations between various social strata (functionally differentiated groups as opposed to classes) were to be governed by the principle of "mutual social responsibility" (*takaful ijtima'i*).[41] Although the Brothers upheld the right of private property as satisfying a basic human impulse, they opposed the materialism, the greed, and the inhumane character of capitalist society. They criticized the "exploitative monopoly companies" and the "big landowners who hide behind white or black wage contracts."[42] The duty of a proper Islamic state was to organize mutual social responsibility. The state was obliged to guarantee an individual's right to work or, failing that, to provide him with an income.[43] The state should also either ensure that the minimum wage be sufficient to support a worker and his dependents or else provide economic assistance.[44] Employers who cut wages (a very common practice in the postwar textile industry) were denounced as overthrowing custom (*thara 'ala al-'urf*).[45]

The Brothers were particularly concerned with the question of mass postwar unemployment. According to an article by Ahmad al-Sukkari entitled "These Workers, How Shall They Live?" the government was morally obliged to find work for the unemployed because it had taken them from their villages to work in the war industries.[46] The "problem of the unemployed" is a recurrent theme in the pages of *Al-Ikhwan al-Muslimun* in late 1945 and 1946.

The Brothers' vision of a just economic and social order regulated by principles of Islamic brotherhood and mutual social responsibility corresponded with a widely shared, if imprecisely articulated, popular and traditional definition of social justice in Egypt. A large number of Egyptians readily identified with the Islamic idiom of the Brothers' propaganda. The Society's criticism of foreign economic domination of Egypt and the impersonal and materialistic values and practices of capitalist enterprises, particularly the firing of workers during recessionary periods, resonated with many workers' sense of what was wrong with the postwar Egyptian economy and society. In this sense the Brothers' vision of a just Islamic society bears a great similarity to the concept of a "moral economy" that E. P. Thompson has used to describe the social consciousness of the eighteenth-century English crowd.[47] This vision held a strong attraction for many workers recently arrived in urban centers, wrenched from their network of rural and pre-industrial social solidarity and confronted with the harsh regime of industrial discipline, job insecurity, and what appeared to be European values and norms.

In practice, however, the Brothers' revulsion against any activities that exacerbated social discord and class contradictions made them back away from participation in and support of strikes and other militant actions that the Shubra al-Khayma textile workers took to win their demands. Having rejected the validity of class as a legitimate category in an Islamic society, the Brothers were unable to comprehend the forces that motivated the Shubra al-Khayma textile workers. They thought of strikes and other expressions of working-class struggle simply as plots of atheistic communism which must be combatted.[48]

The character of the Muslim Brothers' activity among the Shubra al-Khayma textile workers began to change toward the end of World War II in explicit response to the growth of communist influence within the union. This development was related to the deterioration of the Brothers' relations with the Wafd in late 1942 and 1943 and their opposition to the left-wing Wafdist Vanguard and communist forces, which assumed the leadership of the Egyptian nationalist movement during the mass nationalist mobilizations of late 1945 and early 1946. In late 1944, the Society's activities began to assume a more openly political tone. This was reflected in the popular style of the articles in *Al-Ikhwan al-Muslimun* when it resumed publication in December 1944, after a hiatus of nearly a year. The magazine began to report, for the first time, on labor affairs, and on 28 June 1945 a "workers' page" was introduced. In 1944 a Workers' Section headed by Muhammad Sharif was established in the Society's headquarters.[49] These developments tend to validate Taha Sa'd 'Uthman's perception that in late 1944 and early 1945 the Muslim Brothers began to emerge as a distinct political tendency within the GUMTPWGC.[50] Muhammad Sharif himself confirmed that anti-communism was one of the two principal motivations for the activities of the Muslim Brothers in the working class. The other was, of course, spreading the call of Islam.[51]

In August 1945, when the leadership of the dissolved GUMTPWGC was engaged in organizing Yusuf al-Mudarrik's trip to the Congress of the World Federation of Trade Unions and in the discussions leading to the formation of the W.C.N.L., the Brothers launched their first open attack on socialism.[52] Shortly thereafter the Brothers began to engage in activities designed to compete with the existing trade union organization. In December 1945, they convened a meeting of 350 workers in the headquarters of their 'Abdin branch. A large number of workers from Shubra al-Khayma attended this meeting, which adopted a resolution containing a comprehensive list of national political, economic, and trade union demands not very different from those advanced in the electoral platform of Faddali 'Abd al-Jayyid.[53]

On 1 January 1946 a large strike broke out in Shubra al-Khayma. The strike lasted until 9 January and eventually involved 15,000 to 20,000 workers. The main demands of the strikers were to open all the closed plants in the area, to rehire all the fired and laid-off workers, and to end the military occupation of Shubra al-Khayma, which had been in effect since mid-December 1945.[54] Mahmud al-'Askari, Taha Sa'd 'Uthman, and Yusuf al-Mudarrik were arrested and accused of inciting the strike, for which officials claimed the W.C.N.L. was responsible. The trio of W.C.N.L. leaders were held in jail until 30 May 1946.

Although the arrest of the trio resulted in a sharp decrease in the influence of the New Dawn group among the Shubra al-Khayma textile workers, communist influence in general continued to grow. Shortly after the arrests, Muhammad Shatta, a member of the rival communist organization, the Egyptian Movement for National Liberation (E.M.N.L.), was elected secretary of the Stewards Committee of the Shubra al-Khayma textile workers. Several of the stewards subsequently joined this organization.

The Muslim Brothers' response to the arrest of the three worker leaders was to point out that they all belonged to communist cells headed by Jews.[55] The Society did not disagree in principle with the arrest of communists. It merely pointed out that the tactics of the government in fighting communism were defective. Communism, the Brothers argued, could more effectively be combatted by a return to Islamic principles of social justice than by use of police methods.[56] The Brothers' attitude toward this strike was one reason Taha Sa'd 'Uthman gave for cutting all his ties with the Society.[57]

Shortly before the outbreak of the Shubra al-Khayma textile strike, on 20

December 1945, the Egyptian government had sent a memorandum to the British government suggesting that the 1936 treaty between the two countries be renegotiated while maintaining the military alliance which it had established. The British responded that the 1936 treaty provided a sufficient framework for defining Anglo-Egyptian relations. When the contents of this memorandum and the British reply became public, the response was mass outrage at the willingness of the Egyptian government to negotiate with Great Britain while British troops still occupied Egypt. Public confidence in the government's ability to win Egypt's national demands, principally the total evacuation of British troops, evaporated.

The outbreak of the strike in Shubra al-Khayma contributed to the intensification of the atmosphere of political confrontation. The strike was strongly supported by the daily newspaper of the left wing Wafdist Vanguard, *Al-Wafd al-Misri*. Although the paper considered the strikers' demands to be nonpolitical in character, the alignment of political forces in Egypt was unmistakable. The nationalist movement, led by the Wafdist Vanguard and the several communist organizations, was supporting both workers' economic demands and nationalist political demands opposed by the Egyptian government and its landowning and industrialist supporters, the Palace and Great Britain.

The high point of the nationalist agitation and the clearest expression of its new class content and political direction was the formation of the National Committee of Workers and Students (N.C.W.S.) on 18 and 19 February 1946.[58] The Shubra al-Khayma textile workers were especially prominent in the working-class component of the N.C.W.S. The General Nationalist Committee of Shubra al-Khayma Workers participated in the discussions resulting in the formation of the N.C.W.S., and the textile workers were represented on its leading body by two members of the Stewards' Committee, Mahmud al-Dumrani and Sayyid Khudayr.[59] On 21 February, which was designated Evacuation Day, the N.C.W.S. led a successful general strike throughout Egypt. A contingent of 15,000 Shubra al-Khayma workers participated in the demonstration in downtown Cairo that day.[60]

The Muslim Brothers also participated in the general strike and demonstration of 21 February. But shortly afterward they split from the N.C.W.S. and formed a rival National Committee. This was a conscious attempt to combat the influence of the Wafdist Vanguard communist leadership of the nationalist movement. The Brothers also warmly welcomed the government of Isma'il Sidqi,[61] which was brought to office on 17 February in an effort to stem the tide of the nationalist movement. Sidqi was especially unpopular among workers, who recalled his harsh repression of the trade unions during his previous term of office in 1930–33.

These actions created an irreparable schism between the Brothers and the leadership of the nationalist movement and intensified the struggle between the communists and the Brothers among the Shubra al-Khayma textile workers.

The climax of the confrontation between the Muslim Brothers and the textile workers' leadership took place against the background of the strengthening of the left wing of the trade union movement through the tentative unification of the New Dawn– and E.M.N.L.–led trade union federations, the continuing mass mobilization of the nationalist movement, and the active participation of the Shubra al-Khayma textile workers in both arenas.

In the spring of 1946, the Brothers began a full-scale organizing campaign to attempt to supplant the left as the leading force among the workers of Shubra al-Khayma. In March the Society announced the formation of committees in each of the factories and mills in Shubra al-Khayma, as well as a Higher Committee of Factory Representatives.[62] This organization was exactly parallel to the structure of the Stewards Committee, and it is therefore not surprising that the Stewards Committee resolutely opposed these activities of the Brothers and issued the following statement:

> The magazine *The Muslim Brothers* has published that it has formed a committee in each of the factories in Shubra al-Khayma and that a Higher Committee of these committees of Muslim Brothers has been formed. The truth is that committees were not formed despite the strong efforts of the Society. We, the representatives of the workers of Shubra al-Khayma, went to the headquarters of the Muslim Brothers in order to learn the reason for these attempts despite the existence of trade unions among the workers. But we did not succeed in obtaining a satisfactory response. Instead we found them speaking in the language of the imperialists and the bosses. Therefore we informed them that we do not agree to the operation of any [of their] committees whatsoever. We announce this truth to the public. [The statement is signed by Muhammad Shatta and a number of other stewards, including several members of the E.M.N.L.][63]

In mid-May 1946, a strike broke out in Shubra al-Khayma that eventually idled at least nineteen textile mills.[64] The major issue in the strike, as it had been for over a year in most of the industrial struggles of the area, was the threat of closure of the mills and subsequent unemployment. The government saw the strike as a communist-led conspiracy, and the director of the Labor Administration, Hamid al-'Abd, called on Muhammad Sharif in order to enlist the aid of the Muslim Brothers in combatting the communists and ending the dispute. Muhammad Sharif personally attempted to act as a mediator in the strike.[65]

However, all the evidence suggests that, rather than mediate, the Muslim Brothers in fact set out to break the strike and its communist leadership entirely. According to *Al-Wafd al-Misri* and the personal accounts of several participants, the Brothers gave the police the names and addresses of members of the strike committee, and over one hundred workers were arrested as a result of Muslim Brothers' activity.[66] The Brothers also urged the workers to return to work immediately and to sign the no-strike pledge being demanded by the owners and the Labor Administration. The Society expressed the hope that after work resumed the government would act to resolve the problem.[67] As the strike wore on, the conflict between the Brothers and the strikers intensified. Members of the Society attacked a group of striking workers with sticks in an attempt to force them to return to work and accept the no-strike pledge.[68]

The Congress of Trade Unions in Egypt (C.T.U.E.), the communist-led trade union federation, called for a nationwide general strike on 25 June as part of its effort to rally support for the Shubra al-Khayma strike. But the general strike failed and by the beginning of July most of the strikers had returned to work. Following the defeat of this strike, on 11 July, the Sidqi government unleashed a massive campaign of repression against the entire Egyptian left, resulting in the dissolution of the C.T.U.E., the closure of many newspapers and the dissolution of societies, and the arrest of a large number of workers and intellectuals.

In response to daily criticism in the pages of *Al-Wafd al-Misri*, the Muslim Brothers attempted to justify their actions in Shubra al-Khayma in the pages of their own daily newspapers. The Shubra al-Khayma Muslim Brothers Committee published a detailed defense of its actions entitled "The Actions of the Muslim Brothers Promote Higher Interests and Do Not Support Destructive Revolutionary Principles." [69] This article clearly affirms that the Brothers did not support the strike because, in their view, it was provoked by agitators who fabricated reasons to justify it. In response to the accusation of spying for the police, the Brothers replied that their actual role had been to combat the spread of destructive revolutionary principles (that is, communism). The Brothers also admitted that they had opposed the Stewards Committee and gave as their reason for doing so their doubts about its financial accountability. The Brothers had established, in opposition to the Stewards Committee, their own "committee to oversee [*ra'aya*] the affairs of the workers of this area."

The Brothers' use of the term *ra'aya* with its paternalistic connotations of guardianship stands in direct contradiction to the principle of trade union independence from nonworker patrons which the Shubra al-Khayma textile workers had consistently upheld since the establishment of their union. By the use of this term the Brothers indicated that their view of the trade union movement was essentially the same as that of the Wafd and Prince 'Abbas Halim, who also saw themselves as exercising guardianship over the workers.

This conception of the workers' movement failed to recognize that the growth of industrial capitalism in Egypt had begun to create a new class reality in Egypt. Shubra al-Khayma was one of the locations where this development was most advanced. This is precisely why the communists concentrated their activities among workers there. Precapitalist aristocratic conceptions which saw workers only as a group of "the weak" or "the wretched of the earth," requiring the intercession of influential patrons to secure their rights, did not accord with the social reality of Shubra al-Khayma. The success of the communists in 1945 and 1946 in Shubra al-Khayma is due to the fact that their support for independent trade unionism and their recognition of the existence of antagonistic classes, and the consequences of this fact, were more closely in accord with the social realities of Shubra al-Khayma than the theory and practice of the Muslim Brothers.

The failure of the strike of May–July 1946, in combination with the defeat of the C.T.U.E.'s call for a national general strike and the Sidqi government's campaign of repression against the left, dealt a severe blow to the communists' position of leadership in Shubra al-Khayma and allowed the Muslim Brothers to emerge, for a short time in the period 1946–48, as the most influential force in the area. During this period they announced the formation of a new Shubra al-Khayma Textile Workers' Union.[70] Legal appeals against the government's dissolution of the GUMTPWGC were still in process and the New Dawn group in particular opposed the establishment of a new union (even by other communist groups) in order not to give the court an excuse to avoid dealing with the suit against the dissolution of the former union. The Brothers' establishment of a union was therefore viewed as a direct attack on the former union and its leadership.

The only concrete activity of this union which was reported by *Al-Ikhwan al-Muslimun* was the dispatching of a telegram of protest to government officials because of a particularly sharp increase in the rate of unemployment due to seasonal pressures in the textile industry in early 1947. The telegram was signed by representatives of nine Shubra al-Khayma mills, including the secretary of the union, 'Ali Ibrahim Pasha.[71] His title of *pasha* is a certain indication that he was neither a worker nor a foreman. The telegram hints that the union might not have had much influence over the Shubra al-Khayma workers, because it warned that if the government did not resolve the unemployment problem the union could not take responsibility for the workers' actions.[72] Communist sources claimed that the membership of the Brothers-sponsored union was only 200 workers.[73]

The most important activity of the Muslim Brothers in Shubra al-Khayma during this period was the establishment of a textile mill, the Muslim Brothers Spinning and Weaving Company. The decision to establish the mill was made in May 1946 by the Brothers' Shubra al-Khayma branch in order "to protect *its members* from unemployment" (my emphasis).[74] The mill began operation in December 1947 and continued to function until early 1949, when the Society's assets were sequestered by the government following its official dissolution. Muhammad Sharif served as the manager of this enterprise. Since it was one of the smaller mills in the Shubra al-Khayma region, employing fewer than sixty workers on fourteen looms,[75] it can hardly have made a substantial contribution to solving the problem of unemployment. Muhammad Sharif nonetheless felt that the operation of this enterprise conclusively demonstrated the viability of the economic principles of Muslim Brothers.[76]

The defeat and repression of the left and the alliance of the Muslim Brothers with the Sidqi government enabled the Brothers to gain influence in Shubra al-Khayma in 1946–48. They were also aided by the efforts of the mill owners to eliminate communist influence. During this period all the elected stewards who had continued the activity of the GUMTPWGC in late 1945 and 1946 were fired, and many of them were banished to their villages.[77] Shubra al-Khayma itself declined somewhat in importance as a textile center after the strike of 1946. Some of the mills were moved to other suburban Cairo locations, or even as far away as Alexandria, in order to avoid the high level of industrial struggle which characterized Shubra al-Khayma.

The confrontation between the Muslim Brothers and the communists in Shubra al-Khayma in 1945–46 was one of the most decisive struggles in the effort to find a new orientation for the postwar Egyptian movement for national and social liberation. For the left—the Wafdist Vanguard, the progressive intelligentsia, and trade union activists committed to an independent working-class movement, as well as the communists and their followers—the actions of the Muslim Brothers in Shubra al-Khayma and their related abandonment of the National Committee of Workers and Students after 21 February 1946 proved that the Muslim Brothers could not provide a coherent and program-matically effective alternative to the increasingly discredited liberalism of the Wafd. In the trade unions, the Muslim Brothers' reputation was seriously damaged by the charges of strike-breaking and spying, especially since they resurfaced in the major strike at the Misr Spinning and Weaving Mill in Mahalla al-Kubra in 1947. Although these charges did not prevent the Brothers from exercising some influence in the trade union movement in the postwar period, this tended to be confined to localities and industries where particular conditions were especially favorable. The Brothers had only limited influence among textile workers, who were the leading force shaping the character of the workers' movement during this period. Despite a nearly unimpeded opportunity to organize the textile workers in Shubra al-Khayma in the period 1946–48, when the communists and their allies were jailed or disorganized, the Brothers did not succeed in establishing a lasting base of support there. After the Palestine War, when martial law was lifted and political activists were released from detention, the communists reestablished themselves in and around Shubra al-Khayma (especially in the nearby suburb of Zaytun) and in 1950–52 they once again became the leading political force among the suburban Cairo textile workers.

NOTES

1. Egypt, Ministry of Finance, Statistical Department, *Census of Industrial Production, 1945* (Cairo, 1945).

2. Egypt, Ministry of Social Affairs, *The Labour Department* (Cairo, 1951), p. 36. Official figures for union membership are understated because they include only members whose dues are fully paid and they do not include members of officially dissolved unions.

3. Great Britain, FO 371/80580/JE1735 (1950). This refers to the archives of the British Foreign Office in the Public Records Office in London. Subsequent references to this material are given with the abbreviations FO and the reference number.

4. *The Labour Department*, p. 30.

5. FO 141/660/357/8/37.

6. *Shubra*, 18 August 1938.

7. Ibid., 15 September 1938.

8. Muhammad Sharif, personal interview, 28 October 1980.

9. The details of Taha Sa'd 'Uthman's biography, unless otherwise noted, are based on personal interviews on 28 October, 5 November, and 15 December 1980.

10. Mahmud al-'Askari, "Min tarikh al-harakah al-'ummaliya al-Misriya," *Al-'Ummal*, 8 November 1976. Mahmud al'Askari's memoirs were serialized over a period of several years in the pages of the weekly newspaper of the General Federation of Egyptian Trade Unions, *Al-'Ummal*. (Subsequent references to this source are abbreviated al-'Askari, *U*, with the date of publication of the particular installment referred to.)

11. Ibid.

12. Ibid., 1 November 1976; *Al-Ahram*, 17 September 1939; Taha Sa'd 'Uthman, personal interview, 28 October 1980.

13. Al-'Askari, *U*, 27 June 1977.

14. Ibid., 1 August 1977.

15. Ibid., 5 September 1977.

16. *Al-Wajib*, 6, 13, 20 April 1942.

17. *Shubra*, 25 June 1942.

18. Al-'Askari, *U*, 3 October 1977.

19. Ibid., 5 September 1977.

20. Some of Fathi al-Maghribi's poems are collected in the anthology *Ana al-'amil* (Cairo, 1946), which has a biographical introduction by Yusuf al-Mudarrik.

21. This poem was first published in *Al-Yara'*, 1 October 1942, during a hiatus in the appearance of *Shubra*.

22. *Shubra*, 14 May 1942.

23. *Al-Yara'*, 1 October 1942.

24. Taha Sa'd 'Uthman, personal interview, 28 October 1980. The activity referred to is reported in *Shubra*, 30 July 1942.

25. 'Abd al-Samad Jad al-Mawla, *Qadaya al-jabha al-wataniya al-taqaddumiya al-Misriya* (Beirut, 1979), p. 57.

26. Taha Sa'd 'Uthman, personal interview, 28 October 1980.

27. Taha Sa'd 'Uthman, "Mudhakkirat wa-wathaiq min tarikh al-tabaqa al-'amila," *Al-Katib* (July 1971): 175.

28. Al-'Askari, *U*, 28 November 1977.

29. Ibid., 5 December 1977.

30. FO 371/41319/J4548; FO 371/41319/J4615 (1944).

31. FO 371/45978/J1301 (1945).

32. *Al-Waqa'i al-Misriyah*, 21 May 1945, p. 6.

33. FO 921/331 (1945) gives the figure of 263,080 Egyptians employed by the British forces during the war. Approximately 25,000 more Egyptians were employed by the American forces.

34. See, for example, Charles Issawi, *Egypt at Mid-Century* (London, 1954), p. 262; *Al-Ikhwan al-Muslimun*, 10 May 1946; *Al-Wafd al-Misri*, 1 May 1946.

35. Ahmad Sadiq Sa'd, *Safahat min al-yasar al-Misri fi a'qab al-harb al-'alamiya al-thaniya, 1945–1946* (Cairo, 1976), p. 48.

36. Examples of these leaflets can be found in FO 371/45978/J1791 and FO 371/45978/J2001 (1945).

37. Taha Sa'd 'Uthman, personal interview, 15 December 1980.

38. *Shubra*, 10, 17 December 1942, 8 January 1943.

39. The first issue of *Al-Ikhwan al-Muslimun* appeared on 29 August 1942. The magazine continued publication twice monthly until January 1944, when publication was temporarily suspended. In 1946 it became a daily newspaper.

40. *Shubra*, 19 November 1942.

41. Al-Bahi al-Khuli, *Al-Islam ... la shuyu'iya wa al-rasmaliya* (Cairo, 1951), pp. 24, 34, 100. This book, published by the Workers' Section of the Muslim Brothers, contains the fullest official development of this concept as it applies to the relations between employers and employees. It is much more radical in tone than the actual practice of the Muslim Brothers during the period 1944–48, reflecting the radicalization that occurred in some sections of the Society in the 1950s. But the theoretical concepts it employs are valid characterizations of the Society's views in the 1944–48 period.

42. Ibid., p. 108.

43. Ibid., pp. 70ff.

44. Ibid., p. 100.

45. Ibid., pp. 96ff.

46. *Al-Ikhwan al-Muslimun*, 7 May 1946.

47. E. P. Thompson, "The Moral Economy of the English Crowd in the 18th Century," *Past and Present* 50 (1971): 76–136.

48. See, for example, the article "The Actions of the Muslim Brothers Promote Higher Interests and Do Not Support Destructive Revolutionary Principles," *Al-Ikhwan al-Muslimun*, 18 June 1946.

49. Muhammad Sharif, personal interview, 3 December 1980.

50. Taha Sa'd 'Uthman, personal interview, 28 October 1980.

51. Muhammad Sharif, personal interview, 3 December 1980.

52. *Al-Ikhwan al-Muslimun*, 30 August 1945.

53. Ibid., 22 December 1945.

54. *Al-Wafd al-Misri*, 2, 4 January 1946.

55. *Al-Ikhwan al-Muslimun*, 5 January 1946. This accusation was not, strictly speaking, correct: Taha Sa'd 'Uthman did not formally join a communist organization until September 1946.

56. Ibid.

57. Taha Sa'd 'Uthman, personal interview, 15 December 1980. The other reason was their activity in the strike of May–July 1946 (dealt with further on).

58. For a full discussion of the N.C.W.S. and the nationalist movement during this period, see Jean-Pierre Thieck, *La journée du 21 février 1946 dans l'histoire du mouvement national égyptien* (Mémoire de D.E.S.: Université de Paris VII, 1973).

59. FO 371/53368/J1447 (1946).

60. *Al-Ahram*, 22 February 1946.

61. *Al-Ikhwan al-Muslimun*, 26 February 1946.

62. Ibid., 19 March 1946.

63. This leaflet is reprinted as an appendix in Muhammad Hasan Ahmad, *Al-Ikhwan al-Muslimun fi al-mizan* (Cairo, 1946), pp. 98–99.

64. *Al-Ikhwan al-Muslimun*, 2 June 1946.

65. Muhammad Sharif, personal interviews, 28 October, 3 December 1980.

66. *Al-Wafd al-Misri*, 31 May 1946.

67. *Al-Ikhwan al-Muslimun*, 2 June 1946.

68. *Al-Wafd al-Misri*, 16 June 1946.

69. *Al-Ikhwan al-Muslimun*, 18 June 1946.

70. Ibid., 5 July 1946.

71. Ibid., 28 April 1947.

72. Ibid.

73. *Al-Jamahir*, 5 May 1947.

74. *Al-Ikhwan al-Muslimun*, 13 May 1946.

75. Ibid., 5 September 1948.

76. Muhammad Sharif, personal interview, 28 October 1980.

77. Murad al-Qalyubi, *Mashru' qanun bi-shan al-tawfiq wa al-tahkim fi munaza'at al-'amal* (Cairo, 1948), p. 33.

ELEVEN

Muslim Union Politics in Egypt:
Two Cases

Ellis Goldberg

In the literature about Islam and popular social or political movements we often learn much about the theories produced by leaders but very little about what such theories meant to their followers. In this chapter I shall discuss two situations in which a determined leadership fused an explicitly Islamic vocabulary to a movement for social change. The instances I wish to discuss occurred within the trade union movement in Egypt in the 1940s and allow us to see how organizational leaders with a particular ideological commitment—in this case the Muslim Brothers—balanced the competing claims of ideology and organizational maintenance.

We know a great deal about the theories and formal organization of the Muslim Brothers and its charismatic founder, Hasan al-Banna.[1] These studies present a picture of what al-Banna and other leaders thought about "Islamic politics" or "Islamic economics" and attempt to link the grand theory with the gross developments of Egyptian political history: demonstrations, coups, assassinations. In this article I shall focus explicitly on the effort to make the ideology work in the practical realm of trade union activity. This approach leads to a more nuanced picture of organizations such as the Muslim Brothers and a far clearer image of the limitations on the ability of the leaders to turn ideological sympathy or even formal adhesion into practical political consequences. Islam in such a focus appears more like other ideologies which *claim* broad or even total control over members and their activities but which must settle in reality for a partial and limited hold on the energies of those members.

I also hope to show that followers, and especially those followers with organizational commitments outside the religious movement, understand quite well the limitations on their ideology. They especially recognize its limitations in terms of defining either goals or methods of struggle. Those trade union leaders who espoused a militantly Islamic approach to union activity were not only constrained by the economic and social realities of their situation but clearly understood themselves to be so constrained and endeavored to work within those constraints.

The two unions to be discussed in this article are those of the sugar workers at Hawamdiya, a rural area outside Cairo, and the oil workers, most of whom worked along the Red Sea coast. What made these leaders "Islamic?" In an institutional sense they were either members of the Muslim Brothers (as was Anwar Salama, leader of the oil workers) or accepted analyses that closely echoed those expressed in the daily newspaper of that organization, *Al-Ikhwan al-Muslimun* (as did Shaykh Muhammad 'Abd al-Salam of Hawamdiya).

For workers, the salient characteristic of these two industries was that they were foreign-owned. The Egyptian government had significant interests in regard to each industry and was thus willing to intervene in the affairs of the firms involved. Although these industries differed in their technological requirements, both employed an overwhelming majority of unskilled workers from peasant communities who were primarily Muslim.

The ideology of the Muslim Brothers gave local union leaders an analysis of the industrial plant within which men worked and placed that plant in the perspective of an unequal relation between Egypt and the European countries from which the plant owners came. The ideology affirmed that the factories themselves provided valuable assets to Egypt and were an honorable way for workers to provide for their families. At the level of the factory, this ideology conceded that conflict within the plant was real and endemic, but argued that the most oppressive aspects of industrial production were not inherent in the structure of industrial relations. Rather, the Muslim Brothers, Anwar Salama, and Shaykh 'Abd al-Salam argued that the problems between workers and management existed as a result of conflicting cultural outlooks between Europeans and Egyptian Muslims. Implicit in the argument was the idea that some form of Egyptian ownership, including that of the state, was preferable to foreign ownership. Moreover, because these foreign firms were large and relatively wealthy, it was easy to argue that they could afford the concessions which smaller, Egyptian-owned firms could not.

Such an analysis, couched in essentially moral rather than political terms, not only corresponded to the experience of peasants working in industrial settings but was one they could easily accept. These workers were not peasants who had moved to the cities for the risks and rewards of a completely new life. In Hawamdiya they were and remained primarily peasants. Such men did of course move physically from the agricultural regions of Upper Egypt to the oil fields, but the oil fields and refineries embodied neither the tightly structured cooperation of the factory nor the highly political atmosphere of the Cairene or Alexandrian metropolis.

If the leaders and the men were part of the Islamic movement and largely within the orbit (if not always the institutional framework) of the Muslim

Brothers, they were far from being uncritical "traditionalists." They engaged in strikes, signed (and lived up to) contracts, and developed formal organizations and maintained them over fairly long periods of time. If Islam or, more accurately, their interpretation of Islam had a real effect on the political or economic choices of such men, we can only detect it in highly nuanced ways and very specific and perhaps even marginal occurrences. What is most striking about both 'Abd al-Salam and Salama is the degree to which they eventually moved away from an organizational commitment to the Muslim Brothers, whether in response to better deals or simply in search of solutions to new problems.

THE HAWAMDIYA SUGAR MILL

By 1893 when the Société Générale des Sucreries et de la Raffinerie de l'Egypte was founded, there were several large sugar mills spread across Upper Egypt and a large refinery at Hawamdiya, a village in Jiza to the south of Cairo. The workers in these mills were drawn from the local agricultural population, and working in the mills was considered a desirable, although part-time, occupation:

> As long as they have existed, the sugar companies have recruited from among the peasants living near the factories.... The sugar company has an inexhaustible reserve among them because the fathers of the families request, without stint, places for their sons. The "sugar tradition" is established then, in one way or another, in peasant families whose villages or estates lie alongside the factories of the company.[2]

About 90 percent of these workers were unskilled day laborers. As early as the turn of the century, however, there was also a small number of skilled and semi-skilled Egyptians who could entertain the possibility of moving up into jobs held by Europeans. These skilled Egyptian workers and foremen played a key role in all the Egyptian unions. At Hawamdiya they early became conspicuous as offering an alternative to the oppressive rule of European foremen.[3]

Strikes occurred quite early at Hawamdiya and often concerned questions of work rules, discipline, and hours, as well as wages. These strikes partook too much of village social structure to be effective in providing the basis for formal organization. In 1910 a strike was avoided because management "sowed dissension between workers of different villages."[4] Almost a decade later, during the 1919 revolution, the train station at Hawamdiya was destroyed and an attack on the mill was averted only by the intervention of "police officers, the head of the guards, diverse village notables, and a certain number of veteran factory workers who informed [rioters] that the mill assured the prosperity of the region and of an important laboring population."[5] The 1,800 rioters clearly included unskilled workers at Hawamdiya, but for them the mills were too important a source of cash income to be destroyed, much as they were angered by conditions and desirous of higher wages or shorter hours.

The emergence of a union at Hawamdiya depended on skilled or semi-skilled Egyptians who worked in the plants year-round. For these men, however, the critical questions were not so much those of wages and hours but of how they were treated and of their likelihood of promotion. We know something of this period from the unpublished memoirs of "Shaykh" 'Abd al-Qadir Himada. His first job, in 1921, was at Egypt's only sugar refinery, at Hawamdiya: "There were three strikes, one in 1923 and two in 1921, and I personally participated in those strikes and gave what aid I could to the leaders." His explanation of the strike is at some variance with the conventional explanations, which tend to focus on relative decline in real wages in the post–World War I inflation:

> The company didn't respect the work rules. It really tyrannized the workers terribly even though the sugar company was among the first to give its workers better than average wages [*ujur ahsan min ghairiha*] and to provide services to a greater than average degree. However, the workers had more anger than those of other companies and this undoubtedly pushed them to strikes. Besides, the company favored the administrative staff over the workers and this was a big factor in the anger of the workers.[6]

No lasting union organization emerged at Hawamdiya, however, despite continued unrest in the plant which erupted into mass violence in 1934 and again in 1936.

By 1942 a union had come into existence that was firmly enough implanted to register under that year's Wafd-sponsored legislation recognizing unions. How this union became implanted is unclear, but after 1942 it was obviously aimed at structuring a relation between skilled and unskilled workers based on antagonism to foreign foremen and administrators. Thus the union would have severe problems when ownership of Hawamdiya passed from European to Egyptian hands and when skilled workers and foremen came to be Egyptians.

The union was led, from its inception, by Shaykh Muhammad 'Abd al-Salam, who was sympathetic to the Muslim Brothers although not a member. He was a member of the *Jam'iya al-shari'ya al-ta'awuniya*, an organization which provided a reservoir of recruits for and often acted in a "united front" with the Muslim Brothers.[7]

A copy of the union constitution is preserved—the second edition, dated 1950.[8] The newspaper of the Muslim Brothers, [*Al-Ikhwan al-Muslimun*] (*The Muslim Brothers*), carried reports on the activities of the sugar workers' union at Hawamdiya during the late forties. The constitution shows how the Brothers saw the role of trade unions and the organization of the workers in Egyptian society. It contains a preface which explicitly confronts the issue of the situation in which the workers live, their options, and their leaders. This preface dates from 1950 and refers to the period before and after the Wafd "Egyptianization" campaign which brought certain key industries under Egyptian ownership. The sugar mills were bought by 'Abbud Pasha in 1944, and during the next five years European administrators were, in theory, being eased out. The first paragraph asserts, on the part of the union president, that the significant section of the work force to be organized is that of the section chiefs in all crushing factories, including Hawamdiya, although the "message" of the union is not just for them but for every Egyptian and every Easterner.[9] The administration of the plant is perceived as corrupt, given the "distance of these section heads from the teaching of their religion, and following the high and heavenly counsels of the morals of their Prophet."[10] 'Abd al-Salam advises the workers to put themselves under their foremen, listen to them, obey them, and take their direction, so as to "bring back to our country great goodness and general benefit."[11] To the foremen, his advice was to follow good practices and to have the interests of the workmen at heart, especially the problems stemming from misery and poverty; and to recall that workers, too, have pride and dignity and that Egyptian foremen have a special obligation to be gentle and merciful rather than cruel and harsh.[12] At the time the union was formed, the preface asserts that getting rid of foreign domination was the main task confronting Egyptians. In the early 1940s, that is, the days of foreign domination, "we would proclaim in every place, O, you who believe, should you meet those who do not, do not treat them with kindness.... Thus we urged on the faithful to struggle with the colonialists."[13]

The constitution itself gives what must have been an exemplar of a Muslim union, as far as the Muslim Brothers were concerned. It also, given its relative longevity (at least eight years), must have responded to what a significant proportion of the members, many of whom were of peasant background, expected of a union. The constitution sets out the goals of the union as an organization, the rights and duties of the members, and the internal structure of a workers' organization. The first of the three announced goals of the union was to act as a "linking ring" (*halqat al-'ittisal*) between the company and its workers in every field of activity related to work. The second of the union's goals was to defend the material interests of the workers, individually as well as collectively. The third goal was to aid the workers materially and morally.[14] The enunciation of these goals and their ordering reflects both a specifically Islamic vision and one still linked to the world of small production, although in this case, unlike the craft workers, the small producers are peasants, not skilled workers, in origin. Although Islam is not the only religion to proclaim a solidary community as its ideal, the specific vocabulary of Islam conceives the factory as a solidary enterprise, in which workers and management (including not only the foremen but the company administration as a whole) need to be tightly linked in order for production to be maintained.

A significant part of the union's activity was conceived as social aid and support for the workers from their collective resources. The workers, in short, were a collective community inside the factory. After six months of paying dues the workers were entitled to all the union benefits, first and foremost of which was legal aid for any civil or criminal charges brought against them. Many of the other benefits were financial and accrued to the workers in case of need, especially monetary bonds, injury and sick pay, aid to widows, lay-off or severance pay for sick or aged members (at the rate of 3 pounds per year of union membership), loans, and money for weddings. The union also was willing to aid workers arrested on the job as long as they had not done anything provocative. Those arrested could receive monetary aid to the amount of 15 piasters a day for a total of three months.[15]

The union itself was organized on the framework of mass democracy: in the words of the constitution, the general meeting of the membership was "possessor of the highest power."[16] In practice the general meeting was limited to choosing the union's administrative council. The council was elected from a restricted set of nominees and anyone wishing to nominate himself for the administrative council had to be able to read and write, to have been a union member for two years, to be paid up in his dues, and to be able to put up a 20 piaster forfeit should he not gain at least 50 percent of the votes in his shop. Moreover, the council itself was elected by "shop." As there were thirteen "shops" from which a total of fourteen administrative council members were elected, the skilled workers and those in administration elected half of the administrative council.[17]

The general meeting was hardly more than the source of legitimacy wielded by the head of the union, who in 1950 styled himself the *naqib* as well as the president.[18] *Naqib* was a title drawn from the traditional craft-association vocabulary and the title used by heads of such groups in the nineteenth century. In fact, 'Abd al-Salam, the union president, was a worker in the plant and according to reports in *Al-Ikhwan al-Muslimun* himself made only 20 piasters a day.[19]

The president, one of two vice-presidents, the secretary, the treasurer, and the sergeant-at-arms (*al-muraqib al-'amm*) formed an executive committee for the administrative council and decided on its agenda. Of the executive committee in 1950, two had made the pilgrimage to Mecca and two others were considered to be religious leaders (shaykhs).[20] The Muslim Brothers' newspaper, moreover, identified 'Abd al-Salam himself as a shaykh.[21] Thus the leadership of the union at Hawamdiya was considerably more religious in orientation than any other large union in a major industry in the mid-1940s.[22]

In the late 1940s the Muslim activists were leading strikes at Hawamdiya. There was a major, two-part strike in 1945.[23] Evidence of these work stoppages, which must have been led by the Muslim Brothers, appear in the Communist weekly *Al-Jamahir* (*The Masses*). Censorship may have prevented the strikes from being written about at the time they occurred.[24]

Putting together Communist and Muslim Brothers sources, it appears that

1947 marked a high point of activity in the Hawamdiya plant. According to *Al-Jamahir*, in 1947 the company was no longer willing to allow workers' wages to be garnisheed, although living on credit until the pay envelope came may have been the only really universal experience of proletarians. It was then that the leadership began a struggle for a contract that would guarantee the sugar workers benefits similar to those given government employees under the 1942–44 Wafd government. The state set the standard for what workers in private industry could demand, but to the degree that politics and influence with the state were important, the leadership was fragile.

It is clear that the union leadership considered the newspaper of the Muslim Brothers an important, if not the most important, way to reach the general public and perhaps even the factory workers. Clearly, publication of detailed information about the sugar workers, their grievances, and their contracts in the Brothers' newspaper gave public legitimacy to the union. They made sure that the newspaper had access to detailed information about contract negotiations.

On 9 January 1947, *Al-Ikhwan al-Muslimun* published a report concerning the existing wage agreement between the sugar workers' union and the company. There were then 1,613 ordinary workers, 579 trained workers, 608 skilled workers (of whom 408 were "expert"), and 28 super-grade workers. Their pay scales ran from a range of 25 to 60 piasters a day for super-grade workers who were on salary, to 5 to 19 piasters for ordinary workers. The super-grade workers seem to have been a small group who had gotten benefits similar to if not identical with those of European workers. Each classification was broken into subclasses, creating a set of "ladders" from the entry-level wage to the top. It took three to four years to climb one ladder and get into a new category.

The union, in the statements given to *Al-Ikhwan al-Muslimun*, made a detailed criticism of the existing scale. There are several specifically economic criticisms: lack of clarity about raises, including cost-of-living adjustments; the problems of who is included; the question of whether it is retroactive to 1945; the problem of whether workers serving a probationary period are to be paid. There are also several other criticisms, which reflect problems peculiar not so much to Egypt as to any workforce made up of peasants in an uncertain economy. Thus, the workers wanted to be sure that the director, who had the right to choose new workers, would agree to pick them from among the families of those who already worked at Hawamdiya. They wanted the "sugar tradition" to continue.

The skilled workers wanted to be on salary rather than on wage, that is, to have their earnings protected by being given the status of "employees" or "clerks." It seems important to note that all the workers were worried about wages, but that they saw the common solution to their problems in the creation of company "tenure" so that the owners would care for them just as a master craftsman would care for his employees.

The demands of the union seem to have been formulated more with an eye to the needs of the educated or skilled workers than to those of the unskilled. The key issues for the union were equality of Egyptians with foreign employees, the eight-hour day, end-of-service (*nihayat-al-khidma*) compensation, which may refer to either layoff or firing compensation as well as retirement, and the end of benefits for foreigners which conferred an invidious status on Egyptians. Considerable resentment also seems to have been built up during the 1945 malaria epidemic when the workers were made to forego sick pay.

According to *Al-Jamahir*, a strike was threatened in April 1947 and the company agreed not to fire workers whose wages were subject to garnishment. Negotiations over a new contract dragged on, and a new strike deadline was set in October. By the year's end the union had still not won satisfaction on many demands. By then the union was feeling the impact of the nationalist movement.

In an article titled "Sugar from Blood" the Brothers addressed the problem of imperialism and argued that the wage differential between European and Egyptian workers yielded the pernicious imperialist profits to which the company was not entitled. By the end of 1947, however, the pages of *Al-Ikhwan al-Muslimun* were filled with news of the Palestinian war and efforts to recruit volunteers. Under the control of the Brothers it seems likely that the union lasted until the state took control of the trade union movement in 1954.

We can only speculate on why the union achieved such strength in Hawamdiya, but it is apparent that it served more than just the immediate economic needs of the community, a community then (even more than now) made up of peasants and rural workers. The Brothers complained about train schedules which made it difficult to arrive at work on time or to leave. They undertook to build a mosque by the train station. They also probably attempted to have the company provide a restaurant at Hawamdiya, a popular demand in some industries (such as tobacco) but not in all (for example, textile).[25] By appealing to the foremen, who were the skilled workers, the literate, the leaders, the Brothers had identified the key constituency in a factory made up largely of people unable to chart their own course. These workers needed outside help, given their overall poverty of resources. That the Muslim Brothers possessed a newspaper, political clout with the Palace, and an idiom for speaking about oppression was critical. By speaking to the foremen, who were in fact key to union organization in most Egyptian industry at the time, the Muslim activists had also identified a person in the workplace of whom the peasants stood most in awe.[26]

The demands of the union at Hawamdiya were largely in the interests of these men, but by giving them something for which to fight and showing them how Islamic ideology could mobilize a constituency for winning their demands for equality with the Europeans, the Muslim activists established their credentials as a movement fighting in the national interest. The appeal to equity, which

was the stock in trade of the broad Islamic movement and especially of the
Muslim Brothers, furnished a rallying point for both skilled and unskilled
workers. For the new Egyptian owners, Muslim activists provided leadership
which was more concerned with keeping the plants open and saw itself as a link
between workers and management. Precisely because the union saw itself as a
kind of "transmission belt" between administration and worker, Egyptian
owners could rely upon it in contract negotiations. Its political orientation,
against the British and in support of Arab Palestine, did nothing to hinder the
working of the sugar mills.

A BRIEF LOOK AT THE OIL INDUSTRY

The oil industry is second case. There were some 5,100 workers in government-
recognized unions in the "mining and oil refining sector." [27] Not only were
these workers few in number, but they were spread across the relatively isolated sections of Egypt along the Gulf of Suez where oil is located, and in the
Suez Canal refineries. Their weight was so slight that most histories of the working class in Arabic, and even many discussions of Egyptian industry, hardly
mention either oil workers or the petroleum industry. Yet their leader, Anwar Salama, was a member of the Muslim Brothers who ended up becoming
Nasser's minister of labor.

Salama's union, the first among petroleum workers in Egypt, was formed
among Shell workers in 1942, the year the Wafd granted legal status to trade
unions.[28] The impetus seems to have come from a group of workers defending
a man who was fired for making a mistake at work. A strike evidently won the
man's reinstatement and gave the oil workers a sense of their potential collective
power. A first meeting to which ninety men came was held at one worker's
home. At that meeting they agreed to take the roganizational steps, both in
terms of finance and recruitment, to make their union real. They each agreed
to pay initial dues of five piasters and to recruit five new members. The meeting
explicitly rejected the notion—presumably with Salama's approval—of forming a welfare society.

Salama himself made no secret of how he looked at the situation of the oil
workers and how he believed they should see it. In an article in *Al-Ikhwan al-
Muslimun* Salama made three interconnected points: (1) the oil workers are
relatively poor, because (2) the oil companies are exploitative monopolies and
(3) these monopolies make it impossible for Egyptians to provide for themselves.[29] It is worth noting that the first point was no longer true by 1948; the
second point had to do with the relationship of the company to the state and not
to the workers; and the third point indicates the degree to which nationalism,
rather than religious sentiment, was the basis for reuniting the workers. Salama
directed special fire at the companies for not providing amenities as the textile
company at Mehallah had done and at the difficulty in getting paid days off for

local holidays (as opposed to the principle of paid holidays) such as the Prophet's birthday, the king's birthday, or Coronation Day.

The reason for this state of affairs was that an industry vital to modern development—petroleum—was in the hands of the British. This created what Salama saw as a major fiscal problem for the state: the English government, rather than the Egyptian government, taxed the high profits of the oil company. Consequently, the company was "draining the sweat of the workers into gold and silver pipelines." The main difference between the textile and the petroleum industry was that, in the former, the profits were used so that Egyptians could help Egyptians. A nationalist management would avoid the problems of working-class discontent by taking care of the causes of discontent before they become overwhelming. The state, in short, was the natural ally of the workers in the struggle for a better life.

We find other arguments of this genre in *Al-Ikhwan al-Muslimun*. An article several months earlier accused the company of being "an exploitative company which monopolizes the critical petroleum industry and thereby gains terrific profits, and nevertheless never thinks of raising the standard of living of the Egyptian workers." [30] As among the sugar workers, it is the privileged position of the company in national economic life, not its structural relation to its own employees, that makes it exploitative. Also, as with the sugar workers, the company's profits from this privileged monopoly position are misspent because they are not used for the workers themselves. Yet again, the Shell company is attacked for acting in an imperialist fashion precisely because the workers do not share in the profits.[31] Salama explained that it was the *cultural* differences between the company and the workers that made the latter live as they do. Egyptian companies share the profits (we are told), but colonialist companies do not. What is important, then, is to make the company act like a national, properly Egyptian company. After all, "better a noble death in the search for a bit of bread than an ignoble submission to the colonialists in our country." [32]

The immediate postwar situation in the Egyptian oilfields was one of bitter struggle to improve the terms of labor but not to save jobs, which was a key problem for both textile and tobacco workers. There are no reports of widespread layoffs. If consumption was down slightly from wartime highs, it seems that Egyptian internal consumption and world demand were picking up the slack caused by lessened military needs. The first recorded postwar strike occurred in September 1947 and included the occupation of the Shell refineries by the workers.[33] The unity of the Shell workers was impressive. Salama sent a telegram to the Ministry of Social Affairs claiming to represent 3,000 workers. This was rapidly followed by a delegation of Shell workers to the capital to meet with relevant officials.

Government employees and state organizations were forthcoming in their expressions of support for the workers. As *Al-Ikhwan al-Muslimun* put it: "The Egyptian workers who had been forced by poverty, penury, neglect, and illness to an outburst and struck . . . . gained the sympathy (*atf*) of all of the responsible government agencies"—but not that of the company, of course.

The word used, *atf*, has a wide range of meanings running from sympathy to attention. It formed the centerpiece of nationalist as well as Muslim trade-union thinking about relations between employer and employee. It clearly suggests that the moral or ethical framework within which employers operate is far more important than the structured roles they play. It was widely used in the Egyptian union movement, and especially in the Muslim and nationalist sectors, to refer to what was expected from state officials (or individual masters in the crafts) as opposed to capitalist entrepreneurs. By early 1948, strikes had broken out throughout almost the entire industry, although it appears that a general strike never occurred. Thus, the workers at Ras Ghabr were ready to strike in early March but were persuaded not to do so until April 5.[34] In March the employees of the Anglo-Egyptian Oilfields Company, made up of employees of Shell and Socony Vacuum, called for a strike deadline in mid-March and finally struck in the last week of March.[35]

The oilfields were, in short, afire with the unrest and displeasure of the workmen. The strikes often lasted for days and included the militant action of occupying the worksites, both indications (given the relatively weak financial situation of Egyptian workers and unions as well as their vulnerability to state interference) of the level of angry unity that existed. But for what were they striking? In fact, when we examine the contracts it becomes apparent that the workers were relatively highly paid and that the union was very much a "business" union. What is also apparent is that there was a considerable range of wage scales in the oilfields (probably greater than in the textile mills, for example)—from a minimum for the least skilled worker of 14 piasters a day to a maximum for the most skilled of 73 piasters a day.[36] Moreover, cost-of-living increases in the oil fields are greater than in other (especially national) sectors. Many of the wage increases won in the oilfields came as the result of government intervention in the bargaining process when a conciliation commission ordered the firm to pay particular wages. In the case of the oilfields—where the state granted the concessions to exploit the fields—the administration actually had some muscle. Foreign-owned companies such as the Suez Canal complained bitterly—if privately—about this state of affairs: "The owners used to be at the mercy of the functionaries whose principal failing was probably that they indulged in pro-Egyptian demagogy."[37]

Salama and fellow members of the oil workers' unions who were members of the Society found in the anti-colonialist attitudes of the organization a way to attack the companies successfully and win significant demands. They also found an idiom that allowed them to unite workers with very significant gradations in the wage scale (although not quite as severe as the tenfold gap in the sugar workers' range from 5 to 50 piasters). Explaining their situation to the workers in light of the cultural differences between company management and

Egyptians allowed Salama to focus on differences between management and the men. It certainly was not an explanation that used the concept of class, but it was equally certainly one that covered much of the same ground as a class-based explanation. To the degree that a significant proportion of the workforce came from Upper Egypt, where peasant society was more intact than in the Delta, concepts of justice, equity, and the cultural differences between Egyptians and Europeans explained the relative class positions of the workers and the management better than more abstract, and necessarily abstruse, explanations. Besides, Salama's ties to the state, which was even then embarked on a path of Egyptianizing much foreign-owned industry, including the oilfields, got results.

MUSLIM UNION ACTIVISM

Generally we seem to find Muslim leadership where unskilled workers were drawn directly from the peasantry and where ownership of industry was foreign. Muslim activists strove to maintain the unity of the Muslim community in the face of challenge from foreign intervention and social stratification. Their influence was felt wherever pay, status, or working conditions tended to divide Muslims, although they were most successful in social situations like those found among the sugar workers. The Muslim Brothers' newspaper, unlike the left and even nationalist newspapers read by workers and trade union members, spent considerable time defining colonialism as a cultural assault and a matter of personal antagonism and proposing remedies based on cultural cohesiveness and personal dignity.

Despite the vehemence with which the Brothers opposed colonialism, they do not seem to have used violence in the sugar mills or the oilfields; rather, they appear as the workers move beyond unorganized violence to union organization. The violence associated with the Muslim Brothers arose not from the membership at large but from particular sections seeking to eliminate top politicians. The Brothers' members were by no means angels, but they did not resort to force indiscriminately.

The role of the Muslim Brothers and of Islam as an animating ideology in the trade union movement was not too different from the "nationalist" ideology among American Blacks in the 1960s: it provided a way for an educated elite to further its personal interests by giving it a vocabulary likely to appeal to a mass political base. The Muslim Brothers attempted to mobilize workers against colonialism in Egypt. Almost invariably colonialism is that which makes it difficult for skilled or educated Egyptians to step into the positions of Europeans. Thus, in the article titled "Sukkar min damm," the wage differential between Egyptian workers and European personnel in Egypt (rather than between Egyptian factory wage rates and those for similar work in Europe) is explained as the economic basis of imperialism.[38] In "Khalf dukhan al-masani'," colonialism is described as causing the split between skilled workers, who have graduated from technical schools, and clerical employees, so that such workers receive less than their due, namely, wages and security of tenure.[39] It is, the article goes on, "the very essence of colonialism to deny workers the possibility of advancement to higher grades such as engineer or foreman as is the case in their own countries." Unskilled workers, the article goes on, know nothing of culture; the "small worker" is thus like a child when he enters the factory, seeking only satisfaction of his immediate desires.[40] Thus the article counsels, rather like the constitution of the sugar workers, that it is the duty of the owner of the shift foremen to pay attention to the needs of the workers.[41] The paternalist spirit urged by the Muslim Brothers in their newspaper and obviously taken up with success by union leaders in Hawamdiya, in the oilfields, and elsewhere seems to be based on creating a patron-client link between educated, skilled workers (who were likely to become foremen if they were not already) and the mass of men.

This is not the place for an exhaustive analysis of their political vocabulary, but one cannot avoid being struck by how different it is from that of the Marxists. Not only is colonialism, the immediate locus of the peasant-workers' discontent, portrayed in personalized terms, but the nature of that discontent itself is seen in subjective rather than objective ways. Thus, one finds a heavy emphasis in Muslim literature on *dhulm* or oppression, and except in one or two cases (where tax money is paid to a foreign state rather than to the Egyptian one), one does not find the word *exploitation*. *Exploitation* refers to a systemic and organizational concept, whereas *oppression* refers to a personal one. It is not surprising, then, to find that much of the activity of Muslim activists links the educated to the broad mass of workers. All organizations of workers fought for paid holidays, and Muslim trade-union activists did too, but the holidays they fought for, tenaciously, were of course Muslim and Egyptian holidays. Workers at the Bata shoe company as well as in the Shell oilfields and refineries demanded the anniversary of the royal coronation and the Prophet's birthday as paid days off.[42]

If I have any disagreement with the tendency to counterpose class and nation and the presumption that the Brothers organized around the latter, it is simply that for the workers in much of Egyptian industry, what we analyze as "class" was experienced as "national" or, more particularly, "cultural" oppression. The bureaucratic rationality of the factory was seen as a cultural assault on Egyptian folk norms rather than a structured set of economic relations. The Brothers' leadership saw trade unions as just another form of beneficial association, not unlike the Society for Memorizing the Quran, the Society to Aid the Muslim Poor, the Anti-Tuberculosis Society, or the Alms Society.[43] The workers were *makruhun* in the eyes of Hasan al-Banna; on that basis he agreed to cooperate at least briefly with the leftist textile workers' union in Shubra al-Khayma.[44] To that degree one can understand why there was a tendency for union activists such as Taha Saʻd ʻUthman to leave the orbit of the Brothers.

Without a specific vision of workers as a distinct social group with interests in opposition to other social groups, especially owners, it is impossible to create any long-lasting independent economic or political organization based on them. Although leftist organization may, over time, be co-opted, the specific class vision of Marxism and Leninism makes the creation of independent, interest-based (in a broad sense) organization a primary task of trade union organizers. For Muslim activists, on the contrary, maintenance of the Islamic community is primary and reinforcement of the Muslim educated elite is a mode by which to keep the community united.

The structural relations between employer and employee in Egypt made sense in the framework of Islamic moralizing as long as the men in charge of discipline were not Egyptian. Once that changed, moral suasion ceased to be a viable tactic to better the lot of workers.

Clearly, one mode of continuing to improve the conditions of workers was to move the trade unions directly into the state under the auspices of a corporatist nationalism. This was the opinion taken up by Anwar Salama in the mid-1950s when he agreed to head a unified national trade-union movement and to become minister of labor. Precisely at this moment the Muslim Brothers as an organization ceased to have any real viability. Although Salama probably retained ideological affinities to the movement, it no longer held any allure for him as a trade union leader. In Hawamdiya, too, with the Egyptianization of ownership in the 1940s the union leadership experienced a crisis of orientation which continued into the 1952 period. ʻAbd al-Salam never actually joined the Muslim Brothers. After 1950 the union began to seek other allies. Both Salama's move to the state and that of the sugar workers to new allies suggest that the demise of "Islamic" populism around 1952 had roots in the ideology of the organization: unable to create independent, interest-oriented organizations, the Muslim Brothers could only function within the context of a general breakdown of the system.

NOTES

1. For book-length or near–book-length treatments in English see Richard Mitchell, *The Society of Muslim Brothers* (London: Oxford University Press, 1969); Christina Harris, *Nationalism and Revolution in Egypt* (The Hague: Mouton, 1961); Nadav Safran, *Egypt in Search of Political Community* (Cambridge, Mass.: Harvard University Press, 1961). In Arabic there is also Rifʻat Saʻid, *Hasan al-Banna: Mata wa kayfa wa li-madha* (Cairo: Madbuli, 1977).

2. Jean Vallet, *Contribution à l'étude des conditions des ouvriers de la grande industrie au Caire* (Valence: Imprimerie Valencienne, 1911), pp. 83–84.

3. In the end Egyptian foremen were not successful in creating a different way of organizing work in the plant and often treated unskilled and semi-skilled workers in the very ways that

European foremen had, and this provided the impetus for breaking down nationalist or Muslim approaches to union organizing.

4. Vallet, *Contribution*, p. 85.

5. Records of the Ministère des Affaires Etrangères, Paris, K/56/13, sheet 129.

6. Unpublished memoirs of 'Abd al-Qadir Himada, furnished in photocopy by Jamal al-Banna in Cairo, 1981.

7. Jamal al-Banna, interview, Cairo, 22 December 1980. Jamal al-Banna is the brother of Hasan al-Banna, Supreme Guide of the Muslim Brothers. He was active in the trade union movement in the late 1940s and personally knew many of the union leaders of the day.

8. Union of the Workers of the Sugar Factory at Hawamdiya, *Al-la'iha al-assassiya al-mu'addala* (Revised Constitution) (second edition; Cairo, 1369/1950), p. 11.

9. Ibid., p. 2.

10. Ibid., p. 2.

11. Ibid., pp. 8–9.

12. Ibid., p. 9.

13. Ibid., p. 8.

14. Ibid., p. 16.

15. Ibid., "Section Four—The Rights of Members," pp. 18–21.

16. Ibid., p. 23. Other points on the subject of the general meeting are from the same page.

17. Ibid., "Section Seven—The Administrative Council," pp. 24–28.

18. Ibid., p. 10.

19. *Al-Ikhwan al-Muslimun*, 30 December 1947.

20. Revised Constitution, p. 35.

21. *Al-Ikhwan al-Muslimun*, 5 October 1946.

22. The newspaper of the Brothers is said to have had a larger influence than the society itself: interview with Jamal al-Banna, Cairo, 31 January 1981.

23. This account is drawn from Sulayman al-Nukhaili, *Al-harakah al-'ummaliya fi misr wa mawqif al-sihafa wa al-sultan al-misriya minha min sanat 1882 ila sanat 1952* (Cairo, 1967), pp. 253–61.

24. *Al-Jamahir*, 19 May 1947. All events referred to as drawn from *Al-Jamahir* are drawn from a center-spread exposé in the paper on this date. If the Communists had had more connections with Hawamdiya their newspaper would presumably have had more than this one story in two years of publication.

25. See Khairya Khairy, "The Nutritive Aspect of Egyptian Labour," B.A. thesis, American University of Cairo, 1946.

26. Corporal punishment was still employed in Egyptian factories. See Frederick Harbison and Ibrahim Ibrahim, *Human Resources for Egyptian Enterprise* (New York: McGraw-Hill, 1956), p. 76.

27. A. I. Gritly, *The Structure of Modern Industry in Egypt* (Cairo: Government Press, 1948), p. 550. It seems unlikely that there were more than 10,000 workers in the oil industry altogether.

28. This account is taken from Muhammad 'Abd Allah Abu 'Ali, *Al-tanzim al-ijtima'i al-sina'a* (Alexandria: Al-hai'ab al-'ammah al-misriya al-kitab, 1972), p.151.

29. *Al-Ikhwan al-Muslimun*, 20 April 1948.

30. Ibid., 10 November 1947.

31. Ibid., 1 March 1948.

32. Ibid., 5 March 1948. This, it should be pointed out, is from a story on the oil workers in Ras Ghabr.

33. Ibid., 20 April 1948.

34. Ibid., 5 March 1948, where the news indicates that they were convinced by the union leadership not to strike when the company refused to implement a conciliation commission decision. News of the strike appeared in *Al-Ahram*, 5 April 1948.

35. Ibid., reports the strike on 20 March 1948, *Al-Ahram* on March 24.

36. See *Wizarat al-quwa al-a'mila. 'Idarat al-buhuth al-fanniyah wa-l ihsa*, file 11/4/3/5 and 1 (box 2). The comparison would be with the base rates between the National Egyptian Spinning Company

in Alexandria and its union, given in '*Uqd al-'amal al-mushtarik* (Alexandria: Dan Bosco Press, 1949), pp. 26–27.

37. Internal records of the Suez Canal Company, folder 412, no. PO/320/38/CF, dated 11 March 1953, unsigned.

38. "Sugar from Blood," *Al-Ikhwan al-Muslimun*, 30 December 1947; "Behind the Smoke of the Factories," ibid., 30 November 1947.

39. "Hadha al-isti'mar bi-shahmihi wa lahmihi." This is by no means an isolated example. See also "British Monopolies and Egyptian Workers," part of a group of articles on the oil industry, which castigates the British for using cheap Egyptian labor and then asserts that the solutions are, first, to allow Egyptians to become employees and, second, to make their wages equal to those of Europeans working in Egypt.

40. "Only his bit of bread, and no more," to be exact.

41. Given the similarity between the sugar workers' constitution and this article, for example, it seems plausible to assert that although the leadership at Hawamdiya may not have been formally enrolled in the Muslim Brothers organization, they clearly were so close as to be ideologically indistinguishable on issues such as these.

42. *Al-Ikhwan al-Muslimun*, 25 January 8, 12 February 1948.

43. See "Beneficial Societies," ibid., 9 January 1948, where this argument is made.

44. See the memoirs of Mahmud al-Askari, *Al-'ummal*, 8 November 1976, for a description of ties between Muslim and leftist activists. The workers' oppressed status—not class position—provided the theoretical basis for the political tie.

TWELVE

Islamic Political Movements in Northern Nigeria: The Problem of Class Analysis

Paul Lubeck

The object of this essay is to describe and analyze the Islamic component of several political movements that have emerged in the northern, predominantly Muslim region of the West African state of Nigeria. After outlining my theoretical perspective on urban political movements among the popular strata of Kano, the region's largest and most politically developed city, I shall address some interpretive and methodological issues that arose as I prepared this essay. Following this section, I shall analyze the Islamic component of three political movements that have emerged among the subordinate classes since the emergence of nationalist politics in Nigeria. The first of the three movements is Islamic populism: this case study will involve an examination of the role of Islamic ideology and institutions in the program of the radical opposition party, the Northern Elements Progressive Union, during the Nationalist period. The second case study analyzes the influence of Islamic ideology in the effort of first-generation industrial workers in Kano to obtain their legal rights and recognition for trade union organization during the decade of the seventies. The last case study examines the Islamic elements of a violent millenarian movement which erupted in Kano during December 1980. I shall conclude with an assessment of the advantages and the obstacles presented by Islamic political movements for the social and political emancipation of Kano's urban lower classes.

The reader needs to be aware of some bare facts concerning Nigeria, Kano, and the influence of Islam in Black Africa's most populous state (pop. circa 80 million) and most affluent economy.[1] Petroleum exports have altered Nigeria's position in the world division of labor from an agricultural exporting nation (groundnuts, cocoa, and palm produce) to a leading regional capitalist state with a potential for industrial development, if the petroleum revenues are not squandered and if a mutually beneficial relationship can be maintained with multinational corporations whose technology and expertise are required for Nigerian development. After the political chaos and regional tension associated with the Nigerian civil war, successive military regimes have centralized power at the federal level, created nineteen states to replace the original three regions, commissioned a fledgling state capitalist sector, and managed a comparatively orderly transition to civilian rule (in October 1979). While state revenues have soared from approximately one billion dollars in 1970 to a figure approaching 25 billion dollars in 1981, this quantitative economic growth has been achieved only at great social and economic cost. These costs include social disorder in urban centers; widespread public corruption; overly ambitious development projects which, critics charge, are poorly articulated with existing needs and infrastructure; a profound crisis in agriculture, where approximately 75 percent of the labor force is located, thus requiring three billion dollars of food imports in 1980; and deepening social cleavages between the advantaged upper and middle classes and the rural and urban lower classes. Nevertheless, compared to most African states, Nigeria ranks as a regional growth pole that attracts migrants from neighboring countries; for example, it is estimated that over one million Ghanaians now work in Nigeria.

Situated in the northern, Savanna region, Kano is unique in that it offers a rare example of a dynamic pre-colonial Savanna economy which, after incorporation into the world economy, profited from the colonial economy and subsequent changes in transport and communications patterns. With an annual urban growth rate of approximately 9 percent and a population approaching one and a quarter million, Kano has emerged as the center of air and rail communications, as the unrivaled regional commercial center, as the third most important center of industrial production, and as the likely center of Nigeria's agroindustrial production and processing. Always a center of radical politics, Kano boasts a merchant-industrialist class whose origins lie in the early nineteenth century, and a populace whose independence has resulted in a reputation for supporting radical politics and reformist tendencies in Islamic practice.[2] Currently Kano State is the most populous state in the federation (pop. circa 10 million) and the only state to elect a socialist governor and legislature.

Though Islam has been practiced in Nigeria at least since the year 1000, the formation of the Sokoto Caliphate in the early decades of the nineteenth century provided the foundation for an expanding Islamic community. Islam is also practiced beyond the northern region: for example, it is estimated that approximately half the Yoruba peoples practice Islam. Among the entrepreneurial classes of Nigerian cities, Islam is well represented. Further, the militant anti-colonial and anti-imperialist consciousness of the radical Muslim intelligentsia may attract adherents of a similar political perspective. Unfortunately, regional rivalries have undermined the taking of an accurate census so that the exact growth and extent of profession of Islam is difficult to assess.

For the last ten years my research has centered on the relationship of class-

based protest to Islamic institutions and culture in the northern region of
Nigeria. Most political movements in the region are centered at Kano.
Through the use of a wide variety of methods and materials—historical,
anthropological, and quantitative surveys—I have analyzed the manner in
which a class-like, subordinated status group, the *talakawa*, has resisted political, social, and economic exploitation by the dominant classes, as often as not
through the selective use of Islamic ideology and institutions.[3] To be sure,
neither theories of class nor cultural explanations in the Parsonian tradition are
by themselves sufficient to explain the behavior, structure, and consciousness of
the *talakawa* and the emerging wage-earning class of Kano, the urban *leburori*.
Hence, I want to emphasize that *talakawa* and *leburori* are the theoretical and
empirical objects of my research.

In contrast to John Paden's pioneering work on Islam in Northern Nigeria,
which assumed that Kano's dominant and subordinate classes have the same
political culture, my assumption is that Islamic culture is mediated through the
structural and class experience of *talakawa* and *leburori* life.[4] True, political
movements undertaken by the latter usually involve Islamic cultural symbols,
Islamic criteria of legitimacy, and Islamic-sanctioned goals. But in the cases
that I shall describe below, the *talakawa* and *leburori* movements, class-based
deprivation is the prism through which Islamic culture is perceived and upon
which political action is based. The problem, then, is to illustrate in a convincing manner how the selective interpretation of Islamic ideology by subordinate
strata engaged in a political movement—here, *talakawa* and *leburori*—is determined to a significant degree by the social and economic structures that
constrain and shape their participation in political movements which are, at the
same time, informed by Islamic institutions and cultural expectations.

From a macrohistorical perspective, colonial and contemporary political
movements in Kano reflect the interaction, or *articulation*, of two global processes, Islamization and capitalism. The first, of course, is Islamization. Though
Islam was present prior to the jihad of Usman dan Fodio (1804), the Muslim
state system that was ruled by an interurban ruling class of the Sokoto Caliphate both expanded the boundaries of Islam and strengthened the role of
Islamic law and culture within older Muslim communities. Just as is the case in
the centers of Islam, the state bureaucracy and the ulama are the main agents of
Islamization.[5] The second world-historical process that has shaped and continues to shape Islamic political movements in the region is capitalism. Initially
(1900–1904), European capitalism penetrated the social and economic life of
the *talakawa* only in a superficial way. Slavery declined along with slave-
raiding; a colonial bureaucratic system, peopled by the families and, in some
cases, the individuals of the pre-colonial regime replaced the overlapping
jurisdictions of the patrimonial system that M. G. Smith has described so well.[6]
But until the Nigerian civil war and the petroleum boom, mere incorporation
into the capitalist world economy as an agricultural exporter did not in any

significant way alter production relations, forms of consumption, or land tenure, nor did it create a large wage-earning class even in the region's economic center at Kano. Instead, colonial capitalism encouraged a class alliance between colonial administrators and the Muslim aristocracy, whereby the latter "politically" managed a groundnut export economy in return for British recognition of their prerogatives. This alliance eliminated traditional checks on illegitimate authority and actually increased the exploitation of the rural *talakawa*. Indeed, currently, one of the exciting areas of historical research centers on political and agrarian change in northern Nigeria and how this colonial class alliance exposed the *talakawa* to the vagaries of an oligopolistic world market but without any of that corresponding advance in productive technique associated with capitalist development in Europe. Space does not permit a summary of this research, but one of the tentative conclusions suggests that under colonial capitalism the conditions of the rural *talakawa* declined, as did land and labor allocated to produce groundnuts, the proceeds of which were used to pay taxes.[7] In turn, this reduced food production and thus exposed them to the threat of famine following the periodic droughts that are endemic to the region.

To return to the articulation of Islam and capitalism: the fear of Mahdist revolts drove the Muslim aristocracy and the British administrators into an alliance that had the effect of expanding the influence of Islamic law and culture among the *talakawa*. For example, areas that successfully resisted Muslim domination were put under the jurisdiction of Muslim district heads; the British agreement not to interfere with Islamic prerogatives or the affairs of the Islamic religion opened the door for the Muslim aristocracy to interpret their class prerogatives as Islamic in the broadest possible sense; and the relative peace and improved transport created by the colonial order facilitated communication between Islamic communities and expanded the profession of Islam among the rural *talakawa*. Lastly, given the special status of Islam in northern Nigeria, the fact that the region was conquered by Christians, the traditional rivals of Islam, generated among all members of the Muslim community, though less militantly among the ruling class, a movement that I have labeled *reactive Islamic nationalism*. A regional Muslim national identity, it should be emphasized, was not created solely by the expansion of cultural value toward universalism, as Parsons would have it. Rather, the evidence is clear that the Islamic revival was a reaction to Christian conquest and continues to reflect a Muslim nationalist consciousness that often expresses itself as anti-imperialism in overt political movements and, at a more mundane level, in public manifestations for a return to "fundamentalist" Muslim practices.[8]

The methodological point that I wish to make is a relatively simple one. To comprehend Islamic political movements as they actually are, rather than limiting one's analysis to the movement's self-perception, requires that one recognize that most Islamic societies have been subordinated to the capitalist world economy for at least several decades. In the case of northern Nigeria, therefore, Islam and capitalism have been in relationship with each other since 1900. To treat Islamic political movements since that date without reference to the effect of colonial and indigenous forms of capitalism risks serious error; the error is "essentialism," treating historical and contradictory societies as a cultural essence.[9] One must determine whether and how the two social forces, Islamization and capitalist development, have interacted or articulated with each other in generating the conditions that give rise to an Islamic political movement.[10]

Kano, for example, during the pre-colonial and pre-capitalist era continued many of the features described by Lapidus in his study of Muslim cities during the Middle Ages.[11] Ethnic and occupationally specialized wards formed the basic urban unit, which was centrally administered by the authority of the *amir*. Furthermore, not only were wards formally isolated from each other by their direct relationship to the *amir*, but recent oral history collected at Kano has revealed the existence of ritualized warfare between certain wards. Again, occupational associations of craftsmen and traders were not autonomous bodies distinct from the authority of the state. Instead, the officials were appointed by the *amir* to collect taxes, and the urban craft officials engaged in tax-farming activities among the less fortunate rural blacksmiths. And, as always, the only source of independent resistance to the state or an ambitious *amir* came from the ulama, who are called *mallams* among speakers of Hausa. While such similarities suggest that a valuable comparison could be made between two pre-capitalist Islamic cities, without integrating the effect of capitalist penetration into one's analysis one cannot explain colonial or contemporary political movements by abstracting from the ideal-typical features of an Islamic city.

Before discussing Kano's Islamic political movements, I would like to make a point concerning the frontier quality of Islam in northern Nigeria. In a very real sense, Islam and capitalism are the underlying forces that exert a determining influence on Kano's political movements. But one must bear in mind that each influence originates from a distinct and alien society: Islam from North Africa, and capitalism from Europe. In fact, the periphery of Islam and the periphery of the capitalist world economy met at Kano at the beginning of the twentieth century. Yet there are real differences between the two historical processes. Islam was spread by indigenous Africans over the long term through trade contacts, culminating in Muslim mercantile capitalism, Islamic scholarship, and, ultimately, the formation of the Sokoto Caliphate. Hence, the Sokoto Caliphate, with its economic center of Kano, was a cultural periphery but escaped functioning as a political and economic periphery of more advanced North African states. Without the negative aspects of economic and political subordination, therefore, Kano benefited from its peripheral position on the frontier of Islam. In contrast, capitalism was violently introduced by alien Europeans who avoided becoming assimilated into Kano society but instead incorporated the region into the capitalist world economy. Once incorporated,

Kano was subordinated in an economic and political structure that served the needs of the center of the world capitalist economy. While there was transfer of technical and administrative expertise and, most important, a revolution in transport and the expansion of mercantile capitalism, underdevelopment did occur during the colonial period in the areas of agriculture, commerce, and manufacturing.

When one analyzes Islamic political movements in Kano, therefore, one must bear in mind that both capitalism and Islam exist in their peripheral form, rather than in their most advanced and original forms as found at their respective centers. What does this mean in practice? To me it means that the possible political expressions that the combination of peripheral forms of capitalism and Islam may take are virtually unlimited and exceedingly fluid. Not only is each social force weaker than would be the case at its respective center, but each continues to be influenced by events and movements that are disseminated from the center, whether they be new forms of technology or market demands or new forms of urban revolutions or conservative revitalization movements. When we analyze the Islamic social movements that have figured prominently in twentieth-century urban Kano, we must bear in mind not only the effect of Islam and capitalism as they were joined in the same society but also the fact that both are determined or at least influenced by global issues as well as specific changes that occur at their historical centers. With these methodological points in mind, let us turn to the most enduring Islamic political movement among the *talakawa*.

ISLAMIC POPULISM: THE NORTHERN ELEMENTS PROGRESSIVE UNION

As I have argued thus far, colonial rule rationalized and technically improved the ability of the Muslim aristocracy to dominate and to exploit the *talakawa*. British officials were few in number; colonial officers were always accompanied by a representative of the *amir* while touring in rural areas; and the trio of British colonial officers, Muslim aristocrats-*cum*-salaried bureaucrats, and international firms were united in their common dependence on peasant-produced groundnuts and cotton for the export market. Western education was extremely limited and was only available for the dependents of the ruling class. Yet, with the exception of Mahdist movements and rebellious towns who wanted neither Muslim aristocratic nor British rule (erupting during the first few decades of colonial rule), the centralized power of the Native Authority system appears to have been sufficient to prevent any *talakawa* political protest movement from making headway.[12] Yet, at the same time, Islamic teaching and knowledge were expanding among the *talakawa*, through peripatetic *mallams*, through dry-season migration to the centers of Islamic learning, and through the active sponsorship of the colonial state.

It is clear that the first *talakawa* political movement, the Northern Elements

Progressive Union, rooted its ideological critique of the aristocracy and the colonial order in a radical interpretation of Islamic texts. Though founded prior to the party of aristocratic privilege and merchant capitalists (that is, the Northern People's Congress [N.P.C.]), NEPU always remained in opposition and never achieved a credible number of seats in any electoral campaign during the First Nigerian Republic.[13] But as a political movement NEPU was extremely successful in articulating the grievances of the *talakawa* and in convincing the *talakawa* that the perceived abuses—such as forced labor on the farms of the aristocracy, lack of popular participation in selecting Muslim and public officials, unfair distribution of taxation, lack of education and other public services for the *talakawa*, and the myriad privileges enjoyed by the aristocracy at the expense of the *talakawa*—were not only unfair from the political perspective of the *talakawa* but were in fact un-Islamic.

As a political movement, the cadre was drawn from three distinct groups. Most important were the urban petty-bourgeois commercial class who resented their status deprivation, the limitation in economic opportunity represented by the alliance of wealthy merchant capitalists and ruling aristocrats, and, as informed Muslims, the clear breaches of Islamic tradition that were sanctioned by the alliance of colonial administrators and the Muslim aristocrats. A second group emerged from radical, educated civil servants whose families were either attached to the Native Authority system or originated from scholar-trader families. The third group was the *talakawa* ulama, both rural and urban, who preached against the illegitimate practices and exploitation of the *talakawa* by the aristocracy and, most important, the un-Islamic nature of the alliance between the Muslim aristocracy and colonial officials. The social composition, as well as an ideology that attacked imperialism and demanded the abolition of aristocratic privileges and a return to Islamic principles of community, marked the movement as one of Islamic populism rather than a true class-based political movement.

The personality and background of NEPU's spokesman and moral force also make this point emphatically. Mallam Aminu Kano is an educated son of one of Kano's prominent aristocratic lineages who is also descended from a prominent family of *alkalis* (*qadis*).[14] Well versed in Hausa folklore, Islamic scholarship, and Fabian socialism, Aminu Kano's major achievement was to integrate his profound knowledge of Islamic law and tradition into a radical critique of the existing system. Though the political conditions did not permit him to be successful during the First Nigerian Republic, his writings and public speeches encouraged the *talakawa* to reinterpret their understanding of Islamic norms of legitimacy, justice, rights, and equity.

Though it has not been studied in any detail, it is clear that the *talakawa* ulama in both rural and urban areas responded to Aminu Kano's interpretation and became organizers for the NEPU movement. In many ways, they were ideal spokesmen for a political movement that existed under considerable repression from a hostile state apparatus that served the interests of the dominant classes. The peripatetic scholars and their students traditionally wandered from rural areas to cities and to other rural areas during the dry season; it would have been extremely difficult to control them even if the state had dared to repress publicly a whole generation of Muslim scholars who formed an intelligentsia for the *talakawa*.

What Aminu Kano and NEPU failed to achieve during the First Nigerian Republic was compensated for during the election of 1979 when the People's Redemption Party, a populist reincarnation of NEPU, won the governorships of Kano and Kaduna states as well as the state house of assembly in Kano State. Even with manipulation from the electoral commission, support for the PRP in Kano State approached 80 percent of the vote. Clearly, this represented a popular rejection of the aristocratic class and their capitalist allies. But Islamic populism is easier to campaign on than to govern by. Within a year, the class differences, generational aspirations, and inexperience in administration brought about divisions within the party and among the officeholders which have prevented the PRP from implementing its social and economic programs.

Radical tendencies within Islamic political movements tend nearly universally toward populism, a feature I would interpret as determined by the "moralizing" tone that is both their strength and their weakness. Typically, the wealthier and better-educated classes benefit from the successes of the movement, while the poorer and less articulate are unable to form their own movements in part because of the limited vision contained within Islamic populism. Yet, as the following example illustrates, an Islamic populist movement may inform and strengthen the ideological and organizational capacity of an urban working class during its formative period.

ISLAM AND LABOR

The role of Islamic ideology and the mobilization of the *talakawa* ulama in support of NEPU provide an instance of how subordinate classes draw on radical interpretations of Islamic theory in order to emancipate themselves from authoritarian domination and economic exploitation. In the conclusion of this essay, I shall assess the strengths and limitations of this strategy for the emancipation of Kano's *talakawa* and *leburori*. Clearly, radical democratic socialist thought drawn from secular sources in combination with a radical interpretation of Islamic concepts of community, justice, and equity created a potent weapon for the political emancipation of the *talakawa* from patrimonial forms of injustice, if not from market-determined (capitalist) injustices. By 1981, much of the original NEPU program had, in fact, been implemented through the intervention of the federal government and through a generational change in leadership among Kano's dominant classes. Islamic populism, therefore, did eliminate abuses and practices that I would identify as authoritarian or patrimonial, as opposed to forms of exploitation and inequities that correspond to capitalist development. Nevertheless, the obvious problems the PRP has encountered in administering and governing Kano since 1979 indicate the serious difficulties that Islamic populist regimes confront once they gain power and endeavor to implement policies that conflict with the interests of some of their constituents. Unfortunately, the diverse class base of the Islamic populist movement—petty traders and craftsmen, medium-scale merchants and urban landlords, radical civil servants, the rural poor and the peasantry, and the wage-earning class—does not allow a consensus regarding economic or social policies, precisely because so many of the interests of coalition members are opposed to one another. I believe this problem is universal to all Islamic populist regimes.

The dilemma of Islamic populism in the face of divergent class interests introduces the issue of Islamic ideology and institutions among Kano's wage-earning class, the *leburori*. By 1980, industrial workers numbered approximately 40,000 and thus formed a sizable and militant fraction of the *leburori*—which, I should add, is also composed of state-sector workers, casual laborers, construction workers, and a diverse body of laborers employed in the "informal sector." During the decade of the seventies, light and consumer-oriented industries expanded industrial employment such that, with the departure of many southern Nigerian factory workers prior to the Nigerian civil war, a predominantly Muslim industrial labor force was emerging in response to the demand for locally produced industrial commodities during the civil war and to the increase in consumption offered by the distribution of the petroleum revenues.

Because I have described in great detail the structure, behavior, and consciousness of the Muslim industrial working class of Kano in several published papers, I intend to focus attention here on the contribution of Islamic ideology, personalities, and institutions insofar as they articulate with capitalist social relations of production, which, in turn, quite literally created an industrial working class in Kano.[15] Let us begin with labor recruitment. The flow of seasonal peasant labor from the countryside to urban and rural centers of Islamic learning has gone on for centuries, continues at this moment, and functions as an institution of redistribution between the relatively affluent cities and the impoverished peasant communities. Within these mobile Quranic institutions, children, youths, and young adults wander with their *mallam* through networks that exist over several generations. The students study the Quran with their *mallam* and, at the same time, engage in a remunerative activity which, supplemented by formal begging, maintains the *mallam* and his students. Most, but not all, students return to farming when the rains arrive in May or June; stored food is then dispensed from granaries in order to nurture the household labor force while they produce crops during the rainy season. Since the Quranic students do not consume scarce foodstuffs during the long dry season from October to May, but instead sustain themselves through begging and menial labor in such cities as Kano, the resources of the peasant household are extended.

Once in a city, Quranic students perform a wide range of menial tasks, including dying cloth, carrying packages at the market, sewing caps and buttons for tailors, clipping finger- and toenails, or acting as head porters and pushing carts. When Quranic students enter the casual labor market and interact with more seasoned workers they acquire a knowledge of wage rates and an evaluation of work burdens. Many discover that factory work is not only easier than carrying heavy sacks of grain at the market but offers secure work at higher rates of pay. This was evident when I interviewed factory workers: several responded that when they married they knew they needed secure work. How widespread is the phenomenon whereby Quranic student migration becomes a mode of recruitment into the industrial labor force? In a 1971 survey of Kano's five largest employers of industrial labor, numbering 3,075 workers, 13.8 percent of Hausa-Fulani workers, responding to an openended question asking why they migrated to Kano, indicated that they originally came to Kano to pursue Islamic studies. Here, then, is a hidden structure and a neat example of how, without intention or design, a pre-capitalist Islamic institution functions as a mode of recruitment for factory labor and creates an Islamic status-honor group interwoven with an emerging industrial proletariat.

Rural Quranic students were not the only "Islamic" recruits into the industrial labor force. Competition between less charismatic and erudite *mallams* is intense; the production of *mallams* is unlimited, as no certification procedure exists to regulate their number; and the category includes all self-described *mallams*, from charm-makers to legal scholars. Thus the second source of "Islamic" recruits came from the commercial, trading, and *mallam*ic families of the old walled city of Kano. Besides trading, tailoring was important in this regard, for it was considered an appropriate occupation for a *mallam* or an advanced Quranic student, and it was also flooded with recruits. Hence, there were large numbers of former tailors working in factories, many of whom were also *mallams*.

From 1970 to 1979 Kano's industrial workers not only increased in number but also engaged in a series of local and national strikes while struggling, against the resistance of most employers, to form trade unions. While preparing strike and trade union histories of several factories, I discovered that in Kano's oldest textile mill the first trade union was organized by a *mallam* who called a wildcat strike because the management would not allow workers to pray precisely at 2:00 P.M.[16] Following this theme, I discovered that local trade union organizers, most of whom were originally associated with NEPU, used the prayer issue in an attempt to organize trade unions on several occasions during 1967–70. One organizer even reported the manager to the *amir*, and the Local Government Authority intervened to guarantee workers the right to pray at 2:00 P.M. Strikes continued to erupt over this issue throughout the decade of the seventies.

What is important to emphasize here is that the prayer issue was never isolated from typical working-class issues of pay, safety, health, vacations, trade union rights, and freedom from abuse by supervisors. But it was an issue that even the greenest rural recruit could be counted on to support if a strike were called. My own interpretation is that these incidents reflect the inherent alienation contained in factory work, which in turn is expressed through channels allowed by Islamic culture.

While the prayer issue was nearly universal, certain factories were notable in that they contained *mallams* who acted as spokesmen for the workers or because *mallams* were elected to positions in the trade unions. One notable *mallam* was the son of a war *imam*; he had been an organizing secretary for NEPU in his ward and was the only worker in a sample of 140 selected for in-depth interviewing who was literate in English (which he learned from a London correspondence course). Not only did he lead the workers in prayer and take a leading role in the Adebo strikes of 1971, but he was the most popular choice for a trade union leader in that factory.

In order to determine whether the above examples were generalized throughout the sample of industrial workers of Hausa-Fulani origin or, alternatively, if the incidents whereby Islamic issues and Islamic leaders supported class solidarity and class conflict were particular to the personalities or the situation, I undertook a statistical analysis that attempted to correlate Islamic involvement with positive attitudes toward class conflict. I shall not describe the indicators of class consciousness in detail, since I have already published a paper on this topic.[17] Suffice it to say that workers who participated in Islamic brotherhoods such as the Qadiriya or the Tijaniya and those with the greatest degree of involvement in Quranic school education were most likely to support the Adebo strikes, believed "Islam agrees with striking for a fair reason," favored joining worker's organizations and favored workers' engagement in politics. Interestingly, unlike other predictors of class consciousness, such as literacy in Western script, length of time in the city, or length of involvement in wage labor, there was no correlation between the degree of involvement in Islamic organizations and the belief that their pay was unfair. Thus Islamic participation has no effect on the consumption dimension of class consciousness.

The interpretation I offer for this interesting correlation, which turns modernization theory on its head, involves several points. At one level, it is clear that *mallams* and Quranic students have a calling, in the Weberian sense, to lead their communities: others look to them for leadership, and they usually possess the necessary self-confidence to interpret and act on community consensus. At the same time, the statistical data indicate that exposure to urban capitalism and Quranic education simultaneously increases the likelihood that a worker will develop a perspective of class consciousness. Moreover, factory workers refer to modern-sector wage labor as *aikin bature* (literally, "work for Europeans"), while they use a distinct term for rural wage labor on Hausa farms (*kwadego*). My interpretation is that this correlation indicates the continuing strength of reactive Islamic nationalism, where those most integrated into Muslim institutions reject an alien system of industrial inequality and the kinds of social relations that deny the dignity they expect between superordinate and subordinate. Further, because this system—dependent industrial capitalism— is perceived to be imposed upon them and controlled by organizations and interests from advanced capitalist states, Islamic nationalism converges with class consciousness. To put it another way, regional nationalist consciousness arising from a subordinate position in the world division of labor converges with class consciousness arising from a division of labor within a particular organization of production.

Among industrial workers, the class situation predominates over the Islamic, but, while I discovered no political movement that was unequivocally Islamic, the nationalist and anti-imperialist content of Islamic consciousness is present within the industrial working class, and rather than dividing workers during situations of class struggle, Islamic nationalist consciousness reinforces class solidarity.

THE MILLENARIANISM OF THE 'YAN TATSINE

On Friday, 18 December 1980, a militant Islamic (heretical) sect under the leadership of their prophet Alhaji Muhammad Marawa attempted to take over the Friday mosque in the old city of Kano with the intention of seizing control of Kano in order to establish their fundamentalist sect. Blocked from reaching the Friday mosque by the police, the 'Yan Tatsine, as they are known locally, took over a school, fought with and killed at least two policemen, and then, after burning several police vehicles, retreated into the 'Yan Awaki section of the old city. There they fortified their area, seized between fifty and sixty-five hostages, and prepared to fight the authorities for their religion. Ten days of widespread disorder ensued, marked by vigilante groups seizing alleged followers, protracted fire fights between the police and the 'Yan Tatsine, the near-breakdown of public order, and widespread loss of life from clashes between orthodox Muslims and the 'Yan Tatsine. The police were unable to remove the 'Yan Tatsine from their stronghold, which was surrounded by walls and water-filled pits and was accessible only through narrow streets, so the Nigerian army was called in on 28 December to put down the revolt. Using artillery and modern weapons, the army leveled the area and drove the rebels to a village outside of town where their leader died and a large number of his followers were either killed or captured. A tribunal of inquiry has met and gathered evidence and testimony from hostages and followers, but the report is not yet available. Estimates of the loss of life vary from 4,000 to 10,000: the true figure will probably never be known. It was, however, the most significant urban communal disorder in Nigeria since the events leading to the Nigerian civil war in 1966–67.

Let us examine the "new" religious beliefs of this sect. Clearly his followers and Marawa himself believed that he was a prophet, but there is no evidence that he declared himself the Mahdi.[18] Yet this event occurred within one year of the turning of the Muslim calendar to the year 1400, and a popular tradition in the region holds that a reformer will appear at the onset of each century. Thus the "expectation" was present. Marawa's innovations in ritual were simple: a follower need not face the east while praying; only three prayers per day (and fewer still while in his presence) were required. Witnesses at the inquiry suggest that ritual potents, tattoos, and other innovations were also part of his ritual.

For our purposes, his social and political views are much more interesting. The name *tatsine* originates from the Hausa word used to damn someone. This label stuck to him because of his preaching style, which included damning all those who involved themselves with modern materialist objects such as watches, bicycles, or wealth in general. His followers were told to carry only enough money to satisfy their needs for one day. Consequently, during his stay in Kano (and he had been expelled from the city around 1962 as well as from other Nigerian cities), he and his followers verbally and sometimes physically attacked merchants, landlords, and common folk. They had seized property in the area of 'Yan Awaki before the confrontation of 18 December. Hence, mixed with ritual changes and the promise of invincibility from police weapons, which is typical of millenarian movements elsewhere, there was an overt critique of the materialism and inequality that have accompanied the petroleum boom in Nigeria. While I was in Kano during the first days of the insurrection, both observers and a local-vernacular Hausa newspaper verified that prior to the actual insurrection the 'Yan Tatsine had seized property, especially animals for their food, as well as houses and shops. In the latter case, owners were allegedly asked if the shop belonged to Allah or to the owner. If the owner answered Allah, they responded that they were the people of Allah and then seized the house or shop. If he responded that it was his house, they seized the house in the name of Allah and damned its owner as one corrupted by materialism. I am not arguing that the movement was solely a lower-class revolt, but it does contain elements of a political critique of inequality that was directed against the wealthier classes of Kano and especially against those who ostentatiously exhibited Western consumption styles of life.

What can be said of Marawa's followers? Witnesses describe them as *gardi*, a Hausa term meaning an unmarried man who wanders from community to community studying the Quran. Clearly, this is the same institution as the one I described above when discussing the recruitment of industrial labor. But instead of begging with humility, the 'Yan Tatsine seized property and damned the affluent consumers of modern Western styles of living. It appears that Marawa's recruits were drawn from the large floating population of displaced and wandering vagabonds who assume the status of Quranic students or *gardi*.

This is clearly the situation for one Hamza Garba, a water-carrier, originally from Kano but then living in Borno State. According to his testimony at the inquiry, Hamza followed his *mallam* when they received a call from Marawa that his community was about to be expelled from Kano because of the disturbances they had caused in 'Yan Awaki ward prior to the events of 18 December.[19]

The social conditions that provide the underlying material causes for the 'Yan Tatsine movement cannot be dismissed. Prior to the petroleum boom, the means of subsistence in cities of Kano—food and housing—were cheap and available to the *gardi*, younger Quranic students. Since the petroleum boom inflation, drought, and the beginnings of a capitalist transformation of agriculture by the state, by the World Bank, and by private entrepreneurs have exerted pressure on peasant households and undermined the traditional rural economy. These changes can only increase the flow of the rural poor through Quranic and other Islamic networks into cities such as Kano. Once in Kano, however, the *gardi* and Quranic students find the climate much less hospitable than had been the case in the past. This is not so much because of a decline in charity and morality as because of the high price of food and housing in a booming petroleum economy (see Table 1).

Further, the federal government has funded a program of universal Western primary education which has undermined the status and income opportunities of minor *mallams* and the *gardi*. Again, many of the jobs performed by Quranic students have been superseded by new techniques: cement construction, for example, is replacing traditional mud and sun-dried brick construction, mostly

TABLE 1. Food Prices and Industrial Wages in Kano, 1971 to 1978 in Naira (one naira = approximately $1.60 to $1.87)

	November 1971	November 1975	November 1978	Rate of Increase, 1971 to 1978*
Millet (measure)	.17	.50	1.10	5.47
Rice (measure)	.83	1.60	2.50	2.01
Sorghum (Guinea corn) (measure)	.21	.50	1.00	3.76
Beef (kilo)	.93	—	2.50	1.69
Palm oil (beer bottle)	.17	.70	1.55	8.12
Groundnut oil (beer bottle)	.25	.85	1.25	4.00
Pepper (measure)	.33	—	1.00	2.03
Starting wage for industrial workers	.87	1.75	2.25	1.59

$$* \text{Rate of increase} = \frac{(\text{price November 1978}) - (\text{price November 1971})}{(\text{price November 1971})}$$

because of the rise in the price of labor; furthermore, motorized transport is replacing cart-pushing and head porterage. All of this reduces income opportunities for unskilled Quranic students who migrate to Kano. But most important, Kano has become a semi-industrial city, not merely a groundnut-exporting center with household production units. Capitalism is developing alongside overcrowding and increased rural-to-urban migration, which traditional charitable institutions find difficult to continue to support as they had in the past. Though the system is overwhelmed, at the same time there are visible changes in attitude toward the indigent. Violent crime and theft have increased enormously since 1970. For example, the counsel for the PRP at the 'Yan Tatsine inquiry was killed when an outraged crowd mistook him for a thief. In a situation of new and enormous inequality of wealth, rural vagabonds become suspect, and the norms of charity appropriate to an earlier era are eroded by fear of thieves and violence.

As a millenarian movement, the 'Yan Tatsine have had a devastating impact on Kano. Part of the old city has been leveled. Marawa's followers, estimated to number over 5,000 at the time of the rebellion, have either been killed or imprisoned. Public preaching without authorization from the authorities has been blamed. And there is a generalized fear of the wandering *mallams* who, it is said, incite youths and the indigent to attack the wealthy and powerful. What is of interest to scholars of Islamic social movements is the way movements like the 'Yan Tatsine channel despair, frustration, and insecurity, arising out of a deep and far-reaching capitalist transformation of Hausa society, into millenarian fantasy rather than organized Islamic reform or working-class movements. The similarity to the events at the mosque at Mecca during 1979 are obvious, yet there is no evidence that Marawa was influenced by that movement. For the moment, one must wait for the evidence on the social basis of the 'Yan Tatsine to emerge before one can specify the relationship between the transformation of Hausa society and the rise of the millenarian movement.

CONCLUSION

Thus far I have described three Islamic political movements, or at least movements with Islamic components, that have been supported by the *talakawa* of northern Nigeria. It is difficult to be sanguine about the prospects of *talakawa* emancipation from social, economic, and political deprivation in the short run. Capitalist development is only beginning in northern Nigeria. Inequality has increased during the petroleum boom, and, most important, state policy has undermined the autonomous production of the village through policies that discriminate against rural producers, encourage migration of youths, and seek capital-intensive solutions to the food and agricultural crisis. These policies will only expel labor from the countryside at an accelerating rate. One should, therefore, expect more millenarian-type movements in cities, for this movement is one of the few ideological weapons the *talakawa* possess.

What can be said of Islamic political movements and their potential for emancipating the *talakawa*? Clearly, the strength of Islamic political movements lies in their ability to mobilize populations against tyranny and foreign or infidel invaders, rather than in their ability to create a viable political order that will enable a regime to weather the demands placed on the state in the modern world. The paradox, of course, is that the populist movement that is required to rout the opposition is often incapable of organizing a viable state within the ideological boundaries set out by Islamic theory. The tendency for the circulation of elites to occur is extremely high, and the existing body of Islamic thought provides little evidence that new theories of organization are emerging to solve this problem. Hence, in northern Nigeria, and I suspect elsewhere as well, the contribution of Islamic political movements to the emancipation of the vast majority of Muslims will be at the level of resistance to tyranny and injustice rather than the creation of an effective social and economic order.

NOTES

1. For an overview of the decade of the seventies, see D. Rimmer and A. Kirk-Greene, *Nigeria since 1970* (London: Hodder and Stoughton, 1981).

2. For the relationship between Islamic institutions and the merchant class, see I. Tahir, "Sufis, Saints, Scholars and Capitalists," Ph.D. thesis, Cambridge University, 1974.

3. For a discussion of the methodology of this study, see P. Lubeck, "The Value of Multiple Methods in Researching Third World Strikes," *Development and Change* 10 (1979): 301–19.

4. J. Paden, *Religion and Culture in Kano* (Berkeley and Los Angeles: University of California Press, 1974).

5. For the Sokoto Caliphate, see M. Last, *The Sokoto Caliphate* (London: Longman's, Green, 1974).

6. M. G. Smith, *Government in Zau Zau* (Oxford: Oxford University Press, 1960); P. Lubeck, "Islam and Resistance in Northern Nigeria," in W. Goldfrank, ed., *The World System of Capitalism: Past and Present* (Beverly Hills: Sage, 1979).

7. See M. Watts, *Silent Violence* (Berkeley and Los Angeles: University of California Press, forthcoming.)

8. For a complete development and empirical application of this concept, see P. Lubeck, *Islam and Urban Labor in Northern Nigeria* (forthcoming), chapters 1, 4, 7.

9. For a broader critique of essentialism, see Bryan Turner, *Marx and the End of Orientalism* (London: Allen and Unwin, 1978).

10. On articulation, see A. Foster Carter, "The Modes of Production Controversy," *New Left Review* 107 (1977): 47–77.

11. I. Lapidus, *Muslim Cities in the Later Middle Ages* (Cambridge, England: Cambridge University Press, 1984).

12. On colonial rule, see Adamu Fika, "The Political and Economic Reorientation of Kano Emirate, Northern Nigeria," Ph.D. thesis, University of London, 1973; M. M. Tukor, "The Imposition of British Colonial Domination of the Sokoto Caliphate," Ph.D. thesis, Ahmadu Bello University, 1979; and R. Adeleye, *Power and Diplomacy in Northern Nigeria, 1804–1906* (London: Longman's, Green, 1971).

13. On political processes and political parties of the First Nigerian Republic, see B. Dudley, *Parties and Northern Nigeria* (London: Frank Cass, 1968); Paden, *Religion*; R. Sklar, *Nigerian Political Parties* (Princeton: Princeton University Press, 1963).

14. See A. Feinstein, *African Revolutionary* (New York: Quadrangle, 1973).

15. P. Lubeck, "Class Formation at the Periphery: Class Consciousness and Islamic Nationalism among Nigerian Workers," in R. L. Simpson and I. H. Simpson, eds., *Research in the Sociology of Work,* vol. 1 (Greenwich, Conn.: J.A.I. Press, 1981), pp. 37–70; P. M. Lubeck, "Industrial Labor in Kano: Historical Origins, Social Characteristics and Sources of Differentiation," in B. Borkindo, ed., *Studies in the History of Kano* (London: Heinemann Educational Books, 1983).

16. For a detailed description, see P. Lubeck, "Unions, Workers and Consciousness in Kano, Nigeria," in R. Saadbrook and R. Cohen, eds., *The Development of an African Working Class* (London: Longman's, Green, 1975).

17. Lubeck, "Class Formation at the Periphery."

18. On Mahdism, see M. A. Al-Hajj, "The Madhist Tradition in Northern Nigeria," Ph.D. thesis, Ahamadu Bello University, 1973.

19. *Nigerian Standard,* 13 February 1981, p. 1.

PART FIVE

Revolution in Iran

THIRTEEN

Imam Khomeini, 1902–1962:
The Pre-Revolutionary Years

Hamid Algar

It is not sufficiently recognized that Imam Khomeini's leadership of the Islamic revolution of 1978–79, far from being a sudden or accidental phenomenon, was the outcome of at least fifteen years of diligent political, ideological, and organizational work. Nor is it adequately appreciated that when he began his public political career in 1962, he had behind him four decades of close and dedicated involvement in the affairs of the religious institution, of study, teaching, writing, and reflection, and—not least—of concerned observation of the state of Iranian society.

The three main periods of Imam Khomeini's life—the decades of spiritual and political formation, the long campaign against the Pahlavi state, and the years of the revolution and the nascent Islamic Republic—form, in fact, a continuum in which no major interruption or change of direction is visible. At a fairly early age, Khomeini evolved a distinctive vision of Islam, embracing its spiritual, intellectual, social, and political dimensions, to which he has held fast for more than half a century. A high and rare degree of consistency is, indeed, among the most evident traits of his character; the celebrated "refusal to compromise" is merely the political and most noticeable expression of this consistency.

Clearly, no revolution is the work of a single man. Numerous groups, liberal-nationalist and leftist as well as Islamic, had opposed the Pahlavi regime, or at least certain of its manifestations, for many years before the Islamic revolution of 1978–79. Nonetheless, it is arguable that the revolution would not have occurred when it did and as it did without the decisive guiding influence, strategic sense, and moral authority of Imam Khomeini. Certainly the form of government that has emerged from the revolution—the Islamic Republic—has been largely determined by his theories and directives.[1] The designation of

Imam Khomeini that has now become conventional in the Iranian media, "leader of the Islamic revolution and founder of the Islamic Republic," is no mere honorific.

This being the case, a knowledge of the formative years of Imam Khomeini will help us to understand better both the events of the revolution and the new revolutionary order. During those years, all the major elements of his world-view were put into place: a firm belief in the mission of the ulama to guide, lead, purify, and defend Iranian society; a conviction of the need to cultivate the spiritual and even the gnostic aspects of Islam; a hatred and rejection of the Pahlavi state; a determination to rid the Islamic lands of foreign control; and a profound distrust of culturally alienated secular intellectuals. He studied the lives of ulama he regarded as exemplary, pledging himself to emulate them; he developed considerable skill as teacher and orator; he established a rigorous and ascetic regimen of prayer and devotion; and he acquired the core of the devoted following which has provided most of the operational leadership of the revolution. So complete, indeed, is the continuity between the formative years and those of activism and revolution that there are close verbal resemblances between utterances of Khomeini separated by many years.

I do not wish to suggest that Khomeini laid down in his youth a deliberate plan for accomplishing revolutionary change, nor that Iranian society inexor-ably matured through the Pahlavi period to a point where it eagerly embraced his leadership. A host of contingencies made up the historical process leading to the destruction of the Pahlavi state. But with the hindsight now afforded us by the revolution, we may legitimately discern as a leading theme of modern Iranian history the twin processes whereby Khomeini became Imam—that is, became a source of comprehensive and authoritative guidance[2]—and Iranian society became *ummat*—that is, a religiously defined community owing him obedience.

The origins of the Khomeini family lie in India, in the little town of Kintur, about forty miles to the northeast of Lucknow in what used to be the kingdom of Awadh.[3] A Nishapuri family of *sayyid*s, claiming descent from Musa al-Kazim, seventh of the Twelve Imams, settled there sometime in the early eighteenth century, and they soon established themselves both as religious scholars and as cultivators of the land. One branch of the family took root in Lucknow, and both there and in Kintur the family has survived down to the present.[4] The most famous of the Kinturi *sayyid*s is Mir Hamid Husayn (d. 1880), who, conforming to the addictive tradition of Sunni-Shi'i polemics that was preva-lent in Lucknow, wrote a massive work entitled '*Abaqat al-Anwar fi Imamat al-A'imma al-Athar*, defending the Shi'i concept of the Imamate against its Sunni critics.[5] The first word in the title of this work provided his descendants with the *nisba* they still bear, 'Abaqati.

Sayyid Ahmad, Imam Khomeini's grandfather, was a contemporary and relative of Mir Hamid Husayn. In the mid-nineteenth century he went on pilgrimage to Najaf, where he met Yusuf Khan Kamara'i, a leading citizen of the little town of Khumayn in southwest Iran, about 135 miles from Isfahan. Yusuf Khan asked Sayyid Ahmad to accompany him to Khumayn to assume responsibility for the religious needs of its people. Sayyid Ahmad consented, and in addition married Yusuf Khan's daughter.[6] Very little is known about Sayyid Ahmad,[7] but it is possible that it was more than the entreaties of Yusuf Khan that kept him from returning to India. The kingdom of Awadh, a protector and patron of Shi'i scholars, was in an advanced state of political and moral decay, and its full incorporation into British India was only a matter of time.[8] The time may have seemed propitious to Sayyid Ahmad to transplant one branch of the family line back to Iran.

Yusuf Khan's daughter bore Sayyid Ahmad two children, a daughter, Sahiba, and a son, Sayyid Mustafa, born in 1855, the father of Imam Khomeini.[9] Sayyid Mustafa followed the conventional pattern of preliminary study in his hometown followed by advanced training in Isfahan, which was then the major center of religious learning in Iran. His main instructor there was Mir Muhammad Taqi Mudarris, father of Sayyid Hasan Mudarris, well-known leader of the opposition to Reza Shah.[10] Again in conformity with the usual pattern, Sayyid Mustafa went on from Isfahan to the shrine cities of Arab Iraq for the culminating stages of his religious training under the great authorities resident there, above all Mirza Hasan Shirazi (d. 1894), author of the celebrated *fatwa* that inaugurated the tobacco boycott and a figure whose example has often been invoked by Imam Khomeini.[11]

When he returned to Iran Sayyid Mustafa inherited his father's position of religious leadership in Khumayn and its environs. He is said to have exerted himself on behalf of the peasants not only in Khumayn but also in the nearby regions of Arak, Gulpayagan, Khwansar, and Mahallat, protesting against the rapacity of the landlords; foremost among his enemies were a certain Ghulam Shah Khan and Bahram Khan. Sayyid Mustafa's activities finally earned him death at the hands of the landowners. One day when he was setting out from Khumayn for Arak, two men insisted on accompanying him, allegedly to protect him. When they were some distance out on the road, the two men deliberately fell behind Sayyid Mustafa and were joined by a third man, who passed them a rifle. Without delay, they attacked Sayyid Mustafa and fled. Before long, they were captured in the village of Yujan, and the man who had pulled the trigger was transferred to Tehran where he was publicly executed in the Tupkhana Square.[12]

In keeping with the reticence he customarily observes on family matters, Imam Khomeini has never, to my knowledge, made any public reference to the life and death of his father. If the account, frequently heard in Iran, of Sayyid

Mustafa's struggle against oppressive landlords is accurate, we may presume that awareness of his father's martyrdom left a deep and early impression on Imam Khomeini. Certainly the fact that he gave the name Mustafa to his eldest son (who was also destined to acquire the reputation of being a martyr) may have reflected a desire to perpetuate his father's memory. We know too that Imam Khomeini was aware from earliest youth of the oppressive role played by landowners in the Iranian countryside, for he has recalled how they would invariably pervert the electoral process: "The landlords and their thugs would bring people to the ballot boxes and force them to vote the way they wanted." [13]

Sayyid Mustafa left behind three sons, Sayyid Murtaza (better known as Ayatullah Pasandida; well over ninety years old, he is now living in Qum); Sayyid Nur ad-Din (d. 1976 in Tehran); and Ruhullah—Imam Khomeini. [14] He was born on 20 Jumada II 1320/24 September 1902, and was about five months old when his father was killed. His birthdate was the anniversary of the birth of Fatima, the daughter of the Prophet, and some have seen significance in this coincidence of dates. [15] Deprived of a father, Imam Khomeini received his earliest upbringing from his mother, Hajar (daughter of Mirza Ahmad Mujtahid Khwansari, a teacher at *madrasa*s in Najaf and Karbala) and his paternal aunt Sahiba. [16] In 1918, first the aunt and then the mother died, so Imam Khomeini found himself fully orphaned at the age of sixteen. The responsibility for his upbringing now devolved on his elder brother, Sayyid Murtaza. [17]

Sayyid Murtaza recalled, in a conversation with me, that the great determination which has been such an obvious trait of Imam Khomeini's career was already apparent in his childhood. He would apply himself with unusual seriousness, for example, to the games he played with his friends. It is probable that this inherent trait was strengthened by the hardship of fatherlessness and the period of insecurity that followed the deaths of their aunt and their mother. The two brothers found themselves obliged to take turns mounting watch over the family residence, rifle in hand. A sense of disciplined struggle was thus fostered even by the circumstances of family life. [18]

It was also during childhood that Imam Khomeini was exposed for the first time to the arbitrary and tyrannical nature of the Iranian state. Addressing members of the Iranian diplomatic corps on 5 January 1981, he offered the following reminiscence:

> It used to happen that when a new provincial governor was appointed, he would treat the people just as if he himself were the king; that is, he would take no account of the people at all. Once I witnessed the arrival of a new governor for the province of Gulpayagan. The merchants came to meet him and in the presence of them all he gave orders for the chief merchant of the bazaar to be tied to the bastinado and beaten. I was only a child at the time, but even now I can remember how that respectable, pious man was seized and bastinadoed on the orders of that corrupt man, for no reason at all, as if to say, "we can do whatever we want and you have to obey us!" [19]

This was the first of many such experiences that accumulated in the memory of the Imam. He has frequently made reference to this great burden of memory, gathered over more than seven decades, and it is clear that his revolutionary activity has stemmed not least from a long-standing hatred of constantly witnessed arbitrariness.

His early schooling in Khumayn consisted first of classes in reading and writing from Mirza Mahmud, a tutor who came to the home, and later of attendance at a *maktab*, where his teachers were Mulla Abu 'l-Qasim and Shaykh Ja'far. Then he went to a more modern school, recently opened in Khumayn, where he was taught calligraphy by a certain Aqa Mirza Mahallati. By the age of fifteen he had completed his Persian studies and was ready to embark on Arabic and Islamic studies. These he pursued initially with Sayyid Murtaza, but in 1919, when he was about seventeen years old, it was decided he should benefit from the more ample resources of a *madrasa*. At first it was intended to send him to Isfahan, in the footsteps of his father, but ultimately he was sent to the nearby city of Arak, where Shaykh 'Abd al-Karim Hairi—like the Imam's father, a student of Mirza Hasan Shirazi's—had recently arrived from Iraq and begun teaching.[20]

Thus began Imam Khomeini's lifetime association with the religious institution, an association which swiftly became for him far more than a matter of convention or inheritance. Unmistakable throughout his life has been a sense of institutional commitment and loyalty to the ulama as the heirs of the Imams and the Prophet, as the guardians and transmitters of Islamic learning, as those who are both destined and required to restore the fortunes of the Islamic community. In this he differs fundamentally from other ulama who have played significant political roles in recent Iranian history, men such as Ayatullah Kashani (d. 1962) and Ayatullah Taliqani (d. 1979) who, operating outside the religious institution, contracted alliances with a variety of non-ulama groups. For Imam Khomeini, the concept of ulama leadership has always been paramount, and it is significant that when enumerating the antecedents of the Islamic revolution he has always restricted himself to mentioning ulama.[21] The journey from Khumayn to Arak counts as an event of primary significance in his life.

About a year after Imam Khomeini's arrival in Arak, Ha'iri accepted an invitation from the people and scholars of Qum to settle there. Qum, one of the earliest centers of Shi'i Islam in Iran and the site of the tomb of Ma'suma, a sister of the Eighth Imam, had always been a center of learning as well as pilgrimage, but it was largely overshadowed by the great shrine cities of Arab Iraq and even by the *madrasa*s of Isfahan. Hairi's arrival there, followed by his revival of the religious teaching institution, was the first in a series of developments that elevated Qum to the status of spiritual capital of Iran and the first bastion of the Islamic revolution. Hairi was largely quiescent in political matters, but his institutional achievements, confirmed and amplified by

Ayatullah Burujirdi in the years 1945 to 1962, laid the groundwork for the revolutionary role Qum assumed under the leadership of Imam Khomeini.[22]

Four months after Hairi left Arak for Qum, the young Khomeini followed him, taking up residence at the Dar al-Shifa *madrasa*. Applying himself diligently to his studies, in 1926 he completed the stage of the curriculum known as *sath*. Then began a decade of direct study, under Hairi himself, of the subjects that lie at the core of the curriculum, *fiqh* and *usul* (jurisprudence).[23] Mastery of these was essential for the career of *'alim*.

Imam Khomeini was destined, however, to be far more than one *'alim* among a host of others. Despite the proficiency he swiftly gained in *fiqh* and *usul*, he appears always to have been convinced that the study of the law does not exhaust the riches of Islam and that the ultimate concern of religion is situated on a quite different plane from the legal. For during his early years in Qum, Imam Khomeini began a profound study and active cultivation of *hikmat* (philosophy) and *'irfan* (mysticism), related disciplines for the rational and gnostic apperception of ultimate truth that had long flourished in Shi'i Islam. His first guide in this pursuit was Mirza 'Ali Akbar Yazdi, a pupil of Mulla Hadi Sabzavari (d. 1872), celebrated author of the *Sharh-i Manzuma*, one of the basic texts of *'irfan*. It appears that Yazdi died soon after Khomeini's arrival in Qum.[24] Another early guide was Mirza Aqa Javad Maliki Tabrizi (d. 1924), who had been teaching in Qum since 1911. He held two classes on philosophy and ethics, a public one at the Madrasa-yi Fayziya and a private one in his own home, attended by gifted and favored students, including the young Khomeini. He also studied with Sayyid Abu'l-Hasan Rafi'i Qazvini (d. 1975 or 1976).[25] His chief teacher in gnosis and mysticism was Ayatullah Muhammad 'Ali Shahabadi (d. 1950);[26] to him Khomeini deferentially referred in his own writings on *'irfan* as "our master in theosophy" (*ustad-i ilahi-yi ma*).[27] He met Shahabadi soon after his arrival in Qum (probably in the late 1920s), and upon receiving his answer to a question on *'irfan* realized that he was a true master of the subject. Initially Shahabadi refused Khomeini's request to study with him, but then he agreed to teach him philosophy (*falsafa*). It was *'irfan*, however, that Khomeini wished to pursue, and he held out until Shahabadi consented to instruct him in that discipline. Every Thursday and Friday, as well as on holidays, generally alone but sometimes with one or two other students, Khomeini listened to Shahabadi discoursing on the commentary on ibn 'Arabi's *Fusus al-Hikam* by Da'ud Qaysari (d. 1350); *Miftah al-Ghayb* by Sadr al-Din Qunavi (d. 1274); and *Manazil al-Sa'irin* by Khwaja 'Abdallah Ansari (d. 1088).[28]

Despite the deep roots of *'irfan* and *hikmat* in Shi'i tradition, these subjects were studied only sporadically in the religious institution and were more often the object of outright hostility; intervals of favor alternated with longer periods of rejection. Imam Khomeini has recalled the suspicions to which *'irfan* in particular was subject during his early days in Qum:

When I first went to Qum ... the late Mirza 'Ali Akbar Hakim [Yazdi] was still alive. A certain pious individual said, "see the level to which Islam has fallen; the doors of Mirza 'Ali Akbar are open to receive students." For some of the ulama, among them the late Khwansari and the late Ishraqi, would go to Mirza 'Ali Akbar's house to study *'irfan* with him. Now Mirza 'Ali Akbar was a very worthy man, but when he died, there was so much suspicion surrounding him that a preacher found it necessary to testify from the *minbar* that he had seen him reading the Quran.... It is regrettable that some of the ulama should entertain those suspicions and deprive themselves of the benefits to be gained from studying *'irfan*. Similar attitudes prevail toward philosophy, which is actually very straightforward.[29]

Undeterred by such suspicions, and demonstrating the independent and critical attitude toward the religious institution that has always modified his loyalty to it, Imam Khomeini chose to begin his teaching career, at the age of twenty-seven, precisely in this controversial area. He offered classes first in *hikmat*, giving great care to the choice of both texts and students, admitting only those pupils who had the intellectual capacity and spiritual maturity to study metaphysics without endangering their faith.[30]

Shortly after he began teaching *hikmat*, Imam Khomeini organized private classes in *'irfan*, open only to a select few among the students of Qum. The texts taught were the section on the *nafs* (soul) in the *Asfar al-Arba'a* of Mulla Sadra and the *Sharh-i Manzuma*.[31] These private, almost secret sessions continued into the 1940s, and it was in them that Imam Khomeini trained and inspired some of his closest associates, above all the late Ayatullah Mutahhari (whom the Imam described after his assassination in May 1979 as "the very quintessence of my being") and Ayatullah Hasan 'Ali Muntaziri (who has been chosen to succeed to the constitutional position of Imam Khomeini as leader of the Islamic Republic).

The earliest writings of Imam Khomeini were also concerned with contemplative, devotional, and mystical matters.[32] In 1928, he wrote a detailed commentary, in Arabic, on the prayer recited before dawn during Ramadan by Imam Ja'far al-Sadiq (*Sharh Du'a al-Sahar*). In this, his first book, Imam Khomeini demonstrated not only a mastery of the language of *'irfan* but also what has been a lifelong devotion to the prayers of the Twelve Imams as texts for meditation as well as recitation.[33] It was followed, at a date that cannot be precisely determined, by a lengthy and complex analysis, also written in Arabic, of the canonical prayer *Sirr al-Salat*.[34] In this work, the symbolic dimensions and inner meanings of every part of the prayer, from the ablution that precedes it to the *salam* that concludes it, are expounded in a rich, complex, and eloquent language that owes much to the concepts and terminology of ibn 'Arabi. As Sayyid Fihri, the editor and translator of *Sirr al-Salat*, has remarked, the work is addressed only to the foremost among the spiritual elite (*akhass-i khavass*) and establishes its author as one of their number.[35] Soon after completing *Sirr al-Salat*, Imam Khomeini wrote a somewhat more accessible work on the inner meanings of prayer, *Adab al-Salat*.[36]

The gnostic dimension of Imam Khomeini finds its fullest written expression in another Arabic book, *Misbah al-Hidaya ila al-Khilafa wa 'l-Wilaya*, completed in 1930.[37] The book is a dense, systematic, and exhaustive treatise on the major concerns of *'irfan*; its contents defy easy summary,[38] and it cannot profitably be read without prior initiation into the concepts and terminology of *'irfan*. In it Khomeini refers not only to the Quran and the traditions of the Prophet and the Imams but also to such sources and authorities as the Sufis Khwaja 'Abdallah Ansari, Jalal al-Din Rumi (d. 1273), Sadr al-Din Qunavi, 'Abd al-Razzaq Kashani (d. 1330), and Da'ud Qaysari; the Shi'i theosopher Qazi Sa'id Qummi (d. 1691); and contemporary masters of *'irfan* such as Muhammad Riza Qumsha'i (d. 1918) and his own teacher, Muhammad 'Ali Shahabadi. *Misbah al-Hidaya* is, however, less important for the wide erudition it displays than for the complete practical mastery of the art of *'irfan* that underlies it; it is not a digest of received opinions and formulations but the manifest fruit of a powerful and original vision. To quote Sayyid Ahmad Fihri again, "it is apparent that he [Khomeini] has experiential knowledge of all he wrote upon." [39]

Although Imam Khomeini appears to have written other works of a mystic and gnostic nature,[40] concerns of a different kind came to occupy the foreground of his life. Nonetheless, this early and intense cultivation of *hikmat* and *'irfan* should not be regarded as a passing episode, for it contributed powerfully to the formation of his total persona as religious and political leader. The breadth and completeness of his training and interests as a scholar have enabled him to transcend the often narrow concerns of the conventional *faqih*. Very rare indeed have been those scholars, particularly in recent times, who have demonstrated an equal command of *fiqh* and *'irfan*, who have been "possessors of two wings" (*dhu 'l-janahayn*), to use the traditional epithet. When to this mastery of exoteric and esoteric learning is added Imam Khomeini's passionate and revolutionary concern with the political sphere, it becomes comprehensible why many Iranians regard him as a unique figure, one who has ideally merged in his person the roles of contemplative, teacher, scholar, and warrior.[41]

For it has not been a question of simple juxtaposition of *'irfan* with later activities such as the teaching of *fiqh* and the active campaign against the Pahlavi monarchy that unfolded from 1962 onward; those activities have been distinctively tinged by the spiritual orientation of Imam Khomeini. One of the features that made his classes in *fiqh* more vital and attractive to students than those of other instructors was his ability to relate the technical details of the law to the metaphysical and spiritual concerns of Imam, or, as it has been put, "to demonstrate the conformity of the Shari'a to the logic of *'irfan*, as well as the conformity of *'irfan* to the logic of the Shari'a." [42] It has also been said that Imam Khomeini has brought about a "revolution in *fiqh*," [43] through the creation of new categories and the reordering of priorities, and this revolution has been facilitated by his vision of what might be termed, in a certain sense, the relativity of *fiqh*.[44]

As for political activism, the purification of vision and volition that is involved in *'irfan* seems to have served for Imam Khomeini as a kind of inward revolution that in the course of time naturally produced its counterpart on the external plane. It is worth noting, in this connection, that he has ascribed normative value to the conduct of 'Ali ibn Abi Talib, who discoursed on the inner meaning of *tawhid* (unity) while advancing to do battle with Mu'awiya, and observed the following:

> Once a man has become a true human being by means of spiritual discipline, he
> will be the most active of men. He will till the land, but till it for God's sake. He
> will also wage war, for all the wars waged against unbelievers and oppressors were
> waged by men absorbed in the contemplation of the divine unity and engaged in
> the constant invocation of God and the recitation of prayer.[45]

When the Islamic revolution came in 1978, Imam Khomeini described the reasons for its success in remarkably *'irfani* terms, saying that the people had oriented themselves to the divine presence and thereby taken on a divine existence.[46] More recently, he has repeatedly described those who have fallen in the war against the Iraqi invaders as having gone to "the contemplation of God" (*liqa'ullah*), a phrase that furnished the title for one of his early treatises on *'irfan*.[47]

The most substantial recent evidence of Imam Khomeini's lasting concern with *'irfan* is a series of lectures on the interpretation of *Surat al-Fatiha* delivered in December 1979 and January 1980.[48] In sharp contrast to the small, semi-clandestine circle he had once taught in Qum, Imam Khomeini now addressed a nationwide television audience on the perennial themes of *wahdat al-wujud* (unity of being) and the meaning of the divine names, discussing many of the same topics that had first engaged his attention in treatises written more than forty years earlier. The unprecedented circumstances under which the lectures were delivered were a measure of the transformations that had been effected by the revolution.

One early indication of Imam Khomeini's ability to transcend the limits of the *madrasa* and attract a wide popular audience was provided by the classes on ethics he began teaching in Qum in the early 1930s. Taking as his point of reference the well-known Sufi manual of ethical advancement he had studied with Shahabadi, the *Manazil al-Sa'irin* of Khwaja 'Abdallah Ansari, he first gave instruction to a handful of students once a week. Soon hundreds of students and scholars began to attend, including some who were drawn to Qum by the growing reputation of Khomeini as a lecturer. Among them was Sayyid Ahmad Fihri, who has recently written: "I count this time I spent attending those lectures among the most precious hours of my life. In his lectures the Imam taught true Islamic ethics, which cannot be separated from revolution, in such a way that he left a deep impression on all who attended."[49] Then the students and scholars who flocked to the lectures were joined by the towns-people of Qum and even by travelers from other cities who came to Qum specifically to listen to Khomeini. The vast courtyard of the Madrasa-yi Fayziya, where the lectures were held, was filled, and Imam Khomeini was prevailed upon to lecture twice instead of once a week.[50]

Such a phenomenon was unique at the time. The Pahlavi regime was seeking, with considerable initial success, to isolate the religious institution, to discredit it in the eyes of the educated, and even to interfere with its internal functioning. Yet Imam Khomeini succeeded in contradicting this trend with his well-attended lectures on *akhlaq* (ethics). As a result there occurred his first open clash with the authority of the state. When the police chief of Qum told him to stop his lectures, he replied, "It is my duty to hold these assemblies in whatever way possible. If the police want them to stop, they will have to prevent me forcibly from lecturing." Instead of applying force, the police sabotaged the lectures by means of its agents within the religious institution. Imam Khomeini was obliged to transfer his lectures to the Madrasa-yi Mulla Sadiq, a smaller *madrasa* than the Fayziya and more difficult of access. After the Allied deposition of Reza Shah in 1941, the lectures were moved back to Madrasa-yi Fayziya and again attracted large crowds. Once more, however, the regime was able by means of intrigue to secure first the suspension and then the cessation of the lectures.[51]

This termination of the lectures on *akhlaq* did not mean an abandonment of their subject matter.[52] In the same way that Imam Khomeini's teaching of *fiqh* has been colored by *'irfan*, it has been intermingled with the concerns of *akhlaq*. In addition, he has revived the separate teaching of *akhlaq* on at least one occasion. During his exile in Najaf, he delivered to the students at the Masjid-i Shaykh Ansari a series of lectures on ethical self-improvement that were later published in the same city in 1972 under the title *Jihad-i Akbar ya Mubaraza ba Nafs*.[53] These lectures complement in many ways the better-known series of lectures that were published under the title *Hukumat-i Islami*.

Attention may be drawn to one feature in particular of the lectures on *akhlaq* given in Qum, one that has reechoed throughout Imam Khomeini's writings and pronouncements to such an extent that it may be regarded as a kind of personal motto, a summary of spiritual aspirations. He would always close the lectures with the recitation of the following sentence from *Munajat-i Sha'ban*, a litany unique in that it was recited by all of the Twelve Imams:

> O God, grant me total separation from other than You, and attachment to You, and brighten the vision of our hearts with the vision of looking upon You, so that they may pierce the veils of light and attain the fountainhead of magnificence, and our spirits be suspended from the splendor of Your sanctity.[54]

This sentence recurs some thirty years later in the lectures given at Najaf,[55] and then again in the televised lectures mentioned above.[56] It is not the least remarkable feature of Imam Khomeini that he has led a revolutionary movement to success while having his gaze fixed on "the fountainhead of magnificence...and the splendor of [God's] sanctity."

Imam Khomeini's first two decades in Qum coincided approximately with the rule of Reza Shah Pahlavi, and it is not surprising that his attitudes toward the two-man dynasty were formed during this period. His declarations and speeches from 1962 onward are replete with references to the first Pahlavi dictator, and, for Imam Khomeini, Muhammad Reza Shah never ceased to be "the son of Reza Khan."

Imam Khomeini identified the main aim of Reza Shah as the elimination of Islam as a social, cultural, and political force in Iran and was convinced that this aim had been inculcated in him by imperialist powers, above all Britain, who saw in the ulama in particular and Islam in general the only obstacle to the complete fulfillment of their desires. He himself witnessed many of the measures taken by Reza Shah against the religious institution. In an interview granted me, he recalled:

> Reza Khan banned *rauzas* [recitations of elegiac verse commemorating the martyrdom of Imam Husayn at Karbala] throughout Iran; no one could organize a *rauza*, not even if only a few people were present. Even in Qum, which then as now was the the center of the religious institution, there were no *rauza* assemblies, or if there were they had to be held between dawn and sunrise. Before the first call to prayer, five to ten people would gather for a brief commemoration of Karbala, and when the call to prayer was sounded, or very soon after, they had to disperse. Sometimes informers were present, and when they turned in their reports, all who had attended the meeting were arrested. Reza Khan had plans to destroy the religious institution completely.[57]

These measures evoked little open protest, for a variety of reasons. The most important was that Reza Shah had astutely managed to neutralize most of the leading religious scholars at the outset of his reign, despite the well-known tradition, reaching back to the nineteenth century, of ulama opposition to the monarchy. Some of the ulama, including Shaykh 'Abd al-Karim Hairi and *marja'-i taqlid* (authority on *fiqh*) Ayatullah Abu 'l-Hasan Isfahani, had even met with Reza Shah in Qum in March 1924 and pledged him their support on the understanding that he would respect Islamic values.[58] It was not until 1928 that Hairi was moved to protest against the policies of the regime, in mild and circumspect terms, when Reza Shah enacted the Uniform Dress Law.[59] It is unlikely that the young Khomeini should have attempted to impel Hairi in the direction of greater militancy, but he is known to have had contact with various ulama who led short-lived uprisings against the Pahlavi regime.[60]

In 1924, for example, Hajj Aqa Nurullah and Mulla Husayn Fisharaki, two of the ulama of Isfahan, led an uprising that was occasioned in the first place by government attempts to turn opium cultivation into a state monopoly. Other, more general grievances were also voiced, and Hajj Aqa Nurullah was able to gather a throng of merchants, artisans, and peasants, at the head of which he marched on Qum, with the intention of picking up additional support and advancing on Tehran. Once in Qum, the movement stalled, and Hajj Nurullah died under suspicious circumstances.[61] In a speech delivered in Najaf in 1977, Imam Khomeini recalled his participation in this movement.[62]

Four years later, in October 1928, an ulama-led movement of protest against the introduction of compulsory military service took place in Tabriz. The bazaar merchants closed their shops when the chief of a recruiting mission arrived from Tehran, and they were persuaded to reopen them only when three recently imported machine guns were set up at the entrance to the bazaar. The two chief *mujtahids* of the city who had coordinated the movement, Ayatullah Abu 'l-Hasan Angaji and Mirza Sadiq Aqa, were arrested and banished, first to Kurdistan and then to Qum.[63] Angaji ultimately returned to Tabriz, but Mirza Sadiq Aqa remained in Qum until his death in 1932, and Imam Khomeini was a frequent visitor to his house.[64]

A movement in Mashhad was crushed in July 1935 by a massacre at the mosque of Gauhar Shad. One of the chief ulama of the city, Hajj Aqa Husayn Qummi, had gone to Tehran with the intention of presenting certain grievances to the government. There he found himself under virtual house arrest, and when news of his predicament reached Mashhad, people gathered in protest at the shrine of Imam Riza, only to be dispersed by gunfire. A second protest meeting held a few days later at the mosque of Gauhar Shad resulted in a massacre. Two of the leading ulama of the city, Sayyid Yunus Ardabili and Aqazada Kafa'i, were arrested and taken to Tehran. Imam Khomeini happened to be in Tehran at the time, as he later recalled: "I myself saw the late Aqazada, sitting under guard at the side of the road, with his turban removed; no one was allowed to speak to him. Then they dragged him off to the Ministry of Justice for a trial." [65] It is clear that news of the massacre in Mashhad left a deep impression on Imam Khomeini, for when the Madrasa-yi Fayziya was stormed in March 1963 by paratroopers, he repeatedly compared this new outrage to the events in Mashhad in 1935.[66]

The *'alim* whose example of militant opposition to Reza Shah had the greatest impact on Imam Khomeini was, without doubt, Sayyid Hasan Mudarris (d. 1934).[67] He has described Mudarris "the leader of those who stood against oppression, against that man from Savadkuh, the bandit Reza Khan." [68] Mudarris's opposition to tyranny and foreign domination, as well as the simplicity of his way of life, appear to have impressed Imam Khomeini greatly. He recalled, for example, with great admiration, an incident in which Mudarris broke the arrogance of the governor of Isfahan by compelling him to clean out the bowl of his waterpipe. Another memory of Mudarris related by Imam Khomeini is that when he was elected to the Majlis, he bought a cart, loaded his belongings on it, and drove himself from Isfahan to Tehran. There he rented the modest house where Khomeini used to visit him.[69]

Possibly the most significant anecdote concerning Mudarris—one repeated by Imam Khomeini on several occasions—concerns his opposition to a Russian ultimatum. Russian troops had advanced as far as Qazvin to give weight to their demands, but Mudarris rose in the Majlis to oppose any concessions, saying, "If we are to be destroyed, why should we sign the warrant for our own destruction?" Commenting on this, Imam Khomeini said: "That is the conduct of a true religious leader: a thin emaciated man, a mere heap of bones, rejects the ultimatum and demand of a powerful state like Russia." [70] He evoked the memory of this incident during the historic speech of 27 October 1964, in which he denounced the granting of capitulatory rights to the United States. There can be little doubt that he saw it to be his duty, on that occasion, to resist the overweening ambitions of the United States just as Mudarris had successfully resisted Russian demands more than forty years earlier. Concluding his evocation of Mudarris on that occasion, Imam Khomeini said, "The Majlis took courage from his act of opposition, rejected the ultimatum, and Russia was unable to do anything." In a declaration given soon after the occupation of the United States embassy in November 1979, Imam Khomeini significantly used a very similar phrase: "America can't do anything." [71] Like his mentor Mudarris, Imam Khomeini defied the arrogance of a superpower and reduced it to impotence.

In addition to these contacts with ulama who opposed Reza Shah, there is evidence that Imam Khomeini embarked on independent political comment as early as the 1930s. As previously remarked, the classes on *akhlaq* had political implications; they ran counter to the desire of the regime to isolate the religious institution from the people. In addition, Imam Khomeini wrote poetry, privately circulated in Qum, that was often political in content. For example, when Reza Shah sought, by abolishing the capitulations, to present himself as a fervent nationalist, Imam Khomeini responded with a poem that included this verse: "It's true he has now abolished every capitulation, / But only to hide from you the abolition of the nation!" [72]

One complete poem to survive from those years is a *bahariya*, composed to welcome Nauruz (the Persian New Year) in a year when it coincided with the birthday of the Twelfth Imam. The coming of the spring is likened to a divine army that overthrows tyrants, and the peom concludes with an appeal to the Mahdi not to withhold his aid:

O monarch! The affair of Islam and the Muslims is in disarray,
  On a festive day when all should be singing joyously.
See on every side the heads bent down with grief;
  Arise, then, and grant thine aid to the People of Faith;
Especially this Ayat [Ha'iri?], who is the support of the Muslims,
  So that thy rule may be established in this age,
For the sake of Muhammad's prophethood, 'Ali's *vilayat*![73]

Imam Khomeini's most substantial and important early comments on political questions came, however, in the course of a prose work, *Kashf al-Asrar*, first published anonymously in 1944. In essence it is a lengthy polemic against various writers who had attacked or criticized the beliefs and devotional practices of Shi'i Islam. Khomeini's refutation of the views he identifies as erroneous are often preceded by quotations from *Asrar-i Hazar-sala* ("Millennial Secrets"), the work of a certain Hakamzada (the errant son of Hajj Shaykh Mahdi Qumi, an *'alim* in Qum).[74] But the scope of his attack is broader than the work of a single individual. The well-known anti-clerical writer Ahmad Kasravi (d. 1946) is excoriated on several occasions,[75] as is the would-be religious reformer Shari'at Sanglaji.[76] Khomeini's pupose is to give a shattering response to all those who, in his estimation, have served both as the victims and as the agents of imperialism by distorting the beliefs of Shi'i Islam and seeking to discredit the religious institution. Their pens, he charges, are wielded "to arouse corruption, disorder, and disunity, and to destroy the basis of society." [77] Echoes of these accusations are to be heard frequently in speeches of the revolutionary period, when the secular intellectuals are denounced for their elitist refusal to espouse the cause of the Islamic Republic.[78]

In marked contrast to the serene expository tone of the writings on *'irfan*, *Kashf al-Asrar* is written in a fierce and combative style that, again, foreshadows many later speeches and declarations. Marshalling a wide variety of scriptural and rational arguments, and citing authorities such as Avicenna, Suhrawardi, and Mulla Sadra, Khomeini assaults the positions of his opponents generally with great effectiveness, pausing only to regret occasionally the necessity of dealing with such noisome adversaries.

The flourishing of anti-clericalism was, at least in part, the outcome of policies pursued by the Pahlavi regime; the refutation of anti-clerical writings was therefore a political act. But in addition there are sections of the *kashf al-Asrar* that are explicitly and firmly condemnatory of the Pahlavi regime. Reza Shah was attacked for establishing and maintaining a government at "bayonet point," [79] a key phrase that occurs time and again in pronouncements and declarations from 1962 onward that describe the state of every branch of government as deplorable. "Wherever you go, and whomever you encounter, from the streetsweeper to the highest official, you will see nothing but disordered thoughts, confused ideas, contradictory opinions, self-interest, lechery, immodesty, criminality, treachery, and thousands of associated vices." [80]

Such criticism of the monarchy did not yet involve a demand for its abolition; Khomeini even says at one point that "up to the present no member of this class [the ulama] has expressed opposition to the principle of monarchy itself." [81] However, it is plain that the form of monarchy then regarded as acceptable by Imam Khomeini bore little resemblance to the actual state of the Iranian monarchy. For he proposed that an assembly of properly qualified *mujtahids* should choose "a just monarch who will not violate God's laws and will shun oppression and wrongdoing, who will not transgress against men's property, lives and honor." [82] In other words, the king should be the appointee of the *mujtahids*, and his tenure of the throne conditional on the respect of Islamic law. It is apparent, too, that even this arrangement did not constitute the ultimate ideal, for Khomeini made clear that acceptance of the monarchy by the ulama obtains only "as long as no better system [*nizam*] can be established." [83] Possibly, then, Imam Khomeini was already considering the ultimate abolition of the monarchy. Certainly he is a man who knows how to keep his own counsel and to judge, with an unfailing sense of strategy, the demands and objectives to which public opinion will respond.

In any event, we find in *Kashf al-Asrar* the first adumbration of the political doctrine that has come to be the constitutional cornerstone of the Islamic Republic, *vilayat-i faqih*. It is not yet presented as the self-evident and incontestable consequence of the Shi'i doctrine of the Imamate, as it was to be in the Najaf lectures of 1969; in fact, Khomeini opens his discussion of the subject with the remark that *vilayat-i faqih*, "from the first day," has been a subject of controversy among the ulama. [84] However, the main principles of the doctrine are clearly set forth, together with the same arguments and evidences that were marshalled again and in more detail in the Najaf lectures. [85]

In several respects, then, *Kashf al-Asrar* foreshadows what was to come later in the career of Imam Khomeini. There is but one signal difference between the contents of this book and later utterances and proclamations. When discussing in *Kashf al-Asrar* the doctrinal and historical questions that have divided Sunnis and Shi'is, Imam Khomeini exhibits some of the polemical fervor that was traditional in the writings of both camps. [86] In the Najaf lectures, he touched on the same topics in far briefer and more discreet fashion, almost reluctantly, [87] and as his explicit concern for Islamic unity has grown, he has become a major advocate of Sunni-Shi'i rapprochement, particularly after the triumph of the revolution.

Shaykh 'Abd al-Karim Hairi died in 1936. The supervision of the religious institution fell initially to a triumvirate of his closest colleagues, ayatullahs Khwansari, Sadr, and Hujjat, but there was a persistent sense of lack. This sense became more acute after the death in November 1946 of Ayatullah Abu 'l-Hasan Isfahani, the chief *marja'-i taqlid*, who had resided in Najaf. An individual was sought who might succeed both to Hairi and to Isfahani and, living in Iran, give effective and comprehensive leadership under the conditions that had come into being in postwar Iran—a relatively open political system, marked by intense competition among different political and ideological forces and the equally intense involvement of foreign powers.

Ayatullah Burujirdi ultimately emerged as the joint successor. Imam Khomeini, now in his mid-forties, was active in promoting his candidacy and even traveled to Hamadan to persuade the senior ulama of that city to throw their weight behind Burujirdi. [88] While in his native city, Burujirdi had occasionally opposed Reza Shah and had been heard to declare that he "would never remain silent in the face of the wrong and illegal acts of the regime." [89] It was the hope of Imam Khomeini that, once established as main *marja'*, Burujirdi would use the authority of his position to confront the regime more consistently and effectively.

This hope was to be disappointed. Burujirdi proved more thoroughly apolitical than Ha'iri, and his achievements were restricted to an expansion of the religious institution in Qum and its material base.[90] During all the momentous events of the first twenty years after World War II, the voice of the main *marja'* was hardly ever raised to give guidance and direction.

This was not for want of efforts on the part of Imam Khomeini to move Burujirdi in the direction of political activism. For example, he put his signature to a letter dated 21 April 1949 that asked Burujirdi to clarify rumors that he had given his consent to government plans for convening a constituent assembly in order to modify the constitution. Burujirdi replied, in a slightly offended tone, that assurances had been conveyed to him from the Shah that all constitutional provisions touching on religion would remain intact; nonetheless, he had not made any public statements in favor of the government's plans.[91] According to certain sources, Burujirdi occasionally consulted Khomeini in later years on various matters, and despite efforts by agents of the regime to arouse Burujirdi's distrust of his younger colleague, the two men remained close. This has been contradicted by the scion of a prominent clerical family in Qum (in conversation with the present writer). He recalls that Imam Khomeini indeed frequented Burujirdi's house in Qum during the first few months after his arrival, but that Burujirdi, preferring to have less strong-willed people in his entourage, soon discouraged him from coming.

Whatever be the truth of the matter, it is certain that on at least one occasion—the anti-Baha'i campaign launched by the well-known preacher Falsafi—Khomeini sought to exert pressure on Burujirdi. Visiting Tehran during the summer of 1955, he learned from a news report on the radio that Burujirdi had announced his support for the campaign. He was disturbed at the news, for the campaign concerned what appeared to be a secondary issue and was capable of being co-opted by the government. More important, he felt that the prestige and authority of the *marja'* would suffer if Burujirdi failed to carry the matter through to its end. To prevent this, he immediately returned to Qum and stressed to Burujirdi the necessity of firmness in the course on which he had perhaps unwisely embarked. But his efforts were in vain. Back in Tehran, he learned that Burujirdi had withdrawn from the campaign. In bewilderment and frustration, he told an associate, the late Dr. Mufattih: "I don't know what hands are at work in the house of Ayatullah Burujirdi. I go to visit him and talk to him in such a way that he decides to pursue the struggle. But the next day I see he has completely changed his mind." [92]

As Khomeini had foreseen, the anti-Baha'i campaign did indeed terminate inconclusively. In August 1955, orders were issued to all provincial governors to restore Baha'i meeting places to the community, and by 1957, according to an official Baha'i source, "the battle had been won,"[93] making possible the great expansion of Baha'i influence that occurred in the following decade.

There were, of course, prominent religious figures engaged in consistent and serious political activity during the years between the deposition of Reza Shah and the coup of August 1953, and Imam Khomeini appears to have had contact with some of them. Ayatullah Kashani, the chief activist *'alim* of the immediate postwar period, is said to have aided in securing Imam Khomeini's marriage, in 1930, to the daughter of Ayatullah Saqafi, an *'alim* resident in Tehran. Moreover, during his regular visits to Tehran, Khomeini is reported to have stayed frequently at the house of Ayatullah Kashani and to have been there on the night of 31 July 1953, when it was attacked by pro-Mosaddeq demonstrators.[94]

Imam Khomeini was also acquainted with Navvab Safavi (d. 1956), the celebrated founder of the militant Fida'iyan-i Islam. According to the testimony of Navvab Safavi's widow, Navvab would frequently visit Imam Khomeini's house in Qum, under cover of darkness in order to elude the police.[95] In addition, there are many important resemblances between the program of the Fedayan-i Islam and the contents of *Kashf al-Asrar* which may indicate that consultation took place between the two men.[96]

The significance of such contacts with Ayatullah Kashani and Navvab Safavi should not be exaggerated. It is obvious that from 1941 to 1953, Imam Khomeini chose to refrain from large-scale, overt political activity. In May 1944 he issued a proclamation, beginning with the Quranic verse "Say: 'I enjoin upon you one thing only—that you rise up for God, singly and in pairs'" (34:46) and stressing how the prophets had "risen up for God." By contrast, Khomeini claimed, contemporary Muslims "rose up" only for the sake of their worldly interests, with the result that foreigners came to rule over them. Although Reza Shah—"that illiterate Mazandarani"—had gone, the plans that had emerged "from his dessicated brain" would still be implemented if the Muslims of Iran failed to awake.[97]

Several explanations can be hazarded for Imam Khomeini's choice of public silence before 1962. The most important one lies in Imam Khomeini's loyalty to the religious institution, mentioned above, and his conviction that a transformation of state and society in accordance with Islamic precepts could be brought about only under the aegis of the ulama, acting as a cohesive body and led by the *marja'-i taqlid*. Now Burujirdi, as we have seen, was essentially quietist; to have challenged his authority would have been an act of disrespect not only to his person but also the whole function of the *marja'*. Such a breaching of the consensus in Qum would not, moreover, have produced any certain result, for the majority of ulama were distinctly apolitical in their interests and remained so for many years. The laments raised by Imam Khomeini in 1969 concerning the presence of the "pseudo-saintly" in the religious institution (that is to say, ulama who eschewed political involvement because of alleged disdain for the world) were the expression of a long-standing grievance on his part.[98]

In addition, the political and ideological factions operating between 1941 and 1953 were extraordinarily heterogeneous; to have entered the political arena at that time, as did Kashani and Safavi, would necessarily have entailed various kinds of compromise alien to Imam Khomeini's temperament and vision. There was certainly no guarantee or even likelihood that the outcome of the political struggle, which centered ostensibly on the nationalization of the oil industry and the prerogatives of the Shah, would have been the establishment of an Islamic order. It is important to remember that the implementation of the constitution of 1906–07 figured high on the list of demands advanced by various parties, and even at this time it is probable that Imam Khomeini did not hold that constitution in high esteem. In *Kashf al-Asrar* he had proposed the implementation of Article Two of the Supplementary Constitutional Laws of 1907, which provides for the formation of a council of *mujtahid*s to supervise the Majlis,[99] but this proposal was probably tactical in nature. It is true that in some of his declarations made in 1962 Khomeini again invoked the constitution, but the view clearly put forward in the Najaf lectures, that the provisions of the constitution were essentially borrowings from the Belgian, French, and British legal codes, may well have corresponded to the views he held on the subject in the 1941–53 period.[100]

Moreover, the history of the constitutional movement in the first decade of the twentieth century seemed to many ulama to be one of gradual subversion and betrayal, by secularist elements, of a movement that had originally been Islamic. It may well have appeared to Imam Khomeini, together with many others, that a similar process was at work in the early 1950s. Kashani had been highly effective in mobilizing popular support for Mosaddeq and his campaign for the nationalization of the Iranian oil industry;[101] Mosaddeq was then perceived, by many ulama, to repay him with ingratitude, in typical secularist fashion. Certainly such a conclusion must have appeared inevitable if Khomeini was indeed present in Kashani's house on the night of 31 July 1953. That he probably never held Mosaddeq in high esteem or regarded him as a figure worthy of collaboration is confirmed by the gradual discrediting of Mosaddeq that has taken place in the Islamic Republic.

In the years between 1941 and 1953, then, the state of the religious leadership was inauspicious, and the political scene was confused and unpromising. Imam Khomeini's chief activity during those years was the teaching of *fiqh* and *usul*. Such activity was not only a necessary preliminary to his emergence as *marja'*, it was also a powerful means for changing the intellectual and political attitudes prevalent in Qum and for training a whole generation of militant ulama who went forth to play a leading role in the events leading to the foundation of the Islamic Republic.

Imam Khomeini began teaching *fiqh* and *usul* at the *kharij* level in 1946, in response to the urgings of Ayatullah Muntaziri and Ayatullah Mutahhari, who were the closest to him of all his pupils and associates in Qum. The first text chosen was the chapter on rational proofs from the second volume of Akhund Khurasani's *Kifayat al-Usul*.[102] Initially the number of students attending was fairly small: not more than thirty, according to the late Ayatullah Bihishti.[103] Gradually the circle of participants expanded, and by the time Imam Khomeini's second course on *usul* began—roughly in 1951—three hundred students were in attendance.[104] The number rose to five hundred when the course was offered for the third time, making Imam Khomeini's class the largest in Qum, with the single exception of that of Burujirdi, who enjoyed, after all, the prestige of *marja'iyat*.[105] After the death of Burujirdi in 1961, until his exile in November 1964 Khomeini's class remained the largest in Qum. It has been estimated that by 1964 the number attending his classes had reached twelve hundred, an unprecedented figure in the modern history of the Shi'i religious institution.[106]

It was more than the size of his classes that was unprecedented. While he was still a student of Shaykh 'Abd al-Karim Hairi, Imam Khomeini had confided to a classmate, Ayatullah Amuli, his desire to enact a radical reform in the teaching methods used in the religious institution, in order to encourage independent thinking and to make plain to the students the social applicability of what they were studying.[107] His own teaching activity was an important step in the direction of such reform. In keeping with tradition, his classes on *fiqh* and *usul* were centered on the close study of texts: *Kifayat al-Usul*, the *Makasib* of Shaykh Murtaza Ansari, and writings by near-contemporary figures such as Aqa Ziya al-Din 'Iraqi and Mirza Husayn Naini, as well as his own teacher, Hairi. But his attitude to these authorities was by no means one of uncon- ditional acceptance, and he was particularly critical of the assumptions under- lying the theories of Na'ini on *usul*, which were generally accepted in Qum at the time.[108] He encouraged a similar critical attitude in his students; Ayatullah Muntaziri is said to have been a particularly vigorous participant in the discussions that frequently took place in Imam Khomeini's teaching circle.[109]

Other hallmarks of his teaching were simplicity and eloquence of presen- tation; avoidance of technical terminology except when necessary; and, most important, the ability to relate technical concerns of *fiqh* and *usul* to all the other dimensions of Islam—ethical, gnostic, philosophical, political, and social.[110] *Fiqh* and *usul* were the point of departure, but Imam Khomeini's students experienced his classes as a powerful and original exposition of Islam as a whole.

It is well known that the pedagogical norms underlying the *madrasa* system have always required the transmission of more than formal learning from teacher to student. It has been the perennial function of the *madrasa* to cultivate and transmit precise criteria of behavior and thought and, implicitly but strongly, a whole view of the world. But seldom has a *madrasa* teacher had such determining effect on his students and, through them, on the surrounding society as did Imam Khomeini in his classes on *fiqh* and *usul*. In addition to Mutahhari and Muntaziri, a whole host of figures prominent in the Islamic revolution and in the administration of the Islamic Republic were first awakened to the revolutionary potential of Islam by the teaching circle of Imam Khomeini. As one of them, the late Ayatullah Bahunar, told me: "The Imam would instill in us a sense of spiritual nobility, of responsibility and commitment, of spiritual and intellectual richness; his words would resound in our ears for many days after we left Qum to go preaching during Ramadan."[111]

In 1961 Ayatullah Burujirdi died, and Imam Khomeini occurred to many as the possible successor to his position as *marja'*. Initially, however, he appears to have discouraged efforts to promote his candidacy. When a newspaper correspondent asked him for a photograph and a biographical sketch to be used in an article on possible successors to Burujirdi, he refused.[112]

The formal declaration of availability for the position of *marja'* generally consisted of the publication of some work on *fiqh*, particularly the kind of handbook on religious practice known as the *risala-yi 'amaliya*. Khomeini at first refused his close associates permission to publish his writings on *fiqh*, but he relented when they convinced him it was his religious duty to agree. So they published at their own expense first a selection of his *fatawa*, as a supplement to the *Vasilat an-Najat* of Ayatullah Isfahani; next, Khomeini's commentary on the *'Urvat al-Vusqa* of Sayyid Muhammad Kazim Yazdi; and, finally, his own *risala-yi 'amaliya*, entitled, like most works of this genre, *Tauzih al-Masa'il*.[113]

The traditional procedure of declaring availability for *marja'iyat* was thus completed, and many people began to follow Imam Khomeini as *marja'*. But Imam Khomeini's leadership was to transcend the traditional by far, and it was fully appropriate that the true beginnings of his role as religio-national leader should come with a signal act of protest against the Shah's regime. This was the campaign in the fall of 1962 for the repeal of new laws governing elections to local and provincial councils.[114] The issue was trivial in itself, but it provided the point of departure for a movement against the Pahlavi state that, moving through a series of finely calibrated stages, attained its triumph in February 1979. As Hujjat ul-Islam Hashimi Rafsanjani told me, in the fall of 1962 the realization began to dawn that not only had the gap left by the death of Burujirdi been filled, but also that aspirations for a firmer, more comprehensive and effective form of leadership were about to be fulfilled.[115]

For all that has taken place since 1962—the uprising of June 1963, the years of exile and steadfastness, the thirteen months of struggle and sacrifice leading to the overthrow of the monarchy, and the turbulent first six years of the Islamic Republic—the first sixty years of Imam Khomeini's life can be seen as a process of preparation, both conscious and unconscious. The various elements of his worldview were put into place, and he matured to a point of readiness to assume the burdens of leadership—*imamat*, in the original and general sense of the word. Alone among his contemporaries in the religious institution, he conceived for it a sociopolitical role that went against the apparently triumphant secularizing tendencies of the age and conveyed first to his associates and pupils and then to Iranian society at large the vibrant and comprehensive vision of Islam that had first begun to animate his being in youth.

The case of the Islamic Republic of Iran has so far been unparalleled in the modern history of the Muslim lands, and it certainly has features that give it a distinctively Iranian stamp and make its exact replication elsewhere unlikely (most important being the special claims of the Shi'i ulama to the obedience of the community and their marked tradition of hostility to secular power). In a sense, however, the revolution may be regarded as exemplifying one of the most pervasive themes in all Islamic history: that of movements of spiritual and sociopolitical renewal resulting from the emergence of a figure of unquestioned moral authority and the eager willingness of the community to grant him obedience. These movements became particularly numerous when the Muslim peoples faced the full onslaught of imperialism in the eighteenth and nineteenth centuries; from Senegal to Indonesia, a frequent response to the assaults of European powers was jihad under the leadership of Sufi shaykhs. Despite the vast differences in political circumstance and ideological awareness that separate those early movements of jihad from the Islamic revolution of Iran, there is an underlying common factor: the granting of *religious* loyalty, in the course of a *political* struggle, to a figure regarded as a normative embodiment of tradition in its purest and most authentic sense. Placed in this wide perspective of Islamic history, Imam Khomeini may be seen as the heir not only of those militant Shi'i ulama whose example he has invoked, but also of figures such as Sayyid Isma'il Shahid of India, Amir 'Abd al-Qadir of Algeria, and Shaykh Shamil of Daghistan. For the first phase of the Islamic revolution, which led to the destruction of the Shah's regime, was accomplished without the existence of a mass political party, a guerrilla army, or any other form of political organization familiar to the modern world; decisive for its success was the grant of loyalty and obedience by the mass of the Iranian people to a figure seen by them as possessing the whole moral authority of Islamic tradition.

The lasting appeal of Imam Khomeini is by no means restricted to Iran or to Shi'i communities elsewhere in the Middle East. Numerous Muslims throughout Africa and Asia have responded with warmth and enthusiasm to his calls for Islamic solidarity; posters bearing his likeness are to be encountered on the walls of Muslim townships from Mombasa to Manila. Given this widespread popularity of the Imam among the broader *ummat* of Islam, as well as the fragility and artificiality of many existing political and social structures in the Muslim lands, it would be rash to predict that the Islamic revolution of Iran will remain an isolated and anomalous case. The formation of Imam Khomeini's personality as leader may yet come to be seen as a topic touching on far more than Iranian history.

NOTES

1. This statement should not be taken as justifying the simplistic designation of the Islamic Republic as "the Khomeini regime." Such a designation ignores the deep popular roots of the new order and overlooks, among other things, that the present constitution does not do justice, in Imam Khomeini's view, to the doctrine of *vilayat-i faqih* (see his remarks to the present writer in an interview on 29 December 1979; text in Imam Khomeini, *Islam and Revolution*, ed. and trans. Hamid Algar [Berkeley: Mizan Press, 1981], p. 342).

2. It may be as well to clarify that—certain rumors notwithstanding—the application of the title *Imam* to Khomeini does not in any way signify that he is believed to be the Twelfth Imam returned from occultation, or that he is accorded the key attribute of '*ismat* (freedom from error and sin) that characterizes the Twelve Imams. It was first applied to him in poems composed in 1964 and 1969 by Ni'mat Mirzazada, but did not enter general usage until 1977, when the need was felt to accord him some designation to replace or at least supplement the obviously inadequate *Ayatullah*, which is, after all, a title borne by hundreds. *Imam* in its original and general sense—not in its technical and specific sense—was the obvious choice. See Hamid Algar, *Iran va Inqilab-i Islami* (Tehran, 1360/1981), pp. 215–16.

3. *Gazetteer of the Province of Oudh* (Allahabad, 1877), vol. 2, p. 112.

4. See the article "Khomeini Spirit Pervades Family's Ancestral Home," *Kayhan International*, 8 February 1979. According to S. A. A. Rizvi, the Kinturi family arrived in India from Nishapur as early as the fourteenth century: *A Socio-Intellectual History of the Ithna 'Ashari Shi'is in India* (Canberra, 1986), vol. 2, p. 164.

5. Concerning Mir Hamid Husayn, see Muhsin al-Amin, *A'yan al-Shi'a*, vol. 18 (Beirut, 1393/1973), pp. 110–12, and concerning the '*Abaqat*, see Muhammad Riza Hakimi, "Chahar Sad Kitab dar Shinakht-i Shi'a," in Hakimi, ed., *Yadnama-yi 'Allama Amini* (Tehran, 1352/1973), pp. 552–54. Imam Khomeini used to teach the book in Qum in the early 1930s—see interview with Ayatullah Saduqi in *Payam-i Inqilab*, 52 (Isfand 1360/February 1982)—and he made repeated and laudatory reference to it in his early book *Kashf al-Asrar* (Tehran, n.d.), especially on pp. 141 and 157.

6. S. H. R., *Barrasi va Tahlili az Nihzat-i Imam Khomeini* (Najaf, n.d.), p. 20.

7. Muhsin al-Amin mentions in his *A'yan al-Shi'a* (Beirut, 1380/1960), vol. 9, p. 211, a certain Sayyid Ahmad whose great-great-grandfather was Zayn al-'Abidin al-Musavi. This is the name borne by the progenitor of the *sayyid*s of Kintur, so the Sayyid Ahmad in question (who completed in 1886 a book in Persian called *Mu'in al-Varisin*) may have been Imam Khomeini's grandfather.

8. For a graphic account of the final years of the kingdom of Awadh, see Adbul Halim Sharar, *Lucknow: The Last Phase of an Oriental Culture*, trans. E. S. Harcourt and F. Hussain (London: Elek, 1975), pp. 50–75. Hujjat al-Islam Sayyid Ahmad Khomeini, son of the Imam, has suggested that one reason for his great-grandfather's decision to settle in Iran may have been his tense relations with the rulers of Awadh (interview, Jamaran, 12 September 1982).

9. S. H. R., *Barrasi va Tahlili*, p. 23.

10. Interview with the late Ayatullah Sayyid Muhammad Husayn Bihishti, Tehran, 28 December 1979. Bihishti's widow is the granddaughter of Mir Muhammad Taqi Mudarris.

11. Khomeini, *Islam and Revolution*, pp. 124, 334, as well as many other references to Shirazi in his speeches. In addition to his studies with Shirazi, Sayyid Mustafa is said to have received *ijaza*s (certificates of competence) from all the leading scholars of Najaf. See 'Ali Rabbani Khalkhali, *Shuhada-yi Ruhaniyat-i Shi'a dar Yek Sad-sala-yi Akhir* (Qum, 1403/1983), p. 112.

12. Khalkhali, *Shuhada-yi Ruhaniyat*, pp. 110–11, and Heinz Nussbaumer, *Khomeini: Revolutionär in Allahs Namen* (Munich: W. Heyne, 1979), pp. 20–23. A colorful variant on the narrative of Sayyid Mustafa's murder, related to me by Sayyid Ahmad Khomeini (interview, 12 September 1982), has it that Sayyid Mustafa, in his capacity as Shari'a judge of Khumayn, executed a man for publicly violating the fast of Ramadan. The relatives of the dead man plotted their revenge, arranging for the murder of Sayyid Mustafa while he was traveling to Arak. Sayyid Mustafa's sister, Sahiba,

organized a party that tracked down the murderer and brought him back to Khumayn for execution. A strong-willed woman, she presided over the execution, but had first to listen to the entreaties of her daughter for the criminal to be pardoned. For the daughter was enamored of her uncle's murderer, and it was an open secret in Khumayn that her prolonged and excessive mourning was for the murderer, not for his victim.

13. Address to the nation on 11 March 1979; text in *Rahnamudha-yi Imam* (Tehran, 1359/1981), vol.1, p. 39.

14. S. H. R., *Barrasi va Tahlili*, p. 23. Sayyid Mustafa also had three daughters, Mauluda, Aghazada, and Fatima. All six children were borne by the same wife. See Khalkhali, *Shuhada-yi Ruhaniyat*, p. 112.

15. See the anonymous poem quoted in Anon., *Biyugrafi-yi Pishva* (n.p., n.d.), p. 22.

16. Sahiba appears to have been an extremely forceful and courageous woman; for example, in addition to presiding at the execution of her brother's murderer (see n. 12 above), she once interposed herself between two feuding families that were shooting at each other and imposed a reconciliation between them: interview with Sayyid Ahmad Khomeini, 12 September 1982.

17. S. H. R., *Barrasi va Tahlili*, p. 25. The immaculate and orderly habits that the Imam developed later in life were apparently lacking in his early childhood, although his vast supplies of energy were already evident. According to family lore, he would play vigorously all day in the ditches and open spaces of Khumayn, coming home late at night with his clothes dirty and torn; interview with Sayyid Ahmad Khomeini, 18 September 1982.

18. Conversation with Sayyid Murtaza, now Ayatullah Pasandida, Qum, 17 December 1979.

19. Text of address in *Jumhuri-yi Islami*, 16 Day 1359/6 January 1981.

20. S. H. R., *Barrasi va Tahlili*, p. 26. Despite the profound respect that Khomeini developed for the religious teaching institution, he was not overawed by his first contacts with Shaykh 'Abd al-Karim Ha'iri. He reminisced to his son that one day in Arak he was studying Suyuti's text on Arabic grammar, together with other beginning students. Ha'iri was teaching *fiqh* in the same courtyard to a group of advanced students, and the noise made by the class disturbed the concentration of the young Khomeini and his friends. So he turned to Ha'iri and asked him, politely but firmly, to speak more softly: interview with Sayyid Ahmad Khomeini, 12 September 1982.

21. Particularly noticeable is that he has never, to my knowledge, made mention of Sayyid Jamal al-Din Asadabadi, a figure otherwise enlarged to mythic proportions by mainstream Islamic historiography of the modern period.

22. Concerning the life and achievements of Ha'iri, see Muhammad Mahdi al-Musawi al-Isfahani, *Ahsan al-Wadi'a* (Najaf, 1388/1968), pp. 268–69, and Muhammad Sharif Razi, *Asar al-Hujja* (Qum, 1332/1953), vol. 1, pp. 15–72.

23. S. H. R., *Barrasi va Tahlili*, pp. 26–27.

24. Ibid., pp. 26–27. For a brief biography of Yazdi, see Manuchihr Saduqi Suha, *Tarikh-i Hukama-yi Muta 'akhkhirin-i Sadr al-Muta'allihin* (Tehran, 1359/1980), p. 67.

25. Concerning Mirza Aqa, Javad Aqa, see Razi, *Asar al-Hujja*, vol. 2, p. 183; Suha, *Tarikh*, pp. 67, 133–34; and Sayyid Ahmad Fihri's introduction to Mirza Aqa Javad Maliki Tabrizi, *Risala-yi Liqa'ullah* (Tehran, 1360/1981), pp. i–vii. For Sayyid Abu'l-Hasan, see Razi, *Asar al-Hujja*, vol. 2, p. 45; introduction by Sayyid Ahmad Fihri to Imam Khomeini, *Sharh-i Du'a-yi Sahar* (Tehran, 1359/1981), p. iv; and Hasan Hasanzada Amuli's introduction to Sayyid Abu'l-Hasan Rafi'i Qazvini, *Ittihad-i 'Aqil be Ma'qul* (Tehran, 1361/1982), pp. 1–3.

26. On Shahabadi see Suha, *Tarikh*, p. 68; and Muhammad 'Ali Mudarris, *Rayhanat al-Adab* (Tabriz, n.d.), vol. 3, pp. 167–68.

27. See, for example, Sayyid Ahmad Fihri, ed., *Misbah al-Hidaya ila 'l-Khilifa wa 'l-Wilaya* (Tehran, 1360/1982), p. 53.

28. See the reminiscences of the Imam, as related by his son, Sayyid Ahmad Khomeini, in M. Vujdani, ed., *Sarguzashtha-yi Vizha az Zindagi-yi Imam* (Tehran, 1362/1983), vol. 1, pp. 144–45.

29. Remarks made in the last of five lectures on the *Surat al-Fatiha* delivered in the winter of 1980; translation in Khomeini, *Islam and Revolution*, p. 424.

30. S. H. R., *Barrasi va Tahlili*, p. 38.

31. Interview with Ayatullah Muntaziri, Tehran, 12 December 1979; Muhammad Va'iz Khurasani, "Sayri dar Zindagi-yi 'Ilmi va Inqilabi-yi Ustad-i Shahid Murtaza Mutahhari," in 'Abd al-Karim Surush, ed., *Yadnama-yi Ustad-i Shahid Murtaza Mutahhari* (Tehran, 1360/1981), p. 326.

32. According to the Imam's own tentative recollections, his first piece of writing was a commentary on the *hadith* known as *Ra's al-Jalut* ("The Head of Goliath"), but Sayyid Ahmad Khomeini regards this as unlikely. See his remarks in Vujdani, *Sarguzashtha*, vol. 1, p. 43.

33. This work was first published after the revolution, together with an introduction, Persian translation, and notes, by Sayyid Ahmad Fihri (Tehran, 1359/1980). The Arabic original was published separately in Beirut in 1402/1982.

34. Three separate editions exist of this work. One, prepared by Sayyid Ahmad Fihri, contains the Arabic text and a Persian translation only of the Quranic verses and the traditions cited; it was published as a separate book in Tehran in 1360/1980. The other two editions consist only of a Persian translation of the whole work: one appeared as Imam Khomeini's contribution to *Yadnama-yi Ustad-i Shahid Murtaza Mutahhari*, vol. 1, pp. 31–100, and the other in Qum (no date), as a separate book. Both the latter bear the title *Mi'raj as-Salikin va Salat al-'Arifin*.

35. Fihri's introduction to his edition of *Sirr al-Salat*, p. ix.

36. *Adab al-Salat* has remained unprinted as an independent text. Portions of it were included, however, by Sayyid Ahmad Fihri in his *Parvaz dar Malakut*. The first volume of this work was published before the revolution, so quotations from Imam Khomeini were identified only as the utterances of "our master in theosophy" (*ustad-i ilahi-yi ma*). The second volume appeared after the revolution, and there Khomeini is identified by name.

37. It was not until after the revolution that *Misbah al-Hidaya* was published, again through the efforts of Sayyid Ahmad Fihri (Arabic text with Persian translation, Tehran, 1360/1981). Soon after its composition it was, however, circulated in manuscript, and several of Khomeini's elders in Qum thought highly enough of it to write glosses upon it (see S. H. R., *Barrasi va Tahlili*, pp. 56–57).

38. See, however, the useful synopsis prefaced by Fihri to his edition of the book, pp. 9–13.

39. Introduction to *Sharh-i Du'a-yi Sahar*, p. viii.

40. For lists of his writings, see S. H. R., *Barrasi va Tahlili*, pp. 52–53, and Anon., *Biyugrafi-yi Pishva*, pp. 55–61. According to Ayatullah Muntaziri (interview, Tehran, 12 December 1979), many of Imam Khomeini's early writings were lost when SAVAK sacked his library in 1964.

41. It was with reference to this normative completeness perceived in Imam Khomeini that the late Ayatullah Mutahhari said of him: "he is the exact image of 'Ali ibn Abi Talib." Likewise, the expression "prophetlike leadership" (*rahbari-yi payambarguna*), sometimes employed by the Iranian media when speaking of the Imam, is to be understood as an allusion to this completeness.

42. Fihri, introduction to *Sharh-i Du'a-yi Sahar*, p. ix.

43. Muhammad Riza Hakimi, *Tafsir-i Aftab* (Tehran, 1357/1979), p. 152.

44. Law and its application "are but a path or a means in the view of the prophets.... The ultimate goal is a world that lies beyond the present one" (Khomeini, *Islam and Revolution*, p. 331).

45. Third lecture on *Surat al-Fatiha*; translation in Khomeini, *Islam and Revolution*, p. 400.

46. Address to the people of Qum, 22 December 1979.

47. *Liqa'ullah*, published as a supplement to a treatise of the same name by Mirza Aqa Javad Maliki Tabrizi, ed. Sayyid Ahmad Fihri (Tehran, 1360/1981), pp. 253–60.

48. The first lecture was given on 22 December 1979, and the fifth on 19 January 1980. For a complete translation, see Khomeini, *Islam and Revolution*, pp. 365–425.

49. Introduction to *Sharh-i Du'a-yi Sahar*, p. v. Another listener to those lectures, the late Ayatullah Mutahhari, attributed to them "the formation of a good part of my intellectual and spiritual personality"; see his *'Ilal-i Girayish ba Maddigari*, 8th ed. (Qum, 1357/1978), p. 9.

50. S. H. R., *Barrasi va Tahlili*, pp. 39–40; *Anon.*, *Biyugrafi-yi Pishva*, p. 35.

51. S. H. R., *Barrasi va Tahlili*, p. 41.

52. One indication of the importance accorded to ethics by Imam Khomeini is the fact that thirty-three of the forty *hadith* he selected for commentary in an early work (*Arba'in ya Chihil Hadith:* English translation serialized in *Al-Tawhid* 2, no. 3 [Rajab-Ramadan, 1405/April–June 1985]) concern ethical problems.

53. In Najaf in 1973.

54. See Razi, *Asar al-Hujja*, vol. 2, p. 45. For the complete text of *Munajat-i Sha'ban*, see Shaykh 'Abbas Qummi, *Mafatih al-Jinan* (Tehran, n.d.), pp. 213–17.

55. *Jihad-i Akbar ya Mubaraza ba Nafs*, pp. 59ff.

56. In the fifth lecture; see Khomeini, *Islam and Revolution*, p. 420.

57. Interview in Qum, 29 December 1979; text in Khomeini, *Islam and Revolution*, pp. 333–34.

58. Husayn Makki, *Tarikh-i Bist-sala-yi Iran* (Tehran, 1325/1946), vol. 3, p. 15.

59. See Razi, *Asar al-Hujja*, vol. 1, p. 51.

60. Remarkably, there is no record of contacts between Imam Khomeini and the most militant *'alim* of Qum during the reign of Riza Shah, Ayatullah Muhammad Taqi Bafqi (d. 1946), who publicly upbraided women from the court when they visited Qum bareheaded in 1928. See 'Ali Davani, *Nehzat-i Ruhaniyun-i Iran* (Qum, 1360/1981), vol. 2, pp. 156–57.

61. See Yahya Daulatabadi, *Tarikh-i Mu'asir ya Hayat-i Yahya* (Tehran, 1331/1952), vol. 4, pp. 294–97, and Davani, *Nehzat*, vol. 2, pp. 157–58.

62. Text in *Shahidi Digar az Ruhaniyat* (Najaf, n.d.), p. 41.

63. Ahmad Mahrad, *Iran unter der Herrschaft Reza Schahs* (Frankfurt, 1977), p. 98; Davani, *Nehzat*, vol. 2, p. 156.

64. Speech given in November 1977; text in *Shahidi Digar az Ruhaniyat*, p. 42.

65. Ibid. For a full account of the events at Gauhar Shad, see Sina Vahid, *Qiyam-i Gauhar Shad* (Tehran, 1361/1982).

66. See *Sahifa-yi Nur* (a collection of Imam Khomeini's speeches and declarations) (Tehran, 1361/1982), vol. 1, pp. 46, 168, 247, 269.

67. Concerning Mudarris, see Husayn Makki, *Mudarris: Qahraman-i Azadi*, 2 vols. (Tehran, 1358/1979); and Nad'ali Hamadani, *Mudarris: Si Sal Shahadat* (Tehran, 1360/1981).

68. Speech given in November 1977; text in *Shahidi Digar az Ruhaniyat*, p. 43.

69. Ibid.

70. Speech given on 27 October 1964; translation in Khomeini, *Islam and Revolution*, p. 187.

71. Message to the faculty of Isfahan University, 5 November 1979; translation in *Selected Messages and Speeches of Imam Khomeini* (Tehran, 1980), p. 56.

72. S. H. R., *Barrasi va Tahlili*, pp. 102–3.

73. Ibid., pp. 55–59. The poem in question was earlier printed by Razi in *Asar al-Hujja*, vol. 2, pp. 191–96, with the remark that the author had insisted his name remain unmentioned.

74. See remarks of Sayyid Ahmad Khomeini in Vujdani, *Sarguzashtha*, vol. 1, pp. 144–45.

75. *Kashf al-Asrar* (Tehran, n.d.), pp. 73, 133ff.

76. Ibid., pp. 57, 64.

77. Ibid., p. 2.

78. See, for example, the speech delivered on 5 June 1979, on the anniversary of the uprising of 15 Khurdad; translation in Khomeini, *Islam and Revolution*, pp. 270–74.

79. *Kashf al-Asrar*, p. 221.

80. Ibid., p. 222.

81. Ibid., p. 186.

82. Ibid., p. 185.

83. Ibid., p. 186.

84. Ibid., p. 185.

85. Ibid., pp. 187–88.

86. Ibid., pp. 110–19.

87. See Imam Khomeini, *Hukumat-i Islami* (Najaf, 1391/1971), p. 56; English translation in Khomeini, *Islam and Revolution*, p. 57.

88. Interview with Ayatullah Saduqi, *Payam-i Inqilab* 52 (Isfand 1360/February 1982).

89. S. H. R., *Barrasi va Tahlili*, p. 98.

90. See Ayatullah Murtaza Mutahhari, "Mazaya va Khadamat-i Marhum Ayatullah Burujirdi," *Bahsi dar bara-yi Marja'iyat va Ruhaniyat*, 2d ed. (Tehran, n.d.), pp. 233–49.

91. For the text of the letter (signed by five other persons as well as Khomeini) and Burujirdi's reply, see *Majmu'a-i az Maktubat, Sukhanraniha, Payamha va Fatavi-yi Imam Khomeini* (Tehran, 1360/1981), pp. 7–8.

92. Related to me by Dr. Mufattih in an interview, Tehran, 16 December 1979.

93. *The Baha'i World, 1954–1963* (Haifa, 1970), pp. 295–96.

94. Richard Yann, "Ayatullah Kashani—ein Wegbereiter der islamischen Republik?" *Religion und Politik im Iran: Jahrbuch zur Geschichte und Gesellschaft des Mittleren Orients* (Frankfurt, 1981), p. 301. According to another version, it was Ayatullah Lavasani who introduced Imam Khomeini to his future father-in-law (S. H. R., *Barrasi va Tahlili*, p. 31).

95. Interview with widow of Navvab Safavi, *Surush* 130, 26 Day, 1360/16 January 1982), p. 35.

96. There is, for example, much similarity between Imam Khomeini's remarks on monarchy in *Kashf al-Asrar* and the section on monarchy in *Rahnama-yi Haqa'iq*, the program of the Fedayan-i Islam published in 1944 (see pp. 50–51).

97. Text, including a facsimile of the original, in *Sahifa-yi Nur*, vol. 1, pp. 3–7.

98. Khomeini, *Hukumat-i Islami*, pp. 196–99; translation in Khomeini, *Islam and Revolution*, pp. 141–43.

99. Khomeini, *Kashf al-Asrar*, p. 222.

100. Khomeini, *Hukumat-i Islami*, pp. 11–13; translation in Khomeini, *Islam and Revolution*, pp. 30–31.

101. See Mohammad Hassan Faghfoory, "The Role of the 'Ulama in Twentieth Century Iran with Particular Reference to Ayatullah Haj Sayyid Abul-Qasim Kashani," Ph.D. dissertation, University of Wisconsin, 1978, pp. 220ff.

102. Khurasani, "Sayr dar Zindagi," p. 329.

103. Interview with Ayatullah Bihishti, Tehran, 28 December 1979. The steady growth of Khomeini's classes was interrupted in 1949 when, after an attempt on the shah's life, the government is said to have persuaded Burujirdi to ban him from teaching at the Fayziya *madrasa*. He was forced to transfer his lectures first to the Salmasi mosque near his home in the Yakhchal district of Qum and then to the Mahmudi mosque near the shrine. It is not known when he resumed teaching at the Fayziya. See Dilip Hiro, *Iran under the Ayatollahs* (London, 1985), p. 51, quoting an interview with Ayatullah Pasandida.

104. Khurasani, "Sayr dar Zindagi," p. 331. The material presented in this second course was recorded by Shaykh Ja'far Subhani and printed under the title *Taqrir al-Usul*.

105. It is worth noting that in order to avoid any appearance of competition with Burujirdi and to show respect for his seniority, Imam Khomeini would take his entire class to attend the lectures of Burujirdi: see Khurasani, "Sayr dar Zindagi," pp. 329–30.

106. S. H. R., *Barrasi va Tahlili*, p. 42.

107. Interview with Ayatullah Amuli, Qum, 16 December 1979.

108. Khurasani, "Sayr dar Zindagi," p. 330.

109. Ibid., p. 331.

110. Ibid., p. 330.

111. Interview with Hujjat ul-Islam Muhammad Javad Bahunar, Tehran, 15 December 1979.

112. Interview with Ayatullah Pasandida, Qum, 17 December 1979. This refusal to permit the publication of his photograph contrasts strongly, of course, with the ubiquitousness of Imam Khomeini's likeness in Iran today.

113. Anon., *Biyugrafi-yi Pishva*, p. 33.

114. For a detailed account of the episode, see S. H. R., *Barrasi va Tahlili*, pp. 141–216.

115. Interview with Hujjat ul-Islam Hashimi Rafsanjani, Tehran, 22 December 1979.

FOURTEEN

'Ali Shari'ati:
Ideologue of the Iranian Revolution

Ervand Abrahamian

Westerners commonly perceive the Iranian revolution as an atavistic and xenophobic movement that rejects all things modern and non-Muslim, a view reinforced by the present leaders of Iran. They claim that the revolution spearheads the resurgence of Islam, that the revolutionary movement is an authentic phenomenon uncorrupted by alien ideas and inspired solely by the teachings of the Prophet and the Shi'i Imams. This conventional wisdom, however, ignores the contributions of Dr. 'Ali Shari'ati, the main ideologue of the Iranian revolution. Shari'ati drew his inspiration from outside as well as from within Islam: from Western sociology—particularly Marxist sociology—as well as from Muslim theology; from theorists of the Third World—especially Frantz Fanon—as well as from the teachings of the early Shi'i martyrs. In fact, Shari'ati devoted his life to the task of synthesizing modern socialism with traditional Shi'ism and adapting the revolutionary theories of Marx, Fanon, and other great non-Iranian thinkers to his contemporary Iranian environment.[1]

Readers coming to Shari'ati at this point in time face a number of difficulties. The revolution not only made him a household name in Iran but also transformed him into a trophy in the contests of competing political groups. He is more eulogized than analyzed, more quoted—obviously in a selective manner—than published, and more seen in light of immediate conflicts than in the context of his own 1960s and 1970s. Furthermore, dubious works have been published under his name.

Compounding these problems is the fact that there is not one Shari'ati but three separate Shari'atis. First, there is Shari'ati the *sociologist*, interested in the

This chapter appeared previously in *MERIP Reports* (January 1982): 25–28. Reprinted by permission.

dialectical relationship between theory and practice, between ideas and social forces, and between consciousness and human existence. This Shari'ati is committed to understanding the birth, growth, and bureaucratization, and thus the eventual decay, of revolutionary movements, especially radical religions. Second, there is Shari'ati the *devout believer*, whose article of faith it was that revolutionary Shi'ism, unlike all other radical ideologies, would not succumb to the iron law of bureaucratic decay. Third, there is Shari'ati the *public speaker*, who had to weigh his words very carefully, not only because the ever-watchful secret police were eager to accuse him as an "Islamic Marxist," but also because the high-ranking ulama instinctively distrusted any layman trespassing on their turf, reinterpreting their age-old doctrines. As Shari'ati often pointed out to his listeners, contemporary Iran was at a stage of development similar to that of pre-Reformation Europe; consequently, political reformers needed to learn from Luther and Calvin, to take up tasks appropriate for their environment, and always to keep in mind that the Shi'i ulama, unlike the medieval European clergy, enjoyed a great deal of influence over the city bourgeoisie as well as over the urban and the rural masses.[2]

SHARI'ATI'S LIFE

'Ali Shari'ati was born in 1933 in a village near Mashhad. His father, Muhammad Taqi Shari'ati, was a reform-mined cleric who had doffed his clerical garb and earned a living by running his own religious lecture hall and by teaching scripture at a local high school. Because he openly advocated reform, the conservative ulama labeled him a Sunni, a Baha'i, and even a Wahhabi. In later years, 'Ali Shari'ati proudly stated that his father, more than anyone else, had influenced his intellectual development. As a schoolboy, the younger Shari'ati attended discussion groups organized by his father, and in the late 1940s father and son joined a small group called Nahzat-i Khoda Parastan-i Sosiyalist (the Movement of God-worshipping Socialists). This group was intellectually rather than politically significant: it made the first attempt in Iran to synthesize Shi'ism with European socialism.

Following his father's profession, Shari'ati entered the teacher's college at Mashhad and continued to study Arabic and the Quran with his father. After graduating from college in 1953, he taught for four years in elementary schools in his home province. While teaching, he translated—in a somewhat liberal manner—an Arabic work entitled *Abu Zarr: Khoda Parast-i Sosiyalist* (Abu Zarr: The God-Worshipping Socialist). Written originally by a radical Egyptian novelist, Abu'l Hamid Jowdat al-Sahar, the book traced the life of an early follower of the Prophet who, after Muhammad's death, had denounced the caliphs as corrupt and had withdrawn to the desert to lead a simple life and speak out on behalf of the hungry and poor against the greedy rich. For al-

Sahar and Shari'ati, as for many other radicals in the Middle East, Abu Zarr
was the first Muslim socialist. The elder Shari'ati later wrote that his son
considered Abu Zarr to be one of the greatest figures in world history.[3]

In 1958, Shari'ati entered Mashhad University to study for a master's degree
in foreign languages, specializing in Arabic and French. Completing the M.A.
in 1960, he won a state scholarship to the Sorbonne to study for a Ph.D. in
sociology and Islamic history. In Paris at the height of the Algerian and Cuban
revolutions, he immersed himself in radical political philosophy as well as in
revolutionary student organizations. He joined the Iranian Student Confederation and the Nahzat-i Azad-i Iran (Liberation Movement of Iran), which was
formed in 1961–62 by lay religious followers of Dr. Mossadeq. He organized
student demonstrations on behalf of the Algerian nationalists—after one such
demonstration he spent three days in a hospital recovering from head wounds.
He also edited two journals: *Iran Azad* (*Free Iran*), the organ of Mossadeq's
National Front in Europe; and *Nameh-i Pars* (*Paris Letter*), the monthly journal
of the Iranian Student Confederation in France.

Shari'ati took a number of courses with such famous Orientalists as Massig-
non and attended lectures by Marxist professors. He avidly read the works of
contemporary radicals, especially Jean-Paul Sartre, Frantz Fanon, Che
Guevara, Giap, and Roger Garaudy (a prominent Christian Marxist in-
tellectual). Shari'ati translated Guevara's *Guerrilla Warfare* and Sartre's *What
Is Poetry?* and began a translation of Fanon's *The Wretched of the Earth* and the
Fifth Year of the Algerian War (better known to English readers as *A Dying
Colonialism*).[4]

While translating the last work, Shari'ati wrote three letters to Fanon,
challenging him on the question of religion and revolution. According to
Fanon, the peoples of the Third World had to give up their traditional religions
in order to wage a successful struggle against Western imperialism. But, in
Shari'ati's view, the peoples of the Third World could not fight imperialism
unless they first regained their cultural identity. In many countries, this was
interwoven with their popular religious traditions. Thus, Shari'ati insisted, the
countries of the Third World had to rediscover their religious roots before they
could challenge the West.[5]

Shari'ati returned to Iran in 1965. After spending six months in prison, and
on being denied a position in Tehran University, he returned to his home
province of Khurasan. He taught first in a village school and later in Mashhad
University. In 1967, he was able to move to Tehran and take up a lectureship at
the Husayniya Ershad, a religious meeting hall built and financed by a group of
wealthy merchants and veteran leaders of the Liberation Movement. The next
five years were to be the most productive of his life. He regularly lectured at the
Husayniya, and most of these lectures were soon transcribed into some fifty
pamphlets and booklets. Tapes of his lectures were widely circulated and
received instant acclaim, especially among college and high school students.

Shari'ati's message ignited enthusiasm among the young generation of discontented intelligentsia.

Shari'ati's prolific period did not last long, for in 1972 the Husayniya ceased its activities. The hall was closed for several reasons. Shari'ati's popularity aroused concern among the secret police, and the Mujahidin, the Islamic guerrilla organization, was suspected of having a presence there. Intellectual hacks hired by the government accused Shari'ati of "leading youth astray with anti-clerical propaganda."[6] Even reform-minded clerics such as Ayatullah Mutahhari felt that Shari'ati was stressing sociology at the expense of theology and borrowing too freely from Western political philosophy.[7]

Soon after the closing of the Husayniya, Shari'ati was arrested, accused of advocating "Islamic Marxism," and put into prison. He remained in prison until 1975, when a flood of petitions from Paris intellectuals and the Algerian government secured his release. In an attempt to create the false impression that Shari'ati had collaborated with his jailors, the government doctored one of his unfinished essays, added simple-minded diatribes against Marxism, and published it under the title of *Ensan-Marksism-Islam* (*Humanity-Marxism-Islam*). After his release, Shari'ati remained under house arrest. It was not until May 1977 that he was permitted to leave for London. There, only one month after his arrival, he suddenly died. Not surprisingly, his admirers suspected foul play. But the British coroner ruled that he had died of a massive heart attack at the early age of 43.

SHARI'ATI'S POLITICAL THEORY

The central theme in many of Shari'ati's works is that Third World countries such as Iran need two interconnected and concurrent revolutions: a national revolution to end all forms of imperial domination and to vitalize—in some countries revitalize—the country's culture, heritage, and national identity; and a social revolution to end all forms of exploitation, eradicate poverty and capitalism, modernize the economy, and, most important of all, establish a "just," "dynamic," and "classless" society.

According to Shari'ati, the task of carrying forth these two revolutions is in the hands of the intelligentsia, the *rushanfekran*. For it is the intelligentsia that can grasp society's inner contradictions—especially class contradictions—raise public consciousness by pointing out these contradictions, and learn lessons from the experiences of Europe and other parts of the Third World. Finally, having charted the way to the future, the intelligentsia must guide the masses through the dual revolutions.[8]

The Iranian intelligentsia, Shari'ati added, was fortunate in that it lived in a society whose religious culture, Shi'ism, was intrinsically radical and therefore compatible with the aims of the dual revolution. For Shi'ism, in Shari'ati's own words, was not an opiate like many other religions, but was a revolutionary ideology that permeated all spheres of life, including politics, and inspired true believers to fight all forms of exploitation, oppression, and social injustice. He often stressed that the Prophet Muhammad had come to establish not just a religious community but an *ummat* (community) in constant motion toward progress and social justice.[9] The Prophet's intention was to establish not just a monotheistic religion but a *nezam-i tawhid* (unitary society) that would be bound together by public virtue, by the common struggle for "justice," "equality," "human brotherhood," and "public ownership of the means of production," and, most significant of all, by the burning desire to create in this world a "classless society."[10]

Furthermore, the Prophet's rightful heirs, Husayn and the other Shi'i Imams, had raised the banner of revolt because their contemporary rulers, the "corrupt caliphs" and the "court elites," had betrayed the goals of the *ummat* and the *nezam-i tawhid*.[11] For Shari'ati, the *muharram* passion plays depicting Husayn's martyrdom at Karbala contained one loud and clear message: all Shi'is, irrespective of time and place, had the sacred duty to oppose, resist, and rebel against contemporary ills.[12] Shari'ati listed the ills of contemporary Iran as "world imperialism, including multinational corporations and cultural imperialism, racism, class exploitation, class oppression, class inequality, and *gharbzadegi* [intoxication with the West]."[13]

Shari'ati denounced imperialism and class inequalities as society's main long-term enemies, but he focused many of his polemics against two targets he viewed as immediate enemies. The first was "vulgar Marxism," especially the "Stalinist variety" that had been readily accepted by the previous generation of Iranian intellectuals. The second was conservative Islam, notably the clerical variety, that had been propagated by the ruling class for over twelve centuries in order to stupefy the exploited masses. Thus many of Shari'ati's more interesting and controversial works deal precisely with Marxism, particularly the different brands of Marxism, and with clericalism, especially its conservative misinterpretations of Shi'ism.

SHARI'ATI AND MARXISM

At first glance, Shari'ati's attitude toward Marxism seems contradictory. At times he vehemently denounces it; on other occasions he freely borrows from it. This apparent contradiction has led some to conclude that he was militantly anti-Marxist. Others suspect he was a secret Marxist who hid his true beliefs under the veil of Islam. Still others dismiss him as a confused and confusing third-rate intellectual.

These apparent contradictions disappear once one realizes that for Shari'ati there was not one Marx but three separate Marxs, and three separate varieties of Marxism.[14] The young Marx was predominantly an atheistic *philosopher*, advocating dialectical materialism and denying the existence of God, the soul, and the afterlife. According to Shari'ati, this atheistic aspect of Marx was blown out of proportion by European socialists and Communists who, in fighting their reactionary churches, automatically denounced all forms of religion. The second Marx was the mature Marx, predominantly a *social scientist* revealing how rulers exploited the ruled, how the laws of "historical determinism"—not "economic determinism"—functioned, and how the superstructure of any country, particularly its dominant ideology and political institutions, interacted with its socioeconomic infrastructure. The third Marx was the elder Marx, chiefly a *politician* forging a revolutionary party and often making predictions which may have been politically expedient but which certainly did not do justice to his social science methodology. According to Shari'ati, this variety of "vulgar" Marxism eventually overshadowed "scientific" Marxism. Engels, in his view, distorted the central themes. The working-class parties, as they grew, became "institutionalized" and "bureaucratized." And Stalin misused selective aspects of the young and old Marx, at the expense of the mature Marx, in order to reduce Marxism to a rigid dogma that accepted nothing but narrow-minded economic materialism.

Of these three Marxisms, Shari'ati clearly rejected the first and the third but willingly accepted much of the second. He stressed that one could not understand history and society without some knowledge of Marxism. He agreed with much of the paradigm that divided society into a socioeconomic base and a political-ideological superstructure. He even agreed that most religions should be placed in the latter category, since rulers invariably "drugged" the masses with promises of rewards in the next world. He accepted the view that human history was a history of class struggles. In his own words, since the days of Cain and Abel mankind had been divided into two antagonistic camps: on one side stood the oppressed, the people; on the other side stood the oppressors, the rulers. He also dispelled the notion that Marx had been a crude materialist who viewed mankind as cynical, self-seeking animals uninterested in ideals. Shari'ati even praised Marx for being far less materialistic" than most "self-styled idealists and so-called religious believers."

But Shari'ati rejected the "institutionalized" Marxism of the orthodox Communist parties. He claimed these parties had lost their revolutionary fervor and had succumbed to the iron law of bureaucracy. He criticized them for not accepting the fact that in the modern age the main struggles evolved not around capitalists and workers but around imperialists and the Third World. He also accused the Communist and Socialist parties of Europe of not helping national liberation movements in such places as Algeria, Tunisia, and Vietnam.

In criticizing the Communist movement, Shari'ati raised a number of issues against the Tudeh Party, the main Marxist organization in Iran. He claimed that the Tudeh had applied Marxism in a mechanical manner, without taking into account that Iran, unlike Europe, had been molded by the "Asiatic mode of production" and had not experienced the Renaissance, the Reformation, the industrial revolution, and the dramatic transition to capitalism. He also claimed that the Tudeh had failed to teach the public true Marxism and had not even translated such classics as *Das Kapital*. Instead, the Tudeh had offended the country's religious sensibilities by publishing such atheistic-sounding titles as "The Materialistic Concept of Humanity," "Historical Materialism," and "The Elements of Matter."

Shari'ati's main objection to the Tudeh and Marxism, however, related directly to his earlier correspondence with Fanon. For classical Marxists, nationalism was a tool used by the ruling class to distract the masses from socialism and internationalism. For Shari'ati, the peoples of the Third World could not defeat imperialism, overcome social alienation, and mature to the point when they could borrow Western technology without losing self-esteem, unless they first rediscovered their national heritage and their popular culture. In a series of lectures entitled *Bazgasht* (*Return*), he argued that Iranian intellectuals needed to rediscover their national roots and that these were to be found not in Aryan mythology—for such mythology left the masses unmoved—but in Shi'ism, which permeated most spheres of popular culture.[15]

It is significant that Shari'ati, in his polemics, did not resort to the stock argument the clergy invariably used against the left: that Marxists are atheists and *kafer* (blasphemers), and blasphemers are by definition amoral, corrupt, sinful, and wicked. On the contrary, in discussing Marxism he argued that what defined a true Muslim was not possession of a "subjective" faith in God, the soul, and the afterlife, but, rather, the willingness to take "concrete" action for the truth: "Examine carefully how the Quran uses the word *kafer*. The word is only used to describe those who refuse to take action. It is never used to describe those who reject metaphysics or the existence of God, the soul, and the resurrection."[16]

SHARI'ATI AND CLERICALISM

While advocating a return to Islam and Shi'ism, Shari'ati frequently criticized the traditional ulama in order to differentiate himself from conservative clerical Islam.[17]

> It is not enough to say we must return to Islam. We must specify which Islam: that of Abu Zarr or that of Marwan the Ruler. Both are called Islamic, but there is a huge difference between them. One is the Islam of the caliphate, of the palace, and of the rulers. The other is the Islam of the people, of the exploited, and of the poor. Moreover, it is not good enough to say that one should be "concerned" about the poor. The corrupt caliphs said the same. True Islam is more than "concerned." It instructs the believer to fight for justice, equality, and elimination of poverty.[18]

Shari'ati accused the ulama of becoming an integral part of the ruling class, of "institutionalizing" revolutionary Shi'ism and thereby betraying its original goals. He also blamed them for failing to continue the work of such nineteenth-century reformers as Jamal al-Din al-Afghani. He sharply criticized the clergy's opposition to progressive ideas formulated in the West, particularly the radical concepts advocated by the constitutional revolutionaries of the 1905–11 period. He spoke out against their demanding "blind obedience" from their congregations, retaining a "monopoly" over the religious texts, and preventing the public from gaining access to true Islam. He claimed that the clergy refused to look ahead and instead looked back at some mythical "glorious age" and treated the scriptures as if they were fossilized, scholastic parchments rather than inspirations for a dynamic revolutionary world outlook. In his view, they failed to grasp the real meaning of vital terms such as *ummat*, thus forcing Muslim intellectuals to seek the truth in the works of European Orientalists.

Shari'ati often stressed that the return to true Islam would be led not by the ulama, but by the progressive *rushanfekran* (intelligentsia). In *Bazgasht* he argued that the Islamic "Renaissance," "Reformation," and "Enlightenment" would be brought about more by the intelligentsia than by the traditional clergy. In a lecture entitled *Mahzab 'aliyeh mahzab* (Religion against Religion), he claimed that in the modern age the intelligentsia were the true interpreters of religion. In *Cheh bayad kard?* (*What Is to Be Done?*), he insisted that the progressive intellectuals were the genuine exponents of dynamic Islam. Similarly, in a pamphlet entitled "Entezar" ("Expectations"), he argued that scholastic learning could remain in the hands of the theologians but that true Islam belonged to Abu Zarr, the *mujahidin* (fighters), and the revolutionary intelligentsia.

The logic of Shari'ati's agruments clearly threatened the legitimacy of the clergy. If revolutionary Islam was the only true Islam, then scholastic Islam was false Islam. If deeds rather than piety were the sure mark of a genuine believer, then revolutionaries—even if uneducated—were better Muslims than the learned but conservative ulama. If faith rather than learning gave one true understanding, then devout lay fighters had a better understanding of Islam than the scholastic clergy. And if social science was the key to understanding the dual national-social revolutions, then concerned Iranians should study sociology and political economy rather than theology.

SHARI'ATI AND PRESENT-DAY IRAN

During the Islamic revolution, Shari'ati emerged unchallenged as the most popular writer of modern Iran. Tapes of his lectures were widely circulated even among illiterates. His works were frequently republished. His slogans were often seen in street demonstrations. And his ideas were freely discussed by the revolutionaries, especially radical high school students. In fact, his ideas were far better known than those of Ayatullah Khomeini. Shari'ati, therefore, can truly be characterized as the ideologue of the Islamic revolution.

Because of this unprecedented popularity, Shari'ati's name has now become a major prize, fought over by rival political groups. The clerics heading the dominant Islamic Republican party eulogize him, write sermons about his life, and often cite his works concerning Shi'i roots, cultural revolutions, shortcomings of Communist movements, the need to struggle against foreign imperialism. Not surprisingly, they often censor his anti-clerical views and deny that he was ever influenced by the West. The *mujahidin*, on the other hand, emphasize his call for a social revolution and deemphasize—especially since *mujahidin* leader Masud Rajavi fled to Paris—Shari'ati's stress on national unity against the ever-present imperialist danger.

We cannot know where Shari'ati himself would stand if he were alive today. Many of his admirers have joined the *muhahidin*, but many others, despite reservations, continue to back the Islamic Republic. This support of the regime is motivated by several important factors: the need to consolidate the anti-imperialist revolution; the fear of a military counter-revolution; the aggression of neighboring Iraq; and, finally, the mystique that still surrounds Khomeini and influences large segments of the population.

NOTES

1. For works published in English on Shari'ati, see S. Akhavi, *Religion and Politics in Contemporary Iran* (Albany: State University of New York Press, 1980), pp. 143–58; N. Keddie, *Roots of Revolution* (New Haven: Yale University Press, 1981), pp. 215–30; M. Bayat-Philipp, "Shi'ism in Contemporary Iranian Politics," in E. Kedourie and S. Haim, eds., *Towards a Modern Iran* (London: Frank Cass, 1980); and M. Bayat-Philipp, "Tradition and Change in Iranian Socio-Religious Thought," in N. Keddie and M. Bonine, eds., *Continuity and Change in Modern Iran* (Albany: State University of New York Press, 1981), pp. 35–36.

2. 'A. Shari'ati, *Rasalat-i rushanfekr barayi sakhtan-i jam'eh* (Solon, Ohio: 1979), p. 6.

3. Shari'ati, *Abu Zarr* (Aachen: 1978), p. v.

4. One of Shari'ati's followers and former president of the Islamic Republic, Abu'l-Hassan Bani-Sadr, later completed and published the Persian version of *The Wretched of the Earth*.

5. 'A. Shari'ati, *Islam shenasi* (n.p., 1972), Lesson 13, pp. 15–17.

6. M. Muqimi, *Harj-u-Marj* (Tehran, 1972), pp. 13–14.

7. N. Minachi, "Husseinieh-i-Ershad Was Not a Building but a Historic Movement," *Ettela'at*, 21 December 1980.

8. Shari'ati, *Rasalat*, pp. 19–20.

9. 'A. Shari'ati, *Shi'i: Yek hizb-i tamam* (n.p., 1976), p. 27.

10. Shari'ati, *Islam shenasi*, Lesson 2, p. 101.

11. 'A. Shari'ati, *'Ali tanha ast* (n.p., 1978), pp. 1–35.

12. Ibid.

13. Shari'ati, *Shi'i*, p. 55.

14. For this attitude toward Marxism, see 'A. Shari'ati, *Jebr-i Tarikh* (n.p., 1972), pp. 1–72; *Islam shenasi*, Lessons 10–15; *Cheh bayad kard?* (n.p., 1973), pp. 70–75; *Bazgasht* (n.p., 1977), pp. 161–70.

15. Shari'ati, *Bazgasht*, p. 49.

16. Shari'ati, *Islam Shenasi*, Lesson 13, pp. 7–8.

17. For his attitude toward the clergy, see 'A. Shari'ati, *Islam shenasi*, Lessons 2–7; *Cheh bayad kard?* pp. 1–157, *Entezar* (n.p., 1972), pp. 36–37; and *Mahzab 'aliyeh mahzab* (n.p., 1978), pp. 1–19.

18. Shari'ati, *Islam shenasi*, Lesson 13, pp. 14–15.

FIFTEEN

Iranian Revolutions
in Comparative Perspective

Nikki R. Keddie

The Iranian revolution of 1978–79 contained major unique features, but also others that yield to comparative analysis. This essay will venture two types of comparison: (1) internal—comparison, on a few significant points, with other Iranian rebellions and revolutionary movements since 1890—and (2) external—comparison with other great world revolutions, employing theories of revolution that fit the Iranian case. The 1978–79 revolution differed from other "great" revolutions in the centrality of an "orthodox" religious ideology. It also differs from most recent Third World revolutions in being urban-centered.

Iranians, who in peaceable periods seem to disagree openly with the powerful, have in the last ninety years engaged in an unusual number of large-scale popular revolts and revolutions. Except for several northern provincial revolts after World War I, all these rebellions spread to Iran's major cities, and some encompassed tribal areas as well. Indeed, Iran appeared unmatched in the Muslim, Hindu, or Western world for the number and depth of its rebellious and revolutionary movements; only China, Vietnam, and possibly Russia provide competition.

Iran's two major twentieth-century revolutions do not fit very closely widespread ideas of what modern revolutions should be like. Yet there is no doubt that the Islamic revolution in 1978–79 provided a thoroughgoing overthrow of the old political, social, and ideological order. And the constitutional upheaval of 1905–11 was significant enough in participation and in altering the political system to deserve the name *revolution*. Several other movements contained revolutionary elements. The mass rebellion against a British tobacco concession

This chapter is adapted from a longer version, titled "Iran Revolutions in Comparative Perspective," published in *American Historical Review* 88 (1983): 579–98. Reprinted by permission.

in 1891–92, revolts in the provinces of Gilan, Azerbaijan, and Khorasan after World War I, the rebellions in Azerbaijan and Kurdistan after World War II, the mass-supported oil nationalization movement under Mosaddeq in 1951–53, and the popular anti-government demonstrations of the early 1960s all involved efforts to throw off foreign control over the Iranian economy and to build an independent society and state.

To attempt meaningful comparisons among Iran's rebellions and also comparisons with revolts in other Muslim and non-Muslim countries requires locating Iranian movements of the last century within the framework of modern Iranian history. Under the Qajar dynasty (1796–1925), Iran was increasingly subject to Western economic penetration and domination, particularly by Great Britain and Russia. As in many Third World countries, Western powers exacted from Iran treaties that limited customs duties to 5 percent, thus creating a virtual free trade area for Western imports, which often undersold Iranian crafts. Although carpets began to be a significant export around 1875, it is unlikely that the rise in carpet exports compensated for the fall in production of other crafts and the consequent displacement and discontent of their artisans.

The decrease in Iran's handicraft exports was partially offset by rising agricultural exports, particularly opium, cotton, and fruits and nuts. The commercialization of agriculture and carpets, which continued in the Pahlavi period (1925–79), increased economic stratification between the owners of land, water, or workshops and those who worked for them. Whether there was general immiseration or an increase in prosperity is a question on which scholars of the Qajar period have disagreed. But the increase in stratification and the peasants' increased vulnerability to famine, owing to their dependence on land planted in cash crops, such as opium, that were subject to bad market years, brought new sources of discontent to the peasantry, just as the displacement of craftsmen contributed to the grievances of urban residents. Iran did, however, differ from such countries as Egypt and Turkey, which had more European residents and trade with Europe, in that the native Iranian bazaar structure remained largely intact. Wealthy import-export and local merchants proved important in every Iranian revolution.

The Qajars did much less than the rulers of, for example, Turkey, Egypt, or Tunisia to strengthen the government and the army in order to resist further encroachments by Western powers or by their own neighbors. Turkey saw a series of efforts, beginning in the eighteenth century, to strengthen both its military and its technical and educational support structure; those efforts' first stage culminated in the reforms of Sultan Mahmud in the 1820s and 1830s. Egypt under Muhammad 'Ali saw significant transformations until Western powers limited both the economic independence and military strength of the Egyptian government in the 1840s. Iran had no parallel developments. Largely abortive reforms under Crown Prince 'Abbas Mirza (d. 1833) and chief minis-

ters Amir Kabir (d. 1851) and Mirza Husayn Khan (d. 1881) left Iran without
a modernized army, bureaucracy, and educational system. The small Russian-
officered Cossack Brigade, founded in 1879, remained the Qajars' only modern
military force.

This lack of change can be explained. Iran had much less contact with the
West than did Mediterranean and Middle Eastern countries and had an arid
terrain with a scattered population. As a result, the country was very difficult
to centralize. Other countries in similar circumstances—Afghanistan and Morocco, for example—also saw relatively little centralization or modernization
in the nineteenth century. The shahs had to permit a devolution of power to
groups weakly tied in the center. Among these were nomadic tribes (often
organized into confederations mainly for dealing with the authorities), whose
mobility, mastery of gunfighting on horseback, separate languages and cultures, and geographical location (frequently near the borders) made them
semi-autonomous units. Their ties to the government were often limited
to annual payments or to cavalry duties in case of war. Some local governors or mayors had considerable authority, although the central government
exercised increasing control over them, especially under Naser al-Din Shah
(1848–96).[1]

The lack of centralization in Iran was also tied to the increasing power and
pretensions of the Shi'i ulama. By the early nineteenth century, after a long
prior evolution, the *usuli* or *mujtahidi* school of ulama won out over the rival
akhbari school. The latter claimed that individual believers could understand
the Quran and the Traditions (*akhbar*) of the Prophet and the Imams and did
not need to follow the guidance of *mujtahids*, who claimed the right of *ijtihad*
("effort to ascertain correct doctrine"). The *usulis*, in contrast, claimed that
although the bases of belief were laid down in the Quran and the Traditions,
learned *mujtahids* were needed to interpret doctrine for the faithful. As *usuli*
doctrine developed, particularly under Murtaza Ansari, the chief *marja'-i taqlid*
("source of imitation") of the mid-nineteenth century, every believer was
required to follow the rulings of a living *mujtahid*, and whenever there was a
single chief *mujtahid*, his rulings took precedence over all others.[2] *Usuli* ulama
have a stronger position than do Sunni ulama. While not infallible, *mujtahids* are
qualified to interpret the will of the infallible Twelfth, Hidden Imam.

In addition to doctrinal power, which extended to politics as well as religion
and law, the Iranian Shi'i ulama had economic and social power that also
exceeded that of the ulama in Sunni countries. Shi'i ulama, unlike most Sunni
ulama, directly collected and dispersed the *zakat* and *khums* taxes. Like some
Sunni ulama, they had huge *waqf* mortmains as well as personal properties,
controlled most of the dispensing of justice, were the primary educators, over-
saw social welfare, and were frequently courted and even paid by rulers.
Although most of the ulama were generally on good terms with the Crown, they
resisted Qajar encroachments on their power, whereas in most Sunni states the

ulama became more and more subordinate to the government. Some of the Iranian ulama worked for the state, but as the nineteenth century progressed, conflicts between ulama and the secular authorities increased.

The relative independence of the ulama facilitated their alliance with the bazaar—a term used to designate those engaged in largely traditional, urban, small-scale production, banking, and trade—and its artisans, merchants, and moneylenders. The bazaar has long been the economic, social, and religious center of towns and cities, and even in recent times has encompassed a large population and share of the economy. As early as the 1830s bazaaris complained to the government about the large-scale import of foreign manufactures, which undermined their own production and trade. Given the treaties limiting Iranian tariffs, there was little rulers could have done even if they had been more energetic.

Regardless, then, of whether certain individuals or groups were better or worse off as the result of the Western impact on Iran, various groups in society had reason to be discontented with the Qajars and with Western incursions. Displaced craftsmen had clear grievances. Even those merchants who prospered saw Western merchants receiving favored treatment; for example, Westerners were exempt from road and municipal taxes that Iranian merchants had to pay. The ulama opposed the limited steps the Qajars took toward Western education—missionaries were allowed, for instance, to teach Christians in Iran. The ulama also objected to steps toward reform and to concessions granted to Westerners. Peasants were generally too scattered and too subject to landlord control of land and water to organize movements of discontent, although those who migrated and became urban subproletarians participated in urban-based rebellions, both in the Qajar period and, especially, in the revolution of 1978–79.[3]

Among the discontented in the nineteenth century were also a small but growing group of intellectuals, many of whom had mercantile or government positions, who learned of Western ways. Frequently their knowledge of the West was obtained secondhand, by travel to India, Istanbul, or Egypt, or by migration to Russian Transcaucasia. Hundreds of thousands of Iranians, mostly workers, settled semi-permanently in the Transcaucasus, which also supported a few Iranian intellectuals. Several educated Iranians, notably Mirza Malkum Khan and Sayyid Jamal al-Din al-Afghani, also traveled as far as France and England. Those who went abroad were generally struck by Western economic and political development; their writings praise Western ways and criticize Iran's autocratic rulers, petty officials, venal clerics, arbitrary courts, and low status of women.[4]

The recurring alliance between the bazaaris and many of the ulama on the one hand and secularized liberals and radicals on the other has been largely based on the existence of common enemies—the dynasty and its foreign supporters—rather than on any real agreement about goals. The ulama wanted to extend their own power and to have Shi'i Islam more strictly enforced; liberals and radicals looked for greater democracy and economic development; and bazaaris wanted to restrict favored foreign economic status and competition. The alliance formed by many of the ulama, the bazaaris, and a few secular intellectuals first showed its power after the shah granted a British subject a monopoly on the purchase, sale, and export of tobacco grown in Iran. This followed a series of concessions to Europeans but in this case it covered a widely grown, exported, and profitable crop rather than previously unexploited products. Growers and merchants became aroused by the threat to their livelihood as well as by nationalistic fervor. Active and often massive protests in most of Iran's cities in 1891, largely led by ulama in partnership with bazaaris (with some Russian behind-the-scenes encouragement), culminated in a successful boycott of tobacco dealing and smoking (as against the will of the Hidden Imam). The shah was forced to cancel the tobacco monopoly in early 1892.[5]

The tobacco rebellion of 1891–92 shared with later revolutionary and rebellious movements a substantial anti-imperialist and anti-foreign component. Although this component is found in most of the world's colonies and dependencies, anti-imperialism seems to have been stronger and to have resulted in more mass rebellions and revolutions in Iran than in most other Middle Eastern countries. Despite the low degree of direct control that foreigners in Iran have had in comparison with those in many other countries of the Middle East, Iranians have resisted foreign domination more than have most other peoples. Resistance has often been less obvious or militant in Iran than it has in Afghanistan, as in Iran periods of external accommodation to foreigners have alternated with periods of active rebellion. But Iranian anti-foreign feeling has always been strong.

Among the territories subjugated in the original wave of Muslim conquest, Iran was the only large area that retained its own language and a great deal of its old culture, albeit considerably modified by Islam. Iran's state religion since 1501, Shi'i Islam, appears to have been even more resistant to foreign influences than Sunni Islam. Part of Shi'ism's strength in this regard lies in its insistence on ritual purity—prohibiting physical contact with nonbelievers, preventing nonbelievers from entering mosques and shrines, and the like. For many Iranians, the growing economic, political, and ideological influence of Westerners was perceived largely as the usurpation of the rights of believers. Economic, political, and religious resentments were thus intertwined, although different groups stressed different types of grievances. Governments seen as complaisant to foreign nonbelievers were considered almost as culpable as the foreigners themselves. Iranians held their government responsible for Western depredations in 1891, in the constitutional revolution of 1905–11, the oil nationalization of 1951–53 under Mosaddeq, the demonstrations of 1963 around Khomeini, and the revolution of 1978–79.[6] Similar themes have been sounded elsewhere, notably among the Muslim Brothers and other Muslim militant groups in Arab countries and elsewhere, but in Iran the question has attracted a wider and more revolutionary following. Attacks on any regime that permitted Western involvement in Iran have been strongly voiced by respected representatives of the orthodox ulama and the bazaar. The strength of Iranian revulsion to foreign influence arose in part from the long-held belief that Western nonbelievers were out to undermine Iran and Islam. For many, Shi'ism and nationalism were part of a single blend.

The two twentieth-century Iranian movements that clearly merit the title *revolution*—the constitutional revolution of 1905–11 and the Islamic revolution of 1978–79—demonstrate the importance of this Iranian outlook. In part, the events preceding the first Iranian revolution in this century were a continuation and intensification of the tobacco rebellion of the 1890s. The economic and political power of Britain and Russia grew rapidly after 1892. The tobacco "victory" saddled Iran with a £500,000 loan to pay the British company for its lost monopoly. On 1 May 1896, Mirza Reza Kermani, instigated by the anti-shah pan-Islamic activities of Sayyid Jamal al-Din al-Afghani in Istanbul, assassinated Naser al-Din Shah. The shah's weak successor squandered huge sums on courtiers and extravagant trips abroad. The son obtained his money from two Russian loans, granted on the basis of further Russian economic concessions. The British, not to be outdistanced by Russia, retaliated by acquiring further concessions, chiefly the D'Arcy oil concession, which resulted in the first exploitation of Middle Eastern oil (following its discovery in 1908).

The Russo-Japanese war of 1904–5 and the Russian revolution of 1905 gave impetus to an Iranian opposition movement that had been growing since 1901. After a century of successive Asian defeats, an Asian power had beaten a European power, bolstering pride throughout Asia. This feeling was particularly strong in countries, like Iran, that had experienced Russian penetration and oppression. Many found it significant that the only Asian power with a constitution had defeated the only Western power without one, and constitutions came to be looked upon as a "secret of strength" of the West. In Iran, as in several Asian countries, treatises explaining constitutions and their virtues began to circulate, and news of Japanese victories was happily spread. The Russian revolution demonstrated the possibility of a mass revolt weakening a despotic monarchy and forcing it to adopt a constitution. Both the Russo-Japanese war and the Russian revolution also temporarily took Russia out of Iranian internal politics, encouraging those who expected Russia to intervene if the Qajars were threatened.[7]

The constitutional revolution began late in 1905, when respected merchants raised the price of sugar because of rising international prices. The merchants were bastinadoed, and a rebellion broke out in the streets. When some of the ulama took sanctuary (*bast*), the shah promised a "house of justice" and other concessions. But the promise was not fulfilled, and a new rebellion broke out in 1906, highlighted by a new ulama *bast* in Qum and a *bast* by twelve thousand bazaaris at the British legation. The Crown then promised to accept a constitution, and a parliament was elected. The constitution of 1906–07 was modeled on the Belgian constitution, but a provision was added for a committee of five or more *mujtahid*s to pass on the compatibility of all laws with the Islamic Shari'a. The framers intended real power to reside in the parliament and its ministers, rather than in the Crown.

The revolution became violent when a new shah, Muhammad 'Ali, closed parliament by a coup in 1908. Revolutionary guerrillas (*fedayan* and *mujahidin*) held out against the Crown in the north, and then marched south to take Tehran along with Bakhtiari tribesmen moving up from the south. The second constitutional period saw a split between the moderates, led by clerics, and the democrats, who had a program of agrarian and social reform. But the British and the Russians provided the revolution's coup de grace in late 1911. The Russians presented an ultimatum demanding, among other things, that the Iranians get rid of their pro-nationalist American adviser, Morgan Shuster. The British, who had signed an entente with Russia in 1907, supported Russian demands, Russian and British troops moved in during 1911–12, and parliament was closed.[8]

Although parliament passed some social, judicial, and educational reform measures, the revolution was chiefly political, aimed at reducing monarchal and foreign power through the introduction of a Western-style constitution and parliament. These were seen as the best means to limit autocracy. Some of the revolution's participants expected Iran and its people to be able to return to more Islamic ways, while others hoped to become more Western, if only to be strong enough to escape Western control. In this revolution, unlike that of 1978–79, few ulama leaders adopted a new political ideology. Those who supported the revolution were content to occupy a high proportion of the positions in parliament and to have a veto over legislation. One of the ulama wrote a treatise defending constitutionalism as the best government possible in the absence of the Hidden Imam, but there is no evidence that it was widely read.[9] Many ulama accepted the constitution as a means both to limit the Shah's power and to increase their own; some became disillusioned by secularist law and trends and quit oppositional politics.

Just as the revolution of 1905–11 followed smaller "rehearsals"—the movement against the all-encompassing concession to Baron Julius de Reuter in 1872 and the tobacco protest of 1891—so the revolution of 1978–79 built on resentments and organizations that had surfaced in earlier protests and movements. The post–World War II period was marked by the rise of the left, especially the Tudeh Party, whose many strikes included a general strike in the oil fields, and of autonomist movements in Azerbaijan and Kurdistan, which expressed considerable local sentiment. Then came the oil nationalization movement, expressing deep anti-imperialist feeling and culminating in the nationalization of oil in 1951 and the two-year prime ministership of Mosaddeq. He was overthrown with the aid of the United States and Great Britain. Last in the series was the economic and political crisis of 1960–64, highlighted by demonstrations in 1963 that resulted in many deaths and brought about the exile of the religious leader of the movement, Ayatullah Khomeini, in 1964.

Pahlavi rule reversed Qajar policies, and after 1925 Iran was subjected to accelerated modernization, secularization, and centralization. Especially after 1961, the Crown encouraged the rapid growth of consumer-goods industries, pushed the acquisition of armaments beyond even what Iran's growing oil-rich budgets could stand, and instituted agrarian reforms that emphasized government control and investment in large, mechanized farms. Displaced peasants and tribespeople fled to the cities, where they formed a discontented subproletariat. People were torn from ancestral ways, the gap between the rich and the poor grew, corruption was rampant and well known, and the secret police, with its arbitrary arrests and use of torture, turned Iranians of all levels against the regime. The presence and influence of foreigners provided major further aggravation.

Ironically, the OPEC oil price rise of 1973, promoted by the shah, was one cause of his undoing. He used the oil money for radical increases in investment and armaments that the economy could not bear: Iran faced galloping inflation, shortages, and an increase of rural-urban migration that compounded other problems. Iran became economically overcommitted as oil income fell after 1975. To cool the economy, the shah appointed Jamshid Amuzegar prime minister in 1977, but steps he took to bring down inflation brought more hardship and discontent. A major cutback in construction, already in decline, brought massive unemployment, which especially affected recent urban migrants, and a reduction in payments to the ulama increased their discontent. In 1977, partly emboldened by statements by U.S. President Jimmy Carter, Amnesty International, and the International Confederation of Jurists, Iranian intellectuals and professionals began to circulate petitions and letters calling for an extension of democratic rights.[10] A large educated and student class and a newly politicized class of urban poor, aided and influenced by the mosque network, provided the backbone for a new mass politics.

Early in 1978, the semi-official paper *Ettela'at* published an inspired and scurrilous assault on Khomeini, who was then attacking the regime from Iraq. Demonstrations with casualties ensued. Thereafter, on the traditional forty-day mourning intervals, demonstrations recurred, and religious, liberal, and leftist forces gradually coalesced against the regime. Khomeini went to France, where he could easily communicate with revolutionary leaders in Iran; the liberal National Front leadership reached an accord with him; and the shah's concessions were too few and came too late. The shah's gesture of appointing Shahpour Bakhtiar as prime minister led to Bakhtiar's expulsion from the

National Front. Bakhtiar was unable to prevent Khomeini's return to Iran. And the Ayatullah had become, even for many secularists, the symbolic revolutionary leader. In February 1979, air force technicians, supported especially by the Marxist guerrilla Fedayan-i Khalq and the Muslim leftist guerrilla Mujahidin-i Khalq, took power for the revolutionaries in Tehran, and Khomeini's appointed prime minister, Mehdi Bazargan, took office.

Thenceforth, at least until 1983, the revolution moved ever more toward Khomeini's brand of absolutist religious radicalism. First, the National Front ministers resigned. Then, when U.S. embassy personnel were taken hostage by young "followers of Khomeini's line" on 4 November 1979, Bazargan and his foreign minister, Ibrahim Yazdi, were forced to resign in the face of their inability to obtain the hostages' release. Khomeini's choice for president, Abu'l Hasan Bani Sadr, kept his post longer, but with decreasing power, and he was ousted in June 1981. Khomeini's Islamic Republican party came overwhelmingly into control of the cabinet and parliament. Once the party achieved a virtual monopoly on government, however, it lost cohesion, and increasing rumblings have been heard of dissension within the ruling groups on such issues as further land reform, personal power, and foreign policy. While Khomeini-type religious radicals were first in the ascendant, in early 1983 conservatives became more powerful and blocked measures for land reform and a monopoly on foreign trade. Bazaar and other middle-class influences appeared to be growing, and there were moves toward political normalization and central control over religious radicals. By 1985 normalization, in order to encourage Iranians and foreigners to contribute to economic and military reconstruction, was continuing, despite high-level disputes.

Among the theories of revolution that shed light on Iran's two major upheavals in this century are James C. Davies's J-curve theory of revolution and Crane Brinton's *Anatomy of Revolution*. Davies suggests that revolutions emerge after a considerable period of economic growth followed by a shorter, sharp period of economic contraction and decline. C.-E. Labrousse had already described the economic improvements followed by a sharp downswing that preceded the French Revolution.[11] Davies's J-curve matches the prerevolutionary experience of Iran in the 1970s. To a lesser degree, the revolution of 1905–11 may also fit the model, since some scholars see a period of growth in the late nineteenth century followed by economic difficulties that stemmed from the shah's extravagance and Russia's economic and political troubles after 1904.

Apart from Davies's model, the comparative pattern that best fits the revolution of 1978–79 is Brinton's more descriptive than explanatory typology.[12] The political, economic, and financial troubles of an *ancien régime* that made rule in the old way impossible and forced accommodation with new groups were clearly seen both in the lesser crises that preceded the revolution and in the revolution of 1978–79. Such crises, in somewhat different form, were especially characteristic of the financial situation before the English (seventeenth-century) and French (eighteenth-century) revolutions discussed by Brinton. Political alienation of the intellectuals and the elite, including government figures, from the court was as characteristic of Iran in the 1970s as it was of Russia in the early twentieth century. The gradual and somewhat unexpected movement from demonstration to revolution, characteristic of Brinton's revolutions, has also characterized both Iranian revolutions. As late as the summer of 1978, after many major demonstrations and riots, most Iranian intellectuals voiced the view that the movement was over, having achieved its goal of liberalization with the shah's promises, especially of free elections, and many persons close to the Khomeini wing of the movement have said that he and his followers did not expect the shah to be ousted soon.

The Iranian revolution of 1978–79 conforms in part to the pattern of growing radicalization found in all four of Brinton's revolutions. To locate Khomeini on a right-left scale is not easy. On the one hand, he believes in a literalist application of scripture (except when it does not suit him); on the other, he is not only a fierce anti-imperialist, with a particular dislike for the United States and Israel, but also a man with concern for the poverty-stricken, a concern that has been manifested in such programs as free urban housing and state-supplied utilities. Perhaps *populist* is the closest political adjective—with the simultaneous leftist and rightist characteristics and xenophobic and sometimes fundamentalist component that that word connotes in American history. Populist rebellions that have appealed to the subproletariat in the West have sometimes turned into autocratic and even Fascist movements, and some Iranians and Americans would say that this change has occurred, or is occurring, in Iran.[13]

Brinton, in his typology of revolution, posited the fall of the radical element during a Thermidor, in which most people, overtaxed by the rule of virtue and justice, long for more accustomed, laxer ways. This deradicalization is in turn often followed by autocratic, usually military rule; in France, Napoleon succeeded the Directory, and in Russia, Stalin replaced the NEP. Neither of these stages has occurred in Iran as of early 1986, but both are possibilities. Iran has taken major steps toward normalizing its economic and political relations with ideologically divergent regimes—notably Turkey, Pakistan, and some Western and Eastern European countries. And, although much of Iran's internal and external policy has not softened, the growth in strength of the conservative faction in government and the announced merger of the Revolutionary Guards into the armed forces may be signs of a future Thermidor.

With the rise of social history, socioeconomic explanations of revolutions have become more general than Brinton's phenomenological comparisons. Although the revolution of 1978–79 can be explained in terms of socioeconomic causation, Iran fits less neatly into most existing socioeconomic comparative schemes than it does into the basic J-curve or more varied Brinton typology. The closest socioeconomic revolutionary model for Iran's experience appears to be the Marxist formula, without any of the elaborations or modifications added recently.[14] This formula in essence postulates that revolution occurs when the relations of production—particularly the control and ownership of the society's basic means of production—have changed beyond the ability of the old forms of political power and state organization to subsume the new economic order. This situation essentially obtained prior to both Iranian revolutions.

During the revolution of 1905–11 the majority of economically dominant groups and classes—the growing class of big and medium merchants; landlords, particularly those growing cash crops; and tribal *khans*—were decreasingly represented by the Qajars. The Crown did little to create conditions under which trade could flourish or to strengthen the state so as to be able to limit foreign control. Also, the Qajars had no strategy for increasing the loyalty of the ulama; instead, the Crown added to the causes of ulama disaffection while allowing their independent power to grow. Although Iran did not yet have a strong bourgeoisie in the modern sense, groups whose interests lay in rationalizing the economy, encouraging trade and manufacture, and decreasing foreign control were growing in size and influence. But the last Qajar shahs squandered the state's funds on luxurious living and foreign travel for court favorites and members of the royal family.

In the revolution of 1978–79, the conflict between major classes and the autocracy is even clearer. The reversal of Qajar policy toward modernization helped create a sizable, well-educated stratum of society, most of the members of which became bureaucrats and technocrats; others from this stratum entered the professions and arts or private industry. Many industrialists also sprang from humble origins in the bazaar. In addition to the workers' and subproletariat's grievances over the growing privileges not only of foreigners but of the rich as well, the relatively privileged new middle and upper classes and rich bazaaris were discontented. Their economic futures were often determined arbitrarily and irrationally by fiat from the top, while they were denied all real participation in self-government and the political process. Both the successes and the failures of modernization put different classes, from the urban poor to the new middle classes, at odds with the autocratic government. And such contradictions were also felt by national minorities, which were economically oppressed and denied their own languages and cultures.

These various disaffections coalesced in two main ideological strains that had already existed in embryo in the revolution of 1905–11: the liberal or leftist desire for Westernization, and the Islamist wish to return to a "pure" Islam, particularly as interpreted by Ayatullah Khomeini and those around him. The latter won out—hence the appellation *Islamic revolution*—but the grievances behind the revolution were at least as much socioeconomic as cultural.[15]

To compare the revolutions of 1905–11 and 1978–79 to each other can contribute as much to our understanding of twentieth-century Iran as to compare them jointly to paradigms developed by Western scholars. Although many points of similarity and difference can be noted, the most striking point of comparison may be stated as an apparent paradox: the constitutional revolution resulted in an almost wholly Western-style constitution and form of government, while the revolution of 1978–79, occurring after fifty years of modernization, resulted in a self-styled Islamic republic and a constitution stressing Islam. This is not simply a matter of constitutions. The revolution of 1905–11 was secularizing in a number of spheres, while that of 1978–79 was Islamicizing, despite the Westernization of all spheres that had by then taken place. To be sure, the revolutionaries in both the first and the eighth decade of this century were fighting against autocracy, for greater democracy, and for constitutionalism, so there was much ideological continuity. Nonetheless, the ideologies of the revolutionary leaders were quite different in the two revolutions. Why?

The answer to this question lies largely in the nature of the enemy perceived by each group of revolutionaries. In 1905–11, they were fighting against a traditionalist regime and a dynasty that had made very few efforts at modernization or beneficial reforms. Therefore, non-ulama reformers and also some liberal ulama found it easy to believe that the encroaching West could only be combatted if some Western ways were imitated. Reformers called for Western-style armies, legal reforms, a clearly organized government, and modern economic development. When constitutions became of interest after the Russo-Japanese war, the idea of adopting a constitution in order to limit autocracy and achieve the secret of Western strength gained greatly.

Both parts of the 1906/1907 Iranian constitution (which lasted until 1979) were largely derived from the Belgian constitution. The intent was to have a constitutional monarchy of very limited power, a prime minister and cabinet requiring the approval of parliament, and guarantees of basic freedoms. Revolutionary leaders in 1905–11 found their model in Western-style liberalism and constitutionalism, and many of the ulama backed the adoption of the constitution. Others broke away as the implications of secularization became clear, and many tried to block certain aspects of Westernization,[16] but the growth of new bourgeois forces and of secularist ideas continued for many decades after 1911.

In 1978–79 the perceived enemy had changed, and the Iranian response was different. For fifty years the Pahlavi dynasty had pushed the Westernization of Iran. In that period the customs, beliefs, and prerogatives not only of the ulama but of many bazaaris, peasants, nomads, and the urban poor were attacked. The Pahlavis were perceived as tools of Western or Westernized powers, chiefly the United States and Israel. No longer could Iranians accept strong armies, Western-style industries, and modern legal codes and educational systems as solutions to Iran's problems. Even the liberal constitution had been subject to autocratic manipulation. The regime came to be seen as *too* Western, and there began a search for roots and for a return to "authentic" Iranian or Islamic values. The nationalism that had read modern, liberal virtues into pre-Islamic Iran—expounded by intellectuals like the nineteenth-century Mirza Aqa Khan Kermani and the twentieth-century Ahmad Kasravi—had been largely co-opted by the Pahlavi shahs. The shahs promoted pre-Islamic motifs in their speeches and architectural styles, and Muhammad Reza sponsored a mythomaniacal celebration of a fictitious twenty-five-hundredth anniversary of the Iranian monarchy and abortively changed the starting date of Iran's calendar from Muhammad's *hijra* to the foundation of the pre-Islamic monarchy.

Although many educated Iranians clung to their own liberal or leftist versions of Western nationalism, by the 1960s some intellectuals had begun to turn to new ideas. In a famous essay, Jalal Al-i Ahmad attacked "Westoxica-tion," suggesting that Iranians look rather to their own and Oriental ways. Later he tried to rediscover Islam for himself, although his critical account of his pilgrimage makes it doubtful that he succeeded. Clerical and lay religious opposition grew at the same time, publishing new essays and republishing with new introduction works by religious reformers like Jamal al-Din al-Afghani and Ayatullah Naini, who had in 1909 written the first reasoned clerical defense of a Western-style constitution. The Mujahidin-i Khalq guerrillas combined new interpretations of Islam with socialist ideas, inspired by the orator and hero of progressivist Islamic revolutionaries, 'Ali Shari'ati (d. 1977).[17] None of these groups or individuals should be termed *fundamentalist* or even *traditionalist*. Most wished to escape the related evils of internal despotism and of "Westoxication," that is, socioeconomic and cultural dependence on the West.

Increasing numbers of Iranians adopted progressive versions of an Islamic ideology seen as restoring Iranian self-esteem and combatting Westernization. Many liberal and even leftist ideals were found in different strands of the Islamic revival. Liberal ideas were represented by Mehdi Bazargan and Ayatullah Shari'atmadari, both of whom were important in the revolution. Progressive interpretations of Islam came from the popular Ayatullah Taliqani and from Shari'ati, and leftist ones chiefly from the *mujahidin*. Many continued as late as 1978–79 to advocate enforcement of the constitution of 1906–07, although they stressed implementation of its provision for a committee composed of five or more of the ulama to ensure the compatibility of laws with the Shari'a.

Even the interpretations of the Ayatullah Khomeini, which in the end won out, were not, despite their partially fundamentalist emphasis on scriptural morality and punishments, really traditional. They contained new ideological elements appropriate to an Islamic revolution and to direct rule by the ulama.

Khomeini's notion of direct ulama rule is new to Shi'ism, as not only Western scholars like myself but also a Muslim supporter of Khomeini has noted.[18] The victory of Khomeini's more absolutist version of Islam, adding to existing doctrines of ulama power the notion of direct rule, did not come because most people really preferred this to the more liberal or progressive versions of other clerical and lay Islamic thinkers but because, as a corollary to his doctrinal absolutism, his charisma, and his leadership qualities, Khomeini was the most uncompromising opponent of the Pahlavis, of monarchy, and of foreign control and cultural domination.

There is some convergence between the Manichean world outlook of Khomeini and other Muslim thinkers and the more widespread phenomenon of Third Worldism. The Manichean trend sees the world as largely divided into the just Muslim oppressed and the Western or Western-tied oppressors, and the more general ideology of the Third World similarly sees itself as economically drained and culturally colonized by an imperialist West. Such perceptions of "we" and "they," the Third World and the West, evince little appreciation of internal problems and class and other contradictions within either culture. Shari'ati, Bani Sadr, Ghotbzadeh, and others were directly influenced by varieties of Third Worldism, including Marxist-influenced dependency theory and the ideas of Frantz Fanon. Khomeini himself has probably not been immune to such currents.[19] The fusion of "modern," secular Manicheanism, "traditional" Islam, and uncompromising hostility to monarchy, dependence, and imperialism created a revolutionary ideology that distinguished the revolutionaries from Western and Westernized oppressors as much as the constitutionalist ideology of 1906 distinguished revolutionaries from traditional, nonmodernizing autocrats.

The blend of Islam and Third Worldism fits an anti-Western, anti-imperialist mood, particularly among students and those sections of the urban population who were either poor or in the traditional economy. The revolutionaries in 1905–11 disliked Russian and British encroachments, but their main wrath was directed against the Qajar dynasty and its inability to organize a strong and functioning state and nation. Even though the wrath of the revolutionaries in 1978–79 was also directed against a dynasty and a shah, the cases are not really parallel. The late shah was seen as a willing tool of the West, whose culture and economic control had pervaded Iran in a way far more offensive to most than was the case in 1905. Iranians associated things Western with their plight, and they thought their cultural and economic problems could only be solved by a return to what they saw as purely Islamic ways. Hence, the paradox of a more "traditionalist" Islamic, more "anti-modern" reaction in the revolution of 1978–79 than in that of 1905–11 can be explained primarily as a reaction to the rapid, exploitative growth of Western influence, of Westernizing rulers, and of new forms of imperialism in the intervening period.

NOTES

1. See Gene R. Garthwaite, *Khans and Shahs: The Bakhtiari in Iran* (Cambridge, England: Cambridge University Press, 1983), and "Khans and Kings: The Dialectics of Power in Bakhtiari History," in M. Bonine and N. Keddie, eds., *Modern Iran* (Albany: State University of New York Press, 1981), pp. 159–72; Willem M. Floor, "The Political Role of the Lutis in Iran," in ibid., pp. 83–95; Ervand Abrahamian, *Iran between Two Revolutions* (Princeton: Princeton University Press, 1982); John Malcolm, *The History of Persia*, 2 vols. (London: J. Murray, 1815); and N. R. Keddie, *Roots of Revolution* (New Haven: Yale University Press, 1981), chapters 2–3. For additional information, see the numerous anthropological articles on Iranian nomads.

2. Especially see Juan R. Cole, "Imami Jurisprudence and the Role of the Ulama: Mortaza Ansari on Emulating the Supreme Exemplar," in Nikki R. Keddie, ed., *Religion and Politics in Iran* (New Haven: Yale University Press, 1983), pp. 33–46; and Mortaza Ansari, *Sirat an-Najat* (n.p., 1300/1883).

3. On peasants and revolution, see the sources and discussion in Keddie, "Iranian Revolutions," p. 583 n.5.

4. Especially see Hamid Algar, *Mirza Malkum Khan* (Berkeley and Los Angeles: University of California Press, 1973); Nikki R. Keddie, *Sayyid Jamal al-Din "al-Afghani"* (Berkeley and Los Angeles: University of California Press, 1972); and Mangol Bayat, *Mysticism and Dissent: Socio-religious Thought in Qajar Iran* (Syracuse: Syracuse University Press, 1982). Persian works are listed in Keddie, "Iranian Revolutions," p. 584 n.6.

5. Nikki R. Keddie, *Religion and Rebellion in Iran: The Tobacco Protest of 1891–1892* (London: Frank Cass, 1966), and the Persian, French, Russian, and English sources cited therein.

6. Richard W. Cottam, *Nationalism in Iran* (Pittsburgh: University of Pittsburgh Press, 1979); and Keddie, *Roots of Revolution*, passim.

7. The change in Iranian attitudes at this time is clear in documents pertaining to Iran in the British Foreign Office. Also see Nikki R. Keddie, "Religion and Irreligion in Early Iranian Nationalism," in N. R. Keddie, ed., *Iran: Religion, Politics, and Society* (London: Frank Cass, 1980), pp. 13–52.

8. The Persian literature on this revolution is enormous. It includes invaluable classics by Nazem al-Islam Kermani, Ahmad Kasravi, Mehdi Malekzadeh, and Sayyed Hasan Taqizadeh, as well as major background works by Fereidun Adamiyyat and Homa Nateq. For the main books in English, see Edward G. Browne, *The Persian Revolution of 1905–1909* (Cambridge, England: Cambridge University Press, 1910); and Robert A. McDaniel, *The Shuster Mission and the Persian Constitutional Revolution* (Minneapolis: Bibliotheca Islamica, 1974).

9. The work was written in 1909 by Ayatullah Na'ini. Although it is stressed by H. Algar and others, I have seen no Persian or Western book that refers to it before its republication with an introduction by Ayatullah Taleqani in 1955; see Algar, "The Oppositional Role of the Ulama in Twentieth-Century Iran," in Nikki R. Keddie, ed., *Scholars, Saints, and Sufis* (Berkeley and Los Angeles: University of California Press, 1972), 231–55. Na'ini apparently withdrew the book from circulation shortly after its publication; see Abdul Hadi Ha'iri, *Shi'ism and Constitutionalism in Iran* (Leiden: Brill, 1977), pp. 124, 158.

10. The economic and political events of the 1970s are covered in F. Halliday, *Iran: Dictatorship and Development* (Harmondsworth: Penguin, 1979); R. Graham, *Iran: The Illusion of Power* (London: Croom Helm, 1979); and Keddie, *Roots of Revolution*, chapter 7.

11. See Davies, "Toward a Theory of Revolution," in James Chowning Davies, ed., *When Men Revolt and Why* (New York: Free Press, 1971), pp. 137–47; Crane Brinton, The Anatomy of Revolution (rev. ed.; London: Vintage Books, 1965; and C.-E. Labrousse, *La crise de l'économie française à la fin de l'ancien régime et au début de la révolution* (Paris: Presses Universitaires de France, 1944), introduction.

12. James A. Bill has noted the correspondence between Brinton's views and the events of 1978–79; see his "Power and Religion in Revolutionary Iran," *Middle East Journal* 36 (1982): 22–47, esp. p. 30. The closeness of this fit is apparent in Brinton's own summary of the patterns apparent in the four great revolutions he discussed in *The Anatomy of Revolution*, pp. 250–51, 550.

13. Comparisons of Khomeinism and National Socialist movements are found in Richard W. Cottam, "The Iranian Revolution," in Juan R. I. Cole and Nikki R. Keddie, eds., *Shi'ism and Social Protest* (New Haven: Yale University Press, 1986); and Sa'id Amir Arjomand, "Iran's Islamic Revolution in Comparative Perspective," *World Politics* (April 1986).

14. Marx and Engels's basic view is stated, with some variations, in several works from the *Communist Manifesto* onward. Recent theoretical works touching on comparative revolution and influenced by Marx include those by Theda Skocpol, Charles Tilly, Eric Hobsbawm, George Rudé, and Barrington Moore. Although these shed much light on various topics, they have less to say than has Marx on the kind of forces that led to revolution in Iran. Skocpol has modified some of her views in the aftermath of the Iranian revolution; see T. Skocpol, "Rentier State and Shi'a Islam in the Iranian Revolution," *Theory and Society* 11 (1982): 265–83, with comments by Eqbal Ahmad, Nikki R. Keddie, and Walter L. Goldfrank in ibid., pp. 285–304.

15. In addition to the cited books by Graham and Halliday, see Nikki R. Keddie and Eric Hooglund, eds., *The Iranian Revolution and the Islamic Republic* (Washington, D.C.: Middle East Institute in cooperation with Woodrow Wilson International Center for Scholars, 1982), pp. 127–31; Shaul Bakhash, *The Reign of the Ayatollahs* (New York: Basic Books, 1984); and Gary Sick, *All Fall Down* (New York: Random House, 1985).

16. The controversy over the role of the ulama in the revolution of 1905–11 is discussed in Keddie, "Iranian Revolutions," p. 594 n.17.

17. On these intellectuals, see Keddie, *Roots of Revolution*, chapter 8, part of which is by Yann Richard. It includes the most important Persian references.

18. Kalim Siddiqui et al., *The Islamic Revolution: Achievements, Obstacles, and Goals* (London: Open Press in association with the Muslim Institute, 1980), pp. 16–17. Although some Safavid ulama spoke of ulama rule, they still expected a shah to lead in military and other affairs.

19. Gregory Rose, "*Velayat-e Faqih* and the Recovery of Islamic Identity in the Thought of Ayatollah Khomeini," in Nikki R. Keddie, ed., *Religion and Politics in Iran* (New Haven: Yale University Press, 1973), pp. 166–88. Also see Nikki R. Keddie, "Islamic Revival as Third Worldism," in J.-P. Digard, ed., *Le cuisinier et le philosophe: hommage à Maxime Rodinson* (Paris: G.-P. Maisonneuve et Larose, 1982), pp. 275–81. Many of Khomeini's speeches and works are translated in Hamid Algar, ed., *Islam and Revolution: Writings and Declarations of Imam Khomeini* (Berkeley: Mizan Press, 1981).

CONTRIBUTORS

Ervand Abrahamian is Professor of History at Baruch College of the City University of New York and the author of the recently published *Iran between Two Revolutions*.

Hamid Algar is Professor of Near Eastern Studies, University of California, Berkeley, and the author of *Religion and State in Iran* and other works.

Joel Beinin is Assistant Professor of Middle East History at Stanford University and the co-author (with Zachary Lockman) of *Class and Nation: Workers and Politics in Egypt, 1899–1954*. He is an editor of *MERIP Middle East Reports*.

Edmund Burke, III, is Professor of History at the University of California, Santa Cruz, and is the author of *Prelude to Protectorat in Morocco 1860–1912*.

Julia Clancy-Smith is Assistant Professor of History at the University of Virginia. Her dissertation is entitled "Saintly Lineages, Border Politics and International Trade: The Oases of the Algero-Tunisian Frontier, 1830–1881."

Fanny Colonna is Chargée de Recherches at the Centre National de Recherche Scientifique, Paris, and a member of the Ecole des Hautes Etudes en Sciences Sociales. She is also affiliated with the Unité de Recherches en Anthropologie Sociale et Culturelle at the University of Oran, Algeria, and is the author of *Instituteurs algériens: 1883–1939*.

Sandria B. Freitag is currently a Research Associate with the Center for South and Southeast Asia Studies at the University of California, Berkeley, and is completing a volume on *The New Communalism: Public Arenas and Religious Activism in North India, 1870–1940*.

David Gilmartin is Assistant Professor of History at North Carolina State University. He has published articles on Punjab politics and religious organization and on the creation of Pakistan.

Ellis Goldberg is Assistant Professor of Political Science, University of Washington, and the author of *Tinker, Tailor, and Textile Worker: Classical Politics in Egypt, 1930–1954.*

Nikki R. Keddie is Professor of History at the University of California, Los Angeles. She is the author and editor of numerous books, including *Roots of Revolution: An Interpretive History of Modern Iran*; *Sayyid Jamal al-Din "al-Afghani"*; and *Women in the Muslim World*; and she is ex-president of the Middle East Studies Association of North America.

Ira M. Lapidus is Professor of History at the University of California, Berkeley, and is the author of *Muslim Cities in the Later Middle Ages* and *A History of Islamic Societies.*

Paul Lubeck is Professor of Sociology and History at the University of California, Santa Cruz. He is the author of *Islam and Urban Labor in Northern Nigeria: The Making of a Muslim Working Class* and the editor of *The African Bourgeoisie: Capitalist Development in Nigeria, Kenya and Ivory Coast.*

Peter Von Sivers is Professor of History at the University of Utah, editor of the *International Journal of Middle East Studies*, and the author of *Khalifat, Königtom und Verfall: Die politische Theorie Ibn Khalduns* and other works.

Ted Swedenburg is a doctoral candidate in the Department of Anthropology at the University of Texas at Austin.

John O. Voll is Professor of History at the University of New Hampshire and is the author of *Islam: Continuity and Change in the Modern World.*

GLOSSARY OF SELECTED TERMS

'adl	witness to a proceeding before *qadis*
'alim (pl. ulama)	learned man, especially in law and other religious studies
Amir	a general or other military commander; sometimes the title of an independent ruler
ansar	"helpers" of Muhammad at Medina; adopted later to refer to participants in Muslim religious associations
ashraf	those who trace their lineage to the Prophet, his Companions, or, as used in Indian, to the Mughal ruling classes
a'yan	notables
Ayatullah	the highest rank in the Shi'i hierarchy of scholars who are qualified to give independent judgment in religious matters
baraka	blessing, holiness, spiritual power inherent in a saint; more generally, inherent power
Bey	a Turkish title for a military commander, and sometimes independent ruler
biradari	lineage, extended family; term used in India
faqih (faqi)	scholar of Islamic law; jurist
fatwa (pl. *fatawa*)	formal legal opinion issued by a qualified mufti
fiqh	jurisprudence; the discipline of elucidating the Shari'a; also, the resultant body of rules
hadith	reported words and deeds of the Prophet Muhammad, based on the authority of a chain of reliable transmitters
hajj	the annual pilgrimage to Mecca

hamula	a group of people descended from a common ancestor; often a village or territorial community
hijra	the migration of Muhammad from Mecca to Medina; the year it occurred, 622, is the base-year of the Muslim era; migration out of non-Muslim regions or societies
Imam	leader of prayer, founder of one of the major law schools; leader of the Muslim community, especially in Shi'i usage
imambara	building in which the martyrdom of Husayn is commemorated; used principally in India
'irfan	gnosis, mystical science
jihad	war in accordance with the Shari'a against unbelievers; also, the inner struggle against base impulses
khalifa	successor; representative; especially used of the successors to the Prophet; lieutenant of Sufi master
khatib	speaker, preacher, especially the official preacher for the Friday sermon
madrasa	college of law and other religious studies
Mahdi	a personage who will appear at the end of days and establish Islam over all unrighteous forces
muhalla	residential quarter
muharram	first month in Muslim calendar; occasion of mourning for martyrdom of Husayn
mujaddid	the renewer, restorer, reformer of Islam; a leading figure believed to come once in every century
mujahid (pl. *muhajidin*)	warrior for the faith
mujtahid	scholar with authority to reinterpret Muslim law
muqaddam	head of a local Sufi *tariqa*
murabit (pl. *murabitin*)	Shaykh, Sufi teacher
pir	teacher of the Sufi faith, shaykh
qadi	a qualified judge of law (Shari'a)
qaid	district administrative officer
sayyid	a descendant of Husayn, son of the Prophet's daughter, Fatima. Descendants of her other son, Hasan, are often called *sharif*s
shahid	martyr
Shari'a	Islamic law; more broadly, the totality of Muslim belief and practice
sharif	noble; a descendant of Hasan, son of the Prophet's daughter, Fatima
shaykh	an elder; a head; a saint; a descendant of Muhammad's Companions

Shi'is	those Muslims who held to the rights of 'Ali and his descendants to leadership in the community
soff	faction
Sufi	follower of a mystic path
sultan	title of ruler, head of state
sunna	the normative practice of the Prophet and the early community, embodied in the *hadith* literature
Sunnis	the majority of Muslims, who accept the authority of the first generation of Muslims and the validity of the historic succession of caliphs, in contrast to the Kharijis and Shi'is
tariqa (pl. *turuq*)	a way, a Sufi method, a school, a brotherhood of those who follow the same way
tawhid	the unity of God
ulama	see *'alim*
umma	the totality of Muslims forming a community following Muhammad
wali	Sufi master, friend of God
waqf	foundation, endowment of properties to provide income for religious purposes
zawiya	a saint's tomb; a Sufi center and headquarters for teaching and other Sufi activities

INDEX

'Abbas Halim, Prince, 208, 210, 213, 223
'Abbas Mirza, Crown Prince, 299
'Abbud Pasha, 232
'Abd al-Hamid 'Abd al-Haqq, 214, 222
'Abd al-Karim, 189
'Abd al-Karim al-Karmi, 187
'Abd al-Karim Hairi, Shaykh, 267, 273, 277, 281
'Abd al-Qadir, Amir, 40, 43, 47, 61, 62, 69, 73, 75, 94, 283
'Abd al-Qadir al-Husayni, 188
'Abd al-Qadir Himada, "Shaykh," 231
'Abd al-Qadir Yasin, 187
'Abd al-Rahim al-Hajj Muhammad, 197
'Abd al-Rahim Mahmud, 187
'Abd al-Rahman al-Qujtuli al-Azhari, 61
Abu 'Alim bin Sharifa, 49
Abu 'Amama, 51, 52, 54–55, 56
Abu'l Hamid Jowdat al-Sahar, 290–91
Abu al-Khayrat, 100; and Fur sultanate, 103
Abu Himara, 60
Abu Jilda, 188–89
Abu Jummayza, 6, 22, 97–98, 102–4, 109; as the Mahdi's Musaylima, 101, 110; and Mahdists, 100; in millenarian and Sufi populist tradition, 29, 106–7; and Nabi 'Isa revolts, 108; in Sudan, 105–6

Abu Shusha, 53
Abu Zarr, 290–91, 296
Abu Ziyan, 4, 67, 72; Zaatcha revolt of, 70–72
Adam Muhammad: as Prophet 'Isa, 101
Adélia revolt, 50–52
Agricultural self-sufficiency: French fiscal demands on, 47–50; in nomadic and mountain households, 44–45; and political activism, 43–58; private ownership and landlords in, 43; sharecropping, 42–43
Ahl-i Hadith, 152
Ahmad Bey, 43, 47
Ahmad ibn al-Hajj, 40, 73
Ahmad Kasravi, 276, 310
Ahmad Tafish, 183–84
Ahrar party, 158, 164
akhlaq: in lectures and writing of Khomeini, 272, 275
Akhund Khurasani, 281
al-Arb'a tribe, 44–45
Al-Damir, 217
al-Hajj Ahmad. See Ahmad ibn al-Hajj
Algeria, colonial period of, 3, 4–6, 19, 23, 29, 30–31; conditions for independence in, 57–58; under direct French control, 40–41; French and local tribal administrators in, 40, 48, 53; and French capital and industrial

Algeria, colonial period of (*continued*)
goods, 45; and French fiscal demands,
47–50; French influence on political
activism in, 57–58; and landlord
class, 48–49; lineage-based resistance
in, 83; as Ottoman province, 40, 46;
and political action, 39–41, 45–46,
57–58; revolts from French in, 40–41;
and War of Independence, 45–46, 48,
58

Algerian resistance. *See* Resistance
movement, Algerian

Alhaji Muhammad Marawa, 255–56,
258

'Ali Bey (Egypt), 171

Aligarh, College or University, 118, 146

'Ali ibn 'Umar, Shaykh, 65

'Ali Ibrahim Pasha, 224

'Ali Shari'ati, 13, 14, 31, 310, 311; on
Islamic revolution, 295–97; lectures
and translations of, 290–91, 295–96;
as revolutionary ideologue, 296–97;
as sociologist, believer, and speaker,
289–90; teaching and translating
of, 290–92; on Third World and
Marxism, 292–95

Allama Muhammad Iqbal, 164; on
tawhid, 153–54, 164

Amin al-Husayni, Hajj, 183, 186, 190,
191, 192; in Supreme Muslim
Council, 180–81, 188

Aminu Kano, 250–51

amir-i-millat, 9, 159, 160, 162, 163

Amir Kabir, 300

Amnesty International, 305

Amritsar, 148, 162

Anglo-Egyptian Oilfields Company, 238

Anjuman Hizb al-Ahnaf, 153

Anjuman-i Himayati-i Islam, 151

Anjuman Islamia, 149–50, 151, 154,
156, 157

Anjuman-i Tahaffuz-i Masjid
Shahidganj, 156

Anjuman Khuddam al-Din, 153

Ansar, 99, 100, 102, 104, 108

Anti-clericalism: Khomeini on, 276;
Shari'ati on, 295–96

Anti-colonial resistance, Algerian and
Palestinian. *See* Algeria, colonial
period of; Resistance movement,
Algerian; Resistance movement,
Palestinian

Anwar Salama, 229, 230, 236, 237, 238,
239, 241

Aqazada Kafa'i, 274

Aqa Ziya al-Din 'Iraqi, 281

Arab Boy Scouts, 186

Arab Executive (Palestine), 180, 188,
190

Arab Youth Congress, 186

Arms traffic: 'Azzuz in, 66–68, 77; and
European military technology, 65–
66; in the Maghrib, 65–67; among
religious communities, 66–67

Arnon-Ohanna, Yuval, 195

atf: in nationalist and trade-union
thinking, 238

Aurès mountains, 41, 64, 81, 91; Oued
Abdi valley of, 82–84, 86, 90

Awlad bin Sharifa family, 48

Awlad Sidi Shaykh, 54, 55

a'yan, 173, 178, 179, 183, 185, 193;
leadership of, 170; as mediators, 180–
81

Ayatullah: Abu 'l-Hasan Angaji, 274;
Abu 'l-Hasan Isfahani, 273, 277, 282.
See also Ayatullahs Bahunar, Bihishti,
Burujirdi, Hasan 'Ali Muntaziri,
Muhammad 'Ali Shahabadi, Mutah-
hari, Naini, Shari'atmadari, *and*
Taliqani

Badshahi mosque, 149, 160

Baha'i, 278–79, 290

Bahunar, Ayatullah, 282

Balfour Declaration, 179

Bani Sadr, Abu'l Hasan, 306, 311

Banu Sharifa, 50, 53. *See also* Abu 'Alim
bin Sharifa

baraka, 62; of 'Azzuz, 67, 77; and *barud*,
5, 66, 67; of Si Lhachemi, 83, 86

Bardo, Treaty of, 63

Bata shoe company, 240

Bellah, Robert, 20

Berque, Augustin, 90–91
Beso mill, 212, 213, 214
Beylik, 61, 62, 65; in arms traffic and anti-French activities, 63, 68, 69; and later activities of 'Azzuz, 74–76. *See also* Tunisia
Bihishti, Ayatullah, 281
biradari, 7, 118, 149. *See also* Elites, Muslim
Bombay, 115, 129; British authority in, 130, 132–33; communities of, 9, 128, 135; linguistic, ethnic diversity of, 9, 128–30, 141; *muharram* processions in, 9, 129–30, 132–35; and Muslim symbols, 9, 135, 139–40; and 1920s labor movement, 137–38; in 1929 riots, 9, 135–40
Brass, Paul, 147
Braudel, Fernand, 25
Brinton, Crane, 306–8
British Mandate. *See* Palestine
British rule, 7–10, 12, 26–27, 29, 30–31; in Egypt, 108–9, 216–17, 221; in India. 115, 117, 119–20, 128, 132–36, 146, 148–52, 155–60; in mandate Palestine, 178–94
Burujirdi, Ayatullah, 268, 277–78, 281, 282

Cairo, 209, 210, 212, 214, 216, 225
Capitalism, colonial, 246–49, 258
Carter, Jimmy, 305
Charisma, 9, 83, 85, 92, 147, 160, 162, 163, 311; of Sufi shaykhs, 23
Class consciousness: and national consciousness among Egyptian and Nigerian workers, 12, 208–9, 210, 240, 254–55
Collective action, 19, 30, 118, 140; forms of, 26–31; in Muslim societies, 25; in North African *tariqa*, 76–77
Communalism, 115, 136. *See also* Community, Muslim
Communist movement, 137, 297; of class struggle, 11, 294; Egyptian, 207, 209, 216–24
Community, Hindu, 122

Community, Muslim, 8–9, 14, 100, 149, 162, 163, 164, 240; as *millat*, 152; and Islamic community, 146, 164, 173, 241; leadership and education in, 151; in personal practice and public structures, 117–18, 121–22, 127–28, 141; political leaders and definition of, 150–56; and Shahidganj mosque, 157–58; and *tawhid*, 153–54
Condominium. *See* Sudan
Congress of Trade Unions in Egypt (C.T.U.E.), 223, 224
Congress party, Indian National, 122, 137, 152
Cossack Brigade, 300

Dar Fur region, 6; as frontier area, 98; and influences on Islamic practice, 98; local religious figures in, 98–99; Mahdist forces in, 97, 99–100; prophetic claimants in, 102, 105; separatism of, 97–98; teachers and holy men in, 98
Das Kapital, 295
Davies, James C., 306–7
Demography: and agriculture, 41–47; of the Maghrib, 40–41; and population distribution and density, 41–42, 45, 47, 57; and revolts in northern Sahara and North Africa, 40–41
Deoband College, 7, 152
Derduriya order, 5, 6, 22, 29, 82–88, 89
Djendel, 48, 50, 52
Dunn, Ross, 5
Durkheim, Emile, 20
Duveyrier, Henri, 74

East India Company (EIC), 128
Edwardes, S. M., Police Commissioner (Bombay), 130, 133–35
Egypt, 3, 7, 10–12, 15, 19, 24, 29, 105–8, 207–8, 228–31
Egyptian Movement for National Liberation (E.M.N.L), 220, 222
Eickelman, Dale, 101–3
Eisenstadt, S. E., 20
Elites, 3–4, 9, 12, 15, 23, 24, 27, 30;

Elites (*continued*)
  discourse of, and popular discourse,
    24; discourse of, and symbols of
    identity, 21; Mashriq Palestinian,
    180–81; Muslim, 147, 164, 239, 241;
    Muslim, and demand for Pakistan, 8,
    164; Muslim, in Kanpur *ashraf*s, 116;
    Muslim, and religious community, 8;
    Palestinian, 15, 169; political, 24, 26,
    76–77; religious, 26, 259; religious,
    and local politics, 23, 76–77; rivalry
    of Muslim, 15; Sufi, 76. *See also* Sufi
    notables and saints; Ulama
Ethnic minorities: and factionalism in
    Palestine and India, 23–24, 123–25,
    172, 183–86
Ettelaʿat, 305

Faddali, ʿAbd al-Jayyid, 215, 216, 220
Fanon, Frantz, 14, 289, 291, 295, 311
faqih: and local economy, 107–8, 109;
    roles in local religious life, 98–100,
    107. *See also* Ulama
fatawa, 118, 158, 188, 265, 282
Fathi al-Maghribi, 214, 215
Faysal (Syria), 179, 180
Fazl-i-Husayn, Sir, 151, 152, 154
Fedayan-i Islam, 279
Fedayan-i Khalq, 306
fellahin, 170, 174, 179, 176, 179, 182,
    187, 189, 195, 196. *See also* Peasants,
    Palestinian
fiqh and *usul*, 268, 270, 271, 272, 280–81,
    282
French colonial period, 4–6, 29; in
    Algeria, 39–55, 61–76, 82–88. *See also*
    Algeria, colonial period of
Fuad Siraj al-Din, 214
Fundamentalism, Islamic, 20; in Adélia
    revolt, 51

Garaudy, Roger, 291
Gauhar Shad, mosque of, 274
Geertz, Clifford, 20, 21
Gellner, Ernest, 22–23
Ghotbzadeh, 311
Girni Kamgar (Labor) Union, 137

Gramsci, Antonio, 170
Great Mutiny (Indian), 26
Great Revolt. *See* Palestine, Great Revolt
    of; Tunisia, 1864 Revolt in
Guevara, Che, 291
GUMTPWGC (General Union of
    Mechanized Textile and Preparatory
    Workers in Greater Cairo), 216–17,
    220, 224, 225
GUMTWSKC (General Union of
    Mechanized Textile Workers in
    Shubra al-Khayma and Cairo),
    213–15
Gurdwaras Tribunal, 150, 156, 157

Haʿavara, 184
al-Haddad, Shaykh, of Rahmaniya
    brotherhood, 49, 50, 56, 60, 62
hadith, 117
Hajj Amin. *See* Amin al-Husayni, Hajj
Hajj Aqa Nurullah, 273–74
Hasan ʿAli Muntaziri, Ayatullah, 269,
    281, 282
Hasan al-Banna, 189, 211, 240
Hausa: folklore, 250; meaning of *tatsine*
    in, 256; speakers of, 248
Hawamdiya, 229–35, 241
Henni, Ahmad, 92
Henri Pierre mill (Masnaʿ Nasij
    al-Aqmisha al-Haditha), 211, 212
Higher Arab Committee (H.A.C.),
    190–92
Higher Council of Command, 192
hikmat and *ʿirfan*: Khomeini's study of,
    14, 268–71, 272; Sufi and Shiʿi
    authorities on, 270
Histadrut, 184
Hobsbawm, Eric, 20, 22
Hodgkin, Thomas, 190
Holt, P. M., 107
Holy men, Sufi. *See* Sufi notables and
    saints
Hujjat al-Islam Hashimi Rafsanjani,
    282
Husayn, 293; tomb of, 129, 131
Husaynabad tomb, 130
Husayniya Ershad, 291–92

Ibn 'Abbas of Menaa, 85
Ibn 'Arabi: and commentary on *Fusus al-Hikam*, by Da'ud Qaysari, 268
Ibn 'Ayash, 4
Ibn 'Azzuz. *See* Mustafa ibn 'Azzuz
Ibn 'Uthman of Tolga, 64–65
Ibn Abi al-Diyaf, 67
Ibn Badis, 94
Ibn Khaldun, 102
Ibrahim Pasha, 173
Ibraham Tuqan, 187
Ibrahim Yazdi, 306
Ideology: Islamic, 235–36, 239–41, 251–52; Muslim, solidarity vs. class conflict in, 11, 228–29, 239–41
Al-Ikhwan al-Muslimun. See Muslim Brothers
'*ilm*, 87
imambara, 130
Imperialism, 276, 283, 291, 294–95, 311; and Egyptian wage differential, 235
India, 3, 7–10, 15, 19, 22, 24, 29, 30, 115–60. *See also* Bombay; Kanpur; Punjab
Iran, 3, 13–15, 19, 31–33, 265, 267, 289, 291, 294, 296, 306–11; Islamic Republic of, 263–64, 269, 277, 280, 282, 283; Islamic revolution of, 263, 271, 283, 298; political activism in, 271, 278; Qajar, 26, 299–301, 303–5
Iran Azad, 291
Iranian Student Confederation, 291
Iraq Petroleum Company, 191
'*irfan. See hikmat*
'Isa, Prophet of God, 101, 105, 108
Iskandar Sulayman Salib, 214–15
Islah movement, 82, 93
Islamic Republic. *See* Iran
Islamic Republican Party, 15, 297, 306
Islamization: *mallams* in, 246, 248, 250–51
Isma'il Sidqi: government of, 221, 223, 224
Istiqlal Party, 186, 191
'Izz al-Din al-Qassam, Shaykh, 183, 189–90, 195

Ja'far al-Sadiq, Imam, 269
Jalal Al-i Ahmad: and "Westoxication," 310
Jam'iya al-shar'ya al-ta'awuniya, 231
Al-Jamahir, 233, 235
Jamal al-Din al-Afghani, 296, 301, 303, 310
Jama Masjid, 161
jamatbandi, 7
Jamiat-i Ulama-i Hind, 152, 153, 154, 155, 158, 164
Jamshid Amuzegar, 305
Julahas, 116, 128, 131

Kabyle, 4, 44–45, 46, 50, 52
kafer, 295
Kanafani, Ghassan, 187
Kano, 24, 244, 245–47, 251–53, 255–56; food prices and wages in, 257–58; as frontier of Islam and capitalism, 248–49. *See also* Nigeria
Kanpur, 116; caste groups in, 116; factions in, 119, 122–23, 125; and mosque affair, 8, 119–21, 139; municipal leadership of, 122–24; and 1931 riots, 122, 124, 135; Tanzim preaching and processions in, 9, 126–27, 136; universal Islamic symbols in, 8, 117, 121
Kanpur Improvement Trust, 122
Karbala, 130, 132
Kashani, Ayatullah, 267, 279, 280
khalifa, 6, 70, 71, 101–2
Khalifa 'Abdallah, 97, 99, 101, 103, 104, 105, 107; as successor of the Mahdi, 72
khalifa al-mahdi, 72. *See also* Khalifa 'Abdallah
Khan Barkat 'Ali Khan, 149
Khanqa Sidi Naji: saints of, 64
Khatmiya *tariqa*, 106
Khilafat movement, 136, 146, 152, 155
Khomeini, Ayatullah (Imam), 13, 15, 31, 32, 263–83, 296, 302, 305–6, 307, 308, 310–11; classes and lectures by, 269, 270–73, 275, 277, 280–81; devotional and gnostic works of, 269–

Khomeini, Ayatullah (Imam) (*continued*)
70; early life of, 266–67; and family
origins, 264–66; *fatawa* of, 282; on
hikmat and *'irfan*, 14, 268–71, 272;
moral authority of, 14, 263, 283;
on *Munajat-i Sha'ban*, 272–73; on
Pahlavis, 270, 273, 276–77, 279;
political works of, 275–77; public
silence of, 279–80; as religio-national
leader, 282–83; Sayyid Ahmad
(grandfather of), 265; Sayyid
Murtaza (Ayatullah Pasandida;
brother of), 266, 267; Sayyid
Mustafa (father of), 265–66; Sayyid
Nur ad-Din (brother of), 266; in
studies with Shi'i scholars, 267–69;
teaching reforms of, 281–82; writings
of, 269–72, 275–77, 279, 282
Khwaja 'Abdallah Ansari (*Manazil
al-Sa'irin*), 268, 271, 281

Labor movement, Egyptian. *See* Trade
union movement, Egyptian
Labrousse, C.-E., 306
Lahore, 9, 160, 163; British in, 147–49,
157; *rais* and *biradari* in, 149; religious
leaders in, 149–50
Launay, Michel, 92
leburori, 12, 246, 251, 252
London Round Table Conference
(1930), 115

Macchli Bazaar, mosque of, 119, 122,
123
Madrasa-yi Fayziya, 268, 272, 274
madrasas, 87, 161, 281–83
Maghrib, the, 26, 41, 65–67, 69. *See also*
North Africa, colonial period of
Maharaja Ranjit Singh, 148
Mahdi. *See* Muhammad Ahmad
Mahdi, Sudanese. *See* Muhammad
Ahmad
Mahdis, 60, 63, 67, 72
Mahdist movement, 247, 249; and
British fears of Mahdist revival, 108;
and Egyptian rule, 6, 107; Islamic
supratribal message of, 103, 105–6;

and neo-Mahdists, 108; religious
revolts against the, 105; as revolt of
the *faqihs*, 107; of separatism in
western Dar Fur, 97–98, 107–8; and
successors to the Mahdi, 101. *See also*
Muhammad Ahmad
Mahdiya. *See* Mahdist movement
Mahmud al-'Askari, 210–15, 217, 220
Mahmud al-Dumrani, 221
Mahmud II, 17
Majdhubiya, 106
Majlis (Iranian), 274, 275, 280
Majlis-i Ahrar, 153
Majlis Ittihad-i Millat, 156, 158, 162
Malik Firoz Khan Noon, 157
mallams, 249, 252, 257–58; as factory
workers, 12, 254; in unions, 12, 253
marja'-i taqlid, 273, 277–79, 282, 300
Marx, Karl, 19–20, 289; as social
scientist, 294
Marxism, 208, 209, 241, 292, 308; in
Egyptian trade union movement,
208, 215–16, 218; and political
vocabulary of Muslim Brothers, 240–
41; Shari'ati on, 293–95
Mashhad University, 291
Masqueray, Emile, 82
Masselos, Jim, 129, 135
Massignon, Louis, 291
Masud Rajavi, 297
Maulana Ahmad 'Ali, 153
Maulana Zafar 'Ali, 146
Mazil al-Mahn, 102
Medjana-Kabylia revolt. *See* al-
Muqrani revolt
Meerut Conspiracy Case of 1929, 138,
140
Mehdi Bazargan, 306, 310
Meston, Lieutenant-Governor, 120
Metcalf, Barbara, 146
Meynier, Gilbert, 92
millat, 152
Millenarian social movements: as jihad,
5, 23, 72; of Sammaniya and Khat-
miya *turuq*, 106; 'Yan Tatsine as,
25, 29, 244, 255–58
Minault, Gail, 146

Mir Hamid Husayn, 264
Mir Muhammad Taqi Mudarris, 265
Mirza 'Ali Akbar Yazdi, 268
Mirza Aqa Khan Kermani, 310
Mirza Hasan Shirazi, 265, 267
Mirza Husayn Khan, 300
Mirza Husayn Naini, 281
Mirza Javad Aqa Maliki Tabriza, 268
Mirza Malkum Khan, 301
Mirza Reza Kermani, 303
Mirza Sadiq Aqa, 274
Mirza Sir Zafir 'Ali, 149
Misr Spinning and Weaving Company, 209, 214, 225
Moore, Barrington, Jr., 25
Moral economy, Islamic, 22
Mossadeq, Muhammad, 279, 280, 291, 299, 302, 305
Mufti. *See* Amin al-Husayni, Hajj
Mughal empire, 7, 148–49
muhalla, 130, 131, 134, 135, 149, 151
Muhammad, Prophet. *See* Prophet Muhammad
Muhammad 'Abd al-Salam, Shaykh, 229, 230, 231, 232, 233, 241
Muhammad 'Ali (of Bombay), 115, 139
Muhammad 'Ali (of Egypt), 17, 170, 299
Muhammad 'Ali Shahabadi, Ayatullah, 268, 270, 271
Muhammad Abu Allaq, 73
Muhammad Ahmad, Mahdi, 6, 22, 98, 99, 101, 107, 108, 256
Muhammad al-Muqrani, 49; as leader of revolt, 50
Muhammad al-Sanusi, 60
Muhammad bin 'Abbas, 90
Muhammad ibn 'Abdallah, 4, 53, 67, 90
Muhammad Jarallah, 85
Muhammad Khalid: in Mahdist succession struggles, 97
Muhammad Shafi, Sir, 151
Muhammad Sharif, 210, 222
Muhammad Shatta, 220
Muhammad Taqi Shari'ati (father), 290–91

muharram: observances of, 130, 132; processions, 9, 116, 129, 133–34, 135; Shari'ati on, 293; Shi'i rituals in, 130
mujaddid, 67
Mujahidin-i Khalq, 306, 310
mujtahids, assembly of, 276–77
Mulla Hadi Sabzavari, 268, 269
Mulla Husayn Fisharaki, 273
Mulla Sadra, 269, 276
Munazzamat al-Jihad al-Muqaddas, 188, 192
Munich Agreement, 193–94
al-Muntada al-Adabi (Literary Club), 179
al-Muqrani revolt, 4, 87, 89; alliances and causes of, 49–50; Muqrani family in, 43, 48–50, 53; and peasants' interest in political action, 50
Murtaza Ansari, 300
Musa Kazim al-Husayni, 179, 180
Musaylima, 100–105
Muslim Brothers: 11, 189, 209–12, 217–25, 228, 230, 241, 303; anti-colonialism of, 238–41; and *dhulm*, 240; and Egyptian Communists, 24, 208–9, 213–14, 217–25; ideology of, 229, 239–41; and *Al-Ikhwan al-Muslimun*, 218, 219, 222, 224, 229, 231, 233, 234, 236, 237–38; Islamic moral vision of, 11, 218–20, 232; and Islamic politics, 207, 219–20; and *ra'aya* in trade unions, 223; Spinning and Weaving Company, 224; strike-breaking of, 11, 222–25; on trade unions, 231–33
Muslim-Christian Associations, 179, 180, 188
Mustafa al-Nahhas, 212–13
Mustafa ibn 'Azzuz, 4; and 'Azzuziya, 67, 68; in arms traffic, 66–68, 71, 73, 77; defusing rebellion, 75–76; as Rahmani militant, 61–62; and religious notables, 64–65; religious prestige of, 62, 67–69, 73, 74, 77; in view of Tunisian and French, 68–69
Mutahhari, Ayatullah, 269, 281, 282, 292

Nahi 'Isa, cult of, 108
Nachtigal, Gustav, 98
al-Nadi al-'Arabi (Arab Club), 179
Nafta, 65, 87
Nahzat-i Azad-i Iran (Liberation Movement), 291
Nahzati-i Khoda Parastan-i Sosiyalist, 290
Naini, Ayatullah, 310
Nameh-i Pars, 291
Naser al-Din Shah, 300, 303
Nashashibi, 181, 185, 190, 192, 193
Nasser, Gamal Abdel, 236
National Committee of Workers and Students (N.C.W.S.), 221
National Defense party, 185, 190
National Front, 305–6
Nationalism, 303; in Egyptian trade unions, 208, 214–16, 218, 221–22, 225, 235, 237–39, 241; in interwar period, 30–31, 304–5; Muslim, in India, 22, 24, 26; Muslim, in Iran, 13, 300; Muslim, in Nigeria, 247, 255; Muslim, in rural Palestine, 24, 189–90; secular, 207; secular, in mandate Palestine, 24, 185–87
Native Authority, 249, 250
Navvab Safavi, 279, 280
NEPU (Northern Elements Progressive Union), 254; Islamic ideology and institutions in, 244; and populist movement, 12–13, 244, 250–51
New Dawn, 217, 220, 224. *See also* Communist movement
nezam-i tawhid, 293
Nigeria, 3, 7, 12, 15, 19, 24, 31, 244, 246, 248, 255–56; and Islamic considerations, 12, 244, 247–59; and NEPU, 12, 249–50, 253; and opposition to British rule, 12, 247, 249; political movements of, 15, 19, 244, 247–50, 252–54; populist movement in, 13, 251–52, 259; trade unions in, 244, 253–54; working class in, 12, 252, 254
North Africa, colonial period of, 63–65, 70, 76–77

Northern Elements Progressive Union (NEPU): foundation of, 12, 250

Oases, North African: in the arms traffic, 63, 66, 67; in Nafta, 65; in Ouargla and the Oued Souf, 71; in the Ziban, 71. *See also* Arms traffic
Oil workers, Egyptian union of: and foreign management, 12, 237–39; and Muslim Brothers, 12, 229, 236–39
OPEC, 32, 305
Orientalism, 18, 21, 33
Orientalists, 291, 296
Ottoman empire, 24, 28, 29, 155, 170, 178; Algeria as province of, 40; tax policies of, 40–41, 47–48
Ottoman Land Code, 173
Ouarsenis region, 46

Paden, John, 246
Pahlavi regime, 13, 263, 264, 272, 282, 299, 305, 309, 310; and anti-clericalism, 276; Khomeini's views of, 270, 273, 276–77, 279
Paisa Akbar (Penny Paper, Lahore), 153
Pakistan, 115, 162, 163, 164; as national political identity, 8, 10, 141
Palestine, 3, 15, 19, 24, 30; Arab Congress, 179, 180; Arab party, 186; British mandate of, 24, 30–31; 178–84; Communist party (P.C.P.), "Arabization" of, 187, 188, 198; Great Revolt of, 169, 170, 190, 194, 196–98; War, 225, 235
Pan-Islam, 155
Parsons, Talcott, 20, 247
Pathans, 9, 128; as strikebreakers and victims, 137–39. *See also* Kanpur
Peasants, Palestinian, 24, 196; and festival of Nabi Musa, 10, 172–73, 176, 179, 187; *hamula* units and Qays-Yemen tribal moieties of, 10, 171, 193, 195; and patron-client ties, 10, 174–76, 178, 182, 183, 185, 196; in pre-capitalist era, 170–73
Peel Commission, 192

pirs: Chishti, 160; Sufi, 9, 159–61, 163–64
Populism, Islamic, 13, 31, 241, 244, 250, 251, 259; and class interests, 252
prabhat pheris, 123; as Hindu activities, 125–26
Press, Muslim, 118; in Bombay riots, 138–39; coverage of Kanpur mosque affair in, 120–21; in Lahore, 153, 155, 158–59, 161, 162, 163
Prophet Muhammad, 101, 102, 104, 117, 153–56, 161, 163, 164, 172, 270, 289, 290, 293, 300
PRP (People's Redemption Party), 258; and NEPU, 13, 250–51; and reform in populist movement, 13, 251
Punjab, 148, 158, 159, 161, 162, 163; and divisions of Lahore, 9, 148, 150–53, 163; Muslim community in, 150–56; and Muslim community of Iqbal, 153–54; and rural Sufi *pirs*, 9, 159–61, 163–64; and Sayyid Jamaat 'Ali Shah, 9, 159–63; and Shahidgani mosque, 9, 146–50, 156–60, 162, 163, 164; and ulama leadership, 9, 151–53, 158–59, 164

Qadiriya, 67, 82, 254
Qajar dynasty, 299–300, 301, 303, 308, 311
al-Qassam. *See* 'Izz al-din al-Qassam
Qassamites, 190, 191, 192, 196, 197. *See also* 'Izz al-Din al-Qassam
Qum, 266–68, 271–72, 273–74, 281

Rahmaniya: in Algerian resistance movement, 4, 64–65, 76–77; and Si Llachemi, 82; Sufi *tariqa* of, 86, 87, 88; *zawiya* of, in Nafta, 65, 67, 68, 69, 74, 87
Rahmaniya Sufi *tariqa*. *See* Rahmaniya; Sufi brotherhood
Raja of Mahmudabad, 121, 123
Ras Ghabr, 238
Rawalpindi conference, 160, 161, 162
Reform Islamic teaching: and Deoband College, 7, 152–53; of peripatetic

mallams, 249–51; on Quran and example of Prophet, 8, 117–18, 161; and resistance movements, 6, 183, 189, 195–96
Reform movements. *See* Khilafat movement; Mahdist movement; Salafiya movement; Sanusiya; Tanzim movement
Republic, Islamic, 263, 264, 269, 280, 282, 283
Resistance movement, Algerian: in the Aurès, 52–53; of camel and sheep/camel nomads in the Sahara, 53–55; economic conditions of, 52; religious figures in, 55–56; and self-sufficiency, 52–58
Resistance movement, Palestinian, 10, 169, 179–81, 183–85, 195–98; agrarian and urban protest in, 30–31, 170, 178, 183–84, 187–88, 191–94, 196; Islamic reformers in, 10, 183, 189, 195–96; and populist Istiqlal Party, 10, 186; al-Qassam in, 31, 89–90
Reuter, Baron Julius de, 304
Revolution, Iranian: anti-Marxism of, 32, 292–94; ideology of, 13, 267, 283, 292, 308–10; in modern Iranian history, 298–302; as national and social revolution, 14, 292–94; and 1905–11 constitutional revolution, 303–4; as populist rebellion, 307; and post–World War II protests, 304–5; and tobacco rebellion, 298, 302, 304; as urban alliance, 32, 298, 301–2
Reza Shah, 265, 273, 275, 276, 277, 279
Rifaat Abou-el-Haj, 180
Robinson, Francis, 147
Rowlatt Satyagraha of 1919, 136
Rudé, George, 20, 22

Sadr al-Din Qunavi (*Miftah al-Ghayb*), 268
Saint of Nafta. *See* Mustafa ibn 'Azzuz
Salafiya movement, 81, 90, 92, 189
Sammaniya *tariqa*, 106
Sangathan movement, Hindu, 125

Sanusiya, 66, 72, 75, 88
Sartre, Jean-Paul, 291
Sayyid 'Abd al-Rahman, 108–9
Sayyid Abu'l-Hasan Raf'i Qazvini, 268
Sayyid Ahmad: jihad of, 7
Sayyid Ahmad Fihri, 269–70, 271–72
Sayyid Ayatullah Shah Bokhari, 155–56
Sayyid Habib, 158
Sayyid Hasan Mudarris, 265, 274–75
Sayyid Isma'il Shahid, 283
Sayyid Jamaat 'Ali Shah, 9, 159–63
Sayyid Khudayr, 221
Sayyid Yunus Ardabili, 274
Scott, James, 177
Separatism, Muslim: in India, 115, 136, 140, 141
Shaban, M. A., 105
Shah Chiragh mosque, 157
Shahidganj mosque, 146, 149, 150, 162, 163, 164, 156–60; as a Sikh site, 147–48
Shahpour Bakhtiar, 305–6
Shari'a, 152, 153, 154, 270, 304, 310
Shari'ati. See 'Ali Shari'ati
Shari'ati Sanglaji, 276
Ayatullah Shari'atmadari, 310
"sharif's" movement: led by Muhammad ibn 'Abdallah and Sulayman ibn Jallab, 71–74; with support of 'Azzuz and other religious leaders, 71–74; in Tunisia, 73–74
Shaukat 'Ali, 139
Shaw Commission, 184
al-shaykh al-akhbar, 64, 65
Shell (Oil) company, 237, 238, 240
Shi'i Islam, 302
Shi'ism, 14, 289, 311, 302, 303, 311; in ideological struggle in Iran, 14, 31, 276–77, 283, 290, 292–93, 295–96; and Imams, 289, 293; as revolutionary symbol for Shari'ati, 14, 292–93, 295–96; and Shi'i ulama, 13, 276, 290, 300
Shubra al-Khayma, 11, 31, 209–25, 241
Shuddhi movement, of Arya Samaj, 125
Shuster, Morgan, 304
Sidi 'Abd al-Hafidh, 71

Sidi al-'Id, 73
Sidi 'Ali family of El-Oued, 64
Sidi Muhammad al-'Id of Temassine, 68
Sidi 'Umar Abayda of Kairouan, 73
Sikh Central Gurdwaras Committee (S.G.P.C.), 150, 158
Sikh Gurdwaras and Shrines Act, 150
Sikhs, 148, 149, 150
Si Lhachemi, 6, 81, 92–94; and Derduriya in French archives, 84–85; and his grandnephew, 81, 93; on hoarding and accumulation, 89; and June 1879 rebellion, 85, 90; preaching and authority of, 85; as Sufi saint, 88, 90; Tunisian studies of, 87–88
Si Muhammed bin 'Abdallah, 85
Sirr al-Salat, 269–70
Si Saddok bel Hadj, 90
Si Sadiq, 52–53, 56
Si Sulayman, 4, 54
SKMTWU (Shubra al-Khayma Mechanized Textile Workers' Union), 11, 210–13; beginnings of, 210; early leaders of, 212; expansions of, 213, 216; newspaper of, 210, 213, 214, 215, 218; strikes of, 212, 216, 221–23; workers in, 211. See also GUMTPWGC; GUMTWSKC
Skocpol, Theda, 25
Smith, M. G., 246
Social history, 38; and neo-Marxists, 26
Société Générale des Sucreries et de la Raffinerie de l'Egypte, 230
Socony Vacuum, 238
Sokoto Caliphate, 245, 248
Sudan, 6–7, 10, 19, 22, 29, 97, 98, 101, 105, 107; and Anglo-Egyptian condominium, 106, 108; and Islamic renewal, 101–2; political and religious orders in, 106
Suez Canal company, 238
Sufi brotherhoods, 6, 28, 60, 75; in organizing movements, 7, 190, 254; in revivalist mission in the Sudan, 106; in scripturalist and universalist Islam, 6

Sufi notables and saints, 77, 90; in Algerian resistance movement, 62, 75–77; in colonial Algeria, 77; in Tuwala, 69–70

Sufi *turuq. See* Sufi brotherhoods

Sugar workers, Egyptian union of: 229–36; early strikes, 230; foremen of, 235–36; and Muslim Brothers, 11, 229, 230–36; newspaper of, 234; officers of, 233; organization and goals of, 231–33; strength of, 235

Suhrawardi, 276

Sulayman ibn Jallab, 72–74

Sultan Ibrahim, 97

Sultan Mahmud (of Turkey), 299

sunna, 101

Sunni Islam, 302

Sunni Muslims, 24, 129, 130, 131, 133, 134, 141; in early *muharram* processions, 129; from Konkan, 128

Supreme Muslim Council (S.M.C.), 180–81, 188, 191

Symbols, Islamic, 8, 15–16, 117, 121, 122, 132, 135, 141, 146, 155, 163, 164, 246; political role of, in British India, 147; vocabulary of, in Muslim communities, 7, 118, 121

Tabliqh movement, 125

*tabut*s, 130, 131, 132, 133, 134, 135; symbolism of, 129

Taha Sa'd 'Uthman, 211, 213–15, 217–18, 220, 241

talakawa, 12, 246, 247, 249–51, 258–59. *See also* Ulama

Taliqani, Ayatullah, 267

Tanzim movement, 8–9, 26, 125, 136; and martyrdom imagery, 125–27; as Muslim collective activity, 126, 136

tariqa. See Sufi brotherhoods

tawhid, 153–54, 164, 271

Textile industry, Egyptian, 208–9, 240–41. *See also* Trade union movement, Egyptian; SKMTWU

Therborn, Göran, 185

Third World, 14, 289, 294, 298–99, 298;

cultural and religious identity in, 291–92

Third Worldism, 311

Thompson, Edward P., 20, 21, 22, 219

Tibermacine, 82, 91, 94

Tijaniya and Qadiriya orders, 67, 254

Tillion, Germaine, 91

Tilly, Charles, 20

Times of India (Bombay), 139

*toli*s, 130, 133; behavior of, 131–32

Trade union movement, Egyptian, 210, 211, 213, 214, 223, 228; Muslim Brothers in, 11, 207–25, 232; in nationalist movement, 208, 214–16, 218, 221–22, 225. *See also* GUMTPWGC; GUMTWSKC; Oil workers, Egyptian union of; Sugar workers, Egyptian union of, SKMTWU

Tribal and lineage coalitions, 5; in colonial Algeria, 83; and Muslim *biradari*, Sufi *tariqa*, and *jamatbandi*, 7

Tudeh Party, 294–95, 304

Tunisia: in Algerian resistance, 62–63, 64, 65, 75–76; and resistance in the Djerid, 63, 65–67, 69, 87; and resistance in the Ziban, 64, 70–71, 74; Revolt of 1864 in, 5, 75–76; role of 'Azzuz in 1864 Revolt in, 75

Turner, Victor, 20

Twelfth (Hidden) Imam, 275, 284*n*2, 300, 304

Ulama, 8, 9, 13, 14, 15, 20, 30, 31, 32, 60, 75, 117, 147, 161, 246, 248, 290, 308, 309; Barelvi, 152, 153; direct rule by, 310–11; leadership, significance to Khomeini of, 264, 267, 283; opposition to monarchy, 273–77; in Shahidganj agitation, 151–53, 158–59, 164; *talakawa*, 250–251; traditional, 295–96; in urban social movements, 28, 118, 250, 301–2; *usuli* or *mujtahidi* school of, 300

umma(*t*), 9; Islamic Iran as, 14, 264, 283, 293, 296

United Provinces (U.P.; now Uttar
    Pradesh), 115–16, 118, 127, 131,
    132, 136, 141, 149, 159, 161
Universalism, Islamic: as goal of
    insurrections, 56, 58; in Islamic
    brotherhood, 56; and Muslim
    identity, 8; of reform ideas, 10
Urban middle class: and landowners in
    commercial agriculture, 27, 173–74,
    178; and revolutionary ideologies,
    185–87, 195
Urban social movements: ulama in, 28,
    118, 250, 301–2
Urdu: literature, 117; poetry, 155; press,
    155, 163
Usman dan Fodio, jihad of, 246
'Uthman Adam, 97, 99–100

vilayati-i faqih: and Imamate, 277

Wafd, 207–8, 209, 231, 236
Wafd Executive Committee, 212
Wailing Wall (Buraq), 183
Wallerstein, Immanuel, 25
waqf, 149
War of Independence. See Algeria,
    colonial period of
Watt, W. Montgomery, 105
Wazir Khan mosque, 149
Weber, Max, 19, 26, 93
Weberian tradition, 20, 254
Westernization, 308–9; Khomeini's
    opposition to, 14, 273
Williams, Raymond, 170, 195
Willis, C. A., 108
Wingate, Orde, 194, 197
Wingate, Reginald, 99
Wolf, Eric, 25
Workers: class interests of, 138; in
    communal terms, 12, 137;
    Communists' and Muslim Brothers'
    interest in, 11, 208–9, 217–25; and
    Islamic affiliation in Egyptian textile
    industry, 15, 218–20; Islamic goals
    of, 232; in sugar industry, 234–35.
    See also Trade union movement,
    Egyptian; Working class
Workers' Committee for National
    Liberation (W.C.N.L.), 217, 220
Workers' Vanguard, 217, 219, 221, 225.
    See also Communist movement
Working class: and Egyptian workers'
    movement, 208–10, 213, 216–19,
    225; Islamic experience in formation
    of, 31
World Federation of Trade Unions
    Congress, 217, 220
World Zionist Organization, 184

'Yan Tatsine, 25, 29, 255–58
Yishuv, 181
Young Egypt, 207
Young Men's Muslim Association, 10,
    186, 189
Young Turk revolution, 30, 178
Yusuf al-Mudarrik, 210, 212, 217,
    220
Yusuf Darwish, 215, 216, 217

Zaatcha revolt, 65, 70–72
Zafar 'Ali Khan, 155, 156, 158
Zamindar (Lahore), 155, 158–59
zawiya, 5; in contraband arms traffic,
    65–69, 76–77; as institutional
    component of resistance, 62–63,
    69; as insurrectional movement,
    56; and Islamic brotherhood, 55; in
    the Ziban and the Djerid, 61
Zionists, 181, 185, 188, 194, 197
zu'ama, 179, 184, 186

Compositor: Asco Trade Typesetting, Ltd.
Text: 10/12 Baskerville
Display: Baskerville
Printer: Braun-Brumfield, Inc.
Binder: Braun-Brumfield, Inc.